ENVISIONING FREEDOM

ENVISIONING FREEDOM

Cinema and the Building of Modern Black Life

Cara Caddoo

Harvard University Press

Cambridge, Massachusetts
London, England
2014

Printed in the United States of America

Second printing

Library of Congress Cataloging-in-Publication Data

Caddoo, Cara, 1978–
Envisioning freedom : cinema and the building of modern Black life / Cara Caddoo.
pages cm
Includes bibliographical references and index.
ISBN 978-0-674-36805-7 (alk. paper)
1. African Americans in motion pictures. 2. African Americans in the motion picture industry. 3. African Americans—Social life and customs. 4. Motion pictures—Distribution—United States. 5. Motion picture audiences—United States. 6. Race films. I. Title.
PN1995.9.N4C33 2014
791.43'652996073—dc23 2014005703

For my parents

Contents

ENVISIONING FREEDOM

Introduction

Picturing Freedom

Blanche Jarvis may not have known she was pregnant on that autumn day in 1895, when, at seven minutes past five in the morning, she felt the world begin to move beneath her feet. The ground rumbled and heaved, splitting open the earth and propelling geysers of sand and water into the air. Terrified, "people ran out into the streets in their night dress" and huddled in the predawn darkness.[1] Buildings pulled from their moorings, chimneys crumbled, and windows shattered.[2]

A fault line buried beneath New Madrid, Missouri, had catapulted the Mississippi Valley into chaos. From its epicenter, the earthquake reverberated across twenty-four states, to Vicksburg, Mississippi, where Blanche, a thirty-three-year-old mother of three, lived with her husband, Price, in the quickly growing black district on the south side of town. The following day, newspapers across the country reported on the wrecked property, the "violent undulations," and the "roaring sound resembling a heavy train passing through a tunnel."[3]

But even as the earth trembled at its foundations, transformations of far greater magnitude were already afoot. While the earthquake of October 31 sent the Midwest and the South into disarray, it was the tectonic shifts occurring along the fault lines of the nation's racial order that would disperse hundreds of thousands of people, remake entire city skylines, and transform America as a whole. Over the next three decades, black Americans experienced a dramatic change in the way their racial identities were imagined and practiced. The legal, spatial, and institutional structures of black life were irrevocably altered, and the aftershocks of these developments reverberated well into the twentieth century, remaking not only the world in which Blanche Jarvis lived but also that of her unborn child.

Americans living on the threshold of the twentieth century knew "modern times" were underway, but the most spectacular changes appeared in fits and starts.[4] Less than six months after the earthquake, in the spring of 1896, two seemingly unrelated announcements heralded the coming of the new era. As Blanche prepared for the newest addition to her family, Thomas Edison presented the Vitascope to the American public at Koster and Bial's Music Hall in New York City.[5] Edison's machine could project moving images onto a large screen in a dark room instead of through a standard, single-viewer peephole device. For the first time, Americans could watch the moving pictures together. Over the next half-century, filmgoing became one of the nation's most popular leisure activities. Indeed, by the 1920s, politicians and industry professionals claimed that motion pictures were the "nation's fourth largest industry."[6]

Yet it is unlikely that Blanche paid much attention to the news of Edison's new invention. The New York papers raved about the Vitascope, but the Vicksburg press virtually ignored the story. It is more likely that Blanche learned about the motion pictures months later, when W. T. Hook and other traveling exhibitors brought the new technology to theaters across Mississippi.[7] Of more immediate importance to African Americans such as Blanche Jarvis and her family was the legal construction of a new racial order that was taking hold across the South. On the very day that Edison unveiled the Vitascope, a few hundred miles southwest of New York, the U.S. Supreme Court was considering a case filed by a black shoemaker named Homer Plessy. The Court had heard oral arguments on April 13, and a few weeks later, on May 18, Justice Henry H. Brown handed down the Court's decision. In a seven-to-one vote, it upheld Plessy's arrest and conviction for refusing to comply with a Louisiana statute mandating separate railroad accommodations for black passengers. Such laws, the Court explained, were constitutional as long as equivalent facilities were available to both races.[8]

The landmark events of 1896 cast long and overlapping shadows across the twentieth century, but both the Vitascope and *Plessy v. Ferguson* were indications as much as causes of the era's coming changes. Edison's invention was only one among dozens of similar devices that debuted that year, and although the *Plessy* decision would have long-lasting consequences for Blanche's life, she was already familiar with the peculiar system of Jim Crow segregation that the Supreme Court had legitimated. Vicksburg was one of the first cities in which conservative whites disenfranchised the black population and effectively ended Radical Reconstruction.[9] Less than a decade after the Civil War, the state's Democrats conceived of the Mississippi Plan, a strategy of ballot-stuffing and organized violence that prevented black voters from going to the polls. In 1890, the second Mississippi Plan created the blueprint for the South's legal circumvention of the Fourteenth and Fifteenth Amendments, through poll taxes, literacy tests, and other discriminatory legislation. In the following years, Vicksburg's population was moved into racially segregated districts as white redeemers systematically dismantled the considerable accomplishments of the Reconstruction era, excluding black Americans from formal politics and enforcing the racial order through violence.[10]

This was the world into which Blanche's daughter Everline was born on July 16, 1896. The joy of welcoming a beautiful, healthy daughter into the family was short-lived; Jim Crow was moving deeper into the Delta, and soon after Everline was born, Price passed away, leaving Blanche a single mother responsible for her three youngest children.[11] In times like these, Blanche found solace in her church and support from her family, two institutions that together served as the backbone of black life at the turn of the twentieth century. As historians Glenda Gilmore, Leon Litwack, and Michele Mitchell have explained, the period known as the "nadir" of African American history was also one of tremendous growth for black organizations.[12] After a tumultuous half-century of gradual emancipation, a war, and a grueling struggle over Reconstruction, in the face of segregation, black Americans in the 1890s turned to their own institutions as the primary means of achieving their goals for racial progress. Out of both choice and necessity, they strengthened the modern organizational structures of black life—churches, schools, fraternal societies, women's clubs, and businesses.[13]

As the experiences of Blanche, Everline, and millions of African Americans over the subsequent decades demonstrate, the moving pictures played a central role in the processes that reconfigured America's black institutions, its race relations—indeed, its entire cultural landscape. In the years following that fateful spring of 1896, the developments heralded by the headlines "Edison's Vitascope Cheered" and "Supreme Court Rules against Plessy" became deeply entangled with the making of modern black life. In the wake of the *Plessy* decision, as the former Confederate states rewrote their constitutions to exclude black Americans from railcars, schools, city districts, and voting booths, hundreds of thousands of black migrants flowed out of the rural South. When they resettled in southern and western cities, they integrated the moving pictures into their efforts to build up churches, construct new businesses, and stake claims to their lives as free people. As black Americans continued to migrate farther west and north, they carried their aspirations and their moving picture experiences with them, creating national institutions and shared cultural practices along the way.

An adherent of Pentecostalism, which warned against the sins of popular amusements, Blanche Jarvis would have been astounded by the circumstances that brought the 1896 court decision and modern cinema to converge so spectacularly in her own life and that of her newborn daughter.[14] But just a few decades later, Blanche was living in Chicago with Everline, by then known as Evelyn Preer, when the moving pictures changed the course of both of their lives. Blanche's youngest daughter was married to Frank Preer, the proprietor of a well-known café in the city's black entertainment district. Frank was dashing and "widely known to all the sporting men throughout the country," but he was also deeply troubled.[15] While Frank recovered from a series of mental breakdowns, Blanche convinced Evelyn to proselytize for the Pentecostal Church on the streets of Chicago.[16] Crying out to strangers, " 'Sinners, oh sinners, come Home' with her arms outstretched wide in supplication," the beautiful young woman caught the eyes of the black film director Oscar Micheaux. Evelyn accepted a starring role in Micheaux's debut film, *The Homesteader,* and she received rave reviews in the black press.[17] Her success in the newly minted "race film" industry soon made her one of the country's first nationally renowned black starlets of the silver screen.[18] In one unexpected moment, two seemingly disparate developments had collided in Blanche's life and that of her daughter Evelyn. Yet it was far from coincidence that the experiences of these churchgoing black migrant women overlapped with the emerging black film industry. Northern resettlement, black religious institutions, and the race film industry were all integrated into turn-of-the-century efforts by African Americans to better their lives through collective racial progress.

In fact, it is impossible to tell the story of twentieth-century black public life and its institutions without considering the catalytic role of the moving pictures. Shortly after commercial motion picture projectors were introduced to the United States in 1896, black Americans began promoting the technology as a symbol and tool for "racial uplift"—the belief that self-help initiatives were the key to collective racial advancement. Itinerant black showmen and -women exhibited films for black audiences in religious institutions such as the African Methodist Episcopal (AME), African Methodist Episcopal Zion (AMEZ), and black Baptist churches, and in colored fraternal organizations, including the Knights of Pythias, Odd Fellows, and Masons. Motion picture exhibitions not only raised money for black institutions, they also brought black people together for collective enjoyment. When motion pictures began to shift into colored theaters after 1906, these venues, like churches and lodges, brought black city dwellers together as they staked a claim to public space in the Jim Crow city.

The popularity of cinema in black life continued to generate new industries and cultural practices. By World War I, the race film industry soared to unprecedented heights. Its emergence would not have been possible without the capital, skilled professionals, and market for motion pictures created by the earlier practices of itinerant black film exhibition and the advent of the colored theaters. Because the moving pictures moved through so many of the central organizations of twentieth-century African American life, their history provides invaluable insights into the formation of the modern black experience.

Like the constant, building pressure against the Mississippi Valley fault line, the forces of modern life remade the terrain upon which the legal rulings and technological innovations of 1896 unfolded. The dreams and aspirations of black Americans ultimately transformed the moving pictures into a symbol and instrument of racial progress, but three interconnected factors were critical in bringing the black experience into dialogue with cinema: the migration of America's black population from rural locations to urban spaces, the emergence of mass leisure in the United States, and the growth of industrial capitalism.

Perhaps the most critical factor was the phenomenon of rural-to-urban migration that began in the 1860s and continued for more than a century thereafter. America's black population embarked on a massive emigration out of the agricultural South, first into small towns and cities in the South and the West and eventually to the urban North. The exodus from the countryside was unleashed by the Civil War and later fueled by industrialization and the threat of racial violence perpetrated by white vigilantes. In the 1890s, tens of thousands of black migrants left the world of sharecropping, crop liens, land rents, and yeomanry to try their hands at city life. The great upheavals of this period remade cities across the South: Nashville, Tennessee's black population doubled between 1880 and 1910; Atlanta, Georgia's grew from fewer than 2,000 black residents on the eve of the Civil War to 36,000 by 1900; and during this time, a third of Kentucky's black population became urban.[19]

In the city, black migrants staked claims to public space, political representation, and social equality—all of which conservative whites resisted with vitriol and violence. The drive to institute the Jim Crow color line reached a fever pitch in the 1890s as the population of southern cities swelled with black and white migrants from the countryside.[20] Former Confederates and white supremacists gained control of city and state governments and began instituting a de jure system of racial segregation in all areas of public life, from streetcars and housing to the rapidly expanding field of commercial public amusements. Jim Crow segregation was a modern urban phenomenon.[21] The close contact of blacks and whites required by the slave system was replaced by a rigid legal and social order that attempted to eliminate any semblance of egalitarian interracial contact in the wake of emancipation. Antiblack redeemers of the Democratic Party were particularly anxious to prevent the races from intermingling. By physically separating the races, they hoped to thwart the possibility of sexual relations between white women and black men and the threat of biracial political alliances between poor blacks and whites.

White anxiety over interracial contact illuminates a second important aspect of the period's history: the development of a thriving black leisure culture in the cities of new black settlement. Not only were African Americans, for the first time, becoming full-fledged members of the wage labor force, they were also collectively forging through their leisure activities a new culture of freedom.[22] In the city, black "servant girls" cooked, cleaned, washed laundry, and cared for the children of white families. The work was grueling and the pay meager, but as Mandy Smith, a washerwoman from Georgia, explained of her labors, poor folk could not stop "no matter how bad we feels."[23] Black men fared no better. Shut out of higher-paying factory work, they found work instead as draymen, waiters, or "day laborers"—a catchall term that referred to those who toiled as unskilled and poorly paid manual workers.[24] Because black folk had little control over their lives during their working hours, they devoted their nonworking hours to giving meaning to their existence as free people.

Like their white working-class counterparts, African Americans created vibrant leisure practices and institutions in their new cities of settlement. Wage-earning urbanites, excluded from many white venues in the Jim Crow city, organized clubs and joined institutions to derive as much "enjoyment" from their leisure time as possible. These collective black experiences played a critical role in mediating the urban experience of black folk. Poorer migrants caroused in the city streets when not at work, drinking away their worries at the saloon and dancing through their frustrations at the "jook joint."[25] Middle-class blacks were more likely to spend their leisure time at church socials and lectures, but all groups had come to see organized recreation as a fundamental arena of urban life.[26] African Americans gave meaning to their lives as free people, wageworkers, and city dwellers by claiming their "God-given right to play."[27]

The widespread popularity of cinema as a black urban amusement contributed to the social bonds, perspectives, and sensibilities of an emerging modern black public. Across the urban South and West, a black urban leisure culture formed around the moving pictures. Churches and lodges organized these exhibitions not only for their own members but also for the larger black community. Black laborers avoided most other turn-of-the-century amusements promoted by their middle-class counterparts, but they flocked to motion picture shows. The spectacular new form of entertainment appealed to the sensibilities and demands of a leisure-hungry class of newly urbanized black wageworkers.[28] Motion picture shows brought black people together into common spaces of leisure and recreation. The best-known itinerant showmen and -women met these demands by traveling from one center of black settlement to the next, from Havana, Cuba, to Wichita, Kansas, where their thrilling moving picture shows packed churches and halls. Across the informal circuits of itinerant exhibition, filmgoing gave shape to a black urban leisure culture.

Industrial capitalism stimulated—and was transformed by—the large-scale migration of America's black population and the emergence of new leisure practices and institutions.[29] Technological and manufacturing innovations bolstered the productive capabilities of businesses to unimaginable heights, but in order to fully profit from these advances, modern industries were driven to seek out larger markets. The federal government supported these efforts by subsidizing the development of a national transportation and communication infrastructure. The railroads, in particular, benefited from corporate land grants, tax incentives, and protective court injunctions.[30] By 1900, the U.S. railroad system spanned nearly 200,000 miles, not including the thousands of miles of railways that extended into Mexico and Canada. With the emergence of these far-reaching systems of transportation, new industries organized themselves, from their outset, around a model of mass production. The modern motion picture industry, for example, would not have been possible without an efficient and affordable means of distributing its commodities to distant markets. The same systems through which reels of film circulated across the Americas carried black American migrants to their new cities of settlement.[31] Thus emerged an increasingly dispersed black population that was paradoxically more connected than ever before through networks of goods and services—including the moving pictures.

But even as steamboats, trains, and telegraph lines opened up potential new markets, the white American moving picture industry cultivated its consumer base selectively. By the nickelodeon period (1905–1914), middle-class whites had come to view the moving pictures as a less-than-respectable, even immoral, form of amusement. In response, production companies, such as Edison, the American Mutoscope and Biograph Company, and Vitagraph, and white theater owners attempted to appeal to a wider and more affluent audience.[32] They did so in part by alleviating fears over mixed-race interactions. A nationwide cross-class mass market for the moving pictures was achieved by bridging regional differences, chiefly the racial practices of the South and North. Leaders of the white-owned industry pursued a wealthier consumer market by segregating black people within their commercial theaters and justifying this color line by depicting black characters onscreen as inept, promiscuous, violent, and deceitful. By 1920, more than half of the American population attended "the movies" at least once a week.[33] Historians have pointed to the emergence of a cross-class market for the moving pictures as a turning point in American history, but it is equally important to acknowledge that the racial division of moving picture audiences was a prerequisite for this development, not just an unfortunate consequence.[34]

Black Americans were acutely aware of the era's economic transformations. The black middle class, in particular, invested itself in the promises of the new capitalist order. As Kevin Gaines has argued, their philosophy of racial uplift emphasized hard work, piety, education, and black-owned industries as the key to racial progress.[35] The first generation of black film exhibitors likewise embraced the moving pictures as a symbol of black modernity and as a tool with which to publicize and raise money for mainline churches, fraternal orders, schools, and other organizations that espoused the ideas of uplift. When the first colored theaters were constructed, black ministers and entrepreneurs jointly celebrated these businesses as examples of black self-help. But when commercial venues began to compete with churches for the time and attention of the black public, black ministers reconsidered their enthusiasm for the medium. Soon, they were preaching against the inherent evils of the moving pictures—even crusading against the same types of films that had been exhibited, just years before, in their churches. The demands of the emerging black consumer market split the interests of the black middle class and exposed the inherent contradictions in the philosophy of racial uplift, pitting the moral value of piety against the goal for profits.

Excavating the meaning of cinema in black life requires us to remap the geography of the modern black experience. The emergence of black urban cosmopolitanism, commercial leisure, and socially conscious creative arts has been overwhelmingly associated with large industrial cities in the North, the Harlem Renaissance, and the "Great Migration" of 1910–1930. The history of early black cinema challenges such understandings. African Americans first began exhibiting and attending motion pictures in the 1890s, primarily in cities across the South and West. These practices coincided with patterns of black resettlement that preceded the Great Migration: gradual "step-migrations" from the countryside to small towns and cities in the South, North, and West.[36] Black migrants did not simply drop their spades and hoes in the hinterlands of Dixie and hop on the next train to Harlem or Chicago; they tried out city life closer to home before moving on. Their paths were winding and circular, dictated by train routes, family members, friends, labor agents, violence, and the desire for new economic and leisure opportunities. A "Great Urbanization," beginning in the late nineteenth century, better describes the framework in which black Americans staked their claims to modern life.[37]

Despite statistical differences between the earlier and later migrations, the percentage of the black population that became urban during the late nineteenth and early twentieth centuries was not substantially smaller than that of the classic Great Migration: in the period between 1880 and 1910, the percentage of urban blacks rose by 13.1 percent; during the Great Migration, there was an increase of 16.3 percent.[38]

Nonetheless, the later Great Migration still deeply influences how scholars and the broader public understand twentieth-century black modernity and its origins.[39] Popular discourse frequently weaves the Great Migration into a triumphant narrative of black political and cultural renaissance in the North, usually at the expense of a much richer, longer history of postemancipation black mobility.[40] While historians widely acknowledge the patterns of black urban resettlement that began in the late nineteenth century, they also have placed too much burden on the Great Migration as a distinctive period and as an explanatory model. The North was undoubtedly important to the formation of black modernity. Black immigrants and migrants in places such as Chicago and New York fought for equal access to motion picture theaters and fair representations of the race on-screen, pursuing progress through the physical and representational spaces of the cinema.[41] But if the "black meccas" of Harlem and Chicago differed from southern and western black entertainment districts in their size and resources, claims that they represented an entirely new cultural landscape are difficult to reconcile with hundreds of reports of film exhibitions in black churches and halls outside the North, as well as the emergence of the "chitlin' circuit"—the network of colored theaters that spread throughout the South and West.

By the time most African Americans began packing their bags for the industrial North, cinema already figured into their sensibilities, alliances, and material interests. Afternoons at the colored theater and hours spent at church and lodge shows informed the expectations of those who continued along the pathways of migration. From simple storefronts to brick buildings, black churches, lodges, and theaters were built with the dollars of filmgoing migrants. These sites served as the social centers of black urban life and publicly represented the claims black people made to urban space. More than a decade of experiences at the motion pictures shaped how black people responded to two pivotal incidents in American racial politics: black pugilist Jack Johnson's 1910 victory over the white former heavyweight champion Jim Jeffries, and the release of the film *The Birth of a Nation* in 1915. In the aftermath of these events, black people propelled the question of cinematic representation to the center of black concerns about racial progress.

This history not only raises into relief a rich convergence of black cultural practices, community formations, and industry during one of the nation's lowest points in race relations, it also reveals how black people helped to create American modernity. Scholars define "modernity" variously, but historians of the late nineteenth and twentieth centuries most commonly associate the term with a heightened awareness of the era's changes—particularly the ascent of capitalism, urbanization, the emergence of mass media, secularization, and the growing belief in rational progress. Moving pictures were integral to African Americans' responses to the changes of turn-of-the-twentieth-century American life. Early black cinema practices generated a new culture of commercial leisure, black businesses, and circuits of mass media—all of which were incorporated into the era's goals for racial progress. At the same time, black responses to the motion pictures contributed to emergence of the unmistakably modern political demand for fair visual representation on-screen.

Yet the history of black cinema also helps to reconfigure fundamental assumptions about the nature of modernity.[42] For example, the popularity of cinema in black churches troubles definitions of the modern that hinge upon a shift from the sacred to the secular.[43] Black film practices moved across and existed between the arenas defined by tradition and law as private and public, commercial and noncommercial, and sacred and secular. Prohibited from many "public" accommodations, such as the Jim Crow theater, black Americans socialized in private black institutions that functioned as the "public spaces" of turn-of-the-century black life. Religious institutions, in particular, served as gathering places, concert halls, and, by the turn of the twentieth century, moving picture theaters. Historian Evelyn Higginbotham has referred to these sites as a black public sphere, "a discursive, critical arena . . . in which values and issues were aired, debated, and disseminated throughout the larger black community."[44] Built almost entirely after 1865 and organized in the name of racial progress, these were unquestionably modern institutions.[45]

Evelyn Preer lived through a remarkable era. The little girl from Vicksburg, Mississippi, born under the shadow of Jim Crow just months after the public debut of the Vitascope, would live to see her name emblazoned across the marquees of hundreds of colored motion picture theaters across the country. She starred in at least seven Oscar Micheaux productions after *The Homesteader,* including *Within Our Gates* (1920) and *The Devil's Disciple* (1926), and in the late 1920s, began appearing in Hollywood feature films.[46] When Preer succumbed to pneumonia in 1932, her unexpected death was mourned by thousands of black Americans who knew her as the "ideal of beauty, of aspiration—a great hope to a Race born in the ire of prejudice, obstacles and tremendous opposition."[47] Perhaps for some, it seemed the symbolic end of an era. By the time of Preer's death, the independent black film production industry was in its twilight. Black filmmakers outside of the studio system could no longer bear the rising costs of production, especially that of synchronized sound technology. Hollywood was also closing in on the African American market by adopting the mantle of racial integration in order to regain profits lost in the shrinking Depression-era economy.[48] Most of the early independent race film companies shut their doors, ending a significant chapter in the history of black American cinema.

Yet the legacy of events that unfolded during Evelyn Preer's lifetime would continue to live on. The earliest black engagements with the moving pictures transformed the ways in which black people understood themselves and their shared place in the world. They forged social bonds across distant geographies, raised money for the construction of black properties, and supported the development of skilled industry professionals; they formed national and international institutions, consolidated their circuits of exhibition, created new black industries, developed networks of communication, and conceived of a modern black public and its consumer demands. In their debates over the depiction of blackness on-screen, they contested the very meaning of "the race" itself—what it looked like, who belonged to it, and what it represented. These processes created new geographies of black social, political, and economic relations. From New Orleans to Johannesburg and Paris to Jacksonville, Florida, the motion pictures reshaped how black people envisioned their past, their present, and their shared future. Cinema became implicated in the very definition of what it meant to be black and to be free.

I

Exhibitions of Faith and Fellowship

Black churches responded to the upswing in urban migration by using motion pictures to promote their ideas, raise money, and entice fellow members of the race to join their organizations. (Second Baptist Church, Kansas City, Missouri, circa 1913. From Asa E. Martin, *Our Negro Population: A Sociological Study of the Negroes of Kansas City, Missouri* [Kansas City, Mo., 1913], 187.)

On January 2, 1897, black residents of Kansas City, Missouri, gathered at the Second Baptist Church for an evening of entertainment. The edifice, located on Tenth and Charlotte streets, was only partially completed; the second floor was unfinished, and the roof just recently erected. As they entered the building, attendees likely crossed a sawdust-strewn floor or felt a draft of wintry air seeping in from the upper slats of the ceiling. But such trivialities could be easily overlooked, for it was the first Sunday of the new year, and the promised entertainment was unlike anything the church had seen before.[1]

Once inside, the attendees may have noticed a large sheet of white canvas hanging in the front of the room and a curious contraption brought to the church especially for this day. Affixed with glass lenses, pulleys, and a ribbon of shiny material wrapped around a spool, the device was probably about the size of a sewing machine and mounted on top of a table. The room was dimmed, but even in the darkness, the growing excitement must have been palpable as the audience waited for the show to begin. Finally, the machine sprang into motion—a whirring sound emanated from its gears, then a rhythmic click, like the sound of a baseball card clipped to the spoke of a bicycle wheel. Light splashed across the canvas, and immense images moved as if they were alive. Each scene lasted for just a moment—perhaps a breathtaking view of Niagara Falls, a parade of bicyclists, then a ferryboat, a water chute, or fluttering white doves. As the films appeared, one after another, music or a narration might have accompanied the images on-screen, while members of the audience applauded, and awarded the most breathtaking scenes with shouts and cheers.[2]

When the Second Baptist Church announced that it would celebrate the new year by hosting a moving picture show, it must have been stunning news. Only a few months had passed since Thomas Edison unveiled the Vitascope, the nation's first commercially successful device for projecting motion pictures, at Koster and Bial's Music Hall in New York City.[3] Most Americans, especially those in the West, had yet to witness the sensational new technology.[4] In 1897, news of a motion picture show could bring an entire town to a halt. When a traveling moving picture operator stopped by a local opera house in Lancaster County, Pennsylvania, that year, writer Alan Bethel recalled the anticipation: "The courts adjourned, stores closed, the blacksmith dropped his tongs, and school 'let out' at noon."[5] Across the country, Americans rushed to witness for themselves the invention hailed as "one of the wonders of the age."[6]

Only three decades earlier, the Second Baptist Church had been little more than a "stragglers camp," a place where freedmen and refugees from the Civil

War, dressed in rags and clutching their only possessions, gathered to pray together on the "sand, rock, and willow studded banks of the Missouri River."[7] During the war, Kansas City had been a dangerous and unknowable place. Kersey Coates's half-built hotel on Tenth and Broadway, just a few blocks from the river's edge, became a stable for the Union Army; the Longhorn Store and Tavern, once a prison for Confederate spies, had collapsed into a pile of rubble. From the Northland, across the banks of the Missouri, slaves fought pitched battles to reach the south side of the river, which functioned as a dividing line between slavery and freedom. But nowhere was entirely safe. Bounty hunters combed the city streets for black folk to confiscate, guerilla fighters terrorized the countryside, and in the fall of 1864, Confederate troops surged northward across the state.[8] As the war raged on around the members of this humble congregation, they looked to one another and to their faith for guidance and consolation. From the shores of the river, their "melodious song service" and "emotional shouting" could be heard long into the night.[9]

If memories of the Second Baptist's modest beginnings flickered through the minds of the congregants that evening, they may have also taken a moment to marvel at the accomplishments of their church, and the transformation of the bustling western city they called home. Kansas City was a rising star in the "black archipelago," a handful of cities scattered across the Midwest whose black populations had flourished after the Civil War.[10] Growing from fewer than 4,000 black residents in 1870 to nearly 17,000 by 1895, Kansas City vividly reflected the changes wrought by the war, the railroads, and the growing industrial economy during the Gilded Age.[11] The Second Baptist Church had grown in size with the city. After the war, the members constructed a simple frame building of unfinished wood, which by the 1870s was one of the largest black institutions in the city. Although not yet completed, their newest home, a three-story brick edifice, was a testament to their progress as an institution. And that evening in 1897, not only did the congregants witness one of the most exciting new inventions of the era, they were watching it within their own walls.[12]

Set against the long-prevailing narrative of early American cinema, the Second Baptist's film exhibition is an anomaly. Scholars have long believed that African Americans first encountered the moving pictures in commercial venues owned and operated by whites. Black Americans eventually made the moving pictures their own, these studies have argued, but in the beginning, black filmgoers could only attend segregated venues, where they were forced to enter through separate doorways, sit in the worst sections in the house (the "buzzard's roost"), and attend late-night screenings. Even as managers of commercial venues attempted to render black people invisible within the exhibition space, visual depictions of blackness became wildly popular on-screen. Audiences in commercial venues, film scholars have rightly explained, viewed films produced by white companies that profited from fantastical and racist stereotypes of chicken thieves, mammies, Uncle Toms, and violent, city-dwelling "zip coons."[13] While a few film historians have studied colored theaters in the South and the production of a handful of black films before 1910, scholars largely associate black film authorship and the formation of a black cinema culture with the commercial sites that emerged during the northward settlement of the Great Migration.[14] A closer examination of the urban South and West, however, presents a different story—one that complicates our understanding not only of early American cinema but also of migration and black institutional life.

Between 1897 and 1910, hundreds of black film showmen and -women exhibited motion pictures in black lodges, schools, and, most frequently, churches. Early black film exhibition developed in response to the dramatic changes African Americans faced at the turn of the century—migration, hardening Jim Crow segregation, and the growing demand for urban amusements. In new cities of settlement, black religious and club leaders, especially those connected to mainline black Protestant churches, responded to the upswing in black urban migration by using the moving pictures to promote their ideas, raise money, and entice fellow members of the race to join their organizations. These plans were guided by the philosophy of racial uplift—the belief that self-help initiatives were the key to collective racial progress—and the assumption that stronger black institutions were necessary to achieving these goals.[15] The practices of black film exhibition that developed across the urban South and West were not simply borrowed from a world of white producers and showmen. The leaders of the Second Baptist and others like them were at the vanguard of the new motion picture phenomenon. African Americans embraced the moving image before many of their white counterparts because it was suited to the needs and public spaces of modern black life.

In the decades after the Thirteenth Amendment made slavery illegal in the United States, African Americans created the organizations that became the backbone of postemancipation black life: secret societies, mutual aid associations, neighborhood unions, sororities and fraternities, labor unions, pleasure clubs, churches, and professional associations.[16] These agencies grew even more vital when the federal government ended its commitment to Radical Reconstruction and the biracial political coalitions of the following years failed to overturn the wealthy southern white oligarchy. Alienated by the social and economic discrimination of the post-Reconstruction era, black folk turned their conception of racial destiny inward. They embraced a strategy of self-help and came to rely more than ever before on the institutions that stood at the center of black public life: the church, the lodge, and the school.[17]

Yet even as African Americans turned toward one another, their neighbors, and their communities, the distance between them was growing ever greater. Hundreds of thousands of black migrants were leaving the rural hinterland for small towns and cities across the South and West. As W. E. B. Du Bois observed at the turn of the century, "Negroes come from country districts to small towns, then go to larger towns; eventually they drift to Norfolk, Va., or to Richmond. Next they come to Washington, and finally settle in Baltimore or Philadelphia."[18] For these migrants, the urban South and West were stepping-stones on a longer, uncharted journey that led north, farther west, and sometimes in winding circles across the black archipelago. Not all migrants moved directly from the agricultural South to the city. Some returned to the countryside or participated in a "rotational" pattern of migration, while others gradually transitioned into city life. Others stayed in their new urban homes in the South but watched their children and grandchildren venture farther along the pathways of black settlement.[19] America's black population had begun its journey to becoming an urban people. By 1910, 22 percent of the black residents of the South lived in cities.[20]

It was at this crossroads of dispersal and desire for collective social and economic advancement that an enterprising generation of black cinema pioneers first introduced the moving pictures into black churches, halls, and schools. Black leaders such as Samuel Bacote, minister of the Kansas City Second Baptist, realized that his church required new solutions for organizing its members' cooperative efforts and drawing in new congregants. Twenty-nine years old at the time of his appointment to the church, Bacote was as industrious as he was ambitious. His stern countenance and lean frame conveyed his ascetic values; drinking and the pleasure clubs of Kansas City would become a special target of his ire.[21] Hard work and self-discipline, he believed, were the keys to racial uplift, and the values to which he attributed his own success. The son of former South Carolina slaves, he left for college as a teenager with seventeen dollars in his pocket, one pair of clothes, and no socks, and he was "easily recognized as the poorest boy on campus." Nonetheless, he pressed "forward with courage and tireless zeal" to rise to the top of his class.[22] When he arrived in Kansas, he continued to study, eventually earning his master's degree and a doctorate from Kansas City University even as he carried out his pastoral duties.

Bacote's aspirations for the Second Baptist Church were equally ambitious. In 1895, when he arrived at the church, the congregation was in crisis. Its members had planned to construct a new church building on Tenth and Charlotte streets, but could not afford to complete the project. Unable to keep up with the mounting bills, the congregants were forced to worship in the unfinished basement of the structure they had hoped to erect.[23] As minister of the church, Bacote's first mission was to guide the church building project to completion. He quickly resolved to construct a large *brick* church, one that would enable the Second Baptist to grow in size and that would be magnificent enough to serve as a "monument for the Negro Baptists" and "an ornament and a blessing for the race."[24]

Black properties, such as that planned by the Second Baptist, were among the era's most pronounced expressions of the mission for collective racial progress. The construction of cooperatively owned structures was of urgent concern for all African Americans, but especially for those in cities with growing black populations. New buildings replaced the cramped rooms, borrowed quarters, and flimsy A-frame wooden structures that housed most late nineteenth-century black congregations, and black-owned properties served as a repository of the collective wealth of an institution, as public meeting places, symbols of spiritual and racial progress, and physical claims to the geography of the Jim Crow city. Of course, even the first cooperatively constructed properties had constituted a remarkable testament to black collective action, built as they were from the limited resources of those such as the freedmen from Kansas City who scrimped and saved to move their "Stragglers Camp" from the banks of the Missouri into their first small frame building. But in response to the "large emigration to the cities," as Atlanta University reported in 1903, black churches had begun to demand "ministers who could build large church buildings and control large congregations."[25]

Black church leaders across the country responded to the era's segregation and migration by rushing to build larger, more durable structures for their congregations. Across the South and West, in cities of new black settlement, thousands of congregations spent vast sums of money on ornate buildings; brick buildings in particular were celebrated for their structural and symbolic permanence.[26] Because the money raised to build new church buildings was drawn collectively from the race, these structures were celebrated as symbols of black self-determination. Ornate urban black churches exhibited a sort of sacred "conspicuous consumption" that melded older religious sensibilities of constructing prestigious buildings to showcase the glory of God with the modern capitalist desire to publicly exhibit the accumulation of material wealth.[27]

The problem, of course, was that large brick structures were expensive. Although congregations hoped to "glorify God and edify humanity" with their fancy new properties, as black minister Robert A. McGuinn of Maryland explained of the church-building boom, "buildings are too often planned and erected when the resources are not taken into consideration."[28] In fact, some African Americans pointed to the construction of impressive edifices as the most conspicuous problem of the black church. Ministers "are too busy trying to see who can build the finest church," complained a black resident of Illinois.[29] In Kentucky, locals objected to church leaders who tried "to out do each other in raising money and erecting great church buildings."[30] While the upswing in migration had created the potential to construct bigger, more spectacular black churches than ever before, it had also raised the stakes of black church financing—and few burdens were as certain to break the back of an otherwise thriving church as an insurmountable debt. Mortgages, liens, and other property-related debts soon became the most widespread financial burden on black churches across the country.

The leadership of the Bethel African Methodist Episcopal (AME) Church of Indianapolis, Indiana, located nearly five hundred miles east of the Second Baptist by way of the Santa Fe Railroad, was grappling with precisely these same concerns.[31] In 1897, Bethel AME was staggering under the weight of an enormous debt it had incurred through its church-building project. And like the Second Baptist, which needed to raise thousands of dollars to complete its church edifice, Bethel was struggling in its efforts to raise money for its church building endeavors. Bethel's debt topped $6,000, already an enormous strain on the congregation, but it would soon owe more for erecting "one of the handsomest church houses" in Indiana[32] In order to meet these pressing financial burdens, Bethel and other black churches relied on the profits they earned from their fundraising events. One of Bethel's most important charity events of the year was the annual Inter-State Bazaar, a week-long event organized primarily by local black women's clubs, which usually featured concerts, displays of arms, and pageant shows. As the event organizers sought new ways to attract the public to their event, news of the "latest sensation" of projected motion pictures spread across the country.[33]

As soon as Edison debuted the Vitascope, a host of projecting machines—the cinematograph, eidoloscope, biograph, vitagraph, motorscope, and dozens of others—had flooded the market.[34] These film projectors, some of which had been invented before Edison's device, could operate in a variety of venues, and often without electricity. This was important; there were virtually no permanent sites devoted solely to film exhibition until the nickelodeon theaters emerged around 1905. Moving pictures appeared wherever audiences delighted in spectacles and displays. Fairgrounds, amusement parks, dime museums, opera houses, and vaudeville theaters had begun scheduling film exhibitions along with their standard fare of skits, curiosities, and musical performances. A program in one of these venues could consist entirely of motion pictures, but even then, the silent images on-screen were frequently paired with a lecture, live music performance, or phonograph recording. Other times, moving pictures were displayed in programs alongside other acts. These early films often lasted less than a minute, which made the medium relatively adaptable; motion picture projectionists could splice together individual films, made of thin strips of celluloid, into exhibitions of variable length.[35]

In this formative moment of American cinema, black Americans began to incorporate the moving pictures into their larger efforts for racial progress. The spectacular new technology, it seemed, could not only raise money for their collective endeavors, it might also be used to promote their ideas and produce shared experiences. The leaders of Bethel AME may not have known of Samuel Bacote, or have even heard of the Kansas City Second Baptist, but they, too, turned to the motion pictures to solve their fundraising problems. By investing in "a carnival of amusement and display," they hoped to draw crowds to their events and raise more money than ever before. In April 1897, Reverend David A. Graham announced to his congregants that the church had arranged a motion picture exhibition to take place over two days of the Inter-State Bazaar. An entertainment of such magnitude, Graham explained of the film exhibition, had "never [been] attempted before by any of our churches." The plans were met with unprecedented excitement. "No announcement ever made in Bethel church," the *Indianapolis Freeman* announced, had received "more hearty approbation from saint and sinner alike."[36]

Organizing a film exhibition was a gamble. The moving pictures were new and spectacular, but it was not uncommon for the projectors to malfunction, ruining the film or even causing the highly flammable nitrate-treated celluloid to explode. Just a few days after Graham's announcement, a motion picture machine burst into flames during an exhibition at the Bazar de la Charité in France, killing 125 people in a terrible fire.[37] Besides these dangers, the cost of the new technology was prohibitive. Even the most enthusiastic congregants of the Bethel AME had not "dared" to assume the church would "make such a costly venture."[38] In order to turn a profit and ensure a large turnout, they would have to sell hundreds of twenty-five-cent tickets. It was a considerable price, especially for a populace whose families usually earned no more than between five and ten dollars a week.[39] Meanwhile, skeptics shrugged off the moving pictures as a novelty, assuming they would soon be replaced by another fashionable new gadget. At any moment, the fickle public might move on to something else. Reflecting on the "Wonderful Forward Strides" of 1896, the black newspaper the *Cleveland Gazette* followed a short blurb on the Vitascope with a much more gushing description of another revolutionary new invention, the "typewriter bicycle," which enabled an individual to dash off a missive and pedal at the same time.[40]

Despite the naysayers, the Second Baptist and Bethel AME decided to invest their hopes in the moving pictures. Not only would their success help guarantee the survival of their churches, it also reflected the spiritual rectitude of the congregation and its minister. For proponents of the philosophy of racial uplift, outward material success was an indication of inner salvation. "The real price of labor is knowledge and virtue," Bacote once explained, "of which wealth and credit are signs."[41] Graham, too, believed that hard work and true faith would enable the race to "lift ourselves by our own bootstraps."[42] The film exhibition would prove an embarrassing and costly mistake if it failed to earn profits and impress the black public during one of the most important fundraising events of the year—but *if* the technology could draw a crowd, it could bring handsome rewards in the church collection plates, recognition for the church, and glory to the mission of racial progress. With bated breath, the church leaders prayed for success.

The Bethel AME Inter-State Bazaar opened on May 18, 1897. There were displays of arms, pageants, and music, in addition to the eagerly awaited "cinematograph," which played for two nights.[43] By the end of the festivities, when all the fees and ticket sales had been calculated, the church had earned $230. In comparison to Bethel's $6,000 debt, the profits from the fundraiser may appear meager, but the earnings were more than the church could expect to earn over fourteen regular Sunday services, and almost twice the amount the average black worker earned over the course of a year.[44] There are no records indicating whether the Second Baptist's film exhibition directly turned a profit, but in nearby Omaha, Nebraska, the black newspaper *Enterprise* reported that the moving picture show "made a great hit."[45] The day after the exhibition, the industrious Bacote deemed himself deserving of a three-week holiday and departed for the South.[46] And that year, the second of his pastorate, he proved himself an able fundraiser. The congregation saved an impressive $14,000, and was soon able to raise the superstructure for its new edifice.[47] Driven by a spirit of modern optimism and invested in the material and symbolic significance of their properties, a handful of self-fashioned modern race women and men inaugurated one of the most popular black leisure activities of the coming century.

In 1897, church-hosted moving picture exhibitions were an illustration—a particularly novel one—of the role that black churches played as "the central organ of the organized life of the American Negro, for amusement, relaxation, instruction and religion."[48] Church-hosted lectures, pageants, concerts, and plays were important features of black urban life, especially because African Americans were excluded from many of the popular amusement venues frequented by their white counterparts. Black churches arranged amusements for their congregants and neighbors, and their properties constituted some of the few "public venues" available for such performances and exhibitions. Religious leaders of the Baptist, African Methodist Episcopal (AME), and African Methodist Episcopal Zion (AMEZ) churches, as well as other denominations, invited lecturers, entertainers, and ministers from other churches to fill their organizations' social calendars. A well-received calendar of social events helped a church maintain its status as the center of black social and intellectual life at the same time its entertainments raised the "silver offering[s]" necessary to running the church.[49]

To see the most popular traveling lectures and exhibitions of the day, black migrants packed into churches and spilled out into the streets. The best presentations elucidated and thrilled all at once. Before the motion pictures, traveling ministers earned national renown for electrifying their audiences with tales of devilish trickery and holy redemption. Itinerant preachers such as H. Charles Pope of Washington, D.C., might have appeared a bit stiff in the collar, but they had the makings of true showmen. Beneath Pope's starchy moralizing was a charming sense of humor and a flair for spectacle. In Virginia, Pope enthralled his listeners to quit biding their time and spring into action in "Whipping the Devil around the Stump." In New York, he sermonized on "The Devil Making a Motion for a New Trial," and in Kansas, he gave the lecture that earned him scores of admirers and a host of imitators: "The Devil's Cook Kitchen."[50] Pope began by illustrating his colorful lectures about race pride and godliness with a stereopticon, a machine that projected still images onto a large canvas. Other traveling speakers used phonographs or similarly popular devices for integrating sound and still images into their lectures.[51] These technologies added spectacle and excitement to a presentation, and audiences were more willing to pay admission to hear a moralizing lesson when they were being entertained. Ministers rushed to book Pope's "witty" and "wonderful" exhibitions, which enthralled his audiences even as he warned them to stay pious and avoid the popular amusements that beckoned good churchgoers into a life of sin.[52]

By 1905, Pope had acquired a film projector and was exhibiting moving pictures in his show.[53] Like other black ministers, including Romulus R. Richmond, of Chariton, Iowa; J. W. Woods of Mobile, Alabama; and Ellis Drake of Claremore, Oklahoma, all of whom had also begun exhibiting films, Pope had discovered how conveniently the technology fit the needs of the itinerant black speaker.[54] By employing motion picture projectors, itinerants could thrill their audiences with spectacular images while simultaneously communicating through narration or song the importance of thrift, piety, and hard work. Such machines were compatible with the physical layout of cooperatively owned black properties. Most of these modest frame buildings possessed stagelike pulpits and audience-ready pews. And film projectors could facilitate the demands of large groups by exhibiting to an entire roomful of people all at once. Single-viewer devices such as the Mutascope or Kinetoscope, on the other hand, required individuals to line up one by one to peer into a single machine.

The most modern film projection devices were also built for travel. A Kinetoscope might weigh several hundred pounds and stand several feet tall, but film projectors usually weighed less than fifty pounds. Thus projectors could be easily carried from place to place and "set up and removed in ten minutes."[55] A motion picture exhibitor needed only a few pieces of equipment and a simple screen of white fabric, which could be suspended in the front of the room. Suitable for exhibition in churches, halls, and schools and entertaining enough to draw a crowd, the novel technology was befitting of the spirit of modern progress, an idea dear to the hearts of so many turn-of-the-century black church leaders and reformers.

Although a few churches offered their entertainment services free of charge, most required an admission fee or issued strongly worded suggestions for donations.[56] "A silver offering of not less than ten cents {10] for the benefit of the Church is expected of everybody at the door [*sic*]," the Wichita AME Church announced before one of its exhibitions.[57] Black institutions earned money from film exhibitions in three basic ways. They could rent or purchase their own machine and reels of film and have the minister or a church member run their exhibitions. For example, sensing a continuous demand for motion picture exhibitions, Reverend L. L. Blair of Savannah, Georgia, and Reverend Terry of Huntington, West Virginia, decided to invest in their own film projectors.[58] Other churches paid up front for the services of a motion picture exhibitor. Usually, this enabled the church to keep a greater percentage of proceeds it earned from its film exhibitions, but it also entailed a large financial risk. If an exhibition failed to draw interest, the church suffered a larger financial loss. This was likely the agreement that black churches made when they commissioned their first exhibitions in 1897 and the reason why the congregants of the Bethel AME viewed the two-day motion picture exhibition at their church as an especially "costly venture." Finally, an institution could split its profits with a traveling exhibitor who was responsible for providing the technology necessary for an exhibition. In exchange for a percentage of the profits, the church might guarantee to sell a certain number of tickets, in addition to providing the venue for the exhibition and assistance in marketing the show.

Moving pictures were difficult and expensive to produce, but a few black film exhibitors did manage to create or commission their own films. In October 1905, William G. Hynes, "the famous moving picture exhibitor" from Nashville, Tennessee, traveled to Chicago, Illinois, to capture "in moving picture form the National Baptist Convention and Women's Auxiliary."[59] Nowhere was the recent move to consolidate the networks of black life more spectacularly illustrated than at this annual meeting of black Christians. For most of the denomination's history, black Baptists had belonged to separate conventions that had splintered earlier in the nineteenth century from mainline white-led churches. Divided by state and region, and with different leadership and administrative systems, "it seemed impossible," W. E. B. Du Bois recalled, "to unite any large number of them [the black Baptists] in a National Convention."[60] But the desire to strengthen the cooperative efforts of the churches fueled a new campaign to unite the denomination into one organization. In the fall of 1895, the regional conferences made a stunning move by merging into the National Baptist Convention, thereby becoming the third-largest denomination in the United States after the Catholics and Methodists.[61]

A veteran moving picture exhibitor, Hynes understood the demand on the part of black churches and halls to witness the National Baptist and Women's Conventions' annual meeting—"the greatest gathering of the church people of the negro race ever held." Thousands of delegates from every corner of the United States assembled to discuss the pressing issues of concern to black Baptists and the race as a whole. Those present included some of the race's greatest leaders—Booker T. Washington, Reverend Elijah Fisher of the famous Chicago Olivet Baptist Church, and Sarah Willie Layten, Nannie H. Burroughs, and Mary Church Terrell of the Women's Convention, an auxiliary organization of the National Baptist Convention that reflected the desire of black churchwomen to unite the efforts of black Americans and acquire greater autonomy.[62] For the 1.3 million black Baptist men and women who could not afford the time or the ticket to travel to Chicago (even with the Louisville and Nashville Railroad and the Seaboard Airline Railroad offering attendees special round-trip rates to the city), Hynes's moving pictures offered proof of the advancements of the black Baptist church, and a glimpse of some of the most famous church and race leaders in action.[63]

Hynes was not the only exhibitor showing films about race leaders and their accomplishments. H. C. Conley and his wife, Mrs. Conley, managers of Conley's Great Moving Picture Show, Illustrated Songs, and Concert, also produced films that demonstrated "the progress of the successful Afro-American."[64] In 1907, the Conleys convinced Richard T. Greener, the first black graduate of Harvard University and former U.S. counsel to Vladivostok, Russia, to join the company on a lecture tour. With the well-known speaker onboard, the Conleys decided to commission, "at great expense," a series of moving pictures of the "American Negro and the Negro abroad" to illustrate Greener's lecture.[65] Later that year, the troupe brought their exhibition to churches and halls across the South.[66] The program may have also included films produced by white companies, including pictures by the Lubin Manufacturing Company, Pathé Frères, or the Edison Manufacturing Company, which were the staple of most black moving picture exhibitions. Lubin's films in particular were widely available and more affordable than those produced by companies such as American Mutoscope and Biograph.[67]

But even when presenting the films of white production companies, African Americans found creative ways of controlling the meaning of images in their shows. Most films produced before 1906, as cinema scholar Tom Gunning has pointed out, were a "cinema of attractions" that emphasized spectacles rather than story lines.[68] For example, the popular *Black Diamond Express* (1896), which lasted about a minute, simply showed workers scurrying off a railroad track as a train approached at breakneck speed. In *A Happy Family* (1898), two children played with a collie and her litter of puppies. Rather than construct complex narratives with a clear beginning, middle, and end, these films reveled in the technical capabilities of modern cinema to realize the previously impossible—the animation of photographs on an immense scale. Early films titillated their audiences with striking imagery and featured subjects that solicited the attention of the offscreen spectator. While performers of the later classical Hollywood era rarely acknowledged the assumed audience of their films, usually acting as though the camera were invisible, the dancers, body builders, magicians, boxers, canoodling lovers, and even gurgling babies in the "cinema of attractions" seemed to recognize that someone was watching them from behind the fourth wall.

Moving picture exhibitors altered the reception of these films much like a newspaper editor changes the meaning of a photograph by choosing its location on the page or adding a descriptive caption. In the hands of a skilled entertainer, a vast array of moving pictures were infused with new meaning, especially when accompanied by a concert, a lecture, or another performance. For example, a multimedia cornucopia of "timely and instructive" lessons like Pope's "The Devil's Cook Kitchen" might have included a wide and changing assortment of motion pictures.[69] Illustrating his ideas about the "Black Hand"—the role of African Americans in shaping the history of the United States—Pope may have presented a two-minute film like *Panoramic View of the*

Capitol, Washington, D.C. (1901) or *President McKinley and Escort Going to the Capitol* (1901), which showed a military procession on horseback and a horse-drawn carriage carrying President McKinley. As the film played, Pope could have launched into one of his favorite stories, that of James Parker, the black waiter who heroically attempted to thwart the president's assassination.[70] Later, Pope's lessons on the "Ballroom to Hell," which argued that dancing corrupted the soul, could have employed a film like *Bowery Waltz* (1897) or *A Tough Dance* (1902). In both of these films, a working-class couple in garish dress performed a burlesque waltz. The intoxicated couple stumbled and swayed, intermittently groping each other on the dance floor. While the audience giggled at the on-screen antics, Pope may have reminded them that laughing at the follies of a sinner was acceptable, but partaking in such sins was not.

Film exhibitors maintained authorship over their programs by carefully selecting the reels they bought or rented from white production companies. Knoxville, Tennessee–based Harry A. Royston, who explained that his traveling exhibition was designed "to please a colored audience," chose pictures that appealed to his personal sensibilities and that could be incorporated into a program that broadcast his beliefs about racial progress.[71] Royston's pictures were produced by the prolific Jewish German filmmaker Siegmund Lubin, who in 1898 had attempted to film three hundred black men storming across Philadelphia's Fairmount Park in military regalia as "Buffalo Soldiers" in the Spanish American War.[72] Although the production startled a family on a carriage ride and was stopped by local police, the wily director was able to finish his film by moving his actors and crew to the Pennsylvania countryside, where the "war" resumed without further interruption.[73] The resulting moving pictures of "Buffalo Soldiers" so impressed Royston that he purchased a copy of the film and a Lubin Cineograph, a machine that cost about seventy dollars and which projected moving pictures and stereopticon slides.[74]

In 1899, Royston's Chicago Moving Picture Show featured the Lubin pictures in a thrilling celebration of racial progress and black martial manhood. Unlike exhibitions in white commercial venues, which tended to depict black people as unfit for the rights of citizenship, Royston's show underscored the patriotic contributions of black men to the nation's war efforts. In September, Royston reported to the *Indianapolis Freeman,* "We have just closed a two weeks [*sic*] tour of Virginia, which we are glad to say was two weeks of success. We use a Lubin Cineograph [projector], and we are featuring the colored soldiers."[75] The show employed electric light and included, along with the Lubin films, a stereopticon presentation of the "colored Commissioned Officers in the Spanish American War" and an accompanying lecture by renowned speaker Professor James D. Foster.[76] Royston proudly announced that his exhibition's combination of race pride and entertainment received "thundering applause" and was "storming the forts of ignorance nightly."[77]

The William Brothers in Indianapolis, Indiana, and William A. Bettis of Wichita, Kansas, commander of an all-black infantry unit during the Spanish American War, presented similar messages in their film programs.[78] Bettis traveled through Kansas, Oklahoma, northern Texas, and Mexico and reported that his exhibition on "the achievements of the Negro Soldiers" was a success.[79] These films, like the motion pictures exhibited by Conley and Pope, were not only entertaining, they were intended to educate their spectators on the importance of race pride.

Motion picture projectionists edited together their reels for exhibition, which further enabled them to shape the meaning of their films. With a sharp blade and some adhesive, a projectionist could rearrange a series of images, cut out unfavorable scenes, and splice together individual films to create a narrative, blurring the line between filmmaker and exhibitor. But even the simple act of determining where to place a film in a program allowed black film exhibitors to utilize white-produced images to illustrate the ideology of racial uplift, and its middle-class values of thrift, regularity, sexual propriety, hard work, and discipline as essential to collective racial progress. In 1903, Hyde Park Chapel in Chicago, Illinois, featured a multimedia exhibition of still and motion pictures that included a rendition of white novelist T. S. Arthur's *Ten Nights in a Bar-Room*.[80] At the turn of the century, Arthur's popular temperance tale was frequently depicted in photographs, performed onstage, and displayed on the screen (including a 1903 Lubin Manufacturing Company version of the story, which included the tragic tale of a "drunkard's child" and an "exciting scene" in a tavern that referenced Carrie Nation, the teetotaler famous for destroying saloons with her hatchet).[81] Hyde Chapel did not specify whether its version of *Ten Nights in a Bar-Room* appeared in still or moving images, or a combination of the two. The church simply described the program as "beautiful and historical pictures of the race and world together with other moving pictures."[82] Thus however rendered, *Ten Nights in a Bar-Room* was integrated into a multimedia presentation that reconfigured Arthur's story (and any white-produced images included in the exhibition) into a tale of racial harmony and uplift. Dr. A. L. Murray, the exhibitor, may have conveyed these messages with a simple act of visual juxtaposition, with a more complicated technique such as cutting his film together with scenes from other motion pictures, or by employing the capabilities of a machine such as Lubin Cineograph's stereopticon to incorporate projected still images of African Americans into the presentation.

In these early years, religious films were undoubtedly the most celebrated and widely reported type of black church exhibition. Black ministers scrambled to book motion picture depictions of biblical scenes in their churches, especially the wildly popular passion play, which included dramatic reenactments of the life, crucifixion, and resurrection of Christ. Several white-owned film production companies, including Hollaman-Eaves, the Lubin Manufacturing Company, Klan and Erlanger, and Pathé Frères, produced their own version of the passion.[83] They varied in their detail, but most included extravagant tableaus and were less driven by narrative than by the spectacle of their elaborate costumes and lavish sets. After these films were released for exhibition in commercial venues, production companies offered their films to itinerant moving picture exhibitors, who could purchase an entire passion play or select a few scenes to incorporate into a concert or lecture.[84]

In 1899, Reverend Graham of Bethel AME, who had announced the motion picture program at the Inter-State Bazaar, secured a copy of Edison's passion play for exhibition at the Bethel AME. These events were designed to appeal to a broad swath of the black public, young and old alike. Graham may have even brought his two-year-old daughter, Shirley—who would one day marry W. E. B. Du Bois and write her own screenplays—to the exhibition.[85] The black *Indianapolis Recorder* bragged that Bethel was "the first colored church in the country to take it [the Edison Passion Play]" and that it was the "finest spectacle" ever seen at the church.[86] Soon, passion plays could be found in black churches throughout the country; in Florida, C. E. Hawk brought them on a tour from St. Augustine to Sanford, Orlando, Tampa, and Key West.[87] In Washington, D.C., the leaders of the AME, black Methodist, and black Baptist churches all eagerly booked passion play films for their congregants.[88] Other venues, including Colored YMCAs, women's clubs, and universities, also scheduled exhibitions of religious-themed films.[89]

Passion plays, like other motion pictures, were usually exhibited with musical performances. Traveling exhibitor William Craft, the Nashville minister whose film exhibitions captivated Savannah in 1901, toured with his wife, a musician, who presented a musical recital with the passion play in their program. The

Jacksons, a husband-and-wife team who toured black churches in Maryland and Georgia, also combined a "sacred concert" with their moving pictures.[90] Some musical performances, especially those accompanying religious films, may have been similar or nearly identical to those performed in white venues. For example, "The Holy City," a ballad with lyrics written by English composer Fredrick E. Weatherly, was performed with "3,000 feet of highly colored films"—likely *La vie et la passion de Jésus Christ* by Pathé Frères, which had been hand-painted with vibrant tints—at the Wichita AME Church in 1909.[91] When *The Passion Play of Oberammergau* was scheduled at the Bethel AME in Baltimore for the church's Christmas Eve celebration in 1905, advertisements promised a cantata and "lovely music."[92] But even when featuring music deemed "European" in origins, black motion picture exhibitors selected songs tailored for their specific audiences. Leaders of the AME Church, for example, curated the "African Methodist Episcopal Hymn and Tune Book," to include songs that emphasized themes reflective of the particular interests of the race and "the progressive spirit of these modern times."[93]

Like black Americans, white traveling film exhibitors exhibited passion plays under the auspices of their own religious organizations.[94] Indeed, many of the factors that convinced black churches to open their doors to the moving pictures had also informed the decisions of white church denominations to do the same; both black and white religious leaders were alarmed by the growth of popular amusements and hoped that motion pictures would help maintain the status of their institutions.[95] In other respects, however, black and white film exhibition differed greatly from one another. White audiences primarily consumed motion pictures in "public accommodations" such as opera houses, vaudeville theaters, dime museums, and penny arcades. While white churches hosted moving picture shows, most films for white audiences, even those exhibited to benefit religious institutions, were consumed in commercial venues—places where black patrons were usually excluded or forced to sit in segregated seats. These practices became standardized during the nickelodeon era, after 1905, when cheap motion picture theaters spread across the country.[96]

As reports of the "well attended" shows in Kentucky, the "large audiences" in Maryland, and the "filled" churches in Ohio covered the pages of the black press, a growing number of black religious leaders jumped aboard the motion picture bandwagon.[97] These efforts were informed by the same spirit of collective racial progress that inspired everything from neighborhood membership drives to campaigns by high-ranking black officials to create broader, national organizations such as the National Baptist Convention. Driven by a belief in shared racial destiny and the power of cooperative action, ministers met regularly "to consider the best methods possible for bringing us more closely together as churches and as a race."[98] By the turn of the century, all the mainline black churches had joined into larger state and regional conventions, scheduled conferences, and planned cooperative mission work. The consolidation of black church denominations enabled the emergence of auxiliary national organizations, such as youth ministries and publication boards.[99] Black motion picture exhibition developed in dialogue with these changes, both contributing to and facilitated by the personal and professional relationships, forms of media, and collaborative projects that grew out of the efforts for cooperative racial advancement.

Moreover, by organizing these film exhibitions themselves, African Americans actively pursued an agenda of self-help, which they saw as critical to achieving their goals of racial advancement. Black reformer Henry Clay Yerger, the director of the Shover School for black students in Hope, Arkansas, used his 1903 moving picture exhibitions to garner financial support and public recognition for his educational projects.[100] Others personally profited from their film exhibitions, but because the belief in black capitalist enterprise was so deeply bounded to notions of racial progress, this revenue model fit seamlessly into the philosophy of racial uplift. For example, traveling film exhibitor Romulus R. Richmond served both as minister of Chariton, Iowa, Baptist Church and as a leading member of the Negro National Co-operative Development and Manufacturing Association. Despite his unwavering belief in racial progress through economic self-help, Richmond had meager resources (in addition to his other activities, he labored in the Lucas County, Iowa, coal mines for most of his life), but this did not prevent his participating in the phenomenon of motion picture exhibition. An inventor of considerable talent and holder of three U.S. patents, he may have constructed the projector used in his 1903 motion picture operation.[101] His endeavors reflected the sacred triumvirate of piety, industry, and race pride that guided the personal enterprises and participation in black public life of this first generation of black film exhibitors.

Churchwomen keenly recognized the potential of the moving pictures in their endeavors for racial uplift, but they often brought a more practical set of aspirations to their cinema practices than their loftier male counterparts. Black women were more likely to migrate to southern cities and to attend church than their males counterparts. They were also responsible for organizing their churches' social and fundraising activities. By the turn of the century, 119,778 more black women than men lived in southern cities, largely as a result of the urban demand for washerwomen and domestic servants.[102] Women also outnumbered men in black churches throughout the country. The four largest black Christian denominations, which were also the most frequent hosts of moving pictures, all had more female communicants or members than male. In 1906, for example, female membership in the National Baptist Convention was 62.5 percent; women also constituted 62.7 percent of the African Methodist Episcopal Church (AME) and 62.2 percent of the African Methodist Episcopal Zion Church (AMEZ), respectively.[103] These women were the engines not only of their churches but also of the new motion picture phenomenon.[104]

Because the task of arranging charity activities was commonly delegated to female congregants, such as the women who planned the 1897 Inter-State Bazaar at the Bethel AME, the contributions of black churchwomen were crucial to ensuring the success of church film exhibitions. Women such as Mary Page of the Fifth Street Baptist Church in Richmond, Virginia, organized film exhibitions while leading organizations such as the "Rally Club," which, despite its somewhat saccharine-sounding name, played one of the church's most vital functions—the marketing and advertising of the institution's fundraising activities.[105] Likewise, the Rose Bud Club and other women's organizations in Baltimore, Maryland, which hosted film exhibitions at the Whatcoat ME, Bethel AME, Waters AME, and Ebenezer AME, performed the spadework that made their church fundraising activities profitable.[106] Traveling film exhibitors such as Professor Richardson, too, relied on black churchwomen to publicize and sell tickets to their shows. In Philadelphia, he awarded Mildred Whaley an expensive watch for selling the most tickets to one of his programs.[107]

Additionally, black women worked as itinerant film exhibitors. Highly educated and entrepreneurial, black women such as Ednah Jane Walker were well prepared for the business of itinerant moving picture exhibition. After graduating from Oberlin College, she moved to Owensboro, Kentucky, to work as a schoolteacher. She later departed for Chicago, where she managed a grocery store and married her first husband, George W. Price. Within a few years, Ednah was either divorced or separated and operating the business by herself. In 1898, she remarried, this time to former major league baseball star and fellow Oberlin graduate Moses Fleetwood Walker, popularly referred to as "Fleet." But four months after their wedding, Fleet, who was employed by the post office, was arrested for mail fraud and sentenced to prison, leaving Ednah responsible for the welfare of her three stepchildren. With Fleet's career in the postal service over, the couple devised a new plan to make ends meet by capitalizing on his fame and the burgeoning black leisure industry. Soon after Fleet was released from prison, he and Ednah began giving motion picture exhibitions in halls and churches across Ohio and Pennsylvania and throughout the South.[108]

Most black women film exhibitors worked in husband-and-wife teams, like the Walkers, the Conleys, the Jacksons, and the Hawkinses. But a handful of women such as S. A. Bunn exhibited motion pictures independently. One of the most successful black film exhibitors of her generation, "Mrs. Bunn" of Philadelphia operated a motion picture show that toured for at least seven years, perhaps longer. Other performers might have traveled with her between Philadelphia and a circuit of churches farther south, but Bunn was clearly in charge. Her shows were especially popular in Maryland, where she garnered enthusiastic reviews for her "Great Moving Picture Exhibition." In Annapolis, Maryland, locals scrambled to see her moving picture concert and filled the Asbury Church to its "utmost capacity." According to the Baltimore *Afro-American,* the "show was conceded by all present that it was one of the best they had ever seen" and Bunn was immediately invited to return the following month for another exhibition.[109] Bunn's reputation was based not solely on the footage she screened but also on how she programmed the pictures within her larger entertainment program. Like most early exhibitors, she combined music and other live performances into her show. Bunn probably exhibited several short film clips, which she arranged to illustrate the ideas or themes she was promoting. The reputation accorded to Bunn for the quality of her exhibitions illustrates the importance of the exhibitor's skills in arranging a successful program.

Bunn navigated the shifting and often confusing terrain of turn-of-the-century gender relations by identifying herself as a married woman rather than as a "Reverend" or "Professor"—titles frequently adopted by male film exhibitors. Yet Bunn was not hidden behind a male figurehead. Neither did her independence elicit disapproval from the black press nor prevent her from booking her popular shows. The middle-class respectability of black film exhibition venues protected black women from the type of criticisms they may have encountered if they traveled alone to the theater or fairground. Conversely, the fact that films for white audiences were shown mainly in commercial venues constrained the ability of "respectable" white women to participate in the profession as traveling exhibitors.[110] Bunn demonstrated how desires for racial progress refashioned black middle-class ideas about gender—within specific contexts. Contributions by women in "feminine" organizing roles were underappreciated, but women such as Bunn might acquire recognition by stepping into positions that middle-class white and black Americans associated with male leadership. Black women could legitimately take on these roles because they promoted racial progress and religious values, and they performed within spaces associated with sexual propriety.[111]

Nevertheless, women received less public acknowledgment for the contributions they made to successful exhibitions. The black press, for example, usually described women as "assistants" to their husbands. Despite the fact that Mrs. Conley played a central role in Conley's Great Moving Picture Show, she received only a fraction of the attention accorded her husband.[112] Mrs. Conley, who was only identified as "Mrs. H. C. Conley" or the "wife of H. C. Conley," was an accomplished musician who performed in the troupe's concerts. And as an experienced businesswoman who served as a delegate to the National Negro Business League, she likely assisted, if not managed, the booking and marketing of the company's moving picture exhibitions. Mrs. Hawkins also worked with her husband but was rarely mentioned in promotional material or news reports of their exhibitions. Like many women exhibitors, she was identified only by her husband's name, but she may have been Lillian Hawkins, who later gained a reputation "for assisting women in their particular distresses" with her stereopticon illustrated lectures about the "ethics and science of gynecology."[113]

The participation of African American women in the formation of an early black cinema culture underscores one of the most distinctive characteristics of black women's organizational tactics at the turn of the century. By acknowledging the practical needs of their organizations, black women adopted a pragmatic approach to racial advancement. While their male counterparts sometimes noted the role women played in sustaining their churches, black men also ironically viewed the inclination of churchwomen to organize supposedly "trifling" amusements as reflective of feminine frivolity. "Some of the sisters are frequently giving some 'picayune' entertainment," minister Robert A. McGuinn complained in his 1890 tract *The Race Problem in the Churches,* "to get money to pay the pastor's salary, pay the interest on their mortgage, or buy coal to warm them in the winter."[114] But because women understood the challenges of fundraising, the practical requirements of appealing to the broader black public, and the day-to-day obligations of their churches, churchwomen were among the first to recognize the potential of cinema in black life. At the same time, black women advanced their own agendas while they raised money for their institutions. Women such as Frances Smith and Grace White reached across denominational lines to arrange film exhibitions for a special "Women's Day" program "at the John Wesley Methodist Episcopal Church, which was devoted to women's interests," and open to "*All the women of the City.*"[115]

By tapping into the extensive communication networks of black churches, black men and women transformed cities such as Savannah, Georgia, into hubs of itinerant film exhibition.[116] With dozens of black churches, a growing population of migrants, and a widely distributed black newspaper, Savannah was an attractive stop for the Davis Brothers, Reverend Daughtry, Professor Jackson, and J. V. Valentine, sometimes known as "Professor Snow."[117] When Nashville-based Baptist minister William Craft arrived in Savannah in 1901, it took him less than a week to arrange exhibitions of his moving picture show with the city's most venerable black religious institutions.[118] Craft publicized his program through the *Savannah Tribune,* announcing the dates and times of his exhibitions in the "Local Happenings" column of the paper. He also carried "several endorsements of his entertainments," which he used to reach out to other black denominations and secure shows with church leaders to whom he was not formally connected.[119] St. Philip AME Church of Savannah so enjoyed Craft's 1901 program that the following year it hosted several more film exhibitions.[120] By 1905, Savannah's own Reverend L. L. Blair was operating his own motion picture programs.[121]

Most of these early film exhibitors, including Ednah and Fleet Walker, S. A. Bunn, and William Craft, traveled across routes that resembled the intraregional patterns of turn-of-the-century black migration.[122] By the 1880s, trains came to play an increasingly important role in black religious life.[123] Repairs to railways destroyed during the Civil War and the construction of

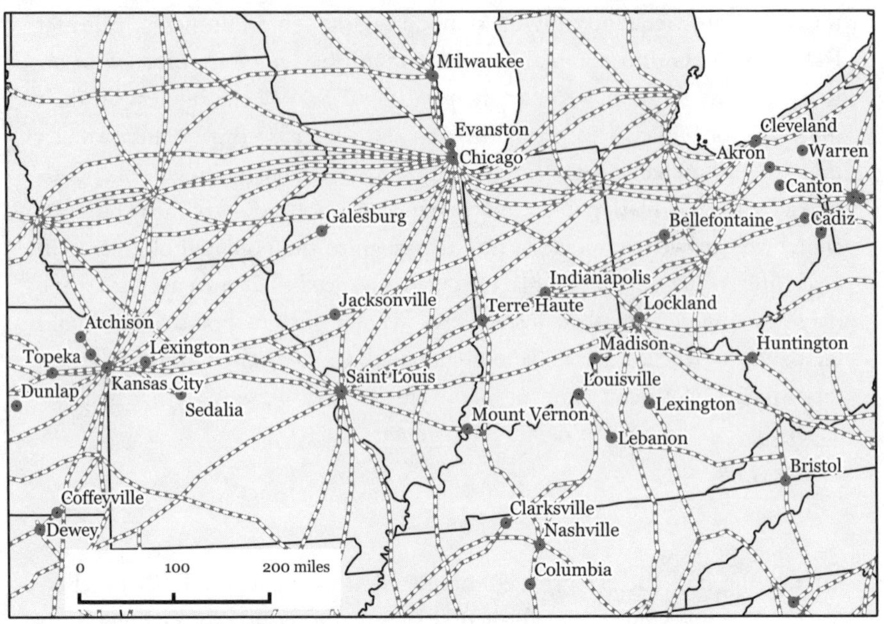

Railways and cities of black church, lodge, and school film exhibitions in midwestern and Upper South states, 1897–1912. Map © 2014 by Cara Caddoo.

new tracks enabled thousands of black ministers, entertainers, speakers, and musicians to earn a livelihood by presenting in black churches and other institutions. Black film exhibitors arranged closely clustered stops in single or adjacent states, and always traveled along the railways. Except for the most intrepid showmen such as H. Charles Pope, exhibitors limited their travels to regional circuits. S. A. Bunn, for example, left "for a tour of the South"; Washington, D.C.–based Richard T. Greener booked exhibitions in "all parts of the South"; and the Jacksons brought their motion picture show on a "tour [of] the South and West."[124] Although there was no formal circuit or route, itinerant exhibition centered in Kansas and Missouri in the West; in the Midwest, the hub was Ohio; in the South, Georgia, Tennessee, and Kentucky were the main centers; and along the eastern seaboard, moving picture show exhibitors traveled between Philadelphia and Baltimore.

The practice of booking tours in sequential stops along the railways—which made traveling film exhibition a feasible endeavor—was possible only with the emergence of an urban black population dispersed across those same

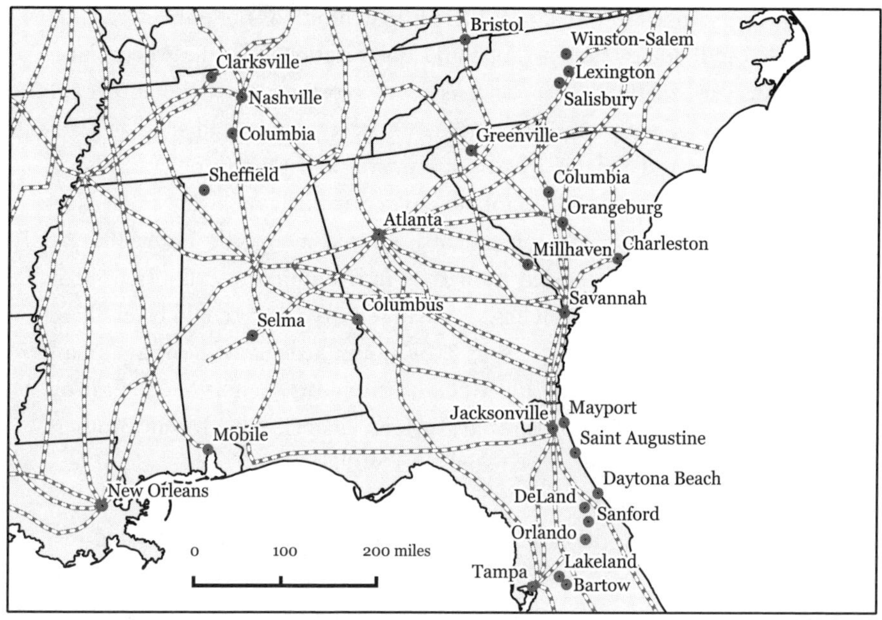

Railways and cities of black church, lodge, and school film exhibitions in southeastern states, 1897–1912.
Map © 2014 by Cara Caddoo.

systems of transportation.[125] Cities near railroad stops were accessible, had higher concentrations of black churches, and were more likely to receive or to publish their own black newspapers. Railroads were also a critical factor in structuring the settlement patterns of migrants in the mid-nineteenth and early twentieth centuries.[126] Boomtowns along these routes attracted pockets of black migrants from the nearby countryside.[127] As migration pushed progressively south and west, cities of black settlement, whose total populations ranged from 2,500 to upward of 50,000 inhabitants, followed the railroads. Large cities such as Richmond, Baltimore, Cleveland, and Savannah, with their multitude of black churches and clubs, frequently attracted film exhibitions because these cities had greater resources to allot to entertainment programs, but along the route, itinerants also included small and midsized towns. Although some exhibitors may have managed to make it to the countryside for the occasional festival or fair, dense pockets of black settlers in towns along the railways were the foundation of the early black moving picture routes.

A well-organized tour of consecutive film exhibitions not only saved time, it enabled individuals such as Pope and organizations like the Allen Christian Endeavor League to meet the considerable cost of a moving picture exhibition outfit.[128] For this reason, cities easily accessible by rail such as Lebanon, Kentucky, and Sedalia, Missouri, attracted a disproportional number of itinerant moving picture exhibitors compared to their relatively small black populations. Lebanon was conveniently located along the Louisville and Nashville Railroad and hosted numerous moving picture exhibitions at its Baptist, Zion, and Stent churches.[129] Sedalia's Katy Depot could be easily accessed on the way to larger cities such as St. Louis. Sedalia, home of the "maple leaf rag," was a popular stop for itinerant exhibitors such as S. M. Pearson, who showed his moving pictures at Taylor's Chapel; the Murray Brothers, who booked a show at Burns Chapel; and William Craft, who held at least two shows there in 1903.[130]

Most importantly, the same institutional connections and personal relationships that shaped black settlement patterns determined the routes of black film exhibition. While planning their tours, black motion picture exhibitors relied on friends, family, and church contacts to vouch for their reputations and assist in booking shows. Letters of introduction, such as those carried by William Craft, enabled newcomers in town to build on trusted relationships and gain credibility for their motion picture operations. S. A. Bunn relied on assistance from the Allen Christian Endeavor League, the youth fellowship of the AME Church, to organize her shows along the B&O rail system between Pennsylvania and Maryland (a route that had also shaped the settlement pattern of AME Church members in the region).[131] Itinerants also depended on kith and kin for lodging. In Washington, D.C., for example, the Lankford family hosted H. C. Conley and his wife for a summer while the traveling exhibitor booked "a long list of engagements for the fall and winter season."[132] While they were on the road, having a place to stay was even more important. A limited number of overnight accommodations, especially in the Jim Crow South, accepted black patrons.

Moreover, when moving picture exhibitors made new contacts with churches and other institutions, they worked to maintain those ties. Washington, D.C.–based H. Charles Pope directed "any minister wishing dates" in Kansas to write Mattie Freeman and Ralston Kenan, who were booking appointments for him at their address in Topeka. The gregarious Harry A. Royston sent dispatches to his friends across the country through the *India-*

napolis Freeman announcing that he would "be pleased to hear from all friends on and off the road" and nudging an acquaintance, E. J. Luney, to "please write."[133] And after Fleetwood Walker visited Cadiz, Ohio, in 1902 with a stereopticon and song show, he arranged to return almost exactly one year later with his wife, Ednah, to exhibit moving pictures in the city's churches.[134] The couple apparently found the town so agreeable they decided to move to Cadiz in 1904.[135]

Perhaps the most remarkable testament to the importance of preexisting networks and connections in determining exhibition routes was the appearance of moving pictures in towns with extremely small black populations.[136] For example, the Second Methodist Episcopal Church of Bellaire, Ohio, hosted an exhibition on March 28, 1902.[137] Bellaire had developed from a six-cabin outpost in the 1830s into an industrial hub after the Central Ohio Railway built a track into the city.[138] Yet its population of slightly fewer than 10,000 included only 428 black residents.[139] Hutchinson, Kansas, the site of several black film exhibitions in 1900, had a similar population; there were only 442 blacks recorded in that year's census. Even more remarkable was the film exhibition for black audiences in Dunlap, Kansas, once an all-black homestead led by Pap Singleton. When a black motion picture exhibitor appeared there in 1900, the town was virtually abandoned and the Freedman's School was shut down. With a population of only a few hundred and fewer than twenty-nine black families, it did not even qualify as "urban" by the modest standards of the U.S. government.

By 1905, across the South and West, in big cities and small towns, moving picture shows were integrated into the fabric of black life. In Topeka, the *Plaindealer* noted the unusually large attendance at the Shiloh Baptist Church in mid-June; the reason was clear to the paper: "A moving picture concern was the attraction."[140] Samuel H. Thompson was reportedly "making a hit" with his motion picture show in Columbus, Georgia.[141] And William Robinson's third show had "crowded" the house in Beaumont, Texas.[142] Newspaper announcements documented only a fraction of the church exhibitions between 1896 and 1910, but the reports nonetheless indicated how networks of communication between black individuals and institutions influenced the spread of film exhibition from one region to the next; the first moving picture exhibitions began in the western states of Missouri, Indiana, and Kansas, then swept through the Carolinas, Kentucky, Georgia, and Tennessee by 1901, reached Washington, D.C., West Virginia, Pennsylvania, and

Ohio by the following year, and moved into California, Florida, and Texas between 1905 and 1906.[143]

In the autumn of 1900, when John E. Lewis purchased a motion picture projector, the local black paper, the *Wichita Searchlight,* declared his deed so noble that he was "sure to go to heaven."[144] How the young migrant, at the cusp of the twentieth century, ended up in Wichita, Kansas, exhibiting moving pictures is a story that reflects the turbulence and the untiring ambition of so many of his generation. His life, which spanned the boundaries of two centuries, three countries, and—according to his obituary in 1920—from earth to a place where "visions of New Jerusalem" guided him to rest, began in Jamaica shortly after the Morant Bay Rebellion of 1865. The intrepid young man spent eight years of his youth living in Mexico before moving to Wichita, Kansas, in 1890, where he settled among the new migrants and an older generation of Exodusters from the upper South.[145] By the age of thirty-two, he had acquired the trappings of a successful nineteenth-century "race man": education, wealth, church leadership, and family.[146]

Lewis and his fellow investor, brother-in-law George Johnston, toured across Kansas in November 1900 with their moving picture show.[147] While on the road, Lewis "set up a new lodge" for the black Knights of Pythias, a fraternal organization dedicated to the progress of the race, and gave several exhibitions of his "instructive as well as amusing" films.[148] Whether he charged an admission fee to the shows or merely used the films to broadcast his beliefs, Lewis had integrated the moving pictures into his mission of racial uplift.[149] It was in this spirit that he served as deacon of his church, hosted events for the Optimate Club, and unapologetically bore the Knights of Pythias pin, which almost got him lynched one cold December night in 1906.[150] Undeterred, men like Lewis looked to the future with optimism, always in search of something exciting and new with which to push the race ahead. Along the way, he found himself, like millions of his counterparts, staring at a moving picture machine.[151]

The tumultuous changes of the late nineteenth century set the stage for black institution building at the regional and national levels, which in turn encouraged and gave shape to the practice of black film exhibition in the urban South and West. Sustained by the railroads and the growing centers of black urban settlement, moving picture exhibitions raised money, broadcast ideas, and brought black people together into common institutions. The church exhibition, in particular, became a common feature of African American urban life before the nickelodeon period—and years ahead of the colored theaters that would one day line the streets of Harlem and Chicago's Black Belt. For some, these first sites of black film exhibition were the only places they would ever watch a moving picture. As Lewis H. Davenport of Baltimore, Maryland, wrote in an editorial to the *Afro-American* in 1910, "Moving picture show houses I never visit, and have only seen the pictures show in churches."[152]

The intertwined development of black cinema and growth of black churches illuminate the role of religion and spirituality in African Americans' responses to modern life and their visions of progress in the postemancipation United States. Like the department store and nickelodeon, the black church, lodge, and school were resolutely modern phenomena. They manifested public black claims for advancement and progress and facilitated the development of a black public sphere.[153] Churches, in particular, "organized efforts of Negroes in any direction"; their buildings were used as gathering places, concert halls, and, by the turn of the twentieth century, moving picture theaters.[154]

Reconsidering the spaces of black public life and the migratory routes that began in the late nineteenth century brings to light a dramatically different and more complex story of black modernity. The formation of a cinema culture in black institutions across the South and West demonstrates that many of the cultural practices and experiences commonly associated with life in the industrial North actually emerged earlier and developed gradually along the routes of migration. In order to understand the boundless creativity of the "Harlem Renaissance" and the cosmopolitanism of the "New Negro," it is necessary to account for the urban experiences, leisure practices, and commercial endeavors that preceded the era traditionally described as the Great Migration.[155] African Americans forged their social bonds and institutions across space and through time. The structures they built and the paths they created gave shape to an ever-changing network of relationships, circuits of communication, and institutions, which would reconfigure the very terms on which black people staked their claims to modern progress in the twentieth century.

2

Cinema and the God-Given Right to Play

Motion picture exhibitors attempted to appeal to a broad swath of black urban dwellers, especially black youth. ("Negro life in Washington, D.C., 1911." Harris and Ewing Collection, Library of Congress.)

On a winter day in 1893, a young black woman from Tyler, Texas, knocked on the door of one of the most prominent white families in town. She was in search of work and wanted to inquire about a position. A few guests were dining at the house that day, including a correspondent for the *Dallas Morning News.* While the young woman waited outside, the guests discussed the "discomforts, vexations and an[n]oyances" to which white southern women were "subjected every day in the year by her wretched [Negro] domestics."

"Happy are those housekeepers who can manage to dispense with the services of those miserable, trifling creatures," the mistress of the house complained.

"They are absolutely good for nothing" a guest agreed, "for besides being untidy, false, treacherous, and generally dishonest, they are entirely too lazy to work."

From where she was standing, the servant girl may not have heard the conversation taking place inside, but she was well prepared to discover for herself the prejudices of her prospective employer. As soon as her interview began, the young woman recited a list of questions: "How many hours in the day will I have to work here?" "Would you let me off on Sundays and on every night when there is a choir rehearsal at the church?" "How much wages do you pay?" The mistress of the house impatiently answered the young woman's questions and promptly ended the interview.[1]

Whether the servant girl was headstrong and determined to find fair-paying work with acceptable hours or simply oblivious (as the *Dallas News* reporter believed) to the irritation of her prospective employer, the young woman's inquiries demonstrated the particular value she assigned to her precious nonworking hours.[2] In 1893, when these events unfolded, modern cinema had yet to enter the landscape of America's leisure activities. But within a decade, the leisure demands of working-class blacks like this servant girl from Tyler would remake film exhibition from a novelty promoted by the middle class into a popular pastime enjoyed by millions of black Americans. By 1906, black Knights of Pythias halls and churches across Texas, indeed the entire South and West, were regularly featuring moving picture entertainments.[3] Nearly a century later, the discovery of rare films produced for black audiences between the 1930s and 1940s in a Tyler, Texas, warehouse hints at the enduring importance cinema may have had for the local black population.[4]

Historians have long debated the meaning of leisure in the lives of turn-of-the-century Americans.[5] Early labor historians argued that leisure tempered the frustrations of American workers, making them less apt to join unions or form political organizations.[6] By the 1980s, however, the work of British labor historians inspired a growing number of American historians to question these assumptions. These scholars argued that nineteenth-century working-class leisure activities actually manifested a rejection of the capitalist values of frugality, efficiency, and industriousness and that it was only with the rise of cross-class leisure venues such as the moving picture palace that the alternative working-class culture fell into line with the ideals of industrial capitalism.[7] Subsequent research has uncovered an even deeper ambivalence toward capitalist values in working-class amusements. By frequenting commercial sites of leisure like dance halls and amusement parks, working-class Americans rejected middle-class notions of proper behavior, while simultaneously buying into the values of capitalist consumer culture.[8] Although such leisure activities tempered certain types of class critique, they also fostered new forms of social and political consciousness. Black workers, for example, expressed discontent and created solidarity through covert forms of resistance interwoven into their everyday leisure activities.[9] Yet as scholars of the postemancipation period known as the "nadir" of race relations have demonstrated, African Americans expressed much more than their acceptance or rejection of capitalist values through their leisure activities. They also gave meaning to their lives as free people and as human beings.[10]

At the turn of the century, black Americans formed an urban leisure culture around the motion pictures. Segregation contributed prominently to these developments. As the class and gender hierarchies that once separated the leisure activities of the nineteenth century began to fade, these divisions were replaced with a system of racial exclusion. But Jim Crow did not single-handedly bring about a shared black culture of leisure; equally important to this formation were the factors that united the sensibilities of black city dwellers.[11] Black laborers constituted the majority of black urbanites, and in general they tended to favor the type of rowdy, sensuous public amusements that conflicted with the outwardly "respectable" behavior advocated by the middle class.[12] The emerging black cinema culture negotiated these tensions by both pleasing the interests of the black middle class and captivating the attention of their working-class counterparts.

Through their interactions with the motion pictures, black Americans forged a collective culture of freedom. As they transformed cinema into a popular urban amusement, they generated new social bonds and subjectivities—the perspectives, sensibilities, experiences, ideas, and demands of an emerging modern black public. These interactions between black Americans contributed to the evolving role of cinema within cities of new settlement, and more broadly across the pathways of black migration. In order to meet the swelling demand for motion pictures, black institutions came to rely on the innovations of a newly professionalized class of itinerant black film exhibitors. These professional showmen and -women competed for church and lodge bookings by incorporating more spectacular films and special features into their exhibitions and by devising an ever-more-dazzling array of marketing and advertising strategies aimed at drawing the black public into their shows.

Having overheard the conversation between the servant girl in search of work and the housewife from Tyler, the *Dallas News* reporter wrote up a timely article—in 1893, the "negro servant girl problem" was a frequent topic of heated conversation among frustrated whites across the South.[13] In the article, names and other clearly identifying information were omitted to protect the identity of the hostess and because the reporter probably felt no need to distinguish this particular "servant girl" from any other. Indeed, the term "girl" was less a reference to age than to status; just a decade earlier, reporters described the black victims of a serial killer as "servant girls," even though several of the women were in their twenties and thirties and married when they were murdered.[14] But even though the *Dallas News* reporter did not cite the name or age of the black woman from Tyler, Texas, the woman's questions about "time off" belied the reporter's description of her as merely a "servant girl"; they indicated the existence of a rich personal life outside of work, which she clearly cherished over her labors as a domestic worker.

Tenacious claims to leisure such as these were woven into the forces that fueled the emergence of a black cinema culture and that would continue to reconfigure its development across the twentieth century. In particular, the urbanization of America's black population informed both the strategies of black institutions as they sought to achieve their goals of collective racial progress and the growing demands of the black working class for urban amusements across the South and West. The acceleration in black migration from the rural hinterland, which occurred in response to the post-Reconstruction racial order and the upheavals of industrialization, signaled a shift in the tactics African Americans used to claim their autonomy as free people. Earlier in the nineteenth century, newly emancipated black Americans, like their white rural counterparts, associated land ownership with freedom. Black resistance to the exploitative system of wage work in the rural South had thwarted early attempts to create a wage-labor force for the cotton economy and ended in a negotiated system of sharecropping and tenant farming.[15] But when the promises of freedom in agricultural life went unfulfilled, a growing number of black folk left the countryside in hopes of building better lives for themselves and their families.[16]

In the city, most migrants became, for the first time in their lives, full-fledged members of the wage-labor force.[17] Despite complaints from Tyler's unhappy white housewives, "servant girls" such as thirteen-year-old Mary Ingram and sixteen-year-old Julia Thompson, who cooked and served meals for white families, were in high demand across Texas, and in fact throughout the entire South.[18] There was also a considerable market for laundresses; for a small fee, black women were expected to make their own lye soap and starch, collect wood, haul buckets of water to fill washing tubs, build fires, and scrub laundry clean in scalding hot water.[19] While there were fewer male than female migrants in the urban South, black men also found work in the city, usually performing backbreaking manual labor.[20] The wages provided some workers with enough income and stability to maintain ties with their families and communities, but the economic advantages they reaped were only relative to their previous exploitation. African Americans were paid less for their time than white workers, even when performing more arduous work.[21]

Relegated to unskilled labor and deemed less valuable on the marketplace because of their race, black urban dwellers anchored their identities and invested their energies in other features of city life. In their new cities of settlement, African Americans gave meaning to their lives as free people, wageworkers, and urbanites by claiming their "God-given right to play."[22] Not only was the "thirst for amusement" a "powerful and in some cases an even more deciding motive" for migration than economic opportunity—as W. E. B. Du Bois once wrote—leisure was also necessary for workers' physical and psychological recuperation after hours of strenuous labor.[23] Like white workers, black folk envisioned leisure as a special sphere of life away from work, a sphere that belonged wholly to themselves. However, unlike their white counterparts, this generation of black Americans and their children were not claiming the lost pleasures of their preindustrial lives—they were instead, for the first time, collectively forging a culture of freedom.

For the servant girl in Tyler, church and leisure were intertwined. Participation in the church choir (an activity she specifically referenced in her request for time off) brought her particular spiritual or emotional fulfillment. Certainly, singing in the church choir could be a religious experience, but such activities were hardly a matter of piety and spiritual uplift alone. Black churches had earned their place as the center of black social life by hosting a vast array of amusements for their own congregants and other local black residents. Indeed, some African Americans believed this was the *most* important function of the black church. Black minister and sociologist W. H. Holloway, for instance, complained in 1903 that young folk looked to the church "more as a bureau whose object is to provide amusement than they do toward it as a holy institution whose high privilege it is to deal with external realities and interpret the weightier matters of the law."[24]

When churches did not satisfy the leisure demands of black migrants, they looked elsewhere for entertainment. Workers formed secret organizations like the "Golden Rod Pleasure Club" and the "Erma Social Club" to make the most of their leisure time in the Jim Crow city.[25] "Lid clubs" and saloons served up intoxicating beverages and opportunities to "slow drag," "fanny bump," or "grind."[26] Those feeling lucky or just plain desperate might slip into a private club for a high-stakes game of three-card monte. With emptier pockets, migrants caroused in the city streets or loitered on street corners.[27] The physical exertion and bodily contact of dance, the movement and thrill of sporting games, and the heady sensation of drink were especially appealing to newly urbanized workers who used leisure to reclaim their bodies after grueling hours of manual and domestic labor.[28] As the world of working-class black leisure, "corner stands," "Negro dives," and dance halls swelled with the influx of black migrants into the city, black reformers and church leaders grew increasingly anxious about the leisure-time activities of their working-class black counterparts.[29]

The amusements of black urban youth presented a special conundrum to the black middle class. By 1900, cities of new black settlement were filled with leisure-hungry young migrants. Even as gender and income demographics varied by region and changed over time, urban migration would continue to be disproportionately a movement of young people.[30] In fact, the scarcity of black youth in rural Virginia once prompted Du Bois to characterize migration as a "perfect stampede of young Negroes to the City."[31] To many older, middle-class blacks, these urban youth seemed absorbed in only the most trivial of pastimes. As one exasperated black observer complained in 1905, young women spent too much time at dances, ice cream parlors, and thoroughfares "clinging to the arm of a dude every night," and young men were "ever ready to go somewhere," so long as it was "a place of frivolity."[32] Youthful revelers nonetheless evoked a great deal of ambivalence from black reformers, who believed that young people were especially vulnerable to the evils of urban life.[33] Social scientist Monroe N. Work, for example, blamed the wayward habits of black youth on a shortage of sufficient leisure activities, and publicly pled with the "Negro Church to attempt to supervise and control, but not with too great rigor, the amusement centers for its young people."[34]

Few and far between were churches that sponsored liquor-fueled "honkey tonks" or an evening shooting craps, but black religious leaders delighted in the moving pictures—a healthy, wholesome form of entertainment easily infused with themes of race pride and piety.[35] By distracting black workers with church-sponsored film exhibitions, the middle class hoped to "offset the saloon and places of amusement."[36] "Gambling, drinking, intoxicating liquors," and late nights at the jook joint were especially troublesome because of the inefficiency of the unregulated motion of dance, the wasted energy of sweating for pleasure rather than profit, and the threat of inhibitions loosened by the bottle.[37] As one black resident of Washington, D.C., explained disapprovingly—and perhaps also with a touch of longing—cheap dances and "syncopated music with its sensual stimulus," attracted "splendid female possibilities with the usual results."[38] Black reformers disapproved of working-class black leisure districts, not only because they supposedly bred iniquity but also because the growing leisure industry seemed to siphon money away from their collection plates. "To maintain its preeminence," sociologist Isabel Eaton observed in 1899, "the Negro church has been forced to compete with the dance hall, the theatre, and the home as an amusement-giving agency."[39]

Religious youth organizations, including the black Baptists' National Young People's Union (BYPU), the AME's Allen Christian Endeavor League (ACEL), and the Methodist Epworth League, which had separate branches for its black members, were especially apt to sponsor film exhibitions.[40] In fact, several of the first black itinerant exhibitors, including L. L. Blair, general manager of the local black YMCA in Atlanta, Georgia; John E. Lewis, president of his local branch of the BYPU; and William Craft, future national secretary of the BYPU, were closely connected to such associations.[41] These black youth ministries, recently created under the denominational umbrellas of mainline black churches, along with organizations such as colored YMCAs, all hosted moving picture exhibitions as part of their mission to attract and maintain the interest of young people.[42] For example, in Baltimore, Maryland, young black adults could attend a moving picture hosted by the Allen Christian Endeavor League, which frequently sponsored S. A. Bunn's shows, or exhibitions organized by the Epworth League, which frequently hosted moving picture shows at the Metropolitan Church, including, in 1907, "Moving Pictures of Africa."[43]

Motion pictures were less controversial than the "turkey trot," the "bunny hug," or even the more "civilized" waltz.[44] Safely confined to the church, hall, or school, films were not intoxicating, nor did they encourage bodily contact like dancing—at least, early church proponents believed this to be true. The themes of church-sponsored programs additionally reflected the values that reformers hoped to inculcate among the black youth. The film exhibition of itinerant film showman H. Charles Pope, for instance, aimed to teach black youth of the dangers of dance. For church leaders who believed that the feet were not meant "to leap imprudently like camels," Pope's presentation of "Ballroom to Hell" was "doing untold good among the youth."[45] Moreover, like film exhibitions for adults, these programs helped churches raise money. A resident of Thomas County, Georgia, described the relationship that had developed between the local black churches and their younger congregants as an especially utilitarian one: "The church amuses the young people," she explained without mincing her words, "and they pay for the amusement."[46]

Of course, some black middle-class reformers saw the project of racial uplift in more cynical terms, complaining that "the better classes [had] a monstrous burden in being made to shoulder the evils of the bad crowd."[47] Sensitive to the growth of scientific racism that reasoned all blacks shared the same moral, intellectual, and physical capabilities, these black reformers feared that the "best" members of the race were associated with the low-class pool hall and jook joint. The upsurge of urban migration deepened these concerns, especially because Jim Crow housing policies began relegating all African Americans to the same residential spaces. In places of amusement, the middle class resentfully watched as the spectrum of divisions of class, ethnicity, status, and income that had previously dictated nineteenth-century leisure practices collapsed into two overarching categories: white and colored.[48]

These fears were compounded by white anxieties over working-class black amusements, especially so-called Negro dives, which had reached a fever pitch with the increase in black urban migration. White politicians revoked the licenses of black businesses, organized police raids on "the dives and saloons frequented by members of the race," and passed legislation that prohibited race mixing in places of public amusement.[49] White newspapers contributed to the hysteria by publishing sensational tales of interracial mixing. Reports of "white slavery" were especially alarmist, describing "weak-minded" young white women lured into the tawdry houses for "immoral purposes," or "young and pretty white" girls who were kidnapped, imprisoned, and forced into prostituting themselves to black men.[50] Cities such as Springfield, Ohio, repeatedly erupted into violence; in 1904, "a mob of 2,000 persons tried to destroy the dives and saloons" of the city's black leisure district, burning down buildings, and killing indiscriminately.[51] Two years later, 6,000 whites marched to a white-owned saloon frequented by blacks, raided it for its whiskey and beer, and then burned it down along with several black homes.[52] The same year, dozens of black residents of Atlanta, Georgia, were murdered in a riot that was fueled by local politicians and reports in the white newspaper, the *Atlanta Constitution,* of criminality and a proclivity for white women bred in the city's Negro dives.[53]

Black reformers preferred church and lodge film exhibitions to the "negro dive," but black workers had their own, often very different, reasons for attending film exhibitions. "Cheap amusements" such as the moving pictures appealed to the sensibilities, and the pocketbooks, of the black working class.[54] For as little as a nickel, or most commonly a dime, black workers could stop by their local church or lodge to view a motion picture exhibition.[55] These programs were substantially less expensive than most vaudeville or theater shows, providing working-class blacks an opportunity to unwind after a hard day of work in places where they could socialize among their peers.[56] In 1906, when C. E. Hawk arrived in Darien, Georgia, with his illustrated motion pictures, most of the town's black population, which consisted primarily of laborers employed in the lumber and naval stores industries, and a good number of visitors from greater McIntosh County, turned out to see the show.[57] Nearly eight hundred people (especially remarkable because Darien's entire black population numbered slightly less than a thousand) reportedly clamored to watch the exhibition of *Daniel in the Lion's Den* and *The Mysterious Handwriting on the Wall,* two religious films that had been released the previous year by Pathé Frères.[58] "The crowds were so great," Hawk bragged to the *Freeman,* that they "had to open the doors and windows and the outdoor collection amounted to twenty-three dollars from those standing."[59]

As individuals, poor black workers had little control over church and lodge matters, but collectively, they wielded considerably more sway, especially in terms of popular entertainments. When the novelty of the moving image no longer piqued their interest, they demanded new and more exciting programs through their patronage. In 1905, locals in Coffeyville, Kansas, for example, chose not to attend a show at their local black Odd Fellows Hall because they assumed the films were "a repetition of the [apparently unimpressive] Saturday night exhibition."[60] Black audiences in Atlanta, Georgia, were even more explicit in their leisure demands after a disappointing show at the Willow Tree Church. Having spent a dime to watch the Christian Exhibition Company's moving picture program, *In His Steps, or What Would Jesus Do,* the unhappy audience, which believed they had been duped into a moneymaking scheme during the show, attacked the two itinerant exhibitors and demanded their ten cents back.[61] In contrast, black spectators were known to follow a "show nightly from church to church" when they were captivated by a particularly enthralling exhibition.[62] These black audiences, through collectively expressing their desires and attending motion pictures together, had begun to articulate themselves as a filmgoing public.

By organizing film exhibitions and other widely appealing amusements, black reformers acknowledged, although somewhat reluctantly, the importance of leisure in the lives of their working-class counterparts.[63] Minister Robert A. McGuinn denounced the "Ridiculous!" priorities of black congregants, who spent thousands of dollars on frivolous commercial leisure activities while their *"unsystematic giving"* left church coffers empty, but he also admitted that profits from club- and church-sponsored entertainments had kept more than a few churches afloat.[64] Reverend George McNeal realized that proselytizing could do little to stunt the appeal of the burgeoning commercial leisure culture, and called on black churches to awaken to "their duty to the rising generation" by offering more "social features."[65] Secular organizations such as the National Negro Business League likewise committed themselves to "providing [the race] suitable places of amusement."[66] In 1910, the league even produced a series of motion pictures with Booker T. Washington, announcing it would "send its pictures about the country and show them in colored churches."[67]

In order to satisfy the demands of their audiences, churches and other black institutions relied on the innovations of professional itinerant exhibitors. From almost the beginning, the practice of hosting traveling film exhibitors had become the most common way for African Americans to organize a motion picture show. Itinerant moving picture exhibitors brought a wider selection of films and more sophisticated exhibitions—generating greater public interest and much-needed capital. Itinerant exhibition also limited the overhead and economic risk for both parties. Churches could incorporate moving picture shows into their calendars without having to purchase a projector, or more prohibitively, constantly investing in new reels of film. Itinerant exhibitors likewise benefited from this relationship. Itinerant showmen and -women with limited capital did not have to risk the investment of purchasing a permanent exhibition space; they could also tap into preestablished networks of local black institutions, such as church membership rolls, which provided free labor and a ready-made audience. Individuals such as Pope, who exhibited *The Devil's Cook Kitchen* for several years, could tour a single moving picture program throughout the country rather than having to continuously change his films to satisfy the demands of a local fixed audience.[68]

Within the itinerants, however, two overlapping groups began to emerge: "institutional exhibitors" and "professors." Institutional black exhibitors included ministers and reformers with formal connections to religious or charitable "uplift" organizations such as John E. Lewis of the Knights of Pythias, Baptist minister William Craft, and educator Henry Clay Yerger. They may have relied partially on the profits they earned from their exhibitions, but their primary goal was publicizing and fundraising for their organizations.[69] Although institutional exhibitors were some of the first people to screen motion pictures, by 1903, they were outnumbered by a new generation of professionals who did not represent specific charitable or religious institutions. Referring to themselves as "professors" rather than "reverends" or "ministers," these exhibitors had more time and resources to devote to their motion picture operations. They booked entire seasons in advance, and their circuits of exhibition followed railroad routes and ports not only regionally but also across the country and abroad. This group included early professionals H. C. Conley and C. E. Hawk, who were later joined by an equally ambitious and highly competitive cohort of film exhibitors including Professor Wade and Professor Richardson, who similarly represented only themselves or their for-profit companies.[70]

In their transactions with churches and other hosting institutions, the professors competed for bookings with forthright descriptions of the profit-orientated nature of their endeavors. After Professor Richardson (later Dr. Richardson) spent more than $250 updating his operation with a "fire-proof cabinet, automatic machines and electric fixtures, to satisfy the new fire law," the self-proclaimed "Religious Show King" announced he was "ready to make dates to show in all churches, with all new pictures," "His name alone means success," Richardson's advertisements boldly declared.[71] The Davis Entertainers also wooed churches by promising to earn "big money" for ministers and church societies. Speaking directly to their customers in the pages of the black press, the Davis Entertainers assured religious and club leaders that the company could "enrich the treasury of *your* church."[72] For the church organizers of black institutions such as the First Baptist Church in Washington; St. Paul Methodist Episcopal in Baltimore, Maryland; and St. Paul Church in Portsmouth, Virginia, which booked these exhibitions, the moral qualifications of film exhibitors and the "uplifting" qualities of their programs were still important, but profits were the first measurement of success.[73] This interdependence of professional black film exhibition and black churches for economic survival sheds light on the pivotal role of black religious institutions in fostering the development of black capitalism.

Only in extraordinary cases did the motivations of for-profit entertainers come into direct conflict with the tenets of racial uplift. Usually this happened when film exhibitors attempted to capitalize on the market of black institutions while brazenly flouting the rules of proper middle-class behavior. One such individual, Mont Morenzo, who claimed to be a "full-blooded African" prince, began making "a special effort to 'show' [his lecture] in black churches," in the early 1890s. He enjoyed a period of relative success before his love of drink and an uncontrolled temper sullied his reputation.[74] Discovered "as full of liquor as he could be and walk" in Ohio and later charged in South Carolina with striking an associate on the head with his walking cane, Morenzo was exposed as a fraud by the black press.[75] The news led to the cancellation of several of his lectures in New York. But in 1905, he was once again appearing in black churches—this time exhibiting motion pictures across Kansas.[76] Although the state, legally dry since 1881, may have encouraged Morenzo's best behavior, his enduring popularity indicates that churches occasionally turned a blind eye to some of the more egregious violations of middle-class mores when film exhibitors turned handsome profits. "There can be one reason given by pastors who persist in the employment of such questionable persons and methods," complained the *Southwestern Advocate* after it uncovered Morenzo's scam, "and that is a desire to make money."[77]

The most successful film exhibitors, however, gracefully navigated between the sensibilities of the black middle class and the demands of their working-class audiences. For example, during film exhibitions, the professors openly encouraged boisterous, outwardly emotional behavior commonly associated with working-class leisure haunts and supposedly "backward" forms of black religious worship. The middle class usually opposed such behavior, especially in black churches; during Sunday services, mainline denominations often prohibited spontaneous noisemaking, bodily movement, and other expressive behaviors described as "getting happy," which reformers viewed as relics of slave worship and rural spirituality.[78] But the often-rowdy reactions of audiences to motion pictures in black venues elicited very different responses from the middle class. In part because the technology cast such behavior as modern, unrestrained demonstrations of rapture were celebrated as indications of successful film shows, and black newspapers applauded film exhibitions that left their audiences "screaming with delight."[79] The professors further encouraged uninhibited expressions of emotion—shrieks of laughter, shouting, and exaltation—with the curiosities and thrilling displays of skill that they presented with their film exhibitions. Reminiscent of circuses and carnivals, these attractions included drag shows, a "celebrated rapid talker," and the "monkey-face boy" who stood at "4 feet high."[80]

The demand for thrilling forms of entertainment drew increasingly spectacular films into black churches and lodges. For black Americans, a population whose lives had been marked by an onslaught of continuous and dramatic change, these types of moving pictures presented the disruptions of modern life reassuringly.[81] The visual spectacle of modern cinema resonated with the sensory experience of city life as experienced by the newly urbanized migrant: in particular, its unfamiliar sights and sounds, constant motion, and spectacular new technologies. Roaring machinery, suffocating smokestacks, crowded city streets, and otherwise threatening spectacles of disjunction that daily confronted the urban dweller could be aestheticized and stripped of their most caustic attributes, leaving the audience to thrill in their cognitive responses.[82] Cinema also presented time and space in a way that resembled the perspective of a railroad passenger watching the world quickly change within the frame of the train window—the very experience that had transported most black migrants from their former homes to their present locations.[83] But as black audiences grew accustomed to the scenes they once found so thrilling and new, the professors rushed in with bolder, fantastical productions and the "latest moving pictures of the day."[84]

By 1903, action-packed narrative films and an array of progressively more sensational motion pictures filled the rosters of black church and hall exhibitions. *The Great Train Robbery* (1903), a twelve-minute film directed by Edwin S. Porter, was especially popular. The Ladies Aid Society of St. John's Church, which showed the film during one of its fundraisers, cheerfully described the picture as having "one thrilling scene" with a "bank robbery and hold-up of an express train."[85] Moving pictures of natural disasters and other catastrophes were also in high demand. Such films, including one of the 1908 Augusta flood, which left more than sixty people dead and the city immersed in six feet of water, screened at the Bethlehem Church in Georgia. The "sinking steamer Titanic, which went down with nearly two thousand on board," was shown in churches across Maryland.[86] In Richmond, Virginia, locals were invited to watch scenes of "the San Francisco Great Disaster" at St. Luke Hall for the benefit of Mt. Zion Baptist Church. "Everybody wants to see the Moving Pictures," the church announced in the *Richmond Planet,* as it was "the very greatest catastrophe of the kind ever witnessed in America."[87] Pared down to their visual elements and reassembled with nondiegetic sound—the melody of a singing choir, a piano accompaniment, or a lecture—these images of modern disaster starkly contrasted with the safe and innocuous surroundings in which they were viewed.

Passion plays and other religious films—the mainstay of the first black church shows—remained popular, but they were combined into eclectic presentations with disaster films, morality tales, and race pride pictures. In 1904, for example, William G. Hynes showed films that depicted two of the most devastating fires in American history: the *Burning of the General Slocum Ship* and *Iroquois Theater Burning,* along with pictures of the "progress" of the race (perhaps similar to his films of the National Baptist Convention and the Baptist Young People's Union), and the first part of the *Life of Christ.*[88] These programs resembled the visual cacophony of turn-of-the-century amusements such as the dime museum, which exhibited an assortment of cultural oddities, human curiosities, and scientific artifacts. But like the segregated theater, dime museums were organized to please the ideal white spectator. Their displays, for instance, commonly portrayed black bodies as the "missing link" in human evolution.[89] In contrast, Hynes's black audiences witnessed inspiring depictions of piety and racial progress amid scenes of a world torn asunder. Juxtaposed against the traumas of modern life, black Americans in these film exhibitions were situated as emblems and agents of modern advancement.

Hawk also showed a combination of religious films, including the *Holy City, Prodigal Son,* and a passion play, along with scenes of military battles, temperance tales, and heist films.[90] By employing an assortment of contrasting images in their programs, especially in regard to setting and location, film exhibitors attempted to replicate sensations such as movement across space, a familiar experience for black migrant audiences. Hawk arranged his films to play on the pleasure of mobility by contrasting scenes of the familiar with the exotic. In Florida, for example, he described an exhibition in which he took his audience to the hills of Manchuria, and then, with great flourish, "brought the spectators back to Missouri."[91] In Richmond, Virginia, Professor M. Jones's film exhibition promised to transport his audience from their everyday lives and make them feel as if they were "actually in the midst of the scenes."[92]

White Americans—especially immigrants and newly urbanized laborers—delighted in many of these types of spectacles, but motion pictures also acquired distinctive, often racialized significance in the context of a black venue, and to black audiences. A film such as *Daniel dans la fosse aux lions* (1905), which Hawk exhibited in Darien, Georgia, depicted a biblical tale that African Americans would have understood in the context of specific cultural references circulating through the black public sphere. Negro spirituals such as "Didn't My Lord Deliver Daniel" told the story of Daniel's deliverance from the lion's den as an allegory to slavery, and the frequent evocations of the biblical figure by black artists, ministers, and other race leaders made Daniel—enslaved, kidnapped from his homeland, and saved by the grace of God—a symbol of the plight of black Americans.[93] Likewise, the black public's reaction to the Russo-Japanese War informed the reception of films such as *Fall of Port Arthur,* which depicted a decisive battle won by the Japanese in 1904. Black Americans, unlike their white counterparts, rallied behind the victory of the Japanese over the white "Russian horde" as triumph for all the "dark race[s]." The "sympathy of the Afro-American is with the Japanese in the present war," declared black newspapers such as the *St. Paul Appeal.*[94] These ideas likely contributed to the response of the black audiences at St. Luke AME in New Augustine, Florida, which in 1905 were reportedly "spell bound" during a motion picture exhibit "when the Japs began to charge at Nanshan Hill storming the Russians."[95]

The motion pictures of ministers such as L. L. Blair of Savannah, who participated in the growing sensationalism, also demonstrate the limitations of analyzing early films without accounting for their exhibition venues. Almost exactly one year after Will Cato and Paul Reed were burned at the stake by a mob of whites in nearby Statesboro, Georgia, Blair announced a "new moving picture exhibition" at St. Philip with "All of the latest scenery." Among the pictures to be exhibited, Blair's advertisement announced, was a film showing "the lynching of Cato and Reid [*sic*] at Statesboro."[96] Blair's film may have been a fictionalized account of the murder, but it was common to visually record actual lynchings.[97] In fact, professional photographers captured still images of Cato and Reed's deaths, which were later disseminated as souvenirs and postcards. Moving picture cameras were technologically sophisticated and transportable enough by 1904 to have filmed Cato and Reed's murders, and the location where the lynching was to take place was publicized well before the murders. Although the men were ultimately killed about two miles away from this site, a camera operator would have had ample time to prepare the film. Finally, because the murders took place at three in the afternoon, there was sufficient light for exposure of the film stock, which would have been much less possible had the murders occurred at night.

There are no further accounts verifying the authenticity of Blair's films or relating how Blair may have acquired them. But records of the film and its origins would still not account for the ways in which Blair might have arranged this film in an exhibition to affect the way the audiences read the images. Neither would records of the film's origins account for the ways that audiences respond to the exhibition of such types of violence, however arranged, in an all-black venue versus the segregated theater. In any case, it does not appear that the church continued to exhibit other films of lynchings, although a few other churches did exhibit moving pictures with fictionalized lynching scenes.

The exhibition site and composition of the audience similarly affected the reception of motion pictures that included racial stereotypes borrowed from the minstrel stage. Black churches occasionally included such films in their programs. The People's Congregational Church in Washington, D.C., for example, featured comedies that depicted African Americans engaging in watermelon-eating contests and stealing chickens.[98] By the turn of the century, several white film companies had produced versions of these films, usually portraying black or blackface characters overindulging in food and dance, behaving foolishly, and getting punished for their crimes.[99] The Edison Company's rendition of *Watermelon Eating Contest* (1896), for example, showed two black men sitting on stools, ravenously eating slices of fruit and spitting out the seeds. Historians have pointed out that these images enabled whites to engage vicariously, through the black characters on-screen, in the preindustrial pleasures of rural life, while simultaneously rejecting the possibility of black social and democratic equality.[100] But black spectators in all-black venues may have not have interpreted the images on-screen as representations of themselves or their racial identities. For example, city-dwelling blacks, much like their white counterparts, reveled in their urban sophistication and frequently regaled one another with tales of their unsophisticated country cousins; stories of Old Aunt Hepsy Garside or Uncle Josh, who could not distinguish between reality and the images on-screen, were oft-repeated celebrations of urban savoir faire.[101] For this reason, some black city dwellers may have found little identification with, or even enjoyed watching, films with rural settings such as *The Watermelon Patch*.[102]

The depiction of racial tropes on-screen was further interceded by the inconsistency of early film grammar: the meaning filmmakers convey with techniques such as the "establishing shot," "cross-cutting," and "close-ups." In fact, until the creation of the Motion Picture Patents Company (MPPC), a trust of America's major film production companies organized by Thomas Edison, most films viewed in the United States were imported from other countries with their own conventions and racial codes. In 1907, for example, American companies produced only about a third of the films released in U.S. theaters.[103] Itinerant film exhibitors such as C. E. Hawk similarly showed a large number of films produced by European companies such as Pathé Frères, and by white immigrant filmmakers in the United States whose productions further compounded the racial ambiguity of early motion pictures. Siegmund Lubin, who had produced Royston's buffalo soldier films, attempted in 1905 to capitalize on the American market for pictures about hapless rural blacks. The German immigrant's films, however, failed to draw the correct cultural references to the American stereotype; the black characters in *Fun on the Farm* were depicted enjoying pumpkins instead of watermelons.[104]

By the mid-twentieth century, black people would widely consider the *screening* of many of these types of films, especially depictions of lynchings, as an act of violence in itself. But in this pre-Hollywood era, the still-emerging American film industry, and the site-specific dynamics of exhibition, made film a relatively incoherent and unstable medium of racial representation.[105] This was further impacted by the fact that individual black spectators experienced and interpreted film differently from one another. Feminist film scholars, for example, have unraveled the notion of a singular "black" filmgoing experience by demonstrating how the intersection of race, gender, sexuality, and class identities informed the responses of individuals to the cinema.[106] These studies bring into relief the problem of defining which images were "positive" or "negative," and the assumption that early black film spectators uncritically viewed negative images until they were "awakened" to racial consciousness. Not only do such narratives divorce cinema from its historical context, they assume a one-dimensional, impossibly distilled black subject that can no more exist than a female spectator erased of her class or racial identity.

After Baptist minister William Craft swept through Savannah, Georgia, with his religious motion pictures in 1901, the city's black churches, including Gaines Chapel, Bethel AME, St. James, New Zion, Union Baptist, and St. Paul, all hosted their own film exhibitions. Few Savannah churches, however, showed films as often as St. Philip AME, especially during its drive to raise money for its New Brick Church fund.[107] Despite the success of St. Philip's first film shows, the church leaders quickly realized that continued success relied not only on the quality of their programs but also on the ability to successfully *market* their exhibitions.[108] Through the pages of black newspapers such as the *Savannah Tribune,* St. Philip began publicly announcing its film exhibitions in advance, urging members to invite their friends and acquaintances to its shows, boasting of its "latest improved" technologies, and claiming to have "the best [exhibition] that has visited this city."[109] To draw in even bigger crowds, the church promised to refund its ten-cent admission to anyone not pleased with its moving pictures—unabashedly acknowledging that its programs would not be measured on the basis of spiritual edification alone.[110] It was acceptable, the church implied, to come out simply to enjoy oneself.

Black church leaders competed with commercial entertainments by adopting sophisticated marketing techniques to publicize their shows. The first published reports of film exhibitions nearly always described events that had already passed. Sometimes articles appeared weeks after a show had occurred. By 1903, black churches were regularly listing their shows in the pages of the black press *before* their scheduled exhibitions. Black newspaper editors aided these efforts by implementing more standardized schedules for publishing and distributing their papers. Public announcements and ticket campaigns encouraged the attendance of church members, but these efforts also sought the attention of individuals who were not formally connected to the institution sponsoring the event. Open invitations highlighted the spectacle and pleasure of filmgoing, reminding would-be attendees that film exhibitions were intended for the public—not just as a service for church members.[111] With slogans like "Everyone welcome," "All are cordially invited," and "Come and bring your friends," churches welcomed strangers who did not feel directly vested in institutions.[112]

The language employed in these announcements mimicked the tone of commercial amusement venues.[113] The Ninth Street Christian Church of Kansas City, Kansas, for instance, exhorted the black public to take part in the sensation of its moving picture exhibition—"to go, see and hear for yourself."[114] In Baltimore, Maryland, the Metropolitan Church bragged that its film exhibition was "the best ever seen in Baltimore City."[115] Itinerant exhibitors, often working in tandem with black churches and halls, even hired advertising professionals to publicize their shows. When Hawk was touring across Florida in 1905, he employed the services of James E. Rodgers, who acted as Hawk's advance agent, in publicizing the troupe's film exhibitions. Hawk was especially pleased with Rodgers's efforts in Jacksonville, where the agent had been "hustling the crowds with heavy advertising."[116] While newspaper advertisements constituted an important forum for publicizing motion picture exhibitions, Rogers may have also relied on broadsides or magazines to publicize his programs. For example, Arthur L. Macbeth, who exhibited films locally in Charleston, South Carolina, and later in Norfolk, Virginia, broadcast his services through publications such as *Who's Who of the Colored Race,* an encyclopedia of race leaders that included the addresses of their businesses along with their biographical profiles.[117]

Black churches and film exhibitors were especially eager to market their motion pictures to black urban youth. When the Conleys exhibited at the True Reformer's Hall in Washington, D.C., they posted recurring advertisements in the black newspaper, the *Washington Bee,* which encouraged parents to "help the children have an outing" by taking them to the show.[118] Children were also offered special admission rates to film programs, sometimes only half of the fee charged to adults. Itinerant film exhibitors attempted to appeal both to the tastes of black youth and to their reform-minded guardians. Pope's exhibition, *The Devil's Cook Kitchen,* may have included moralizing themes on drink and dance, but his flashy marketing campaign promised fun and excitement. His advertisements, for example, included cartoon images of Satan, replete with handlebar moustache, chef's hat, and apron, beckoning from the fiery bowels of hell.[119] Images such as these in advertisements were a relatively new phenomenon. Until the late nineteenth century—and particularly in the black press—most advertisements provided straightforward text that described the products up for sale.[120] With the growth of industrial capitalism, new forms of advertising emerged as businesses sought to expand the consumer market to meet their increased manufacturing capabilities.[121] Pope borrowed from these strategies and added a bit of his characteristic flair with copy that was unmistakably his own. His "Wonderful Moving Picture and Stereopticon Exhibition," he promised, would show the impressive "26 ways in which there is harm in dancing."[122]

Professional exhibitors such as Harry Royston, who doubled as an agent for the *Freeman,* developed these marketing strategies with the help of the black press. Communicating through the nationally distributed *Freeman,* Royston advertised his exhibitions and stayed in contact with his business contacts even while tending to his popular tamale business in Knoxville, Tennessee.[123] Others relied on black newspapers for the latest news on potential venues of exhibition, the demands of the black public, and employment opportunities. While on tour in 1905, film exhibitor Ed C. Price wrote a column for the *Freeman,* which ended with a personal request to C. E. Hawk, asking, "Why don't you write and tell us the news?"[124] Hawk responded with an update of his show, and signed off by stating, "Would like to hear from Ed C. Price, B. T. Harvey, Kemp and Lang while here."[125] For these itinerant showmen and -women, black newspapers were among the most reliable means by which they could keep in contact with one another while on the road.

The black press benefited from this relationship not only because itinerant film exhibitors paid to list advertisements in their pages but also because as agents, itinerant exhibitors gathered news and introduced potential subscribers to their papers. Former newspaper editor William A. Bettis sent news dispatches to black papers in his home state of Kansas while he was on tour across the South and in Mexico.[126] In Bartow, Florida, Hawk (who like Royston doubled as an agent for the *Freeman*) distributed twenty copies of the *Freeman* to local residents who were "delighted to learn of the national illustrated colored paper."[127] And when he visited Darien, Georgia, he explained, "The

Freeman was introduced and went well."[128] The itinerant exhibitors with the closest connections to the black press, especially those who served as agents, had some of the farthest-reaching circuits of exhibition. The routes of William Bettis and Professor H. C. Conley included Mexico, and C. E. Hawk regularly visited Cuba with his famous "Electrical Display of Life Motion Pictures."[129] When Hawk announced he was "en route to Cuba our fourth time, where success awaits our arrival," he did not indicate his distribution plans, but the national and international circulation of U.S. black newspapers might be attributed to some of these cosmopolitan individuals.[130]

As black migrants flowed into cities in the 1890s, leisure became a critical site for black cultural and social formation. African Americans jealously guarded the moments of their days that were unfettered by the demands of employers or the unending obligations of manual and domestic labor.[131] Organized strikes by black workers in Apalachicola, Florida, in 1890 and by black and white laborers in New Orleans in 1892 supported explicit demands for higher wages and shorter hours.[132] Nevertheless, most black men and women negotiated their freedom in their everyday interactions. They quit, slowed down, bargained, and "borrowed" to make ends meet. And they sought leisure activities which enabled them to give meaning to their lives as autonomous human beings and free people.[133]

For black reformers, the dreams and desires of these leisure-hungry migrants were both a boon and a burden. With thousands of potential new members, black church and club leaders hoped to strengthen their institutions and ultimately achieve their goals of collective racial progress. At the same time, the middle class feared that misdirected poor black migrants would be a liability to the entire race. While desperately seeking ways to divert their working-class counterparts from "iniquitous" amusements that were "the particular property of the devil" and the "diversions of Satan," black reformers and church leaders were ecstatic to discover that their moving picture exhibitions drew crowds to their doors.[134] Although some white American showmen assumed that "moving pictures do not appeal to the masses of negroes," others knew better; it was "here," in the black church, that the "moving picture is seen," white sociologist W. D. Weatherford wrote in his 1910 study, *Negro Life in the South*.[135] The promotion of this "intellectual, amusing and Christian entertainment" grew as uplift reformers fought to maintain their precarious status amid the incursions of Jim Crow and the allure of commercial enjoyments. But as moving picture exhibitions rose in popularity, both the exhibitors and the content of many exhibitions began to change. The increasingly sensational nature of the films reflected the demands of the black public as church leaders and traveling exhibitors conjured up new ways to attract crowds and earn profits from the ever-growing market of black filmgoers.

Cinema evolved as African Americans confronted the ever-changing landscape of modern American life. The malevolence of Jim Crow segregation, the exploitation of wage labor, the threat of violence, violence itself, the comfort of companionship, the meaning of laughter, the thrill of something new—it was in response to, and in spite of, these aspects of modern black life that the moving pictures grew in popularity, and with them, a black leisure culture that served as an emblem of the investment black people made to their lives and their futures as free people. Implicit in these developments was a new social imaginary, a new way that black people conceived of their relationships to one another. A largely working-class audience of filmgoers not only expressed their leisure demands by selectively patronizing amusements in black churches and halls, they also articulated themselves as a public, which in turn galvanized the growth of a black amusement industry, its performers, and a professional class of showmen and -women. Less than a decade after the first black church exhibition, cinema was already a vivid illustration of the intertwined history of black businesses, institutions, and media during the "nadir." But this was only the beginning of a much longer story; over the subsequent half-century, even more seemingly disparate aspects of black life would converge in the malleable and ever-changing practices of black cinema culture.

3

Colored Theaters in the Jim Crow City

Members of organizations such as the National Negro Business League invested in the new colored theater boom. (National Negro Business League Executive Committee, date unknown. George Grantham Bain Collection, Library of Congress.)

Growing up, Tish Hubbard may have looked past the fields of her father's farm in Sangamon County, Illinois, and wondered where her future would take her. Born into an educated, property-owning family, she could entertain a broader horizon of possibilities than most black women of her generation. The popular young socialite might have married a minister or a wealthy shopkeeper; she could have become a colored women's club leader in nearby Indianapolis, or a schoolteacher in Chicago. But Tish ventured down another path. In 1907, she married Eddie D. Lee, a well-known vaudevillian, and entered the fast-paced world of show business. Soon, she was writing and performing in her husband's vaudeville troupe. Her wicked sense of humor and uncanny impersonations charmed black critics and audiences alike, making the statuesque twenty-three-year-old a respected actress and renowned playwright by the time she and Eddie arrived in Louisville, Kentucky, in 1908 to open the city's first colored moving picture and vaudeville theater.[1]

The Lees' Thirteenth Street Theater signaled a new era of black moving picture exhibition and commercial entertainment. Previously shown under the auspices of churches, halls, and schools, motion pictures for black audiences began appearing in theaters around 1906. These venues not only featured motion pictures but also vaudeville performances and musical acts. Only a handful of similar sites, such as the African Grove Theatre, which briefly staged plays such as *Othello* in antebellum New York City, offered a precedent for the new industry. As Tuskegee Institute's *Negro Year Book* explained in 1912, "there was hardly a theatre for colored people in the entire United States" before the turn of the twentieth century.[2] Once inaugurated, however, the colored theater industry made impressive gains.[3] In Louisville, a series of black-owned and black-managed theatrical enterprises followed the Lees', including the Lincoln and the Taft in 1909, the Lyre (later Lyric) and the Houston in 1910, the Garden and the Evanston in 1911, and the Walnut Park, the Olio, and the Ruby in 1912.[4]

These theaters emerged at a moment business historian Juliet E. K. Walker has referred to as the "golden age" of black entrepreneurship.[5] A proliferation of black businesses—insurance agencies, barbershops, beauty companies, grocery stores, shipping lines, funeral parlors, banks, and newspapers—created and reinforced black community bonds and a belief in collective racial destiny.[6] Black-owned and black-operated theaters performed these functions, but they also presented black city dwellers with unique opportunities for interaction with one another. Situated at the nexus of black social, economic, and cultural life, they brought African Americans together across class and gender lines into common spaces that were constructed for the purpose of social interaction and pleasure. As both a physical location and an arena of the black cultural and economic exchange, the colored theater became an especially critical site in the black public's ongoing negotiations over the meaning of race progress.

More than two hundred black-owned and black-managed colored theaters opened in the United States between 1906 and 1914.[7] They took on all shapes and sizes, from brick playhouses with marble interiors, to rickety storefronts, to seasonal open-air pavilions. These new businesses owed much to the churches and lodges that had pioneered black film exhibition by fostering a skilled class of motion picture professionals and cultivating the market for black cinema. Indeed, black film exhibitors in commercial venues continued to rely upon these institutions. It was far from coincidence that colored theaters first appeared in the established centers of black cinema across the urban South and West. At the same time, however, the industry expanded in new directions. Colored theater proprietors, including a wealthier class of black investors, considered shifting patterns of migration and the changing local climate for black entrepreneurs when deciding where to establish their businesses. Would-be theater owners were particularly eager to open their establishments in black "boom" towns, places where colored theaters served as literal investments in the future prosperity of the black population. Locals eagerly awaited these amusement venues, which expanded their leisure opportunities and indicated the cultural and material advancement of their communities.

Cinema not only moved across the pathways of black migration, it also traveled between the spheres defined by tradition and by law as private and public, commercial and noncommercial, and sacred and secular. Indeed, it was this very mutability that enabled cinema to flourish in black life at a moment when African Americans had limited access to both public space and the consumer marketplace. Black audiences first encountered "public amusements" like the moving picture exhibition in private institutions, which served as proxy public spaces in black life.[8] Within these institutions emerged a vibrant for-profit film exhibition industry. When these businesses moved into commercial spaces—colored theaters—they remained dependent on the sacred black church and the private black lodge. "Public accommodations," which were legally defined as facilities "open to common use," segregated and excluded black patrons. At the same time, local and federal laws restricted the commercial activities of black people by preferentially granting licenses, tax breaks, and lucrative incentives such as land grants to white business owners.[9] African Americans were commonly denied permits or were prohibited leases by white landowners. Those charged with minor infractions of the law (often fabricated) were frequently forced to close their businesses. In other cases, mob violence punished the successes of black business owners. As Ida

B. Wells explained in *Southern Horrors,* the lynching of three prosperous African American grocers near Memphis, Tennessee, served as a "lesson of subordination."[10] These factors shaped the development of black cinema in the "private" spaces of black institutions and the "public" sites of commercial enterprise.[11]

Racial segregation and cinema swept into the twentieth century on the same currents of modern change—migration, urbanization, and the rise of industrial capitalism—but the creation of a segregated mass leisure culture was far from a clear-cut process. Although America's racial order and Jim Crow segregation ensured that cinema would cater to black and white audiences separately, nothing guaranteed that either group would have sustained interest in the medium. In fact, after the novelty of film projection faded, white theatrical film exhibition practices began to stagnate at the turn of the century. Vaudeville theaters, among the most common sites for commercial film exhibition, relegated the moving pictures to the bottom of their programs. Film historians have described these first few years of the 1900s as the "chaser era." Vaudeville theaters offering "continuous" entertainment programs used moving pictures as "chasers," which signaled the audience to clear the theater.[12] Although the term "chaser" was not always used as a pejorative—a spectacular moving picture might offer a thrilling end to a vaudeville bill—these practices did not bode well for the medium's appeal as a feature attraction. Even less auspicious for white film exhibition, motion picture–only venues, such as storefront theaters, rarely survived for more than a few months before closing down.[13]

Meanwhile, black cinema practices developed along another path. Even as white film exhibition dwindled, reports of black church, lodge, and school exhibitions continued to climb. Black showmen and -women responded very differently to the fading novelty of motion pictures. Instead of withdrawing or pushing the medium to the end of their programs—as was the case with white commercial amusements—black itinerants threw their resources into enhancing their film exhibitions with more spectacular subjects, up-to-date technologies, and creative methods of exhibiting their motion pictures. They devised tantalizing narratives and integrated music and lectures into their programs.[14] A well-designed film exhibition and a few key performers (often a sibling or a spouse) were far cheaper and easier to take on the road than a big vaudeville troupe.[15] Most importantly, these shows appealed to the demands of the black public. Aided by the institutional needs and resources of black institutions, itinerant showmen and -women continued to enjoy a thriving market for their entertainments.

In fact, white exhibition was arguably technically and narratively less innovative, on the whole, than black film practices during the chaser period. Locked to a stationary site, white theaters and film exhibition services (the local distribution branches of motion picture production companies) appealed to the same customers week after week. For example, vaudeville houses were organized around the model of "continuous entertainments" and had to constantly update their repertoire. Thus, unlike the touring film professional, the locally based projectionist had very little time to devise and rework a film program. A few white traveling film exhibitors such as Lyman Howe created sophisticated motion picture shows by arranging various nonnarrative films, the "cinema of attractions," into story lines.[16] But by 1900, most motion pictures for white audiences screened in all white or segregated theaters and were conducted by local exhibition services. The use of motion pictures as chasers in these venues further indicates that white theater projectionists rarely integrated the medium into intricate, labor-intensive (thus more expensive) feature acts or story lines. Cheap, nonlinear acts were selected to end vaudeville programs, which urged the audience to gradually transition into and out of the theater.

In contrast, most black film exhibitors during this time were itinerants. These individuals presented the same films seasonally or annually, which supported their ability to integrate the moving pictures into their performances with greater sophistication. This also enabled them to create more elaborate programs over time, adding or subtracting elements based on the responses of local audiences. Additionally itinerant black film exhibitors honed their skills by repurposing films by white production companies. Integrating such films into stories and messages specific to the mission of racial progress likely required careful planning and sophisticated technical know-how. The white filmmakers whose pictures appeared in *The Devil's Cook Kitchen* undoubtedly would have been astounded to see their work illustrating H. Charles Pope's exhibition about racial uplift. William Hynes's programs, which combined white- and black-produced films, may have employed advanced editing techniques.[17] The most popular film exhibitors such as M. Posey, Arthur Laidler Macbeth, and Harry Wallace—"one of the best moving picture machine operators in the business"—earned widespread admiration for their considerable abilities as film projectionists.[18] Touring and the mission of racial progress, in essence, encouraged black film exhibitors to invest more resources into refining their film programs. When a local audience tired of the repertoire, black exhibitors moved on to their next stop.[19] These practices were far from mimetic of the white film industry. Black people were drawn to motion picture shows in black institutions not only because they were excluded from other venues but also because of the vibrancy of black cinema culture.

By 1906, however, the tide began to turn for theatrical exhibition, reconfiguring both black and white filmgoing. For the first time, stand-alone motion picture theaters became a viable investment. Film exchanges were established, which provided theater proprietors a more affordable means of obtaining motion pictures. Previously, film production companies required theaters either to purchase their reels of film or to hire the services of a local film exhibition service. The film exchange inaugurated a rental-based system of distribution, which made acquiring films easier and often more affordable.[20] Additionally, the creation of longer, multiple-reel moving pictures and the growing popularity of narrative film made it possible to feature movies with fewer accompanying live acts.[21] These changes renewed the interest of white Americans in the medium, swelling the market for moving pictures and new commercial venues of exhibition. The cheap neighborhood theaters known as nickelodeons rose to meet this demand. Millions of white laborers and immigrants flooded into these storefront theaters, transforming the moving picture theater into a successful business. While moving pictures continued to appear in other sites, the nickelodeon became the primary venue for white filmgoers.

The nickelodeon crystallized the racial divide in American cinema and popular culture.[22] A host of Jim Crow policies and practices came into alignment, some of which appeared only remotely related to commercial amusements. The racial segregation of public education, for example, worked in tandem with discriminatory housing policies to reconfigure the racial geography of America's cities. Black and white families moved closer to their children's schools, real estate developers and white property owners refused to sell or rent to black residents, and the limited economic opportunities of black tenants constrained them to poorer neighborhoods.[23] Although the role of the government in encouraging residential segregation was especially visible in the Jim Crow South (where slavery had once reinforced the custom of residential mixing), racial segregation was also a northern phenomenon. When these national developments converged, the repercussions of *Plessy v. Ferguson* and the earlier *Slaughterhouse* and *Civil Rights* cases in the 1870s and 1880s (which effectively refashioned the constitutional rights of black citizens into new protections for American businesses) were fully unleashed upon the American film exhibition industry.

The cheap neighborhood moving picture theater was built into a landscape reconfigured by Jim Crow. The *Motion Picture Handbook* referred to this racially ordered urban geography when it described the "ideal location" for a motion picture house in 1910. The "first and most important consideration" for prospective theater owners should be location, F. H. Richardson's popular guide for industry professionals explained: "Any considerable number of negroes will queer a house with all other races; and there are other races to which you must cater exclusively or not at all, so that the matter deserves close investigation when seeking a city nickel theater site."[24] By describing black audiences as alienating to all other groups and suggesting that prospective proprietors open theaters in racially homogenous neighborhoods, the manual's prescribed business practices not only were constructed around an already racialized built environment, they added another layer to it. Working in conjunction with Jim Crow legislation, white theater owners made the segregated motion picture theater an industry-wide standard. Throughout the South, black Americans were legally required to sit in segregated seats in the "buzzard's roost" or "nigger's heaven," located in theaters' balconies, or to attend off-hour screenings of films.[25] Residential zoning laws, instituted in the South during the 1910s, would further entrench Jim Crow. In the North, white theater proprietors adopted the policies of discriminatory seating, asserting they had no other choice.[26] One Ohio theater manager, "compelled by public prejudice to reserve a part of the house for white people," argued that he was "more deserving of pity than censure" because economic survival, not racism, dictated his seating practices.[27]

The policies and practices of the North and South were mutually reinforcing.[28] To justify their legal system of Jim Crow segregation, white southerners pointed to the "Unofficial 'Jim Crow' Laws" of northern theaters. In places such as Massachusetts, the "fountainhead of abolition and the defender of equal rights for the black man," southern reporters smugly announced, white locals were gradually "drifting toward the 'color line.' "[29] The *Montgomery Advertiser* reprinted an article from the *Chicago Tribune* describing the widespread discrimination faced by black residents of that supposedly progressive city. By employing "underhanded and indirect methods," white theaters in the North achieved the same ends as the legal system of the South. Frequently, northern theater proprietors devised elaborate performances to disguise their policies of racial discrimination. This began at the box office, which was directed to falsely inform black theatergoers that all seats on the main floor were sold out. If black patrons somehow managed to procure a ticket on the parquet, they were led to specially prepared seats that "g[a]ve way beneath them." The usher would feign surprise, and apologetically tell them that the only other available seats were in the gallery.[30] As the reporter concluded of these charades, "It is hard to see any great difference between this procedure and that employed in the South." By bridging regional differences, including the racial practices of the South, these theater proprietors laid the groundwork for the development of a white mass leisure industry in the United States.[31]

As segregated theaters spread across the North and South, they became an increasingly urgent political concern for African Americans.[32] But without a federal commitment to protecting black rights under the Fourteenth Amendment, the penalties for racial discrimination were limited, even when local and state courts ruled that theaters had violated the rights of black Americans. Northern courts began awarding as little as one cent in damages.[33] In Washington, D.C., a political row in 1908 between lifelong Republican W. Calvin Chase, editor and publisher of the *Washington Bee,* and Sidney Bieber, chairman of the local election board for the Republican National Committee, demonstrated the obstacles that black Americans faced in mounting campaigns against Jim Crow theaters. In the spring of that year, Chase was furious to discover that Bieber, whom Chase had publicly endorsed, owned part of a chain of moving picture theaters instituting Jim Crow policies in the capital. Chase marched to Bieber's office and later headed to the Senate chambers, where the editor hovered around the doors and entrances, hoping to track Bieber down. Unsuccessful in his mission, Chase drafted a public letter and published it in the following Saturday edition of his newspaper. "The colored people can not support your ticket," Chase announced, as "you are the owner or proprietor of the many moving picture theaters in the city that 'Jim-Crow' respectable colored citizens, and you claiming to be a Republican."[34]

Over the following months, Bieber responded with a series of political machinations that reflected the waning ability of black Americans to address inequality through the traditional channels of formal politics. Apparently fearing a backlash from the black citizens of the capital, Bieber arranged for the manager of one of his theaters, A. C. Myers, to speak with a representative from the *Bee.* Myers explained that he only prohibited "disorderly" blacks from his establishment but had "never objected at any time to respectable colored Americans."[35] Convinced of Bieber's sincerity, Chase reversed his accusations. He publicly applauded Bieber for correcting "all irregularities when his attention was called to this discrimination" and even encouraged the black public to attend Bieber's theaters. After the endorsement, however, Bieber reinstated the policy of segregation, first secretly and later without apology.[36] A frustrated Chase resumed his campaign, reminding Bieber that "if a colored man is good enough to 'vote' for you, he ought to be good enough to be allowed to sit anywhere in a theater he is able to pay for a seat."[37] Yet the futility of the efforts was becoming increasingly clear, and Chase had begun to wonder if the Jim Crow theater might be undermined in other ways. An outspoken proponent of the philosophy of racial uplift, his belief in collective self-help would inform his response to the new colored theater industry.

The surging black demand for motion pictures and other commercial amusements and the rise of the segregated white moving picture theater convinced countless black film exhibitors, jazz and blues musicians, and vaudeville performers—including Tish and Eddie Lee—to rush into the colored theater. Many black theater professionals, especially those who exhibited motion pictures, hailed from the church and lodge show tradition. Others had gotten their start hocking tonics at medicine shows, appearing in burnt cork on the white vaudeville and minstrel stage, or playing in jook joints, the often illicit gathering places for dance and drink associated with the black working class.[38] Agents that once advertised and scheduled shows for traveling film exhibitors translated their experiences into gigs as managers and booking agents for commercial venues. Together, these black entertainment professionals ventured into the colored theaters, venues that featured an eclectic array of media and live performances and were dedicated to the entertainment of black and mixed-race audiences.

Although colored theaters were commercial, public spaces, they continued to rely on the support of religious and fraternal organizations.[39] The Lees, for example, opened their theater in a building belonging to the Grand United Order of Odd Fellows, a black fraternal organization and women's auxiliary with more than 50,000 members and a thousand lodges across the United States, Canada, and the Caribbean.[40] The Order of Odd Fellows was one of the oldest black institutions in Kentucky. Shortly after the Civil War, members of Louisville's Center Street AME Church had organized the first branch, which in 1885 joined several other local orders in purchasing a three-story building on Thirteenth and Walnut streets. After a tornado destroyed the building, the Odd Fellows constructed a new property that included the storefront space in which the Lees would open their theater.[41] The interconnected development of these institutions and businesses exemplified the entangled history of black religious, economic, and social life at the turn of the century. The organizational structures of Louisville's black churches informed the creation of its mutual aid societies, which jointly supported the emergence of the black film industry. These contributions, of course, worked both ways. Black film exhibition assisted black lodges and churches in raising money and building their edifices. And some individuals were church members, fraternal brothers, and theater proprietors all at the same time.

By reserving space in their lodges for black businesses, black cooperative and fraternal organizations played an important role in the growth of the burgeoning colored theater industry. Dozens of colored theaters opened in lodges across the country. In Frankfort, Kentucky, Lucien Taylor conducted a moving picture show in the Odd Fellows Hall; in Rocky Mount, North Carolina, W. A. Baynard managed the International Order of Odd Fellows and Picture Show; and in Atlanta, Georgia, S. L. Lockett ran a moving picture exhibition in the Odd Fellows' auditorium.[42] Besides the Odd Fellows, other black fraternal organizations including the People's Benefit and Fraternal Society, the Elks, the Masons, and the Knights of Pythias also sponsored exhibitions and leased space to theaters in their lodges.[43] G. H. Green, the principal of the Douglass School in Lexington, Missouri, announced he would open a theater in the Masonic Hall in 1911.[44] Ill health and a campaign to clean up the local black cemetery, which was littered with unburied human remains, may have distracted him from his plans to open the theater. But in a small town such as Lexington, with few well-maintained spaces open to the black public, the lodge was an especially viable home for new businesses. In Charleston, West Virginia, and Sherman, Texas, colored theaters were opened in Pythian temples.[45] The Knights even made it on the big screen themselves; in 1913, Daly's Theater in Baltimore featured "race scenes" including a Knights of Pythias parade in Baltimore and the National Baptist Convention in Nashville.[46]

These black-owned properties offered considerable advantages for commercial enterprises like the colored theater. Fraternal organizations built their lodges near black residential neighborhoods and in colored business districts, centrally situated and conveniently accessed by potential theatergoers. Moreover, having long hosted itinerant motion pictures and other entertainments, lodges were already established sites for black social interaction. In some cases, these organizations catalyzed the transformation of their neighborhoods into centers of black entertainment and commercial activity. In Louisville, Kentucky, the Odd Fellows Hall and the black Knights of Pythias Temple (also the site of a colored theater) gave shape to the city's black business district. Black lodges also housed other types of businesses, including barbershops and banks, which in turn attracted more black companies and additional foot traffic into the neighborhood. The fact that black lodges were "race" operations was of no small consideration to colored theater proprietors. Leasing space in such structures enabled black business owners to circumvent some of the discriminatory treatment they faced, especially the suspicions commonly directed at black amusement venues. Finally, theater proprietors put the philosophy of racial uplift into practice by entering into cooperative financial agreements with fellow members of the race. The mutually beneficial exchange provided revenue for black lodges, which they used to pay their mortgages and maintenance expenses.

A few fraternal and mutual aid organizations elected to open their own theaters. For those organizations that frequently hosted itinerant motion picture shows, constructing more permanent spaces for film exhibition in their halls may not have required extensive remodeling. A slapdash storefront theater could be erected in a matter of hours by blackening windows, hanging up a canvas screen, and setting out some foldable chairs.[47] But fraternal orders, viewing the colored theater as a serious investment and symbol of racial progress, often chose to construct more elaborate facilities. In 1906, the Mobile, Alabama, Odd Fellows voted unanimously to invest $40,000 on a colored theater, which the fraternal organization decided to operate itself.[48] An even more elaborate venture, the Temple Theatre in New Orleans, Louisiana, was scheduled to "throw open its door to the public" in January 1909.[49] "Owned and controlled by the colored Knights of Pythias of Louisiana," the handsomely appointed theater possessed a fifty-one-foot stage, a grand proscenium arch, and "every facility for the convenience and comfort of the patron."[50] The Knights intended to primarily feature concerts and stage performances, but they eventually began showing more motion pictures.[51] When black fraternal organizations directly invested in colored theaters, the lines between the public and the private were obscured even further.

One of the most famous colored theaters of the early twentieth century was owned by a working-class organization that straddled the boundaries between mutual aid society and corporation. Formed in 1906, the Laborer's Building and Loan Association of Washington, D.C., began as a savings and lending cooperative for black construction workers. John Whitelaw Lewis, a former bricklayer and janitor, spearheaded the association as a means for black laborers in the building trades to "combine their humble resources and put them into something tangible."[52] Two years later, the association had successfully erected a residential building on Eleventh and U streets, and its membership numbered four hundred.[53] They next decided to construct a commercial property, and the crowning jewel and centerpiece of the structure would be a "magnificent theatre" with a "seating capacity of 2,500." The plans and the sizable amount of capital they hoped to raise for the project, $400,000, reflected how deeply the association's working-class members had invested their visions of freedom and autonomy in the promises of the colored theater. Their beliefs were conveyed explicitly in the association's advertisements, which solicited investments in the project through the purchase of stocks. A theater and office building "built by Negroes, for the use of Negroes is a NECESSITY," they asserted, for both the "welfare" and "self-respect" of the race. The demand for public spaces of leisure had been integrated into a larger vision of black economic and political equality. While the Jim Crow galleries "colonized" black patrons, the association promised that a black-owned and -operated property was "THE NEW EMANCIPATION PROCLAMATION."[54] Although the group struggled to raise enough money to fully implement its plans, it finally opened the Hiawatha Theatre in 1909, and expanded its facilities the following year.[55] During the 1910s, it became one of the capital's most popular black venues for motion picture exhibition.[56]

The circuits of the black church and lodge show further contributed to the colored theater by fostering the development of a highly skilled class of black film exhibitors. These professionals had built reputations, raised capital, and gained industry experience through itinerant film exhibition before opening commercial venues. Former traveling film exhibitors Fleet and Ednah Walker gradually transitioned into more permanent sites of business. They moved to Cadiz, Ohio, where they had once successfully exhibited their moving pictures in the city's churches, first leasing the Wonderland Moving Picture Theater and later the Cadiz Opera House.[57] Another former itinerant exhibitor, Arthur Laidler Macbeth, began showing films in 1899 near Charleston, South Carolina. His reputation in the photographic arts and his uncanny resemblance to Theodore Roosevelt had made him a popular public lecturer.[58] Macbeth, as a church leader and black Mason, fit the profile of the first generation of itinerant film exhibitors. But he also shared many similarities with the new cohort of colored theater professionals; he was an accomplished professional photographer (his motto was "If you have beauty we'll take it, if you have none, we make it"), and he belonged to professional organizations such as the National Negro Business League.[59] In 1909, Macbeth opened up a colored theater in Norfolk, Virginia. Located on the ground floor of L. W. "Lem" Bright's Mount Vernon Hotel, the building (like the Odd Fellows building in Louisville) was one of Norfolk's landmark black properties, thus providing Macbeth's Mount Vernon Theatre with both name recognition and an established location.[60]

Other itinerant companies lacked the resources or desire to settle into permanent spaces but expanded their business operations to serve the commercial black theatrical circuit. C. E. Hawk continued to travel across the United States and into Cuba and Mexico but began scheduling appearances in commercial and noncommercial venues.[61] In the spring of 1910, Hawk was still running advertisements geared toward the black church circuit, which announced, "Pastors may have this entertainment at any time or place." But whereas religious and lodge venues had once been the bread and butter of traveling companies, Hawk had added "opera houses" to his customary list of "churches, halls, schools," and parks.[62] When not touring the black church and hall circuit, he worked stints in Savannah's black theaters. In 1910, he spent eight weeks in Savannah, delighting the locals with a program that reportedly consisted of 12,000 feet of film, six illustrated songs, and a choir of jubilee singers.[63] The traveling moving picture exhibitor W. W. Horner transitioned from itinerancy to a permanent venue when he opened a moving picture house in Denton, Maryland, but even then, he occasionally brought his films into black churches.[64] This practice of mixing traveling shows and theater management may have been common; Eddie and Tish Lee, like Horner, remained active in the traveling exhibition circuit, bringing their popular moving picture program to colored festivals and fairs across the state after they opened their theater in Louisville.[65]

The skills and experiences of itinerant black film exhibitors facilitated not only the growth of the colored theater industry but also the technological development of American cinema on the whole. Fleet Walker's expertise enabled him to invent several mechanisms for improved motion picture exhibition. He received patents from the United States, France, and Canada for devices that allowed film projectionists to quickly and safely switch between multiple reels during an exhibition. One of his most important inventions was the reel "alarm" system. When a predetermined length of film had passed through the projection machine, a spring arm fixed to the reel would sound an alarm, thereby signaling the projectionist to switch to a new reel of film. For Walker, an audible prompt indicating a certain point in a reel of film may have been especially useful when integrating film into his multimedia and song performances on the road. In any case, these types of technologies became indispensable across the film industry as longer multiple reel features grew in popularity. Descriptions of Walker's invention were mentioned in Eastman Kodak Company publications, and in the 1920s, the Globe Machine and Stamping Company of Cleveland apparently began manufacturing the device.[66] Similarly, Arthur Laidler Macbeth drew on his skills and experiences, both in the field of photographic arts and as a touring film exhibitor, to develop "Macbeth's Daylight Projecting Screen." With a series of partitions and a translucent screen, the invention allowed for the display of moving pictures and stereopticon slides in full daylight. Macbeth received a patent from the U.S. government for a version of the invention, which was listed as a "Picture-Projection Theater."[67]

Along with the industry professionals, a new class of entrepreneurs began investing in colored theaters. "DO YOU KNOW THE POSSIBILITIES FOR MONEY MAKING IN OWNING AND OPERATING A THEATRE IN BALTIMORE," William H. Daly asked the readers of the Baltimore *Afro-American* in 1910, hoping to entice outside investors into the colored theater business.[68] As the commercial film industry expanded, businessmen such as Daly promised boundless opportunities in the black consumer mass market. These entrepreneurs hoped to emulate the financial success of white showmen like B. F. Keith, a onetime circus grifter, who earned millions by organizing a chain of "continuous entertainment" vaudeville theaters. Whereas a previous generation of capitalists invested in steel, chemicals, and manufacturing, commercial amusements had become a lucrative new industry for those in search of national prominence and unimaginable wealth.[69] Of course, achieving success was easier said than done. Truman Kella Gibson, a future insurance mogul and proponent of racial progress through black industry, dove into the moving picture business directly after graduating from Harvard University. Prohibited by his parents from the distraction of commercial amusements for most of his childhood, Gibson was hardly prepared for his new career. He later recalled his brief foray into the industry as an "interesting though unprofitable moving picture venture."[70] Nevertheless, inexperienced would-be investors had some hope; for those wet behind the ears, veterans of the industry offered help—for a price. John Spotts of Topeka, Kansas, for example, began selling a motion picture how-to guide with "full instructions, tips, [and] pointers" to hopeful colored theater managers through the black press.[71]

The new investors included a wealthier class of black men and women, many of whom had earned their money in other "race enterprises." Reports of the potential for colored theaters circulated at the meetings of the National Negro Business League and other professional organizations. In 1904, the league's annual meeting brought together established film industry professionals H. C. Conley and Arthur Laidler Macbeth, and future colored theater proprietors, such as A. C. Howard, the "shoe polish king," from Norfolk, Virginia.[72] Also present was Booker T. Washington, the league's founder. Washington became involved in several motion picture endeavors over the following years, including the "'Tuskegee' moving picture show outfit [he carried] with him on his lecture tours" in 1910.[73] Investors from outside the world of commercial amusements such as Howard, a Pullman porter before earning his fortune manufacturing shoe polishes, relied on these connections to learn about the colored theater industry. The most astute newcomers partnered with or hired the assistance of individuals more experienced in the industry. For example, former savings and loan officer Charles H. Douglass of Macon, Georgia, enlisted the help of the traveling film exhibitors and musicians Ludell and Ed C. Price in 1904.[74] "The Two Prices" moved to Macon, where they provided Douglass's Ocmulgee Park Theatre with invaluable resources—assistance and industry advice. The Prices, in turn, owed much of their knowledge to another industry professional, C. E. Hawk, whom they had once toured with and who likely introduced them to the practice of film exhibition.[75]

An evening at the Thirteenth Street Theater in Louisville was, by all accounts, a "corker." Situated in what would soon become the center of the city's black business district, the theater literally sparkled with its "brilliantly illuminated entrance" and "handsome box office."[76] By the fall of 1908, Tish and Eddie Lee had expanded their stage and added new backdrops, scenery, and electrical effects. After purchasing a ticket at the box office, guests were ushered through the front door of the theater where, on a busy evening, six hundred black patrons awaited the Lees' famous "riproaring show" of "side-splitting" comedy, "the finest and best moving pictures of the age," and "wonderfully clever songs and dances." The Lees did not regularly advertise the titles of their moving pictures, but one of their first exhibitions was the Oberammergau passion play, *Life of Christ.*[77] Their other films, described as "the latest moving pictures," may have included titles similar to those screened at other colored theaters that year, including Segundo de Chomon's *An Excursion to the Moon* (a reproduction of French filmmaker Georges Méliès's popular trick film *A Trip to the Moon*) and Edwin S. Porter's *Nero and the Burning of Rome.*[78] With Tish and Eddie at the helm, there was never a dull moment—amateur nights and pie-eating contests were "a roar from start to finish." On other evenings, guests were treated to vaudeville acts performed by "first-class" artists.[79]

Colored theaters presented new possibilities for social exchange in the city. They were where "everyone goes and where you meet everyone," as proclaimed by the society columnist for the *Washington Bee.*[80] Young urbanites gathered at these theaters to show off their finest clothing or to attract the attention of potential suitors.[81] The most upscale theaters became meeting grounds where the "popular dreamy eyed belles, and the young men of our race, intelligent, dignified," mingled.[82] Fashionable venues such as Washington, D.C.'s Douglass Theatre on U Street drew out the stylish set—ladies adorned in soft turban hats and high-waisted skirts finished with ecru lace, gentlemen in tailored suits with fancy waistcoats of silk or velvet—who attracted just as much attention as the spectacle on-screen. And on summer evenings, outdoor motion picture gardens served ice cream to young women in neatly hemmed sailor dresses with wide collars of white piqué, while men smoked and meandered through the crowds, their olivewood canes tapping to the live musical accompaniment.[83]

Such displays were virtually impossible in segregated theaters, which were organized to make black patrons invisible to the white audience.[84] Back entryways, hidden staircases, and upstairs galleries shuffled black patrons to the margins of the theater and out of sight from the preferred ground-level seats reserved for whites. The dark, cramped space of the "buzzard's roost" structurally reinforced the racial hierarchy. Noises emitted by black patrons were more difficult to control, but the physical distance between blacks and whites buffered the black aural presence. White theater owners discouraged talking, laughter, shouting, and screaming by black audiences, and seldom hesitated to usher out black patrons or further segregate their theaters when white patrons complained about the unruly "gallery gods."

Of course, certain black patrons actually craved anonymity, but as Charles Baudelaire once wrote of the nineteenth-century city-dwelling flâneur, the colored theatergoer hoped to be "in possession of his incognito."[85] In colored theaters, black people celebrated their ability to willfully blend into a crowd, and most importantly, to move freely through space without reproach. Black men and women could "march through the door without fear and trembling" in "theaters of their own," explained one newspaper writer from Birmingham, Alabama.[86] By mediating the visual experience of being black in the city, the public spaces of the colored theater turned upside down the meaning of surveillance and display, being unseen and rendering oneself inconspicuous. Whereas a white patron might saunter unwatched and unhindered across the parquet floor of a Jim Crow theater, a black patron nearing that same section of the house would evoke, at best, disapproving stares. When not closely monitored by the white theater manager and ushers, black theatergoers in the colored theater could more freely explore the *pleasures* of being anonymous so often described by their white urban counterparts. Young men and women, for instance, socialized in the moving picture theater, away from the prying eyes of their elders. When the lights went out, the darkness offered a cloak for "spooning" and other types of forbidden physical contact.[87]

"First-class" colored theaters like the Lees' hosted moving picture exhibitions with an array of performances and exhibitions including jazz, ragtime, and vaudeville.[88] Black cinema developed in dialogue with these other cultural forms. On the road and later in the theater, black musicians practiced their craft and paid their bills by playing at motion picture shows. Charles McAfee, one of Ohio's most popular black musicians, was frequently hired to perform concerts along with Vitascope picture shows.[89] Blind Harris, "a pianist of some note," played with an itinerant church moving picture show in 1906, winning him favorable reviews in the black press and publicity for his talents.[90] Professional musicians like the Conleys and the Prices had advanced both the screen and sound practices of black cinema by integrating motion pictures into their concerts. Similarly, black film exhibitors, writers, musicians, and actors, along with their respective arts, continued to grow together in the colored theater.[91] These common spaces facilitated the cultivation and cross-pollination of a broad range of cultural productions. American jazz, for example, appeared in black theaters before splitting into its own clearly defined cultural form, which became popular enough to sustain venues solely dedicated to its performance.[92] The financial exigencies of colored theater proprietors factored into these developments. When Howard Powell of Carrolton, Missouri, decided to open a new motion picture house in East St. Louis, Illinois, he sought business partners experienced in a variety of arts, preferably a "colored man and wife one that can double stage or piano."[93] Limited resources demanded a great deal of professional dexterity, as attested by Tom Gales of Cincinnati, Ohio. The multitalented Gales was not only the Gaither Theater's moving picture operator, he was also the porter, stage manager, usher, booking agent, ticket teller, and actor in the company's vaudeville performances.[94]

Industry professionals identified colored theaters as either vaudeville or picture houses, but most vaudeville theaters after 1908 exhibited moving pictures.[95] In fact, theaters that claimed to be vaudeville houses often booked relatively few, if any, live performances.[96] Vaudeville troupes generally required more overhead, labor, and time to organize and book than did moving pictures. Black theater owners, nonetheless, sought vaudeville identification to distinguish themselves from cheap nickel theaters, which were quickly earning a reputation for seediness among middle-class white reformers. The desire for "respectability" was not just rooted in a desire to attract a wealthier class of patrons; it was also essential for warding off the suspicions of angry whites who readily accused black business owners of operating "negro dives." For example, black theater owner J. T. Coleman of Columbus, Georgia, was forced to close his business in 1912. In response to complaints of "noisy conduct" at his theater, police arrested Coleman, charged him with running a "disorderly house," and held him on a $100 bond. Two other employees were charged with "simple larceny." The eagerness of city officials to shut down the establishment may have stemmed from a fear over race mixing, as a group of whites living across the street reportedly patronized the colored theater.[97] Of course, black business owners could not assume that abiding by the rules of proper racial etiquette and appropriate middle-class behavior guaranteed protection either. The Dreamland Theater in Tulsa, Oklahoma, was a model of middle-class respectability, with its two-story brick edifice (rather than a cheap storefront), "high-class" entertainments, and the most "proper" type of management—a husband-and-wife team. Despite this (or perhaps because of it), white mobs targeted the theater during the 1921 race riots, and completely destroyed the building.[98]

At the same time black theater owners had to shield themselves from attack, they also had to attend to a very different problem—that of attracting customers into their venues. Theater proprietors could not afford to exclude working-class patrons from their businesses. Both the "toughs" and the "aristocratic" members of the race attended colored theaters like the Globe in Jacksonville, Florida. "Although there is a decided difference between the elements," one local remarked, "it is so drowned beneath the genereal [*sic*] feeling of pride in the place that it is discernable only to those who really know the difference from years of acquaintance with the city and the people."[99] While white venues ranged from opera houses that featured "high-class" live performances for wealthier audiences to nickelodeons that appealed to working-class and immigrant audiences with their cheap, continuous film exhibitions, black proprietors had to market themselves to a broader class demographic.[100] At times, this meant juggling between claims of "refinement" and the demands of the working class.[101] Black managers needed to "suit all kinds of people and cater to everybody" in order to stay in business.[102] Even the fancy New Royal Theater in Asbury, New Jersey—famous for its distaste of "crudism" and "vulgarity"—relied on the general public for support and could only hope that its audience would "*gradually* be composed of the better class."[103]

Attending to the desires of female patrons was an equally important consideration for colored theater managers. Women continued to outnumber men in cities, even in some places in the North—and thus constituted a considerable percentage of the potential audience.[104] Moreover, the presence of women provided a mark of respectability that protected the theater from many of the criticisms lobbied at all-male spaces of amusement.[105] A. B. Grant's moving pictures in Kansas City, Missouri, were "a credit to the colored people," the *Wichita Searchlight* reported, suggesting "every man should take his wife and children to see them."[106] Theater managers did not defer only to men as the arbiters of women's social lives; advertisements also directly addressed women consumers. "Ladies, make this your theatre," urged the American Theatre in Indianapolis, Indiana, appealing to the black female public.[107] Black theaters also attempted to lure in female customers with gifts and prizes. "A useful and beautiful souvenir," one theater promised, "will be presented to each lady on opening night."[108] Sometimes, the deference to women amounted to frivolous reinscriptions of middle-class ideas of femininity such as when managers promised to feature "inoffensive" pictures without images of crime or sexual themes. Yet even these considerations acknowledged certain deference to the black female consumer.

The majority of black theaters were constructed—as Juli Jones, the theater critic for the Indianapolis *Freeman,* pointed out in 1909—in "small cities of the West and the South."[109] Cities with thriving black populations might see a proliferation of theaters along a certain thoroughfare within a matter of months. Colored theaters appeared almost overnight when cash-strapped proprietors leased storefront spaces instead of building entirely new structures. A little over a year after the Queen Theatre opened in Baltimore in 1907, five other colored theaters opened in quick succession: the Renard, the Home Theater, Daly's, the People's Amusement Company, and the Eagle Moving Picture Parlor.[110] Some moving picture theaters were part of even grander ventures to provide amusements for the black public. For example, two of the wealthiest black residents of Dayton, Ohio, Mose Moore and his "energetic wife," Marion Smart Moore, opened Dahomey Park in 1909. Along with "the theatre and moving picture show," the park featured bowling alleys, shooting galleries, and a scenic railway. "Everything will be decidedly Colored at this park," the Moores announced, "from the lemonade to the doll babies."[111] Located on the outskirts of Dayton, places such as Dahomey Park appealed to churches and lodges organizing "excursions," group leisure tours to out-of-town locations.

One of the most vibrant black cinema cultures in the country emerged in the capital city, after tens of thousands of new settlers poured in from the Maryland and Virginia hinterlands after the financial panic of 1893. Before the Harlem Renaissance, Washington, D.C., was the capital of black life in America.[112] Home to the nation's largest black urban population before World War I, Washington housed Howard University and other renowned black intellectual and artistic institutions.[113] Cinema quickly became an integral aspect of black life in the capital. Itinerant exhibitor H. Charles Pope and one of the most famous and long-lasting traveling showmen, H. C. Conley,

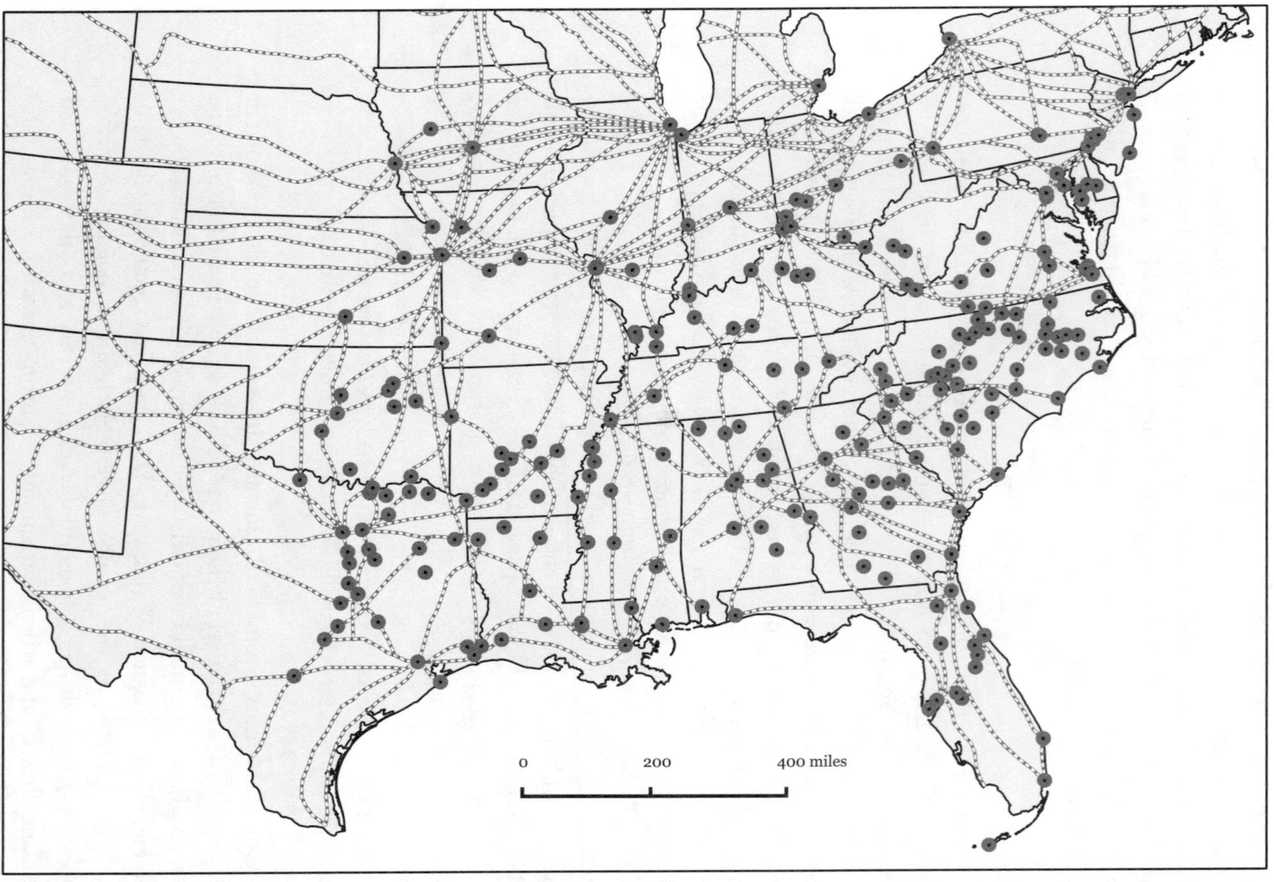

Railways and cities with colored theaters and black commercial venues, 1900–1922. (*Note:* Boston, Los Angeles, and San Francisco not shown.) Map © 2014 by Cara Caddoo.

based their operations in the city. The black theater magnate S. H. Dudley also got his start in Washington. By 1910, there were more black theaters in the capital than almost anywhere else in the country. Theaters such as the Maceo, the Hiawatha, and the Douglass enabled the "proscribed Negro race in Washington to solve their amusement problem" and were trumpeted as symbols of black progress and accomplishment for the entire race.[114]

The locations of colored theaters reveal how black Americans imagined the geography of racial progress. The industry was fundamentally speculative, forcing investors to make predictions about the future prosperity and vitality of black settlements. Prospective theater owners looked regionally, nationally, and across the Americas for cities where they believed their businesses could thrive.[115] Cities such as New Orleans, Louisiana, "with her 90,000 colored population" eager for "colored attractions" and Washington, D.C., with "100,000 amusement loving people deprived of every form of theatrical entertainment" attracted a healthy number of black investors.[116] However, a sizable black population was not enough to guarantee a colored theater's success. J. D. Williams, for example, decided that Cleveland, Ohio's Central Avenue was too saturated with black businesses, and he chose to depart for a "small town in the state" to open his motion picture show.[117] Several theater proprietors departed from northern cities for the South, including the Lees, and Marion A. Brooks, who left Chicago, Illinois, to open a colored theater in Alabama in 1908.[118] As the move from large urban centers in the North to smaller southern cities indicates, individuals traveled curving and sometimes circular routes as they navigated in the direction of black progress.

Violence was also a critical force in locating the colored theater industry. Confronted with police hostility, riotous crowds, or the abuses of a resentful white business competitor, black business owners were frequently forced to abandon their hard-earned commercial enterprises. One such individual, Charles Moseley, a native of south Georgia, maintained his Atlanta business for years, despite being subjected to almost constant harassment. Moseley owned the Vendome, the only licensed black drinking establishment in the city. Police nonetheless raided the saloon on a regular basis and arrested and fined Moseley on numerous occasions.[119] Still, in 1904, Moseley decided to open a second business in the city—a colored motion picture theater and amusement park. He hoped the benefits of locating the new endeavor in Atlanta would outweigh the considerable obstacles he was sure to face there as a black business owner. But in the fall of 1906, as he was preparing to open his new business, a riot erupted in the city. Dozens of black people were murdered and the entertainment district along Decatur Street was decimated. Fleeing the city "on account of the September mob rule," Moseley was lucky to escape with his life.[120]

Moseley resettled in Virginia. Although the Atlanta riot had dashed his dreams of opening a colored theater and amusement park in the city, Moseley was determined to put his plans into motion elsewhere. He decided to open his first theatrical enterprise in Richmond. Moseley had arrived at the location through a combination of circumstances and considerations. This included his previous experiences in Atlanta, which convinced him to leave that city, and the factors that drew him to Richmond: his kinship networks—likely his wife, Hazel (a native of Richmond), and W. L. (his brother and business partner in Richmond). It was also important to assess of the cost of real estate and labor and to measure these expenses in relation to predictions about the local black consumer market. An astute businessman, Moseley likely considered these and countless other factors before deciding to open the first colored theater in Virginia. In 1907, equipped with a motion picture projector and $700 in ball-bearing roller skates, Moseley finally opened up his long-awaited business, the North Side Rink, which brought together two of the era's most popular amusements: roller-skating and moving pictures.[121]

Entrepreneurs turned to the black public sphere for advice and information that could help them determine where to locate their new businesses. Theater owners and managers, for example, announced their business plans and solicited for information through the black press. George Ross of Chicago advertised that a group of electricians and a licensed moving picture operator were looking for a "small town" where they could practice their trade.[122] And because so many moving picture professionals were newcomers to town, they also depended on black papers to connect them to local black consumers. When A. B. Grant, a "stranger in the city," opened the M. and O. Theater in Kansas City, Missouri, he introduced himself and marketed his business through local black newspapers.[123] Such publications also helped prospective theater proprietors forecast patterns of black migration and settlement. Rapidly growing pockets of black settlement were appealing because new black communities usually presented less competition and lower real estate expenses. For example, James H. Huddnel of Washington, D.C., and Edward Nelson of Baltimore, Maryland, recognized the local demand for colored theaters in these cities but decided to set up their businesses elsewhere. Huddnel moved from Washington to Anderson, South Carolina, a "thriving little town" with "no moving picture theaters," to open up his colored theater.[124] Nelson decided to establish his parlor in Winston-Salem, North Carolina.[125] Just as colored theater proprietors relied on the more established structures of black religious and fraternal organizations, the overlapping networks of the black press fostered the growth of the new colored theater industry. Besides printing reports about black settlements from across the country, this arena of the black public sphere enabled black theater owners to make contact with other professionals in the field business through advertisements and entertainment reports such as the "Stage" section of the Indianapolis *Freeman.*

Increasingly conspicuous features of black urban settlement, colored theaters became coveted monuments of racial progress. Like the black church, colored theaters exhibited optimism, capital, and a physical hold on urban space.[126] The Jacksonville Globe Theater was celebrated as a "pioneer" and "model" of black progress, and its proprietor, Frank Crowd, was "to be congratulated for the great service he [was] rendering his people and his growing city."[127] In cities suffering from the incursions of Jim Crow, such as Birmingham, Alabama, black residents were encouraged to construct colored theaters as a "practical settlement of their amusement problem"—the widespread "necessity" for leisure activities amid the limitations of Jim Crow segregation.[128] Although colored theaters were not essential for survival, they were—as the members of the Colored Laborers' and Loan Association had asserted—necessary for "welfare" and "self-respect."[129] Venues such as the Lincoln Theatre in Knoxville, Tennessee, with its "beautiful brick structure . . . centrally located with electric cars passing the front entrance every few minutes," were "justly proud" accomplishments for the race.[130] The New Royal Park Theatre, owned by A. C. Fletcher, "an Afro American gentlemen who believes in race pride," was even more opulent. The "handsome fire-poof building, composed of pressed brick and stucco exterior, and finished inside in a color scheme of triple mahogany," displayed a public image of black wealth and refinement.[131]

Locals hoping to draw black settlers and additional colored businesses to their communities were particularly eager to attract colored theaters. One agent for a black settlement in Louisiana, for example, touted his city's attractions in dispatches to national black publications: "Those desiring a change for either pleasure or business" ought "to try Lake Charles," he announced. The city had nearly 10,000 residents, was conveniently located on the S. P. & W. Railway, and would soon "have a moving picture show for colored people only."[132]

Farther west, James McFall and his business partner, John McMurray, arranged to bring a colored theater to the all-black township of Boley, Oklahoma.[133] The burgeoning city had recently incorporated and was energetically promoting further settlement.[134] In 1913, Fortune J. Weaver, president of the Afro-American Realty Company, excitedly reported that McFall and McMurray had secured the services of film projectionist Harry Wallace. They were "spending the week in Kansas City with the Motion Picture men," where they purchased the "latest and most up-to-date paraphernalia."[135] The colored theater, in essence, not only followed migration patterns, it also contributed to them. In their search for new cities of settlement, migrants sought out cities not only for the sake of subsistence but also where they could live rich and fulfilling lives.

"Mr. Lee is certainly doing a world of good for the amusement loving public of Louisville," the *Freeman* announced of the Thirteenth Street Theater in 1909.[136] Black locals proudly pointed to the well-appointed theater as a symbol of racial progress and hailed the Lees' long-term investment in the cultural and material advancement of black Louisville.[137] Nationally distributed black papers described the Thirteenth Street Theater as an example for the rest of the country. In Chicago, Illinois, and Savannah, Georgia, black papers credited the entirety of Louisville's black population for opening the new theater. Without any specific mention of the Lees, the papers explained that it was the "Negroes of Louisville, Ky." who had "recently opened a theatre, owned and controlled by themselves."[138] Such reports contributed to the growing consensus that colored theaters were not merely individual enterprises, but rather the culmination of the collective progress of black Americans. In Topeka, Kansas, the black press observed, "The colored people of Kansas City ought to congratulate themselves and feel highly elated over the fact that they have a high class place of amusement of their own."[139]

These words echoed the response of W. Calvin Chase, enmeshed in his campaign against Sidney Bieber and his Jim Crow theaters in Washington. Proponents of the philosophy of racial uplift welcomed the arrival of new colored theaters, which brought together two of their core beliefs: race pride and profits.[140] Viewing their dollars as weapons and believing that entrepreneurship was a key ingredient in the recipe for black progress, middle-class blacks enjoined fellow race men to "go and open these places and make [themselves] rich."[141] Across the country, they endorsed the opening of black theaters such as the

Elite, Douglass, and Maceo as respectable alternatives to segregated venues.[142] "It is the wish of every good citizen," an enthusiastic supporter of the Lees' theater explained, "that fortune and luck follow this enterprise as it is in every way worthy."[143]

For overlapping reasons, black religious leaders joined the celebration of the new colored theater industry. William H. Council, president of Alabama State Normal and Industrial School at Huntsville and an organizing member of St. John African Methodist Episcopal Church, hailed the emergence of the colored theater industry as a long-overdue antidote to the degrading Jim Crow theater.[144] Additionally, black ministers still viewed motion pictures, at least those shown in colored theaters, as offering a healthy and more self-respecting pastime than either the dance hall or the saloon. Having first championed the moving pictures as a diversion from the "Negro dive," church leaders continued to encourage the growth of the industry. In fact, not only did black churches and theaters book programs from the same film exhibitors, religious leaders were also invited to take an active role in the construction and support of the commercial theater industry. Owners and managers promised to screen pictures "suitable to be shown in any church or parlor," and theaters such as the Airdome in Atlanta, Georgia, encouraged ministers to attend their shows.[145]

Black churches even began holding events in colored theaters. In Louisville, members of the Fifth Street Baptist Church organized a fundraiser at the Lees' theater. The Thirteenth Street Theater also hosted benefits for the Eighteenth Street Church, the Emmanuel Baptist Church, Quinn Chapel, and several other congregations during the summer of 1908.[146] In Dayton, Ohio, churches such as the Hamilton, Ohio, Baptist Church organized excursions to Dahomey Park. These were the same religious institutions whose properties had fostered the emergence of the black film exhibition industry, but now black church events frequently convened inside the structures of the colored theater. Managers of colored theaters eagerly demonstrated how they had inherited the moral values and social obligations of black religious institutions. The Thirteenth Street Theater used some of its receipts to maintain a "potato barrel" and "flour bin" for the benefit of local "orphans and old folks."[147] Mose Moore and Marion Smart Moore's advertisements indicated their deference to religious organizations, and the reliance on such institutions for patronage, when the couple promised that a "liberal percentage on the receipts from the various amusements [would] go to churches, lodges, etc." They even announced that church societies and clubs would have the option to buy stocks in Dahomey Park should it go public, "thereby giving to each organization an equal chance to encourage a race enterprise" and an opportunity for "controlling a feature that speaks well for the energy and thrift of Ohio negroes."[148]

For the middle class, critiques of discriminatory cinema practices and celebrations of colored theaters expressed interconnected concerns about class and gender, which were almost invariably tied to the physical space of the theater. Middle-class blacks were especially sensitive to theater seating policies since the cultural privileges once associated with class were physically manifested in the theater. Nineteenth-century theaters had customarily seated "the better classes" away from the "unruly masses."[149] The gallery and the dress circle separated the "respectable" from the "disreputable." The wealthy occupied the first floor, while the "gallery gods" sat up above and poorer or even middling whites could be turned away from theater doors.[150] For instance, class conflict turned into a near riot in Albany, Georgia, in 1890, when a white police officer was denied admission to the city's elite opera house on a Friday evening. When the chief of police was notified of the insult upon his class, he called upon the entire police force to push their way past the doorkeepers and into the theater.[151] By the twentieth century, these class-based seating customs were replaced by a system of racial segregation.

Middle-class blacks criticized white theater managers for their unwillingness to acknowledge class distinctions within the race. In 1907, a special correspondent for the *Freeman* even blamed Cincinnati's recently instituted practice of excluding all blacks from the city's moving picture houses on the "shiftless, no-account Negro," who was a "most formidable drawback to the onward march of the race."[152] Moving picture halls that catered to poor whites but discriminated against all black patrons, regardless of class, were especially intolerable. Lawsuits and other grievances against white moving picture venues cited the tendency on the part of theater managers to favor the poorest whites and immigrants above the "best" members of the race. The *Topeka Plaindealer* took aim at the "poor white men" who discriminated against blacks in their cheap moving picture and vaudeville theaters. "If these theatres were operated by educated, wealthy, refined white people," the paper argued, "everybody would be accorded the same treatment."[153] In nearby Wichita, the *Searchlight* took "special pride" in announcing the opening of Captain Sam W. Jones's black moving picture show "in view of the fact that all the little cheap John moving picture houses in the city has seen fit to draw the color line."[154]

Thus, although black elites rejected scientific claims of black biological inferiority, they did accept many of the tenets of social Darwinism, the belief that the most talented, hardy, and intelligent people naturally rise to the top of society. The black middle class advocated "color blindness" to obliterate racial distinctions, not class ones.[155] Uplift reformers—including the Jacksonville theatergoer whose belief in "racial progress" mitigated the displeasure of having to attend exhibitions alongside working-class "toughs"—connected their interests to those of their poorer brethren but still promoted social distinctions. Those who had accumulated wealth and education, or who worked in respected occupations, took particular pride in their accomplishments. These black elites petitioned for better treatment and more respect than their poorer black counterparts were given, believing they had risen up wholly on account of their hard work, moral rectitude, and piety.

Additionally, middle-class black men viewed segregation as an insult to their manliness. Anglo-American expressions of gender and leisure, as historian Martin Summers has argued, were different from those of many black men, but for both groups, middle-class ideas of gender were reformulated as the social and economic standards that defined nineteenth-century masculinity became less relevant in the urban industrial landscape of the new century.[156] Manliness became based more explicitly on outwardly expressive characteristics of aggression, physical power, and sexual virility. Partially in response to blurred lines between "feminine" and "masculine" labor activities, leisure became a critical space for articulating these new ideas of manliness. Middle-class black men expressed their masculine identities through activities such as boxing, hunting, and the consumption of material goods that reflected one's power in the marketplace.[157] The color line was a form of submission and an assault on their manliness, they argued, deploring those who begged for admission into white amusements as "incapable of controlling themselves and standing up for honor and manhood."[158] Such behavior went against nature, William H. Council announced. Linking black manhood to defiance of racial submission, Council argued that the black man who submitted to Jim Crow threatened to "unrace himself"; he "will make himself despicable in the eyes of other races and deserve the curse of God."[159]

According to the Indianapolis *Freeman*, there were at least 112 black-owned and -managed colored theaters operating in the United States in 1909.[160] The new colored theater industry was informed by a multitude of factors, all of which pointed to the complex calculus at the heart of black conceptions of progress. These formulations had little regard for the traditional categories of consumer or producer, sacred or secular, and public or private—terms that could describe neither the location nor the role of colored theaters in black life. Colored theaters served both as physical sites of convergence and exchange in the city, and as arenas of the black consumer marketplace. Individuals such as Juli Jones believed the colored theater industry was long overdue, but in reality, the currents of black urban migration and the development of a market for black moving pictures had only recently created this "most needful vacancy."[161] These changes developed alongside the transformation of cinema into one of America's first mass leisure industries, which was contingent upon the exclusion of black people from public spaces and pleasures supposedly open to everyone.[162]

As colored theaters emerged from and contributed to the development of new black social bonds and public spaces, they fostered a sense of national black culture and identity. For example, film scholar Dan Streible has observed, "the name Pekin became a signifier of African American popular culture."[163] By 1909, there were more than thirty Pekin theaters across the country, including official Pekin franchises and independently owned venues. Marion A. Brooks departed for Alabama in 1908 with "the best wishes of all the [Chicago] Pekinites" for his new "Pekin" theater in Montgomery.[164] Tish and Eddie Lee in Louisville, Kentucky, renamed their Thirteenth Street Theater the New Pekin.[165] And Charles W. Moseley, who fled Atlanta after the 1906 riot and opened the Rink in Richmond, Virginia, moved to Norfolk in 1909, where he opened a second amusement venue, the New Pekin Theatre.[166] Other Pekin theaters were opened in Atlanta, Georgia; Fort Worth, Texas; and Cincinnati, Ohio.[167] The "Dunbar" was also a popular name. There were Dunbar Theatres in Georgia, North Carolina, Ohio, Pennsylvania, Alabama, Washington, D.C., and Michigan.[168] These common names presented the vision that African Americans across the country participated in a shared leisure culture. Additionally, in 1913, black musician and theater manager Sherman H. Dudley helped form the Southern Consolidated Circuit, which further facilitated the growing networks of the black entertainment industry.[169]

Cinema wore a Janus face as it traveled across the borders of nineteenth- and twentieth-century black life. Traveling showmen and -women brought film exhibitions across the growing pathways of black migration. Moving pictures appeared before the approving eyes of church elders and drew crowds of pleasure-seekers. Films were projected inside church and lodge buildings that were built up with the dollars from these shows. In colored theaters, they played with jazz and ragtime, vaudeville skits, and musical acts. Their audiences sat in rickety storefronts, danced in outdoor gardens, and could even be found gliding in roller skates as the pictures flickered away on-screen. Never settling too long in any one current of modern life, cinema took on many forms and incarnations. And as black life set sail for uncharted and unexpected territories, cinema continued to evolve. Black Americans, reflecting on these transformations, would come to realize that they too had changed.

4

Monuments of Progress

From rickety storefronts to imposing brick buildings, black churches and theaters looked remarkably similar by 1910. The Howard Theatre, Washington, D.C., circa 1915 (top); and (bottom) a contemporary image of Quinn Chapel AME Church, constructed in 1891. (Howard Theatre image courtesy of Grace Ridgeley Drew, Historical Society of Washington, D.C. Quinn photograph taken by Tania Lee.)

Elijah John Fisher's health was failing him, but he was determined not to let it alter his plans for the day. Tenacity had served him well in life. It had won him the hand of his wife, Florida, whom he trekked forty-five miles to see every month of their courtship, arriving with feet so blistered they had to be greased with mutton suet. It enabled him to walk again at the age of twenty-one after he lost his left leg under the wheel of a speeding train whose conductor refused to slow down because Fisher was black. And it was with dogged persistence that he weathered the storms that periodically swept over Chicago's Olivet Baptist Church during his twelve-year tenure as minister. By 1915, the former slave from the red-clay hills of Georgia had risen to become one of the most prominent black citizens of Chicago. But Fisher still had much to do—and with this in mind, he picked up his crutches and headed out into the bustling streets of Chicago's South Side toward the Pekin Theatre.[1]

A decade earlier, it would have been unthinkable for Fisher to enter the Pekin. In 1905, he and Reverend A. J. Carey, minister of the nearby Quinn African Methodist Episcopal Chapel, had mounted a campaign against its owner, Robert T. "Bob" Motts.[2] For years, Motts, a man infamously connected to the Chicago underworld, had maintained a saloon and gambling hall on South State Street. It was such "commercialized vice" that Fisher believed cursed "the weaker element of his race" and marred "the splendid record of Negro achievement."[3] After Motts opened the Pekin Theatre in 1905, and Ida B. Wells agreed to lend the establishment an air of credibility by hosting a fundraising event at the venue, the ministers were outraged. Fisher ordered his congregants never to step inside the theater and added that if *he* ever did, "he hoped that his tongue would cleave to the roof of his mouth and his right hand forget its cunning."[4]

Much had changed in the intervening years. Fisher had clearly reconsidered his shibboleth against the theater, or he at least made an exception on that April day. And the dusty old theater was, in any case, far past its glory days. Fisher walked to the stage and began to speak when he suddenly swooned and then collapsed. He was rushed to a drugstore around the corner, where he regained consciousness. A nurse was called to tend to him day and night, but Fisher never recovered. In July, he was buried at the age of fifty-eight.[5] Fisher's death was mourned across the city and thousands gathered for his funeral procession.[6] But in hushed voices, the black residents of Chicago recalled the words that Fisher had spoken during his campaign against the Pekin, and they wondered what it all meant.[7]

What led Fisher to speak out so vociferously against the Pekin when so many of his counterparts were celebrating the construction of colored theaters, and how had he ended up there on that ill-fated day in 1915? His tale must be told against the backdrop of the long migration, the growing commercialization of black cinema culture, and black Americans' responses to the growth of moving pictures after the initial theater-building boom that began after 1906. The desires, resources, and sensibilities of the modern black public had produced the circumstances from which a black cinema culture emerged, but the evolving demands of black filmgoers and the exigencies of commercial capitalism eventually forced black film practices to diverge along two competing conceptions of black progress.[8] Black film professionals and church leaders, once united in their economic interdependence and their shared belief in the philosophy of racial uplift, suddenly found themselves at odds with one another as they each vied for the attention of the black public. Black migrants were at the helm of these developments. They brought their leisure demands and cinema practices across the South and West and into new centers of black life in the North. In these places, colored theaters became monuments of racial progress and black settlement. The cinema culture that emerged in the urban North during the 1910s trickled upward—geographically from the South, and from the working class to the middle class. As their cinema practices remade cities along the migratory trail, black men and women also remade themselves.

———

"I pick up my life / And take it with me / And I put it down in / Chicago, Detroit / Buffalo, Scranton," Langston Hughes once wrote of the mass exodus of black Americans from Dixie.[9] Written in the 1940s when Hughes was spending most of his time in Harlem, the poem described an influx of black migrants who were making their way out of the Jim Crow South. But even as black migration began to bend more acutely northward by 1910, the gradual movement into southern cities did not cease. Elijah John Fisher had treaded these paths; he moved from his master's plantation in Georgia to the coal mines of Anniston, Alabama, and then on to Atlanta and Nashville before the Olivet called him to Chicago.[10] Langston Hughes was familiar with these routes, too. In fact, Hughes's personal experience was far from the straight South-to-North journey depicted in his poem. The Missouri-born poet lived in Kansas, Ohio, Nebraska, Mexico, England, and Washington, D.C., before settling down in Harlem in the 1920s.[11]

Hughes's poem "One Way Ticket" nevertheless conveyed an enduring truth about the movement of black people from one place to another. As Hughes and other black Americans moved farther along their migratory paths, they did not go empty-handed. Even the most modest, poorest migrants brought more than the clothes on their backs and the shoes on their feet when they journeyed northward. They carried their sensibilities, experiences, and dreams with them. At the threshold of the industrial North, these ideas did not disappear. Rather, many of the developments associated with northern modernity—urban cosmopolitanism, black commercial amusements, and the assertiveness of the New Negro—were fashioned *along* the pathways of the long migration. In each new location, migrants unpacked their lives and made them anew, but what would be was also fashioned out of what had been.

One stream of northbound migration followed the tracks of the Pennsylvania railroad toward the Eastern Seaboard; others drifted westward or even across the border to Mexico.[12] Perhaps the most famous route followed the Illinois Central, which moved up the spine of the Midwest, from the Gulf of Mexico to the Great Lakes. The flood of people and cultural practices from the South gave cities such as Cleveland, Ohio, the moniker "Alabama-North."[13] Even in the farthest reaches of the industrial North, black folk recognized the enduring sway of southern black culture upon their lives. Of course, southern influence was most often described in pejorative terms. The *Philadelphia Tribune,* for example, acknowledged that "the majority of our people here are from the south and . . . many of the proprietors of the places referred to are also southern," but went on to warn that "we don't want any Southern Laws or Rules enforced in the State."[14] Deference to whites, poor manners, enthusiastic church worship, and ignorance were all pegged as "southern" characteristics in the pages of the black press. But other cultural practices were begrudgingly acknowledged as southern, too.[15] For example, good food and music that you could dance to came from the South. Of no minor significance, southern religious practices remade spirituality in the North.[16] Zora Neale Hurston argued in her 1942 autobiography that language and aesthetics deemed black were in fact simply "southern."[17] Hurston may have oversimplified the role of race in making "southern culture," but she was pointing to a much broader process of cultural production that race alone could not explain.

Black film practices evolved as they circulated between Atlanta, Georgia, and New York City, or Montgomery, Alabama, and Cleveland, Ohio. By the time colored theater districts had sprung up across the industrial North, African Americans had already spent more than a decade at the cinema. They were familiar with the passion play, spectacles of disaster, comedies, melodramas, and Westerns. They had watched the moving pictures on Sunday afternoons at their churches, during fundraisers at the local Masonic lodge, and from the cramped balcony seats of the segregated venue. The more recently opened colored theater presented even more filmgoing options. Even rural black folk were gradually discovering more opportunities to see the medium, which they viewed during the colored fair and at church, or during trips into town. Black migrants attended films in small cities, and those who resettled in large urban centers asked their friends and their neighbors where to go for the best pictures and the liveliest crowds. By 1910, the black theatergoing public possessed a cosmopolitan outlook and discerning expectations of the filmgoing experience.

To capture this market, investors constructed theaters in growing cities of black settlement and devised programs suited to the tastes and lifestyles of the migrant populace.[18] Some theaters opened with "continuous" entertainments that ran every day from morning until late into the night in order to accommodate the schedules of wageworkers, housewives, and schoolchildren.[19] Black filmgoers demanded a continuous supply of new features and higher-quality programs. "While we enjoy moving picture shows," the *Savannah Tribune* complained, "it gets rather tiresome to observe 17,635 different ways of upsetting a peanut stand by unsteady bicyclists or motorists."[20] In 1907, the Avenue Theater in Baltimore had bragged that its pictures were changed three times a week, but just two years later, local theaters were boasting that their films were changed daily.[21] To draw crowds, colored theaters installed electric cooling systems and soda fountains, and offered gifts and raffles. The amenities and special attractions in venues across Chicago's Black Belt and Harlem borrowed from successful businesses elsewhere. Following in the footsteps of theaters in Savannah, Georgia, and Indianapolis, Indiana, which awarded door prizes to their patrons, Chicago's Merit Theatre presented a canary to a lucky theatergoer once a week.[22] By implementing these practices, black commercial amusements appealed to the converging demands of the migrants who constituted their consumer market. These businesses could not have survived, much less thrived, without the dollars and the dreams of the new migrants who sustained them.

"We tho[ug]t State Street would be heaven itself," Mrs. Lynch explained in 1917 of her family's motivations for moving from Hattiesburg, Mississippi, to Chicago.[23] The aspirations of settlers such as Lynch, who arrived flush with rumors of the fantastic pleasures to be had in the city, helped transform Chicago into a glittering hub of black cultural life. Black migration began to remake the South Side in the 1890s. With the assistance of a white supporter, the Quinn AME Chapel was able to surreptitiously purchase the deed for the plot at the corner of Wabash Avenue and Twenty-Fourth Street in 1891.[24] The church was one of the first major black institutions to lay claim to what would become the "black belt"—a three-block-wide stretch of city streets from Twenty-Second to Thirty-First Street. Within a decade, colored restaurants, groceries, and shops dotted the thoroughfare. The Binga Bank, Provident Hospital, and the *Chicago Defender* were touted as symbols of racial progress crucial to the health of the black population. But without a doubt, theaters and churches were the center of black social and cultural life in the city.

It was in this venerable district, near the intersection of State and Twenty-Seventh streets, where Fisher and Robert T. Motts first clashed in 1905.[25] At that time, the Olivet Baptist Church and the Motts Theatre had only recently ventured into the neighborhood, and their fate there was far from certain. The Olivet's problems had begun before Fisher arrived at the church. In 1893, under the direction of its prior minister, John Francis Thomas, the Olivet had purchased three lots at the corner of Twenty-Seventh and Dearborn streets. The church then contracted one of its members, Jasper Higginbotham, "to erect a stone and brick building on the site."[26] The construction debt would place an enormous burden on the church, but its members believed the expensive edifice was necessary for the institution's future growth and prosperity. Nothing could have been further from the truth. Over the following years, a series of unpaid bills, liens, and lawsuits drove congregants away; the church's membership decreased by almost half over the next few years.[27] The few members who regularly attended services worshipped in the drafty, half-completed structure until 1903, when they were prohibited from entering the site on account of Olivet Baptist's unpaid debts. Thomas decided to abandon the property, but several heartbroken members refused to leave the partially constructed building. They had struggled to purchase the property and construct the new church edifice for almost a decade, and they saw it as a symbol of racial progress and spiritual glory that was inseparable from the mission of their church. The congregation split and Elijah John Fisher was called to minister over Olivet Baptist, while those loyal to Thomas left to form the Ebenezer Missionary Baptist Church.[28]

As Fisher struggled to rebuild the Olivet Baptist Church, Motts was waging his own battle. He had made his money in the Chicago underworld, first under the tutelage of "Mushmouth" Johnson, the infamous kingpin of the city's black gambling houses, and then by opening his own saloon and gambling hall on South State Street.[29] Motts was regularly lampooned by the local black press and attacked by various religious leaders for running a "hell-hole of iniquity."[30] In 1905, he attempted to improve his reputation by transforming his saloon into a more respectable music and vaudeville theater, but Fisher and fellow minister Archibald Carey interpreted the plan as a scheme for surreptitiously corroding the morals of Chicago's black citizens.[31] Yet this conflict between the pastors and Motts was not specifically waged over the issue of film exhibition. The Pekin featured a combination of motion pictures and vaudeville performances. The pastors' reaction was remarkable nonetheless, particularly because it was so unrepresentative of the general response of black leaders to the announcement of new colored theaters. During the initial building boom, Ida B. Wells expressed a sentiment that was much more typical of the general attitude toward colored theaters when she declared, "The race owes Mr. Motts a debt of gratitude for giving us a theater in which we could sit anywhere we chose without any restrictions."[32]

Motts, however, had an unsavory reputation, and this was further magnified by his decision to construct the new Pekin Theatre on the suspicious site where his saloon was previously located.[33] Even before the theater opened, Motts's venture was situated in the territory of "degrading" commercial amusements that black churches had been campaigning against for years. And unlike many colored theater owners and managers, Motts was no stranger in town, but instead a well-known debaser of black middle-class values. His venture therefore inspired an almost immediate backlash—the sort of response that was usually drowned out by celebrations of race pride when it came to colored theaters. Moreover, personal animosities between Carey and Motts stoked the flames. Ida B. Wells believed Quinn's minister had a personal vendetta against

Motts, and she blamed Carey for turning Fisher against the Pekin and her charity event at the theater. The fact that Motts had been congenial with Thomas, the former minister of the Olivet Baptist Church, did not further incline Fisher to be sympathetic.[34]

Just a few years later, however, both institutions had recovered from their shaky beginnings. In fact, they had grown into two of the most important monuments of black racial progress in the nation. The ongoing influx of migrants enabled Fisher and Motts to prosper and earn national renown as race leaders.[35] Migrants helped expand the membership of Olivet Baptist and greatly reduce its debt. It would soon become the largest black church in the country. By 1920, with 10,000 members, it was one of the largest Protestant churches (black or white) in the world. After Wells's charity event at the Pekin, Motts transformed the theater into a nationally acclaimed and much imitated entertainment venue. It was Motts's renown that had inspired Tish and Eddie Lee, and dozens of others, to name their own colored theaters "the Pekin." Black Chicagoans proudly pointed to the two institutions as illustrations of the advancement of black residents and their hold over the geography of the city.[36]

Other northern cities, including New York, were also remade by the accelerated northbound migration. By 1910, black migrants, immigrants from the Caribbean, and locals from the Tenderloin and San Juan Hill moved into Harlem after falling real-estate prices and a new uptown subway opened up the area to black settlement. Harlem had once been a predominately middle-class neighborhood of "old stock" white Americans and immigrants from England, Ireland, and Germany. These white property owners and residents resisted the "Negro Invasion" by organizing the Harlem Property Owners' Association, the Save-Harlem Committee, and the Property Owners' Protective Association of Harlem. But black migrants continued to assert their claims to the city streets by attending theaters and building churches in the neighborhood, including "Mother Zion" and the St. Mark's Methodist Episcopal, Abyssinian Baptist, Bethel African Methodist Episcopal, and St. Philip's Protestant Episcopal churches. "By becoming landowners," historian Gilbert Osofsky explained in his seminal 1966 study of the neighborhood, "Negro churches helped transform Harlem to a Negro section." By World War I, black churches were among the largest property owners in Harlem.[37]

Colored theaters also contributed to the transformation of Harlem into a "black mecca."[38] The neighborhood's first theater to cater to black audiences, the Crescent, was opened in 1909, an event that drama critic Lester Walton applauded as a sign of the future.[39] By attracting large numbers of black people into the neighborhood, colored theaters provided lively arenas of social and intellectual interaction for the city's black residents. Like Daly's open-air moving picture theater on Baltimore's Pennsylvania Avenue, where patrons could "sit and smoke or drink sundaes and soda" while mingling with their peers, or the Lees' multipurpose venue in Louisville, colored theaters in New York offered an ever-broadening array of pleasures and experiences along with their motion picture exhibitions.[40] For example, the Crescent Theater began operating a "country store" on Saturday nights. Each week, the management offered southern treats such as hams and sausages to lucky ticket holders. It was so popular that the theater soon announced another weekly event: "poultry night—when live chickens are given away."[41] When theaters across the country began hosting their own "country stores," they demonstrated how popular industry practices circulated across the pathways of migration.

The churches and theaters that framed the thoroughfares of black neighborhoods enabled black folk to "stroll" through their city streets. While sauntering leisurely through Harlem, along U Street in Washington, D.C., or down Pennsylvania Avenue in Baltimore, Maryland, the black city dweller was surrounded by an array of colored institutions that marked the vibrancy of black life in the city. "A stroll down Pennsylvania avenue these days reveals interesting signs of race progress," observed a writer for the *Afro-American,* whose opportunities for black social interaction and urban flanerie—the *pleasure* of observing and being observed—were facilitated by the numerous colored theaters and churches that lined the black blocks of Old West Baltimore. Heading north from Dolphin Street, the Pennsylvania Avenue A.M.E.Z., Renard Theatre, Sharp Street Memorial Church, and the Home Motion Picture Palace could be seen in a short, three-minute walk.[42] Not only did these religious and entertainment venues stake a claim to public space through their material presence, they drew in black people who congregated inside their doors, loitered outside their steps, and circulated through their surrounding streets.

Migrants provided the capital and energy that made it possible for these centers of modern black cultural and social life to thrive. As black folk settled amid the growing number of rickety storefronts and imposing brick buildings that housed Chicago's black churches and colored theaters, Fisher, Carey, and Motts found themselves fellow inhabitants of a corridor along State

Street quickly becoming known as "The Stroll"—proudly described by the *Chicago Defender* as "the most wonderful thoroughfare populated with Afro-Americans in the United States."[43] While the men did not see eye to eye, the rift between them was smoothed over sufficiently to prevent another explosive public skirmish. But as these leaders of black Chicago navigated across the black metropolis, their roles as arbiters of black social life became entangled. Indeed, even the buildings that housed their institutions looked similar to one another. The Quinn Chapel's avant-garde interior, designed by black architect Henry F. Starbuck, featured a two-tiered auditorium space with seating for more than 900 people. The sturdy oak pews were fixed with brass plates, each listing a seat number. At the front of the church was a ticket booth.[44] Mott's Pekin Theatre was similarly outfitted with balconies and enough seating to accommodate nearly a thousand patrons.[45] By 1910, the demands of the largely working-class black migrant population had convinced the managers of the Pekin and other colored theaters along the Stroll to eliminate many of their vaudeville headliners to make room for more film exhibitions. Staying in business, they understood, meant "paying some attention to the public or their patrons."[46]

Motion pictures vividly illustrated the overlapping functions of black churches and theaters. By hosting film exhibitions, black churches had earned their place as "the social center of the community, the place of amusement and of gathering information" by hosting popular entertainments. Fisher's son recalled how his father fashioned himself a modern race leader "in accord with the advancement of the times" by inviting some of the era's "most noted singers, musicians and entertainers" to perform at the church. These phrases—"social center," "place of amusement," and "noted . . . entertainers"—reverberated in the language of the colored theater industry.[47] In fact, Fisher's words might have been plucked from an advertisement for Motts's theater. Had Motts not shared those aspirations—to create the center of the city's black social life when he opened up Chicago's first colored theater across the street from the Olivet? And was it not Motts, rather than Fisher, who was earning national renown for fulfilling this goal?[48]

In 1907, the *St. Louis Palladium,* a black newspaper in Missouri, printed an article with the ambiguous title, "Not So Long." It told a story that went something like this: a few weeks earlier, congregants of a church in New York City gathered to lay the cornerstone for their new building. A moving picture cameraman was called to film the ceremony. He was so impressed by the pomp and circumstance of the dedication that he felt it "warranted to take a couple miles of photographs." Later, members of the church gathered to watch the film. They were pleased with the pictures, which were of high quality and very realistic.

> "I like the moving pictures better than I did the original service" confessed a prominent member of the congregation.
>
> "You do," gasped a devout elder. "I'm surely pained to hear you say so. Why should you prefer the pictures?"
>
> "Because the picture man," answered the prominent member, pleasantly, "cut out all the sermons."[49]

Black papers around the country reprinted the story for several years. It humorously conveyed the ironies that many turn-of-the-century Americans experienced as they encountered technologies such as the moving image. For one man, the film was a memento of a significant event; for another, the film was its idealized version. Black residents of St. Louis, Missouri, and Cleveland, Ohio, or any of the other cities where the story was published could interpret it variously. Was the prominent member of the congregation a spiritual fraud, or was he coyly commenting on the long-winded and overwrought sermons so common to church services? Did the church elder represent the bygone days of piety, patience, and respect, or was he just a stodgy old-timer? The wit of the story was its flexibility; it retained its humor amid a spectrum of sensibilities. More importantly, its significance resonated beyond the metaphoric. It gestured toward a more immediate truth about the changing role of cinema and the church in black life.

H. Sylvester Russell, the drama critic for the *Chicago Defender,* was surely among those who would have sided with the church elder. Russell believed in tradition, and besides, he found the moving pictures distasteful. Russell was a fan of the stage, however, and on a chilly February day in 1910, he made his way up South State Street to the Grand Theatre for a vaudeville performance by Wallace and Company.[50] He may have been dressed as he was shown in his published photographs—suit and tie, an elegant fold of the cuff, impeccably groomed, but whatever he was wearing, it was surely selected as a display of his refinement. As he walked into the Grand, Russell likely sized up his fellow theatergoers.[51] He intended to spend the evening with the "respectable elements" of the city's black population, and he was probably relieved to see that other upstanding black citizens were present at the theater. For years, the only option for black theatergoers had been segregated seats in the worst sections of the house. When the Pekin, Grand, and Monogram opened, Russell applauded them heartily.[52] Healthy, classy entertainment, Russell firmly believed, was the key to uplifting the race.

Russell left the theater that night sorely disappointed. One of the vaudeville performers, Miss Wallace, had performed a "disreputable dance" that Russell believed "would not be allowed in any other city."[53] Greatly disturbed by the performance, Russell promptly composed a review of the program in which he placed the blame for the undignified entertainment squarely on the Grand's association with moving pictures. "No wonder that Dr. Fisher extols the people of his church not to go to those wicked moving picture theaters," he wrote in reference to the minister of the Olivet Church.[54] By specifically describing the venue as a "moving picture" theater, Russell, an avid patron of the stage, implied that the unseemly behavior of the vaudeville dancer, Miss Wallace, was somehow connected to the fact that the Grand also exhibited films. In his complaint, he made no mention of whether any moving pictures had been shown that evening.

At first glance, Russell's response appeared to mirror white Progressives' criticisms of the motion pictures. White church leaders and reformers had already launched several highly public campaigns against commercial theaters—one of which famously led Mayor George B. McClellan to shut down all the moving picture houses in New York City in December of 1908. But critiques such as Russell's had emerged from a set of concerns that did not simply echo Progressive complaints against moving pictures. Russell's confusing critique of the theater, which blamed the evening's scandalous vaudeville performance on the venue's status as a motion picture theater, reflected an ambivalence shared by many of his black middle-class counterparts. Disconcerting reports of less-than-respectable happenings at colored theaters were beginning to trickle in from the thriving centers of black cinema culture across the country. In places such as Wichita, Kansas, the *Searchlight,* the same black paper that enjoined its readers to attend colored theaters as an indication of their race pride and that once announced that John E. Lewis and his brother-in-law were "sure to go to heaven" for operating the "greatest show on earth," the moving pictures, had begun to describe the most avid supporters of the medium as "young negroes who are professional loafers." Such individuals, the paper argued, should be hauled from "moving picture shows and street corners and carried forty miles into the country and dumped upon the turning rows of some farm and made to go to work."[55]

In Louisville, Kentucky, Tish and Eddie Lee announced that they were thinking about opening the Pekin Theater on Sunday nights.[56] Their earlier decision to close the theater on Sundays may have been prompted by low attendance or their own busy schedules, not by deference to local church leaders. But when the Lees considered opening on the Sabbath, they certainly put themselves in competition with the local churches that also hosted Sunday evening entertainments. Indeed, black church leaders across the country had noticed that commercial moving pictures were diverting attendance away from their church-sponsored events. For example, Mr. and Mrs. M. E. Douglass of Columbia, Missouri, realized only too late that they had scheduled an event for the Might Missionary on the same evening on which a show at the opera house and a moving picture were being held. "Few attended this social," the downtrodden couple reported of their sparsely attended church party.[57]

In Washington, D.C., the bustling center of black cinema culture, tensions grew sharper. The starry-eyed vision of colored theaters was clouded only a few months after the celebrated string of theater openings on U Street when the *Bee* published a disturbing account of a moving picture exhibition. The author of the article was most likely W. Calvin Chase, the editor of the paper, who was known for his stinging attacks, which "expose[d], in the most condemnatory manner, any fraud, unjust attack or evil, that caught his vigilant eye."[58] Chase held back the name of the venue, but he did not spare other details. In-the-know locals must have had a good suspicion as to which venue he was referring when he described the "certain moving picture theatre" which had "offered as its bill last Sunday evening a series of pictures not calculated to raise the standard of morality." The Sunday afternoon program of the unnamed theater (most likely the Douglass, which was managed by schoolteacher George D. Jenifer) included a vaudeville skit and a series of moving pictures. The article deplored the live performance in which "colored fellows, outlandishly attired" performed "a lot of stale chestnuts, which were a mockery on the race."[59] Chase linked the indecorous atmosphere to the venue's status as a motion picture theater. Like Russell's critique of the Grand in Chicago, the headline ignored the live performance. Instead, it was the "Degrading Moving Pictures" that were to blame. The most problematic features in the exhibition included a film of a robbery, another with a double murder, and scenes from a lightweight prizefight between white boxer "Battling" Nelson and black pugilist Joe Gans.[60]

Russell and Chase were not only concerned by the colored theaters' failure to uplift the "immoral classes." The moral standards of the working classes seemed to be affecting middle-class behavior. The comments of the supposedly "prominent member of the congregation" in New York City and the response of the "respectable elements" in Chicago suggested a change in the role of moving pictures in black life. Perhaps colored theaters and film exhibitions were not acting as forces of progress; they might even be bringing out the basest impulses of the middle class. What disturbed Russell the most was the effect of the evening's entertainments upon the city's most refined black citizens—the "falling off of the respectable element." The *Bee* similarly pointed out that the proprietor of the moving picture show was a public school teacher, a profession that was the epitome of the black middle class. The *Bee* launched into a personal attack, again arguing, "No teacher should be allowed to remain on the payroll of the Washington schools who will offer such a bill for week days, much less on a Sunday." Anxieties about the wayward moral habits of urban children and public decency clearly expressed the paper's middle-class sensibilities of religious uplift. The author implored the parents of these misguided youth to prohibit their children from attending such pictures, which were "disgusting and degrading even to adult persons." The *Bee,* nonetheless, did not completely write off the value of all moving pictures. Instead it advocated on behalf of the "highly educating and educational" pictures and scolded the proprietor of the house for behaving like a "consciousless fak[e]r." The article closed with a warning: in "the interest of the children and public decency, the *Bee* proposes to keep tabs on these moving picture shows."[61]

At stake in such controversies was the shifting role of black cinema culture, which had roots in two sacred areas of black life: enterprise and religion. For nearly a decade, while the moving pictures had resided comfortably in the realm of the church, religious leaders viewed film as a tool for uplift—even as the themes of exhibitions grew increasingly secular. When black-owned moving picture theaters first opened in 1905, ministers assumed the entertainment programs were safely under the responsible guardianship of the middle class. These assumptions shielded colored theaters from the criticisms typically directed at white nickelodeons. Moreover, black critics of moviegoing in white theaters emphasized the degradations of the segregated theatrical space. Black reformers' ire targeted the ignorant white proprietor and an absence of race pride, manliness, and self-respect—not the power of the medium to represent the race. When colored theaters first opened, class tensions were usually pushed aside in the name of racial progress. Recall that when the Globe colored theater opened in Jacksonville, Florida, the "decided difference between the elements which frequent the Globe" was "drowned beneath the general feeling of pride in the place."[62] But as the black cinema industry's profits came to depend less on the black church, these tensions could no longer be ignored. The moving pictures brought into relief differences in the sensibilities and material interests of black urban dwellers.

At the heart of these tensions over moving pictures were contradictions within the middle-class's vision of black progress. One set of middle-class interests resided squarely in the material and philosophical requirements of the church; the other was invested in black enterprise and its vision of racial progress. Middle-class blacks who sided with the church believed that ministers and religious leaders should dictate how the black public spent its time and money. These church-minded reformers had long promoted the development of black enterprise, which they viewed as congruent to their beliefs. A haircut, a bag of flour, or a funeral service purchased from a black business was not only a means for avoiding white racism but also a strategy for financial enrichment, one that would bolster the economic base of black churches. For this reason, ministers had enthusiastically endorsed the first black-owned and -operated theaters. But the optimism that inspired the *Bee* to write, "All that the enterprising colored man wants is to be let alone. He is paving his own streets. He knows just what his people want and they are satisfied" was mired in idealism. Who would take the lead when entrepreneurial race men and women followed the black Methodist Episcopal Reverend Mathew Clair's suggestion for "a closer cooperation in educational and social movements as well as industrial and economical"?[63]

These conflicts were playing out in many areas of black life—especially in religious and educational institutions—but the tension between church leaders and theater professionals was especially evident because motion pictures appealed so strongly to the middle class. This group was less likely to be drawn off from the mainline denominations to the Pentecostal or Holiness movements, or filtered into small storefront churches, which were attracting a growing number of working-class congregants.[64] When it came to commercial amusements, however, it seemed as if the middle class was following in the footsteps of their working-class brethren, not the other way around. The split was not only about ideology or influence, it was also about attendance and church coffers. In 1909, James Conway Jackson of Washington, D.C., wrote a poem assailing the effect of motion picture theaters on black churches: "The Christian people in this city should see to it that a law is passed / prohibiting the moving pictures shows from showing on the Sabbath." Noting the empty church pews in Washington, Jackson continued: "Just watch those dens of Satan, those moving picture shows / That desecrate the Sabbath, they are Christians' foes."[65] Since the opening of moving picture theaters, church attendance had decreased, claimed Clair. He and his allies blamed Sunday shows for cutting into church attendance and inculcating bad morals upon the black public.[66]

When material interests were not at stake, an apology and clarification might temporarily smooth over ruffled feathers. A week after the *Bee* published its condemnation, the "misunderstanding" between the paper and the theater was corrected. A representative of the schoolteacher contacted the *Bee* to deflect blame for the immoral program.[67] The individual disavowed the evening's entertainment, explaining that some employees had organized the program without the knowledge of the schoolteacher. Nothing of the sort would happen again, the representative assured the paper, as the theater was safely back in the hands of the proprietor. Meanwhile, the *Bee* continued to be an avid proponent, at least in theory, of black-owned and -operated moving picture theaters. As theaters continued to open in the following years, the paper promoted them and boasted of "refined and up-to-date, and original" entertainment.[68]

Although the *Bee* forgave the exhibition of the immoral program by shifting blame to the theater's employees (who were presumably of a lower class, and thus of more questionable moral aptitude), close readers of the paper may have noticed a seeming hypocrisy. Just a few weeks before the report of the "Degrading Moving Pictures," the paper had reported in fawning language that, on a recent September evening, Washington, D.C.'s finest colored citizens had gathered to watch a moving picture show at the Douglass Theatre. The theater crackled with excitement as the audience gasped and cheered as black pugilist Joe Gans attempted to defend his title as lightweight boxing champion of the world against "the battling Dane," Oscar "Battling" Nelson.[69]

The crème de la crème of black Washington was watching the Nelson-Gans prizefight—the same entertainment that the paper described as "disgusting" on October 2. Completely absent from the "This Week in Society" report of the Douglass exhibition was the condescending tone of the report published just weeks later. The earlier article instead described with colorful language the excitement of the evening: The responses were so visceral and the tension so thick that "one would have imagined it was a real fight to hear the expressions from the audience."[70] Among those caught up in the excitement of the evening were several distinguished gentlemen, including W. T. Vernon, colored register of the Treasury, and renowned musician and public school educator John T. Layton. The theater was also packed with scores of respectable young women who took particular interest in the fight, including socialites Annie Murdock, Daisy Craighton, and the Wormley sisters, who hailed from one of the wealthiest black families in America.[71]

What did the film of Joe Gans represent in these two instances? In one theater, Gans was an emblem of degradation, but when observed by Washington's elite, he was a symbol of race pride. The paper had either overlooked this discrepancy or accepted a different set of values for the two audiences. If the *Bee* had accepted two sets of standards, they were not merely based upon the age of the theatergoers. The fight film had been criticized as degrading "even for adults."[72] Besides, the fawning report of the social elite emphasized the age of the audience—"the young folks are coming."[73] Several of the young socialites in attendance, including eighteen-year-old Emmie Kibble, were barely adults. Taken together, the two articles demonstrated the middle class's ambiguity regarding the qualities they believed constituted a "moral" film. Perhaps the editor assumed that *certain* audiences were responsible and refined enough to watch these sorts of entertainments? The wayward youngsters at moving picture theaters, implied the paper, were not the children of responsible middle-class families. Such fears over the morality of black youth were a response to the social and economic changes that city life and wage work had had upon family life, but these concerns also served as a synecdoche for class and gender anxieties.[74] Referencing the less-developed capabilities of children to resist immoral behavior was a common middle-class rhetorical device that gestured toward more general anxieties over the easy corruptibility of the masses.

Black reformers argued that young people who spent their Sundays in theaters rather than in churches were especially likely to engage in deviant sexual behavior. A common accusation placed blame on the predatory and irresponsible behavior of young women and girls who frequented motion picture theaters. Darius Webb Johns, a thirty-nine-year-old father from Baltimore, primarily blamed "the girl that went astray," when describing the harm to black youth, "especially boys," that was posed by the "existing evil" of moving picture houses.[75] Johns had attempted to prevent his twelve-year-old son from attending moving picture shows by lodging complaints with the Child's Labor Bureau and the Juvenile Court. Both informed him they were helpless in the matter as they lacked the legal grounds and the resources to monitor the social activities of children. Although Johns was apparently unable to control the behavior of his own son, the frustrated father warned fellow black parents to better "draw the demarcating line between good and evil" by prohibiting their children from attending moving picture shows.[76]

Johns was not alone in his concerns about the moving pictures' effects on the behavior of black youth. In Ohio, black reformers pleaded with parents to prevent their children from attending motion picture shows where black youth reportedly made "engagements for immoral purposes."[77] "Not many weeks ago we were passing a well-known moving picture theater on Central avenue and we heard from the lips of a young girl, not more than 14 years of age, the most obscene language that could ever fall from the lips of the most hardened tough," a black resident of Cleveland lamented.[78] The next month, the *Cleveland Gazette* reported that a fourteen-year-old girl had stabbed her "sweetheart," Ferdinand Bowman, "in or near the moving picture show . . . so badly that the blood bespattered the sidewalk" down Central Avenue.[79] In Mineola, New York, the downfall of twenty-one-year-old Henrietta Tyson was also linked to the moving pictures. According to the black *Savannah Tribune,* Tyson spent so much time at the cinema that her neglected infant son starved to death.[80]

These reports circulated conspicuously in places with a high ratio of colored theaters to black churches. By 1910, there was approximately one theater catering to black patrons for every ten black churches in Washington, D.C.[81] Meanwhile, urban church film exhibitions dipped dramatically in proportion to theatrical exhibitions for black audiences. During June 1910, the *Freeman,* which was published weekly, made only two references to church film exhibitions. Moving pictures in commercial venues were mentioned specifically about a dozen times, and more than fifty references were made to colored theaters.[82] Although black religious institutions continued to host moving pictures throughout the twentieth century, these practices would primarily shift to the countryside, especially as new forms of transportation such as the automobile made it easier for itinerant film exhibitors to reach rural churches.

In 1923, white Moravian minister and sociologist Edmund de S. Brunner's study of black churches in three rural southern counties noted that "three [Negro churches] have moving-picture machines, which is a record twelve times better than that made by white churches in the six counties studied."[83] But by 1910, it appeared unlikely that church film shows would ever again outnumber colored theatrical film exhibitions in the city.

At the same time, colored theaters were subject to the changing demands of the black public. Had their patrons been satisfied with passion plays and other benign entertainments, many theater managers would have been relieved to dodge the discontent of their local religious leaders by featuring only such programs. Even the famous Robert T. Motts had to adapt his program to suit the growing migrant population. The new settlers preferred cheaper entertainments, which forced the Pekin to add more moving pictures to its repertoire. The tradeoff was an unhappy one for Motts, a proud patron of Chicago's finest stage performers, but the black public wanted cheap entertainments and would "not pay any more big prices to see ordinary shows."[84] "The Moving Picture House Is Taking the Day," announced the *Freeman* of the black public's ever-growing appetite for the moving pictures. The elaborate vaudeville shows that had commonly accompanied moving picture exhibitions were fading: "To-day is different. Every one of the small houses is playing quick vaudeville at small prices, and pictures. The latest craze has come to stay; the managers are making money out of it; the public is satisfied. This fad has spread all over the country."[85] Like the mainline churches that competed with smaller storefront churches, big venues like the Pekin were forced into competition with cheaper storefront theaters.

The networks of black churches that once popularized moving pictures were now used to mount the campaign against them. Individuals such as Mathew Clair of the Methodist Episcopal Church transported the earliest and most heated debates over motion pictures across the migratory belt. The Methodist Episcopal denomination worshipped in separate congregations but had not officially split, and white church leaders' public criticisms of moving pictures probably influenced Clair, but his complaints did not turn into a concerted campaign, nor did he receive much support until the building boom of colored theaters. Clair was stationed in Washington, D.C., when he began preaching most stridently against moving pictures. In fact, since Chase and Clair traveled in the same circles and were associated with the Niagara Movement (the civil rights organization that later formed the NAACP), Clair's ministrations may have influenced Chase's campaign against the "sinful" pictures in the capital. When Clair visited New York City in 1910, he ignited a public debate between the city's clergy over the influence of moving pictures on morality and church membership. Although some sided with Clair, other religious leaders such as Reverend Adam Clayton Powell defended motion pictures.[86] Nonetheless, the skepticism shared by many black church leaders toward popular amusements pushed motion pictures away from the realm of the church. Traces of the earlier history eventually faded for many black Americans, who came to associate moving pictures solely with commercial theaters.

Colored theaters and black churches had grown up together. They hosted the same social entertainments and supported each other financially; they had even helped to build each other's homes. Together, they formed the backbone of social and cultural life for early twentieth-century black city dwellers. But having matured, they grew apart. Both sought to be the center and meaning of black social life. As moving pictures and black churches outgrew each other, they pulled at the seams of the beliefs in racial uplift that had once brought them together. Lodges and other secular uplift organizations weathered film's shift to commercial theaters with less public ambivalence. Not only had halls and lodges profited from the emergence of commercial theaters, members of organizations such as the Negro Business League invested cooperatively in moving pictures.[87] Nevertheless, the contradictions in the philosophy of racial uplift exposed by colored theaters placed pressure on the entirety of the "respectable" class. The high expectations for and celebrations of colored theaters implied that middle-class blacks assumed their peers would manage theaters that abided by their shared interpretation of the philosophy of racial uplift. If they could persuade their working-class counterparts to "see the light," black reformers could guide the race toward progress—a route that was paved with middle-class moral standards of sexual behavior, hard work, frugality, and discipline. But the core values of racial uplift were not always profitable. In 1907, when Booker T. Washington spoke at the Olivet Baptist Church, how did Fisher and his congregants interpret Washington's request "to see a black man in every commercial enterprise"?[88] Washington must have noticed the flashy moving picture theater just two hundred feet across the street from the church. If Fisher was able to square his beliefs with Washington's request in theory, the minister found it much more difficult to do so in practice. As the Renard Theatre in Baltimore once advertised, "We change our pictures to please our patrons"—not to please their ministers.[89] In the end, the changes in black cinema culture contributed to the realignment of the black middle class based on black middle-class conceptions of racial progress. In deference to their patrons and desirous of profits, black business owners promoted their own vision of racial advancement, which they hinged to their capitalist enterprises. Black religious leaders who disdained moving pictures, meanwhile, found welcoming allies in the white Progressive movement.

———

When Oscar De Priest campaigned to become Chicago's first black alderman, he knew he could count on his old friend, the highly respected Reverend Elijah John Fisher of the Olivet Baptist Church, for help. It was for this reason that Fisher, on that fateful day in 1915, mustered up his energy and headed to the Pekin Theatre to speak in support of De Priest's candidacy. When Fisher arrived at the theater, Robert T. Motts was long gone. Laid to rest in 1911 after a battle with leukemia, the site of his memorial service, Quinn Chapel, was no less ironic than Fisher's presence at the Pekin that day. As the minister walked to the stage and felt himself grow faint, did he recall the battle that he had waged a decade before? Perhaps a verse from the *Book of Psalms,* which he had cited so long ago, faintly echoed in his memory: "If I forget thee, O Jerusalem, let my right hand forget its cunning. If I do not remember thee, let my tongue cleave to the roof of my mouth."[90]

But had Fisher not fainted in the midst of his speech, his appearance at the Pekin Theatre would have raised few concerns. By 1915, what was once a clash between two different visions of racial progress was now old news. Soon after Mott's death, the Pekin had fallen into a state of disrepair. By the time Fisher entered its doors, it was only another cheap five-cent motion picture house; bigger, brighter venues had long since surpassed the once grand theater. In a year, the seats would be removed, and in another decade, it would be gutted and made into a police station. The ailing minister and the crumbling theater were veterans of an ancient war, brought together for a moment of reconciliation. On the day that Fisher visited the theater, another monumental symbol of racial progress commanded the attention of the city: the election of a black politician. De Priest's campaign was successful; to be sure, he owed his victory in part to the support of Fisher and to the theater that Motts had constructed, but above all, he owed it to the thousands of migrants who settled in the city and voted for him.[91]

As they traversed the pathways of the new century, African Americans discovered that the ground beneath their feet had also shifted. Yet even as their alliances and beliefs continued to change, the moving pictures would come to play an even more critical role in how black Americans responded to the changes of modern life. "One cannot run toward heaven and Satan's Kingdom at the same time," Reverend Corbett J. Edward of Orangeburg, South Carolina, warned in his 1912 sermon denouncing the "great evil" of moving pictures.[92] But how could one navigate toward heaven if the path to hell was paved with the same intentions? And how could the ideas of racial progress be squared with those curving, drifting paths of black modern life? For many black Americans, there was no clear answer. Only time would tell where their paths were headed—and as always, the devil was in the details.

5

The Fight over Fight Pictures

After Jack Johnson's 1910 victory, working-class black Americans began to view the motion pictures as a critical site of racial representation. ("Struggling to get a chance to shake the hand of ex-champ Jack Johnson in New York, 1921." Library of Congress, Prints and Photographs Division, NYWT&S Collection.)

On July 4, 1910, a resounding left hook catapulted the race question to the center of public debates over the moving pictures. In the most anticipated match of the sport's history, black pugilist John Arthur "Jack" Johnson knocked the "Great White Hope," Jim Jeffries, nearly unconscious. A dozen motion picture cameras stationed at the arena in Reno, Nevada, captured the action: Johnson's playful banter, a furious crowd, and Jeffries limp against the ropes.[1] "Before the sun had set over the western hills," a black reporter from Wilmington, North Carolina, marveled, the announcement "flashed in every little town in the United States . . . Johnson, the great Negro pugilist, had knocked out Jim Jeffries in the fifteenth round."[2]

Brilliant, dashingly handsome, and skilled enough to bring the best fighters in the world to their knees, Jack Johnson was the first black heavyweight boxing champion of the world, and not coincidentally, its first black moving picture star.[3] Through his victories in the ring, he came to symbolize an assertive, physically powerful vision of black masculinity, but it was his bold and unrepentant public persona that kept him in the spotlight.[4] In an era of racial segregation, imperial ambitions, and heightened gender anxieties, Johnson was both revered and reviled for his refusal to abide by the rules of white supremacy. Hours after his victory in Reno, race riots and antiblack violence exploded across the United States.[5] On July 6, a group of angry whites attempted to break into Johnson's railroad car in Ogden, Utah, and lynch him.[6] Three days later, a man named Richard McGuirk slipped into Johnson's home in an attempt to assassinate the pugilist.[7] The nation was up in arms. Quickly, the controversy transformed into a battle over Johnson's image in moving pictures, which was waged on the streets, in theaters, and on the U.S. Senate floor.[8]

The Johnson–Jeffries prizefight was a pivotal moment in the intertwined history of modern cinema and race. Within days, politicians in North Carolina, Tennessee, and Connecticut announced plans to block exhibition of the films of the fight.[9] Ultimately, legislation passed in response to Johnson's victory created mechanisms at the local, state, and federal levels to regulate images of blackness on-screen. Local laws, folded into larger Progressive-era efforts to regulate morality, suppressed the fight pictures by prohibiting their exhibition in theaters. Courts validated such policies by affirming the right of local and state jurisdictions to film censorship. Meanwhile, federal legislation targeted the interstate distribution and circulation of prizefight pictures. The most far-reaching measure was the Sims Act, which made it unlawful to transport pictorial representations of prizefights across state and national borders.[10] In legally defining film as commerce, rather than art, the federal government determined its constitutional right to regulate motion pictures. By doing so, it shaped the very nature of cinema in the United States, and bound the motion pictures to the maintenance of the existing racial order.[11]

These scrambling and desperate attempts to control on-screen images of blackness responded to an even more fundamental transformation in the way that African Americans understood the motion pictures. For the black public, Johnson's victory and the events that unfolded in its wake established the screen as a discursive field for the production of racial knowledge. In other words, these developments crystallized cinema into a "place of blackness." These ideas can be fully understood only by examining the changing meaning of the moving pictures within black life. The infighting of the black middle class, inaugurated during the conflicts over the colored theater, spilled into the debates over the prizefight pictures. Meanwhile, as working-class blacks rallied in support of Johnson and his films, they came to invest their own racial identities in the screen. Neither group could agree on the type of racial representations that should, or should not, appear in the motion pictures. Despite the multiplicity of these responses, the debates over Johnson and the prizefight pictures turned the attention of the black public to issues of racial representation on-screen. The longtime investment in the *physical spaces* of the film exhibition (church properties, lodges, and colored theaters) as representations of racial progress had broadened to include the *moving image* itself as a critical site of racial representation.

Threatened by the implications of these new sensibilities, white supremacists responded with antiblack violence and laws to regulate motion picture depictions of blackness. But such reactions only furthered the black public's belief that images of race on-screen generated, reflected, or were otherwise inexorably linked to the larger racial order. The assumption that it was essential for black people to have access and control over their depictions in the motion pictures served as the basis for the emergence of an unmistakably modern conceptualization of rights—the belief that visual self-determination and fair representations on-screen were essential to civic equality and belonging. These claims rippled across the twentieth century, eventually altering the terms by which a broad swath of Americans would come to stake a claim to their own citizenship, equality, and freedom.

On July 13, 1910, Jack Johnson and Etta Durya arrived at East Fourteenth Street in Brooklyn, New York, the site of the Vitagraph film company's sprawling motion picture studio. They were a striking couple, even more recognizable than top-billed actors of the era like the stylish Florence Turner, known as the "Vitagraph Girl," or the "matinee idol," Maurice Costello. But even if Johnson had not just won the heavyweight title, his name emblazoned on headlines across the world, the couple would still have elicited stares. Johnson was black, and Durya, white, at a time when the color line between black men and white women was drawn with miscegenation laws and enforced by lynching. Even more conspicuous in their fur coats and diamond jewelry, Johnson and Durya presented the type of otherworldly opulence soon associated with "movie stars," those famous—or infamous—individuals whose names alone, like Johnson's, drew fans to the box office. As the couple strolled through the famed archway of Vitagraph Village, they drew gasps from admirers and detractors alike.

Johnson and Durya had arrived to watch the film of the July 4 prizefight. The production company arranged the private exhibition for the filmmakers, the couple, and a few close associates handpicked by Johnson, but others, insatiably curious, slipped into the back of the screening room. Johnson sat close to the screen, next to Durya, and waited until the invited guests were seated before he took off his coat. The lights were dimmed, and Johnson's larger-than-life image flashed across the screen. As the figures jostled and swayed, the delighted champion provided the audience with a running commentary on the match. While watching the second round, Johnson may have recounted how he teased his opponent in the ring: when Jeffries desperately attempted to hold him in a clinch, Johnson had famously joked "Please, Mr. Jeff, Don't love me so!"[12] Later, Jeffries landed a square punch on the black boxer, eliciting a sympathetic "Ouch!" from a member of the audience. "He didn't hurt me much that time," Johnson amicably explained. "The black champion seemed much pleased as he watched himself in action," newspapers reported of the film exhibition, especially as Johnson "watched his own arms deliver" the final blows.[13]

While Johnson watched his image flicker across the screen, millions debated the meaning of his victory. "Jack Johnson and Jim Jeffries have been on every tongue since the fourth of July," the *Indianapolis Freeman* reported of the fervor.[14] Although polarizing, the debates over Johnson did not merely pit black opinion against white. A week after the title match, the *Afro-American* of Baltimore published a full-page spread documenting the differing "views of the Afro-American press on the Johnson–Jeffries Fight."[15] Black Americans connected the event to everything from temperance to religious hypocrisy. The "racial significance" of Johnson's victory should "impress the importance of resisting dissipation, avoiding dirt and disease" upon the black public, a correspondent for the *Southern Reporter* curiously suggested, perhaps unaware of Johnson's affinity for the bottle. Another writer opined that boxing was "a menace to the peace and happiness of the races and ought to be abolished." Some attempted to reconcile their distaste for boxing with a defense of the celebrations that followed Johnson's victory. The *Atlanta Independent* argued that it was "quite natural that the blacks should sympathize with Jack Johnson and the whites with Jim Jeffries," but as a "moral question" it was undeserving of the conflicts it had caused among "decent people." The *Philadelphia Tribune* was more celebratory, lauding Johnson as the "black Samson" who had "knocked out the white Goliath."[16]

These opinions were already being linked to the moving pictures and their role in representing blackness. For most of the medium's short history, black Americans had been preoccupied with the physical spaces of exhibition—the location of colored theaters or the seating policies of segregated nickelodeons—when considering the "race question" and moving pictures. Middle-class blacks began collectively critiquing negative images of the race on-screen when colored theaters came into competition with black churches, but even then, the physical space still loomed large in public discourse.[17] For example, celebrations *and* criticisms of Robert T. Motts focused on the location and architecture of his Chicago theater. The Pekin was built on the site of Motts's former gambling hall, critics pointed out, but advocates claimed the handsome brick building also publicly displayed the progress of the race.[18] Theater critic Sylvester Russell did not bother to mention whether a film was exhibited at the Grand Theatre on the evening he attended the "disreputable" show in 1910; rather, he implied that the "wicked" moving pictures had somehow sullied the physical space of the theater.[19] Black legal petitions and public pronouncements against moving picture theaters likewise emphasized access to public accommodations protected under the Fourteenth Amendment. While white Progressives petitioned to regulate depictions of sex, alcohol, and violence in moving pictures, black lawsuits almost always targeted unfair ticketing and seating practices.

Of course, the content of moving pictures had not been completely ignored. Discussions of cinema and race did consider the medium's representational power, but they did so most often when moving pictures highlighted black achievements. Harry A. Royston's pictures of black soldiers, C. E. Hawk's scenes of race progress, William G. Hynes's films of the National Baptist

Convention and Women's Auxiliary, and Booker T. Washington's pictures of Tuskegee all emphasized the positive representational value of the moving pictures.[20] Campaigns and legal actions against negative representations of blackness in the cinema were uncommon and very much improvisational, as when public school teacher Harriett K. Price lodged a complaint with the manager of Ohio's Luna Park in 1908 after seeing an advertisement for the film *The Black Viper* illustrated with "a picture supposed to represent a colored man choking a white woman."[21] Price sent a letter to Harry Clay Smith, editor of the *Cleveland Gazette,* who promptly wrote Cleveland's mayor, Tom L. Johnson, complaining that Luna's "hellish exhibitions" were a threat to "the safety and morals of the community."[22] It is unclear, however, if Price or Smith (or indeed the illustrator of the advertisement) ever viewed *The Black Viper.* The villain of the film, a "viperous, venomous creature in human form," and his gang were swarthy in complexion, but they were depicted as Italian, not black.[23] The editor's failure to investigate before mounting his campaign against the film may have stemmed from his relative inexperience in critiquing moving picture content; much more often, Smith's reports and lawsuits cited unfair seating policies.[24] This changed in the years following Johnson's victory, when the editor shifted his strategy and organized some of the era's most politically sophisticated campaigns against racist images on-screen.[25]

In the months following the prizefight, the black public's discussions of cinema and race overwhelmingly focused, for the first time, on the representational power of the moving image. Several processes long in development informed this dramatic shift. Important among these was the longer history of visual culture in the age of emancipation across the Americas. By dismantling systems of chattel slavery, governments unwrote many of the legal mechanisms used to control the lives and labor of black people. Racial ideologies thus grew increasingly reliant upon a system of visual codes.[26] Western science and popular culture catalogued physical differences and correlated them with supposed mental abilities and moral rectitude, and the results were disseminated through new technologies that mass reproduced images, including still photography and motion pictures.[27] But this alone does not explain why the Johnson–Jeffries prizefight pictures would incite such spectacular and widespread public responses.

The events of 1910 and their aftermath were catalyzed by the convergence of two rapidly growing global consumer industries, cinema and boxing, and their popularity among turn-of-the-century black Americans. The same processes of industrialization and urbanization that fueled blacks' demands for the motion pictures and the rise of cinema in the United States had contributed to the surging popularity of moving pictures across the world—in Cape Town, Barcelona, Kingston, and Moscow. Although wealthier audiences also attended the cinema, the widespread, global appeal of the medium for working-class city dwellers gave it a reputation as the "theatre of the masses."[28] The powerful French, English, and U.S. film industries vied for control of highly lucrative and rapidly expanding foreign markets by establishing branches overseas and attempting to aggressively block out their competitors by forming trusts, filing lawsuits, and lobbying for legislative protections. Meanwhile, film producers in the smaller Russian and Italian industries fought tenaciously to maintain a share of their domestic markets while aspiring for larger international vistas. By 1910, the motion picture industry spanned the globe.[29] The producers and promoters of the Johnson–Jeffries prizefight pictures expected the footage to earn them hundreds of thousands of dollars in Canada, France, England, Australia, and the United States alone.[30]

Boxing, much like cinema, had grown into a global spectator sport powered by the expansion of commercial capitalism and its attendant values of leisure and consumption. By the turn of the century, the boxing industry captivated audiences across the world and generated millions of dollars in revenue each year, a large percentage of which came from prizefight films.[31] Once primarily associated with working-class aggression and brutality, boxing had grown in popularity during the late nineteenth century as a generation of middle-class men began eschewing the Victorian values of emotional and physical self-restraint. These traditional determinants of masculinity no longer made sense in a landscape dominated by corporate bureaucracies and factories or amid the ascendant values of leisure and consumption.[32] By the 1890s, arbiters of this new middle-class culture promoted an aggressive, sexually voracious, and physically powerful image of masculinity as an antidote to the "feminizing" aspects of modern civilization.[33] They defended pugilism against the attacks of more traditional middle-class reformers by describing boxing as a contest of both mental acuity and physical stamina, and thus a natural expression of masculine power. White supremacists fused eugenics to these new ideals of masculinity. Ignoring the fact that heavyweight boxing champions before Johnson had simply refused to fight blacks who sought to vie for the title, they claimed that the long-standing history of white champions proved that white men were biologically more virile and more powerful.

Before the opening bell rang in Reno, the cultural significance of boxing had begun to overlap with that of the moving image. A month before the prizefight, black New Yorkers flocked to the Palace Theater, a few blocks north of the Tenderloin neighborhood in Manhattan, to witness the moving pictures of Johnson practicing with his sparring partners in preparation for his fight with Jeffries.[34] If boxing was a spectator sport arranged around the display of powerful masculine strength, early motion pictures similarly presented spectacles of exceptional human bodies to the public. The film *Eugene Sandow,* for example, welcomed the public to gaze upon the German bodybuilder's nearly naked physique as he flexed his muscles for the camera. The entangled nature of these two commercial leisure activities, along with Johnson's exceptional talents, factored into the willingness of black people to reconceptualize the screen as a site of racial meaning. In celebrating the visual display of Johnson's masculine power, black supporters of the pugilist described his manliness as representative of the entire race. "Stand up, thou brawny son of African lineage, and let the world see thee!" the *Birmingham Reporter* exclaimed; "let all admirers of the physical hero behold thy muscular frame."[35] For these black fans of pugilism, the image of Johnson's championship both challenged the presumption of white physical and biological superiority and served as a monument to the strength and virility of black manhood.[36] Witnessing the motion pictures of Johnson's victory, they argued, would make "the white children grow up with certain fear or dread of the colored boy."[37]

Not everyone, however, agreed with these assessments. As Johnson's victory became a lightning rod for public debates over race and representation, middle-class blacks found themselves, once again, forced to reconcile contradictions in their ideas about racial progress. Middle-class black progressives, unswayed by the merits of pugilism, joined black religious leaders and white progressives in older, more established campaigns against moving picture houses. Together, these groups channeled their discontents into a movement to censor the prizefight films. "Almost every sort of person," explained the *Afro-American,* "white and black, more especially the white folks, have kept up a constant agitation against the showing of these pictures."[38] But not all religious leaders found it so easy to choose sides. On July 11, African Methodist Episcopal ministers from Pennsylvania, New Jersey, Delaware, and New York voted *against* a resolution calling for censorship of the prizefight pictures. Explaining his position, Bishop B. T. Turner vehemently denied he supported prizefighting but admitted he had "prayed for Johnson to win."[39] Mary

Church Terrell, former president of the National Association of Colored Women, found boxing distasteful and had "no special admiration for Jack Johnson." Nonetheless, she found herself coming to Johnson's defense. "There is not much fuss made when men fight and mobs destroy, or when colored men are even shot and burned," she explained, "but when a big black man licks a big white man there is all kinds of action. Laws are passed, and moving pictures suppressed."[40] The *Richmond Planet* took a similar stance, referring to the censorship of the film as "Hypocrisy That Shames the Devil."[41] Sidestepping the ethics of pugilism and moving pictures, the newspaper printed an illustration of a white moralist preaching about the "immoral, unchristian, brutal" films with his back turned to the bodies of four lynched black men.[42]

Even the conservative Wizard of Tuskegee, Booker T. Washington, had reason to be ambivalent. Publicly, Washington "declined to express an opinion" about Johnson, coyly confusing the champion's name with another boxer's and telling a white journalist that he knew "little about pugilism."[43] But he acknowledged the importance of Johnson's fight to the students at Tuskegee and allowed them to set up a telegraph system to transmit live results of the match.[44] In fact, Washington may have been just as eager to hear the outcome of the prizefight. Although Johnson flouted the norms of respectable middle-class black behavior (especially by openly cavorting with white women), he had risen up to become one of the wealthiest black men in the world. Leaders of black industry such as Washington idealized this type of "pull yourself up by the bootstraps" upward economic mobility.[45] Especially impressive were the fees that Johnson demanded from motion picture producers for the rights to his image. Although Washington refrained from explicitly supporting the pugilist, the two men were in communication for at least a year after the 1910 prizefight. That December, Johnson invited Washington to dine at his home in Chicago. Washington cancelled at the last moment but sent his regrets, and later described an incident in which he witnessed the champion donate a considerable sum to a black church.[46] By publicly expressing his hope that Johnson would continue to invest in institutions working to uplift the race, Washington cautiously left the door open for future collaborations.[47]

Meanwhile, a much more vocal group of supporters launched a public campaign in defense of Johnson and in opposition to the criticism of the Johnson–Jeffries films. On the evening of the prizefight, 2,000 people packed themselves into Motts's Pekin Theatre, where they chanted "Jack, Jack, J-a-j;

Jack, Jack, J-a-j!" while Robert T. Motts read aloud the results of the fight.[48] It wasn't just black leaders like Motts who supported Johnson. Religious leaders, too, viewed his victory with pride. Minister Harvey Johnson of the Union Baptist Church in Baltimore, Maryland, referred to Jack Johnson as "the greatest hero the colored race has ever had."[49] Reverend Johnson even encouraged his congregants to teach their children how to box "for their moral and physical uplift" and argued "authorities in many places were a little too hasty in stopping the motion pictures."[50] For Harvey Johnson, the prizefight pictures offered unmistakable proof "that ability [not race] is the chief factor in any struggle for superiority."[51] As theater critic Lester Walton wrote shortly after the fight, "there is no doubt in the minds of thousands that Jack Johnson's victory has caused the white race to entertain a higher respect for the Negro. Before the Johnson–Jeffries fight the white brother, in general, seemed to be puffed up with the idea that color alone counted."[52]

Most dramatically, working-class black support of Johnson paved the way for their reconceptualization of racial representation on-screen. This group had previously shown little interest in collectively contesting cinematic representations of blackness. Working-class blacks' responses before 1910 suggest they may not have viewed depictions of "black" figures on-screen as representative of all black people, or of their own racial identities. In 1906, for example, two thousand black attendees of a moving picture exhibition at the Fifth Street Baptist Church in Richmond, Virginia, reportedly cheered a lynching scene in a film: "When the negro was finally caught and swung up, the entire audience of negroes arose and gave vent to their indignation at the crime by applauding as the negro was dangling from a tree."[53] Though details of the account may have been exaggerated or misinterpreted by the *Baltimore Sun,* the white newspaper that reported the story, similar reports corroborate the exhibition of such films in black churches. In other cases, as in the 1905 motion picture exhibition of the Cato and Reid murders in Savannah, Georgia, films may have been viewed as illustrations of white brutality against black people, but neither the exhibitions nor the images themselves were broadly described as inherent acts of violence, as they would later be understood.[54] Such interpretations were not inevitable; they would emerge only as a result of larger historical processes, as a series of factors transformed the screen into an overdetermined site of black identity.

The literal investment of working-class blacks in Johnson and his image as representative of the race contributed to their altered perception of the screen.

Months before the 1910 prizefight, working-class blacks began wagering hundreds of thousands of dollars on the match. The middle class also indulged in the "vice," but black reformers generally frowned upon the working-class proclivity for gambling.[55] Although outwardly "secretive" about their wishes for Johnson, black residents of Savannah, Georgia, showed their support of the pugilist by betting on his victory. The *Savannah Tribune* predicted, "If Jack Johnson is defeated the negroes stand to lose thousands of dollars. If he wins, there will be many negroes who will quit their jobs for the time being and loaf until their winnings are spent."[56] In Santa Fe, Cuba, poor blacks formed the "Jack Johnson Betting Pool." "We have not much money, but will bet what we have," one of the members explained.[57] In fact, even those without any disposable income found ways to gamble on the fight. One man from Omaha literally bet the house on Johnson; he gathered together everything worth value in his home in order to place his wager.[58]

On the evening of Johnson's victory, those who had bet on the champion were handsomely rewarded. "Almost every celebrator has a pocket full of money," the *Indianapolis Freeman* reported; "the black belt had everything down to its shoestrings on Jack."[59] By "the most conservative estimate," the paper continued, black residents of Chicago had won half a million dollars on his victory. A white newspaper, the *Aberdeen Daily News,* reported that triumphant blacks were using their winnings to quit "their jobs, declaring the day of the black race has come."[60] Yet for the black folk who gambled on Johnson, "there was more at stake than just a few dollars," Ruby Berkley Goodwin recalled; "the fate of an entire race hung in the balance . . . one lone black man had the power to make us a race of champions."[61]

As black Americans began to collectively identify with the image of Jack Johnson, riots, beatings, and other forms of intimidation raised the stakes of racial representation. In the hours after Johnson's victory was announced, angry white supporters of Jim Jeffries embarked on "negro hunts," which targeted working-class black leisure and residential districts in cities such as St. Louis, Missouri, and Roanoke, Virginia.[62] In New York City, "a gang of white men in the 'black and tan belt' set fire" to a "negro tenement on the middle west side."[63] Farther south, on Barren Island, poor black laborers barricaded themselves inside their homes after a fellow worker was stabbed in a brawl following the prizefight.[64] Black workers who lived in outdoor encampments were particularly vulnerable to white violence. In Uvaldia, Georgia, black laborers living in a construction camp enraged the local white population with their "insolent remarks about Jeffries."[65] A party of whites attacked the camp, killed three black workers, and sent the rest fleeing into the woods.[66]

This violence was accompanied by dehumanizing images of the champion in white newspapers, and messages that desperately attempted to empty Johnson's championship of racial significance. Jeffries, once the "Great White Hope," was suddenly described by his former supporters as an ordinary fellow who just happened to be white. "The conflict was a personal one, not race with race," insisted an editorial writer for the *Los Angeles Times* after the prizefight. Black people should "not point your nose too high," the writer warned; "remember you have done nothing at all . . . your place in the world is just what it was."[67] The bitterness stemmed from not only white resentment of Johnson's victory but also the racial significance that many black Americans had publicly attached to the event. Random attacks were far from uncommon, but white attackers were especially apt to target black people who publicly rallied in favor of Johnson's victory.

Such sentiments, especially among the black working class, were made evident in their numerous public festivities and revelries celebrating the pugilist.[68] In Du Quoin, Illinois, a coal belt town located along the Illinois Central Railroad, where work was grueling and deadly mining accidents were a regular occurrence, black laborers viewed Johnson's victory as an accomplishment for the entire race. On the day of the fight, an unusual silence descended over the city. Black men and women, too nervous to eat or drink, quietly gathered outside in anticipation of the news. As soon as the *Du Quoin Call*'s office received the telegraph of Johnson's victory, a group of men rushed down the streets, spreading the news. The black folk broke out in jubilation. Joyous shouting and dancing commenced in the streets. Jerome Banks, a black laborer who had lost a leg in a mining accident, rushed outside with his crutches waving in the air. "Everybody wanted to buy someone else a dinner, a glass of beer, or a shot of whiskey," Ruby Berkley Goodwin recalled.[69] Underneath the grape arbor, tiny Harriett "Grandma" Thompson, eighty-nine years old, lifted her head of snow-white hair and began to sing, "Hallelujah, hallelujah."[70] The crowd joined her, singing in unison, "The storm is passing over, Hallelujah!"[71]

Johnson's victory was celebrated in disregard of or even in direct opposition to white standards of proper racial etiquette. One eighteen-year-old domestic worker, Jeannette Chapman, believed that Jack Johnson's victory should be fêted in style. Without permission, she borrowed the silk dress of her white employer, which she wore on the evening of the prizefight, "surrounded by a crowd of her admiring friends" before being discovered by the police.[72] Public festivities, spontaneous parades, and street gatherings took place in black neighborhoods across the country.[73] Revelers in black districts were highly public, even provocative, in their celebrations of Johnson's victory.[74] Black correspondent Cary B. Lewis emphasized the "good natured" spirit of the ebullitions but added that naturally the bootblack who earned only a few cents a day shining shoes was not "expected to act any other way but foolishly" when he had "just cashed in a betting ticket and had plenty of Johnson money in his jeans."[75] Ten thousand people gathered on the Stroll in Chicago, where "white people passing through the crowd on street cars, in automobiles, on foot, were made the butts of black folks' boisterous wit."[76]

Later, the celebrations resumed during exhibitions of the fight pictures. "Do not be impatient but just wait," the *Cleveland Gazette* soothed its anxious readers in late July 1910; "we will all have an opportunity to see those moving pictures of the Johnson–Jeffries fight, yet."[77] In August, advertisements for large-scale outdoor exhibitions of the "original MOTION PICTURES" of the Johnson–Jeffries fight in Reno began appearing in the *New York Age*. The films screened nightly at Meyerrose Park in Brooklyn, and in Manhattan, a grand exhibition was planned for the evening of August 8 at Olympic Field, a baseball stadium in Harlem that could hold more than 10,000 people.[78] Just days after, advertisements indicated the Olympic Field exhibitions had been extended to "every evening."[79] When the pictures arrived in Moundsville, West Virginia, an especially eager black schoolteacher dismissed classes an hour early "for the purpose of taking his pupils to witness the Jeffries–Johnson fight pictures."[80] And "practically the entire census of the negro population" of Tucson, Arizona, "jammed and pushed" into an exhibition of the Johnson–Jeffries prizefight pictures, though police stationed at the theater prohibited them from applauding.[81]

The Johnson–Jeffries fight pictures evoked a spectrum of responses from the black public. Working-class black folk vociferously celebrated Johnson's victory and clamored to view his moving pictures. While some middle-class blacks had joined white Progressives in opposing the prizefight pictures, others responded to the films with ambivalence, or even enthusiasm. But even within these various factions, debates fractured into ever-more-nuanced disagreements about how the race should be properly depicted on-screen, or why, exactly, Johnson's image should serve as a representation of all black people. Black Americans would never agree on the meaning of Johnson's image. Yet, paradoxically, in the aftermath of these controversies, a commonality was slowly emerging in the black public's conception of the cinema. They had begun to link the meaning of blackness itself to the screen. This new way of thinking would continue to evolve, developing in dialogue with desperate efforts to establish white order over this uncharted landscape of racial meaning.

On October 15, 1910, four months after Johnson's victory in Reno, a train pulled out of Pittsburgh, Pennsylvania, and passed into Ohio, then Indiana, and finally on to Illinois. Aboard was a twenty-four-year-old white woman named Belle Schreiber.[82] Her race did not garner her any special attention that day, but such was not always the case. A year earlier, while traveling in the company of Jack Johnson, her whiteness had been a spectacle.[83] Although the two were separated by the time she departed from Pittsburgh (in December, Johnson would marry Etta Durya), Schreiber had borrowed money from the pugilist to purchase her train tickets to Chicago.[84] Uneventful as it appeared at the time, her journey would be written into the intertwined history of race and the moving pictures in the United States.

In the months between Johnson's victory and Belle Schreiber's journey by train to Chicago, white Progressives and politicians had clambered to control the exhibition of the prizefight pictures. The otherwise avid boxing enthusiast Theodore Roosevelt immediately called for a legal ban on the exhibition of fight films.[85] Censorship legislation enacted by state and local governments deemed the pictures "immoral" and thus unsuitable for public viewing. As black observers noted, whites were investing "time and space endeavoring to prevent the exhibition of the moving picture of the Johnson–Jeffries fight."[86] Within a year of Johnson's victory, the fight pictures had been banned by local governments across the United States and in several countries abroad. It was not until 1912, however, that the U.S. federal government finally enacted its two-pronged strategy aimed at regulating the threat Jack Johnson posed. One aspect of this strategy was firmly rooted in the nineteenth-century practice of controlling the movement of black bodies; the other attempted to regulate the motion pictures—a new site of blackness, whose mobility came to be seen as equally dangerous. These twinned efforts signaled a growing anxiety over the power black people had assigned to Johnson and his on-screen image as representative of the race, and the federal government ultimately sought in both instances to limit the mobility of blackness across state and national borders.

On November 7, 1912, Johnson was arrested and confined to the Cook County Jail in Chicago, Illinois. Federal prosecutors charged him with violating the Mann Act for having sent Belle Schreiber the seventy-five dollars that she used to purchase her train ticket to Chicago in 1910. Also known as the White Slave Traffic Act, the Mann Act prohibited the transportation of "any woman or girl for the purpose of prostitution or debauchery, or for any other immoral purpose" across state borders.[87] Although it was widely understood that Schreiber had been Johnson's romantic partner, the case rested on the popular narrative of black male sexual aggression and exploitation of white women. The prosecution argued that Johnson intended to involve Schreiber in "prostitution and debauchery," which essentially defined Johnson as a slave trader and Schreiber as a slave. Although it was based on the interstate movement of his former lover, the indictment was part of a concerted government effort to control Johnson's own mobility.[88] Imprisoning him would not only physically separate him from his white wife; it would also prevent him from participating in other boxing matches that would elevate his notoriety and wealth.

Most importantly, however, demobilizing Johnson was an act of symbolic power. When Johnson was convicted in 1913, Harry A. Parkins, assistant U.S. district attorney, explained:

> This verdict will go around the world. It is the forerunner of laws to be passed in the United States which we may live to see—laws forbidding miscegenation. This Negro, in the eyes of many, has been persecuted. Perhaps as an individual he was. But his misfortune is to be the foremost example of the evil in permitting intermarriage of whites and blacks. He has violated the law. Now it is his function to teach others the law must be respected.[89]

Parkins's description of the "law" referred not only to Johnson's violation of the Mann Act but also to the unwritten rules of the racial order, which forbade interracial marriage. Enforcing that order by imprisonment recalled a much older heritage of restricting black mobility. Movement across space, both free and coerced, has long been a defining characteristic of the black modern experience. From the middle passage to the Great Migration, the dislocation of black people from one place to another has been accompanied by an alteration in status, whether for better or for worse.[90] Slavery and postemancipation regimes alike were maintained by controlling the mobility of black people.[91] Indeed, it is impossible to speak separately of free and forced migration while accounting for the duress that set modern black subjects into motion.[92] Neither erasing the agency of migrants nor framing their actions as wholly willful accurately describes their movement, which was shaped by both subjugation and aspirations for a better life. Mobility thus lies at the center of the history of black engagements with the motion pictures. Popularized in cities of new black settlement, and utilized as a means of disseminating positive depictions of blackness across the vast pathways of migration, the mobility of the motion pictures was tied to black movement across space and aspirations for upward mobility.

Well aware of the correlations between mobility and status, Johnson fled the country in 1913. Aided by Andrew "Rube" Foster, manager of the Chicago American Giants, who disguised Johnson as a member of the baseball team, the fugitive slipped undetected across the border of Illinois northward to Canada. From there Johnson traveled to Europe, Mexico, and South America, where the boxer spent much of his next seven years in exile.[93] The Federal Bureau of Investigation tracked Johnson's movements, hoping to extradite the prizefighter back to the United States.[94] As the prosecuting attorney, Parkins indicated in his description of Johnson's "function" that the federal government's desire to incarcerate the "individual" Johnson was linked to the pugilist's status as a representational black figure.[95] But the government also recognized that physically capturing and imprisoning the fighter could not, by itself, sufficiently contain his representative power. In the modern world entwined with cinema, patrolling the sites of racial meaning required new strategies. Johnson's deviant blackness was written on his body, but it was also mapped onto the moving pictures.

In 1912, the same year Johnson was arrested for "white slavery," Congress passed the Sims Act, which prohibited the transportation of fight films across state and national borders. Like Johnson's conviction under the Mann Act, the Sims Act was rooted in a desire to maintain the established racial order, but rather than disciplining black bodies, it controlled moving images. Prior to 1910, Congress had rejected proposals to censor pictorial depictions of prizefights.[96] The shift in the federal government's position on the matter acknowledged how highly contested and how central cinema had become in mediating the public meaning of race. In describing the Act, Representative Thetus Sims of Tennessee, House cosponsor of the bill, explicitly referenced Johnson. The bill intended to block "moving-picture films of prize fights, especially the one between a negro and a white man, to be held in New Mexico on the 4th of July, [1912]," Sims explained in reference to Johnson's upcoming prizefight against a white boxer, Jim Flynn.[97]

The Sims Act initiated the federal government's involvement in film censorship and tied it explicitly to the maintenance of the existing racial order.[98] In order to regulate the meaning of blackness on-screen, Congress defined, for the first time, the legal status of motion pictures. Film was not "art," but commerce, the law established, and thus was subject to congressional regulation.[99] Subsequently, politicians would continue to support legislation that disciplined black people by both controlling on-screen and embodied representations of the race. Southern Democrats such as Representative Seaborn A. Roddenberry of Georgia collapsed the regulation of these two sites of blackness into their larger mission to keep black people in their place. After supporting censorship regulation and laws targeting Johnson's on-screen images, Roddenberry's disgust with the pugilist induced the congressman to propose a constitutional amendment prohibiting interracial marriage, which he defended on the floor of the House with an impassioned speech denouncing the ability of the "brown hued, black skinned, thick lipped brutal hearted African" in Chicago to "walk into an office of the law and demand an edict guaranteeing him wedlock to a white woman."[100]

The Sims Act targeted the movement of particular images of blackness by prohibiting their transportation between states or across national borders. It was not only the material object—the film reel—that was subject to federal control. So, too, was the cinematic expression, as "pictorial representations."[101] In *Pantomimic Corp v. Malone,* Judge Augustus N. Hand of the federal district court ruled against a group of white businessmen who had attempted to profit from the 1915 Willard-Johnson prizefight pictures by evading the Sims Act. The men had brought the reels of the prizefight filmed in Havana, Cuba, to the Canadian border, where they duplicated the film:

> A motion picture projecting machine containing the original films of the [Willard–Johnson] fight was set up on the Canadian side of the line, and on the American side within 12 inches of the other machine, a motion

picture camera was set up. Powerful electric lights were used to transfer the pictures from the projecting machine to the sensitized film in the camera.[102]

Because the reels of film never cross the border, the businessmen believed they had discovered a novel means of circumventing the Sims Act's prohibition against transporting films across state and national borders. Judge Hand decided otherwise. Although the "traveling rays of light" that constituted the pictorial image were not physically tangible, he explained, they were still subject to federal regulation.[103]

The *Pantomimic* case revealed the extent to which screen images had become a critical site of racial meaning. The Sims Act represented a new conception of racialized space, which nevertheless borrowed from established disciplinary mechanisms. The federal government elected to police both the embodied and on-screen representational sites (the "pictorial representations") of race by selectively defining the objects of regulation and then constricting their mobility across space. The lengths to which the government went to control the circulation of the film responded to the importance black Americans had endowed in the motion pictures. Nonetheless, the efforts of white politicians to establish control over motion picture content far from disabused black Americans from investing their racial identities in the screen. In fact, the censorship regulations passed in response to Jack Johnson's prizefight pictures only further entrenched the motion pictures as a site of racial significance.

During the debates over censorship of the prizefight pictures, black Americans introduced the language of natural and civil rights into conversations about on-screen representations. These beliefs began unevenly but grew increasingly common as injunctions against Johnson's image spread. Although black critiques emphasized the visual, these ideas overlapped with economic and political concerns. Black critics were acutely aware of the manner in which white supremacists had been able to mobilize the political system to serve their goals. Censoring certain types of black images on-screen would constrain the opportunities of black Americans in the lucrative leisure industries of moving pictures and pugilism. The law should allow people to "enjoy their natural rights" protected by the Constitution to watch the moving pictures of the Johnson–Jeffries fight, argued a reporter for the *Freeman,* framing the question as one of "civil equality of the races."[104] A few weeks after Johnson's victory, the *Broad Ax* wrote of the injustices of censoring the pictures, arguing that the hypocrites who "roll up their eyes Heavenward in holy horror at the very idea of permitting the exhibition of the moving pictures" would bring their "sweet little children to witness the Negro being burned at the stake."[105] Like the brick church, the colored theater, and the city street, the moving image had become a site upon which black Americans staked claims to their rights of citizenship.

At the same time, concerns about the representation of blackness on-screen generated a transatlantic discourse about the moving pictures. Images of black achievement were censored, critics pointed out, but racist depictions of black people circulated freely across the world. "To every section of the globe are these motion pictures sent," the critic Lester Walton wrote, lamenting that "in England, Germany, France and Russia the natives see only pictures of the worst of us."[106] As reports of the censorship on Johnson's fight films emanated from all corners of the globe, critics connected the phenomenon to the racial oppression of black people in the United States and the oppression of colonial subjects across the world.[107] The censorship of the prizefight pictures, they argued, indicated a shared global oppression of "the darker races." Such critiques articulated a diasporic vision of oppression that transcended national boundaries and connected the experiences of black Americans to those of dispossessed populations across the globe. South African newspaper editor Sol Plaatje described the British Empire's response to the pictures as a form of colonial control. Permitting exhibition of the films in South Africa, he wrote, "will mean that the Natives will secure pictures of whites being chased by coloured men, and who knows what harm such pictures may do?"[108] The *New York Age* linked the United States' control over the visual representation of blackness to the social and economic control of colonized Africans and Asians:

> The fight pictures were shut out of everywhere that the law and public opinion could accomplish it; especially was this done in European Africa. Johnson's single victory had the same shocking, awful influence on the English speaking peoples towards Africa and the black peoples that the Japanese victory over the savage Russian hordes had on the rest of Europe and America towards the red, the yellow and the black people of Asia.[109]

The borders of this transnational blackness were mapped variously. While the *Age* categorized Asians as black, red, or yellow, other papers categorized certain Asians as "white." The *Chicago Defender* pointed out "the white people of the world, except France, China, and Japan don't like [Johnson's victories]."[110] Through this discourse, moving pictures served not only as a representational site but as a venue for considering the very meaning of what constituted blackness.

Johnson's emerging career as a motion picture actor contributed to this ongoing conversation. Pictures of his 1910 prizefight were especially popular, but the black demand for Johnson films extended to other fight pictures, documentary footage, and fictional stories featuring the champion.[111] Although largely censored in his home country, he continued to appear in motion pictures, first in exile, and later, back in the United States. In 1912, he starred in *Une aventure de Jack Johnson,* directed by Henri Pouctal.[112] A few years later, he performed alongside Spanish actors in a four-part serial, *Fuerza y nobleza.*[113] Johnson reveled in the spotlight and profited handsomely from his appearances on camera. World Colored Heavyweight Champion Joe Jeanette pejoratively referred to Johnson as a " 'moving picture' fighter."[114] But nobody could deny that he was, as the *Chicago Defender* described him, a "moving picture star."[115] Only when moving picture cameramen descended upon Duryea's funeral after her suicide in 1912 did Johnson briefly regret the public demand for his on-screen image.[116] He secured an injunction against the new owners of the Pekin in Chicago when they began advertising the picture at their theater.[117] Motion pictures of his second marriage to another white woman, Lucile Cameron, however, were exhibited in theaters across the country.[118]

Johnson returned to the United States in 1920, exhausted and homesick after seven years in exile, to serve his prison sentence for violating the Mann Act. After he was released, film promoters may have hoped U.S. film censors would be more lenient with his pictures. *The Black Thunderbolt* (likely a recut version of *Fuerza y nobleza*) appeared in the United States in 1921. The Lenox Theatre in Augusta, Georgia, claimed to have "turned hundreds away," from the popular picture.[119] But *The Black Thunderbolt,* too, faced censorship. In Maryland, the State Board of Censors deemed the film immoral for its heroic depiction of the "former convict."[120] A frustrated black writer who went by the nom de plume William E. Ready complained of the "inconsistency of the verdict"; films lionizing white outlaws such as Frank James (Jesse James's brother) and Al Jennings, a former train robber, Ready explained, appeared "time and again" on-screen.[121] Johnson nonetheless continued his film career in moving pictures such as *As the World Rolls On* and *For His Mother's Sake.* At the age of fifty-four, he was still performing "strong man" parts in the moving pictures, or rather, the "movies," as the medium had become popularly known.[122]

Meanwhile, black people's reconceptualization of film had come to inform an increasingly widespread demand for visual self-determination. In Chicago, black residents vociferously petitioned for representation on the Film Censor Board as a political right. "The colored citizens of Chicago have won their fight to have one of their race made a member of the Film Censor Board," the *New York Age* reported triumphantly, explaining that the new censor "will be in a position to object to all pictures ridiculing the Negro."[123] The individual assigned to the Film Censor Board was none other than A. J. Carey, the minister who in 1905 had convinced Elijah John Fisher to jointly mount a public campaign against Motts's Pekin Theatre.[124] Just as this earlier campaign had been, Carey's tenure on the board of censors was fiercely contested. But despite the disagreements over how the race should be represented, African Americans continued to connect their conceptions of freedom to the representational space of the silver screen. "Misrepresentations" of the race in film—however that might be perceived—soon prompted black Americans to speak of "civil death," a "new slavery," "violation[s] of our natural rights, and the despoliation of our citizenship."[125]

On-screen, Jack Johnson was a thousand men: he was a sinner, heaven sent, a black colossus, a provocateur of racial tensions, a way to make an extra dime, a reason to be proud, a shame to the race. How black Americans perceived him and why they held those opinions changed by the minute. Johnson's dynamic public persona contributed to these diverse sentiments. His successes in the ring were matched by a bravado that directly challenged both white masculinity and the black uplift values of thrift, sexual propriety, and modesty. While one group of supporters claimed that his pictures should be promoted as a positive way to represent the race, another faction demanded that his films be burned and censored. Amid the broad interest the cinema evoked, innumerable ideas about blackness coexisted and competed. Even those who agreed on a specific policy or solution often arrived at their conclusions through vastly different routes and for very different reasons.

Yet, beneath these fissures, a perceptible shift had occurred in the black public's conceptualization of cinema. Even as black Americans debated Johnson's worthiness as a representative of the race, the debates folded back into themselves. The burden of representation was heaped upon the medium, rather than the physical space of the venue. Developments prior to the 1910 prizefight had set the stage for this pivotal moment. The ascendance of the visual in the age of emancipation, an emergent system of global consumer capitalism, and the formation of black cinema culture all set into motion the particular responses of black Americans to Johnson's victory, and in turn, the federal legislation aimed at controlling moving pictures. These factors converged to generate public discourse about race and the content of moving pictures that would have been impossible just a few years earlier.

Black Americans participated in and were subject to the creation of this modern visual world. Their investment in the screen as a representational site built upon earlier black aspirations for racial progress linked to the moving pictures. From the first film exhibitions sponsored by black churches and lodges to the rise of colored theaters and lawsuits over seating policies in segregated theatrical venues, African Americans asserted their rights as citizens and as free people by exhibiting and attending motion pictures. But with the dramatic events that surrounded Johnson's victory, these earlier concerns, which were preoccupied with the physical sites of film exhibition—the church building, the colored theater, and claims to public space in the segregated city—had broadened to include a more concerted investment in the representational power of the medium.

A year after the passage of the Sims Act, the black entrepreneur and filmmaker William Foster wrote that motion pictures, more than anything else, awakened blacks to "race consciousness." Yet the moving pictures had done more than simply rouse a sleeping populace. Black engagements with the motion pictures had produced a new racial site whose power only became fully actuated once the race had fully invested its racial identities in the screen. As Foster went on to explain, the black American was "hungry to see himself as he has come to be."[126] Blackness was not static. As black people reconfigured their understanding of the motion pictures, they negotiated their relationships with one another, and the common issues and concerns that united them. Indeed, their debates about *how* the race should be represented simultaneously contemplated the public meaning of blackness itself.

After the events of 1910 forced the issue of racial representation to the center of national attention, the earlier site-specific concerns over race and cinema expanded into a more widespread consideration of questions regarding film content and its value. Black Americans, moviegoing or not, would find their lives increasingly intertwined with that of the moving pictures. The belief in fair representation and visual self-determination would make possible the emergence of a new, unmistakably modern conception of freedom and civil rights, inspiring a broad spectrum of Americans, who integrated these demands into their own struggles for citizenship and belonging. Just five years after Johnson's 1910 victory, those beliefs would ignite one of the most spectacular protest movements of the twentieth century.

6

Mobilizing an Envisioned Community

Between 1915 and 1917, protests against *The Birth of a Nation* in nearly sixty cities in the United States, the Canal Zone, and Canada drew in black people from all walks of life, including railroad porters, housewives, domestic workers, poets, ministers, gangsters, janitors, and schoolchildren. ("The protest on Boston Common, 1915." From *The Crisis,* June 1915, p. 88.)

In the spring of 1915, as students prepared for their summer holidays and farmers finished sowing their fields with alfalfa, announcements for *The Nigger* began appearing in newspapers across Cedar Rapids, Iowa. The notice in the *Coe College Cosmos* ran alongside advertisements for graduation jewelry and straw hats. In the *Daily Republican,* the Palace Theatre described the picture as "one of the most talked about dramas of the year."[1] The film was slated to begin a four-day run downtown starting on Wednesday, May 5. Almost immediately, the women of the Cedar Rapids Bethel African Methodist Episcopal (AME) Church began organizing against the film. Elnora Gresham, Carrie Perkins, Julia McGee, Mattie Morgan, and Morgan's daughter, Audrey, drew up a list of the film's offensive aspects and resolved to present their complaint to the Cedar Rapids City Council. They wanted the film, which graphically depicted the lynching of a black man, removed from the Palace Theatre and banned from future exhibition in the city.[2]

On that day, the women of Bethel AME joined thousands of African Americans across the South, West, and North who were simultaneously organizing against "pictures tending to arouse race hatred."[3] The locus of these campaigns was D. W. Griffith's photoplay *The Birth of a Nation,* a revisionist tale of the Civil War and Reconstruction that depicted valiant Confederate soldiers and Ku Klux Klan nightriders fighting to protect the virtues of white womanhood. Although the protestors in Cedar Rapids organized against *The Nigger,* the actions of the AME women were inseparable from the larger movement against *The Birth of a Nation.*[4] As black people mobilized across distant geographies, the local campaigns, which began shortly after the New Year, converged by the following winter into the century's first mass African American protest movement. By 1917, the national movement had engaged hundreds of organizations across the country, involved tens of thousands of black protestors, and established demands for visual self-determination that endured well into the twenty-first century.

The mass protest movement had wide-ranging political, cultural, and social implications. The National Association for the Advancement of Colored People (NAACP) became the era's most powerful civil rights organization as a consequence of the campaigns—but even broader transformations were at work. As the earlier history of cinema in black life clearly demonstrates, mobilizations against racial images in film were far from inevitable. Motion pictures before Griffith's 1915 photoplay contained similar characterizations of black people, but on-screen depictions of the race rarely aroused collective responses from the black public before 1910. And when racial representation in the motion pictures did become a widespread public concern, black reactions to what they saw on-screen were diverse. Five years before the premiere of *The Birth of a Nation,* African Americans had engaged in passionate debates about the proper representation of blackness on-screen during the controversies over pugilist Jack Johnson's 1910 prizefight pictures. While some black reformers joined white Progressives in opposing on-screen depictions of the match, many middle-class blacks defended the exhibition of the films. Still other African Americans of all classes vociferously celebrated Johnson's victory and his moving pictures. The only commonality that emerged in the aftermath of the Jack Johnson moving picture controversy was a shared conception of the moving image as a critical site of racial representation.

What compelled so many black Americans to act together—to collaborate, form organizations, and invest their time and money—in collective protest against *The Birth of a Nation*? The mobilizations were astounding not only for their geographic breadth but also for the diversity of the participants. As the campaigns unfolded across nearly every major city in the United States and two U.S. territories, the movement drew in black people from all walks of life—railroad porters, housewives, domestic workers, poets, ministers, gangsters, janitors, and schoolchildren. These individuals employed tactics in their local campaigns that reflected their respective abilities and interests. While lawyers filed legal briefs in St. Paul, Minnesota, church leaders in Savannah, Georgia, collected signatures for petitions, and working-class women in Philadelphia, Pennsylvania, hurled stones at theaters exhibiting *The Birth of a Nation.* The factors that brought these individuals and civil rights organizations together call into question a linear, teleological narrative of modern black politics. The protest movement against Griffith's film did not grow out of a political consciousness that emerged from the late slave community, weathered the fall of Radical Reconstruction, and then reawoke, battle worn and militant during World War I. Instead, the movement against *The Birth of a Nation* reveals an evolving process of black racial formation that was always messy and fraught with contradictions.

The general outline of the protests against *The Birth of a Nation* is familiar to scholars of twentieth-century African American and film history.[5] In 1977, pioneering film historian Thomas Cripps first uncovered the truly exceptional nature of these campaigns in his groundbreaking study of early African American film, *Slow Fade to Black.* Writing at a moment in which issues of racial representation were at the forefront of black politics, Cripps emphasized in his research the protest movement's ability to challenge negative images of blackness on-screen. For Cripps, the campaigns were an important exercise in black political activism, but they were too often marred by infighting and misguided ambitions. The "branch presidents [of the NAACP] found it too easy to concern themselves with *The Birth of a Nation,*" he explained, "which could swell their membership rolls, rather than the larger question of the blacks' role in the movies."[6] Cripps suggested that in the end, the protest campaigns may have been counterproductive, providing publicity for Griffith's film at the same time the energy and resources of black Americans were diverted away from producing their own, competing film industry. Following in Cripps's footsteps, subsequent scholars have provided important insights into the organizational tactics of the NAACP and the effect the campaigns had on Griffith's film and the formation of the black "race film" industry.[7] Yet there is still more to be gleaned from the events that unfolded between 1915 and 1917, especially in consideration of the complex history of cinema and black life that preceded this moment.

Disagreements, infighting, and misunderstandings—all of these persisted, but in 1915, a mass movement formed in response to *The Birth of a Nation.* Fueled by the longer history of cinema in black life and magnified by the growing power of Hollywood, the pivotal events of 1915–1917 generated organizational strategies, networks of communication, alliances, and critiques that informed the abilities—and limitations—of subsequent mass black mobilizations in the twentieth century. In order to organize the campaigns against Griffith's film, African Americans utilized existing networks of communication and institutions, including the black churches and fraternal orders that grew up alongside and in conjunction with the moving pictures. New civil rights organizations emerged to link previously unconnected individuals and organizations. Because the film was ubiquitous, protestors could challenge it locally while simultaneously participating in a national movement. Yet as African Americans collectively articulated their conceptions of "the race" by joining together in a mass mobilization, they also selectively engaged in negotiation, benign neglect, and willful misunderstandings in order to transcend their disagreements with one another. Their collaborations served as a crucible for the public articulation of modern black politics.

Los Angeles in 1915 was a patchwork of settlements edging into the San Fernando Valley and down the Pacific Coast to San Pedro Bay. Railroads, and increasingly automobiles, linked the city's sprawling agriculture, oil, and manufacturing sectors. The recently annexed township of Hollywood added a touch of glamour to the city's motley character. As independent production companies began migrating from the East Coast (and out from the purview of Thomas Edison and his litigious motion picture trust), Los Angeles beckoned with its antiunion policies, cheap labor, and mild climate.[8] Also enticed by the promises of brighter days and new beginnings, black migrants streamed into the city from the upper South, the Midwest, and the Caribbean to a place the black press described as "the Most Prosperous City in the Far West for Afro Americans."[9] Among the recent arrivals was Nassau-born E. Burton Ceruti, who had recently graduated from Brooklyn Law School. The city's sunshine and natural beauty pleased the young lawyer, but he was troubled by the rising tide of Jim Crow segregation. A Jamaican-born dentist, John Alexander Somerville, and his wife, Vada, shared Ceruti's concerns. In 1914, they organized a local branch of the recently formed civil rights organization based in New York City, the NAACP.[10]

These black migrants in Los Angeles launched the first local campaign against *The Birth of a Nation* in January of 1915, but from the start, the protests were rooted in networks that reached far beyond the borders of California. By the end of the following year, African Americans organized public mobilizations—lawsuits, petitions, parades, rallies, and picket lines—in nearly sixty cities across the United States.[11] Dozens of other protests, including the campaign organized by the women of the Bethel AME Church in Cedar Rapids, Iowa, and a walkout staged by African American servicemen in Hawaii in 1915, cited Griffith's film but targeted discriminatory images in other moving pictures as well. Black protests against *The Birth of a Nation* also occurred in the Panama Canal Zone and in Toronto, Canada, in 1915.[12] After World War I, the protests continued across the United States and in cities such as Paris, where a contingency of Senegalese deputies pressured Premier Raymond Poincaré to ban the film from the country.[13]

When members of the Los Angeles branch discovered that *The Birth of a Nation* was scheduled to premiere at Clune's Auditorium in downtown Los Angeles in early February, they were already familiar with the film's basic story line. Griffith's film was based on two novels by Thomas Dixon, *The Clansman* and *The Leopard's Spots*. *The Clansman* had been adapted into a play, which previously evoked local protests among black Americans who denounced Dixon's heroic Klan protagonists, predatory black characters, and scenes of lynching.[14] In late January, E. Burton Ceruti and Los Angeles NAACP branch president Charles E. Locke, a white Methodist minister, joined other local civil rights organizations in submitting a petition to the city's board of censorship to ban the picture.[15] When their protests went unheeded, they contacted the mayor, the chief of police, and the city council with their appeals. On February 2, the Los Angeles branch wired the NAACP's headquarters in New York City with a report of their efforts. For the next few weeks, a whirlwind of correspondence circulated between the two offices as the Los Angeles branch and the national NAACP organized a broader national campaign against the film.[16]

The campaign in Los Angeles and subsequent legal actions employed the rhetoric, strategies, and precedents established by the courts during the 1910–1912 controversies over Jack Johnson's prizefight pictures.[17] Los Angeles had been hit especially hard by the violence and threats in the aftermath of Johnson's victory against Jeffries. Memories of racial violence and warnings by whites to black residents not to point their "nose[s] too high" or "swell [their] chests too much" likely made the campaign against Griffith's picture all the more pressing.[18] Citing the threat of violence and racial tensions, protestors argued for the suppression of Griffith's film. Locke, for instance, claimed that the photoplay was likely to encourage riots and "racial antagonism."[19] Subsequent organizers in other American cities similarly argued that *The Birth of a Nation* and other racist films should be banned because they incited hatred among the races. When the campaign moved to New York, James Weldon Johnson, the poet and a contributor to the *New York Age,* echoed the demands—and language—used by critics of Jack Johnson's prizefight pictures. "The Mayor issued orders that the Johnson pictures should be suppressed as they would create racial antagonism," he announced. "We are asking that the *Birth of a Nation* be stopped for the same reason."[20]

Locke, a minister of the Methodist Church, which had long prohibited its members from attending commercial theaters, may have wholeheartedly believed that *any* moving picture with the potential to cause racial strife should be censored. But national leaders of the NAACP including W. E. B. Du Bois, and other opponents of *The Birth of a Nation* such as James Weldon Johnson, had opposed—and would continue to oppose—the ban on the Johnson–Jeffries prizefight pictures.[21] The promotion of censorship by these opponents of *The Birth of a Nation* was not merely a replication of the ideologies of 1910 but a tactic that helped smooth over differences among campaign organizers who varied in their motivations for joining the battle against Griffith's film. In this case, they shared the immediate goal of banning *The Birth of a Nation.* However, their overall vision of the morality of the moving pictures was not nearly as aligned. Johnson and Du Bois legitimated their call to suppress *The Birth of a Nation* by citing a legal precedent established by the censorship of the 1910 Johnson–Jeffries fight pictures, while simultaneously highlighting the hypocrisy of those who would ban one film and not the other. In differentiating the two films, black critics frequently focused on analyzing the content of the films, not only on the reactions of the white public, which in both cases had been violent. "How great is the difference between this picture [of the Johnson–Jeffries prizefight] and Birth of a Nation?," a correspondent for the *Chicago Defender* asked rhetorically. "In the former we view the camp life of trained athletes and subsequently their wonderful skill. In the latter the terrible picture of white men raping colored girls and women and burning them at the stake."[22]

At the same time, protestors were vividly aware of the fact that the American film industry that produced the Johnson–Jeffries prizefight pictures was vastly different from the one that created *The Birth of a Nation.* "While less than twenty years old, [the motion picture industry] stands fifth among all the industries in the United States," the *Broad Ax* told its readers in 1916, continuing, "twelve million people in this country go to the picture theatre every day."[23] As World War I destroyed Europe's ability to produce films and access its export markets, the United States powered to the forefront of the global film industry. European companies produced at least half of the films exhibited in the United States in the first decade of the century. During World War I, however, Europe's share of the American and international film markets virtually disappeared. In the United States, the domestic film industry was further bolstered by an expansion of its market as a greater number of middle-class and wealthier Americans began attending moving picture exhibitions. Together, these changes ushered in the emergence of Hollywood as the geographic center of American film production and as a set of industry practices dominated by big-budget studios, movie stars, and a global distribution system.

Recognizing these changes, local activists and national civil rights organizations conceived of their campaigns in broad geographic terms. The film "concerns the whole country," Ceruti explained in his suggestion that the national headquarters of the NAACP organize "local fights wherever the 'Clansman' [*The Birth of a Nation*] is introduced."[24] Moreover, even before *The Birth of a Nation* became a runaway hit, protestors distinguished the picture from other forms of media, arguing that cinema was different from live performances and novels. As James Weldon Johnson explained in March, "*The Clansman* did us much injury as a book, but most of its readers were those already prejudiced against us. It did us more injury as a play, but a great deal of what it attempted to tell could not be represented on the stage. Made into a moving picture play it can do us incalculable harm." Johnson argued that the cinema differed from the pages of a book or a performance on stage because in motion pictures "every minute detail of the story is vividly portrayed before the eyes of the spectators."[25] By describing Griffith's characters as "out of proportion to the history," Johnson implied that on-screen images had more power to represent blackness than the actions and behavior of actual black people.[26]

Black critics also argued that cinema had exceptional powers to alter the public perception of the race. As Johnson explained, the impressionable masses "constantly go to the 'movies.' "[27] Besides making class-based assumptions about the gullibility of the masses, these arguments assessed the powerful connection between the emerging economic dominance of Hollywood, its systems of distribution, and the exhibition practices of the moving pictures. Building upon earlier criticisms of the censorship of the Johnson–Jeffries fight films, protestors spoke out against the dissemination of racist films and their role in reinforcing the belief that black people were "unfit for citizenship."[28] The "widely viewed" moving image was especially influential because it was not tied to a single location, protestors argued, but rather could exist everywhere.[29] In this way black critics identified in the moving pictures many of the qualities that Walter Benjamin attributed to art in the age of mechanical reproduction: it was relatively accessible and infinitely replicable, and possessed an exhibition value that had come to replace the "aura," or uniqueness, attached to less democratic forms of art.[30] Unlike theatrical performances, which were locked into a single place and time, or the printed word, which presupposed the reader's solitary and intimate relationship with the text, the movies could be distributed and exhibited to thousands of people all at once. The ability of the masses to simultaneously access works of art in the age of mechanical reproduction enabled new forms of collective response not only within the exhibition space, as Benjamin emphasized, but also across the black public sphere.[31] Because Griffith's photoplay was exhibited throughout the country, participants in the movement contributed to the national goal of blocking the film at the same time they mobilized on the grassroots level against it, the neighborhood venues in which it was shown, and the local politicians and business owners who promoted its exhibition.

In late February 1915, the Los Angeles branch of the NAACP notified the central office that it "had been unable to suppress the play because it has the approval of the National Board of Censorship."[32] The organization's national leadership immediately began proceedings to block the film from moving into New York City.[33] On February 27, the NAACP contacted Frederic C. Howe of the National Board of Censorship, whose Fifth Avenue office was located in the same building as the NAACP headquarters. The NAACP also reached out to "all churches, clubs, and organizations interested, in New York and vicinity to unite" at a hearing before the New York City mayor, John P. Mitchel. On March 30, representatives from the NAACP, the Citizens Club of Brooklyn, the Committee of One Hundred of Hudson County in New Jersey, the National Urban League, the United Civic League, the Columbia Hill Civic League, and the Northeastern Federation of Colored Women's Clubs gathered for a hearing at Mayor Mitchel's office.[34] The ability to rapidly organize the campaign in New York attested to the region's efficient and wide-reaching channels of communication. In the following months, members of the A.M.E. Minister's Alliance, the National Baptist Convention, the National Federation of Colored Women's Clubs, the Knights of Pythias, the National Equal Rights League (a civil rights organization that often rivaled the NAACP), and of course the NAACP itself would spread reports of the campaign across the country.

Nationally distributed newspapers fed the momentum of the movement by keeping protestors and would-be participants in the fold. Campaign organizers relied on the black press to publish dispatches on new developments and to rally support for the cause. On March 23, the NAACP sent a letter to five hundred newspapers across the country with a copy of a scathing review of *The Birth of a Nation* originally published in *The New Republic*.[35] By late March, black newspapers were teeming with reports about the campaign in New York: the decision of the Board of Censorship, criminal proceedings against D. W. Griffith and producer Harry Aitkin, and responses from the commissioner of licenses and the New York mayor's office. Black journalists called for local participation in the national movement against the picture. "It is up to the colored people in every town and city, north, south, east and west" to block the film, exhorted the *Freeman* in an effort to rally its readers.[36] Lester Walton of the *New York Age* was supportive of the campaigns but critical of what he believed to be the apathy of fellow black New Yorkers. Expecting few results, he attempted to shame his readers into action. "If a movement was started to raise a fund to bring injunction proceedings against the producers of *The Birth of a Nation*," he railed in late March, "it is safe to assert that out of all the colored people in Greater New York $500 could not be raised."[37]

Walton underestimated the response. Hundreds of black and white protestors crowded into Mayor Mitchel's reception room on the day of the hearing. The "colored citizens, choking with indignation," explained that they disapproved of Griffith's picture because it "characterized them as beasts."[38] Mitchel then announced that "the owners of the vicious film and the managers of the Liberty Theatre [where the picture was schedule to play] had decided to eliminate the two most objectionable scenes." Although the protestors were disappointed, they accepted the mayor's decision as a partial victory.[39]

While the NAACP decided on its next move, the campaign on the ground continued to attract new supporters. On April 14, a young white man named Howard Schaeffle and at least one black man traveled to Times Square, where they had front row seats in the gallery of the Liberty Theatre.[40] During a climactic moment in the film, Schaeffle hurled two eggs at the screen, blotting out part of a scene in which a young white woman leaps off a cliff to her death in order to save herself from being raped by her family's former slave. Schaeffle was a member of the Industrial Workers of the World (IWW), a racially inclusive union with anarcho-syndicalist leanings and a penchant for direct action. Such tactics were generally disapproved of by the NAACP's national leadership, which favored more conservative legal strategies. But while the NAACP's leaders claimed to be at the helm of the national movement, they were clearly not the only ones determining the direction of the struggle.[41]

The police quickly tackled Schaeffle, who shouted "Rotten! Rotten!" while detectives pushed him down the stairs of the theater. Close behind, his black acquaintance cried out, "That play's a *libel* on a race. It's got to be stopped!" as he too was ushered outside.[42] Having rid the Liberty of the IWW rabble-rousers, the police left and the exhibition continued as planned. Several minutes passed without incident until another black man in the audience stood up suddenly and began shouting, "On the anniversary of Lincoln's assassination . . . it is inappropriate to present a play that *libels* 10,000,000 loyal American negroes. I think President Lincoln wouldn't like this play." As the man was promptly removed from the theater, he identified himself as Cleveland G. Allen, "head of a colored news agency."[43]

What happened at the Liberty Theatre that day? Newspaper correspondents and later historians have collapsed the two outbursts into one event, overlooking the very peculiar mixture of individuals who had acted against the photoplay.[44] It is highly unlikely that Howard Schaeffle and Cleveland G. Allen jointly planned their actions at the Liberty. Allen, a prominent young member of St. Mark's Methodist Church and publicist for Booker T. Washington, would have been risking both his career and his reputation by orchestrating a direct action with radical members of the IWW. Allen's conservatism was reflected in an editorial he once wrote to the *New York Times,* lauding it for its "clean and conservative policy" designed for a "refined and learned" readership.[45] Schaeffle traveled among IWW activists such as Elizabeth Gurley Flynn and Frank Tannenbaum, who chained themselves to lampposts and stormed churches as they agitated for workers' rights.[46] While Schaeffle claimed his actions were unplanned—that he had purchased the eggs for breakfast and only decided to throw them because Griffith's film made his "blood boil"—it was Allen who was perhaps the most spontaneous that day.[47] Allen had probably arrived separately at the Liberty, unaware of the IWW's plans. He may have coincidentally planned his own intervention, or perhaps the Wobblies' actions roused his vocal protest. By emphasizing Abraham Lincoln's assassination, Allen's diatribe was highly personal. At the time, he was planning an event in honor of the Emancipation Proclamation. In any case, Allen's actions exhibited both caution and an upswell of emotion.[48] He waited until the police had left the theater before he engaged in his own polemics, but he did not hold back as he delivered his passionate speech. He felt it necessary to speak out and place his name on record in opposition to *The Birth of a Nation.* He knew the risk of connecting himself to the earlier egg-throwing incident, but he nonetheless placed himself on the side of the agitators.[49]

As the protest in New York grew stormier, another campaign was simultaneously brewing in Boston. On April 17, nearly two thousand black Bostonians crowded in front of the Tremont Theatre, which was scheduled to exhibit *The Birth of a Nation.* Sixty plainclothes police officers stationed in the lobby and two hundred uniformed officers along the Boston Common guarded the theater.[50] A group of protestors gathered to watch as W. Monroe Trotter, editor of the *Guardian,* a black newspaper known for its militant stance on black equality, attempted to purchase tickets to the show. When booth vendors refused to sell him a ticket, he protested, and a crowd rushed into the theater in his defense. Trotter was then struck in the jaw by a plainclothes police officer and arrested for "disturbing the peace."[51] Still, nearly two hundred black men and women managed to enter the theater that evening.[52] As the film was exhibited, demonstrators hissed and exploded about twenty "stink pots," forcing members of the audience to cover their faces from the choking odor. At ten o'clock in the evening, a black waiter named Charles P. Ray threw a "very ancient" egg at the screen.[53]

In Boston, the National Equal Rights League (NERL), radical church leaders of the African Methodist Episcopal (AME) Church, and a broader black populace spearheaded the campaign. The outspoken AME minister and NERL leader Montrose W. Thornton opposed the conciliatory tactics of Booker T. Washington. He had once made headlines for referring to white people as "the demon of the world races" (and supposedly commanding his black parishioners to "drink [the] blood of whites") during a passionate and pained sermon made shortly after a mob of 5,000 lynched a black laborer named George White in Delaware.[54] William Monroe Trotter, another NERL leader, was also no stranger to controversy. Trotter advocated direct action, especially when other avenues of protest were unavailable.[55] In fact, he had secretly purchased a few "fresh eggs" and some "odiferous bombs" before heading into the Tremont on April 17. Despite the critical role played by these other participants, the NAACP claimed credit for organizing the mobilizations. When asked if the demonstration on April 17 was prearranged, William D. Brigham of the Boston NAACP slyly replied, "You can see for yourself. . . . I don't think any formal vote was taken, but the word may have been passed along."[56] In truth, neither Brigham nor even Trotter could claim leadership of the Boston campaign. Although some pockets of the protest were planned out, the movement in Boston was above all "SPONTANEOUS," as black newspaper editor Harry C. Smith pointed out.[57]

While direct action and spontaneous mass mobilizations did not sit well with the NAACP, which feared that the unmonitored involvement of inexperienced organizers might spoil the reputation of the national movement, the ragtag spirit of the Boston campaign indicated the future direction that the national movement would take.[58] Local protests varied. In Portland, Oregon, middle-class black professionals led the movement. In Cleveland, Ohio, a contingent of working-class protestors organized their own protest parades. And in Philadelphia, a mixed crowd of workers and middle-class reformers campaigned together. Given this diversity, the national campaign could not be characterized as conservative or radical, elite or working class. The campaign facilitated the participation of a diverse range of protestors because blocking the film could be accomplished through a range of strategies and tactics, from petitions to lawsuits to local direct action. This enabled people with different resources to become involved in the broader fight. Depending upon one's circumstances, participation might entail writing a legal brief, petitioning to censorship boards, boycotting the film, handing out pamphlets, marching in a parade, making a donation, defacing a theater marquee, or threatening would-be patrons of the film.

Another reason the campaign attracted such a large and diverse range of protestors was the film industry's exhibition and marketing practices. By design, advertisements were intended to be conspicuous and to reach as broad a market as possible. Anyone who purchased a white newspaper or passed by a theater marquee had access to critical information needed to launch a local campaign: the place and the time of an event down to the exact minute. Protestors were thus aware of the specific event they wished to prevent in advance, rather than after the fact, when the possibilities of recourse were much more limited. Organizers such as Mary Childs Nerney, the national secretary of the NAACP, monitored white newspapers to determine when to schedule the next leg of the national campaign. On April 7, Nerney sent a notice to the branches and local members asking if they had seen *The Birth of a Nation* "being advertised for production and on what date."[59] About a week later, Jennie M. Proctor, secretary of the Pittsburgh branch of the NAACP, responded, "The play, 'THE BIRTH OF A NATION,' has not been played in Pittsburgh. . . . The pictures are advertised two weeks in advance and we can therefore keep posted."[60] As Proctor's letter indicated, the film industry's marketing and exhibition practices provided a timetable, replete with a countdown and zero-hour, that added to the urgency of the ticking clock as organizers rallied support for the cause.

In fact, even before theater managers began advertising their films, black organizers learned of exhibitions through the censorship bureaucracies that were implemented in the aftermath of Jack Johnson's 1910 victory in Reno. In order for Griffith to screen his film, he had to obtain approval from local censorship boards wherever he wished to exhibit *The Birth of a Nation*. This factor staggered the release dates for the exhibition of his picture and enabled national organizations to develop their tactics over time and to focus their resources on specific mobilizations. The NAACP was adept at tuning into this process of censorship, especially because its lawyers could interpret recondite legal rulings and procedures. When the National Board of Censorship, a powerful self-monitoring organization formed by the nation's major motion picture producers, refused to disapprove of *The Birth of a Nation,* the NAACP immediately sought "a list of the states where bills for public censors are pending."[61] In Hot Springs, Arkansas, local "race men" formed a new civil rights organization in advance of *The Birth of a Nation's* premier and petitioned the mayor and district attorney to prevent the film from exhibition.[62] Griffith later learned to keep his dealings with local censorship boards as discreet as possible, but the bureaucratic hurdle still enabled black organizers to intercept his film through these channels and to plan their mobilizations prior to local releases.[63]

Consequentially, in cities across America, black protestors wrote declarations against the film and organized demonstrations before the photoplay locally debuted. In July of 1915, months before the Ohio Board of Censors ruled against *The Birth of a Nation,* board chairman Charles G. Williams had already received numerous letters calling for a ban. "We can say nothing of its merits or demerits," he wrote in a letter to Governor Frank B. Willis, explaining that Griffith's production company had not even submitted the film yet for review.[64] In response to these protests, Griffith and his representatives complained that criticisms of the film's themes of race hatred and historical inaccuracy were based on hearsay. There was a measure of truth to this claim.[65] The story line of *The Birth of a Nation* was widely known, and trusted leaders and journalists had described its problematic features, but many protestors had never seen the film before they joined the campaign against it. The willingness to invest countless hours and to risk arrest and violence required a great deal of faith by participants, many of whom had little firsthand knowledge of the film. The preemptive strikes against it thus suggest a growing trust forged across the networks of black life. The protestors based their actions on the assumption that African Americans shared a common black aesthetic, sensibility, and politics.

In other cases, participants overlooked potential differences between their goals and that of other protestors as they eagerly joined the national movement, whether for power, legitimacy, or a sense of belonging. In Cedar Rapids, protestors used newspaper articles to justify their demands and link their campaign against *The Nigger* to a broader mission. The women carried a copy of the *Chicago Defender,* by then the most widely circulated black newspaper in the Midwest, to their meeting with the city council. Pointing to an article about the censorship of *The Birth of a Nation* in New York City, the women insisted that the town follow suit and ban *The Nigger.* The women's decision to link their activities to the larger movement against Griffith's photoplay was undergirded by the belief that the campaigns shared common political and aesthetic sensibilities. Elnora Gresham's husband, Fred, used language employed in other protests: "libel" and "insults to the race." He called for a dialogue between the Cedar Rapids movement and other faraway supporters. "We would like to hear from some of the race men and women, on what we have done as it may open the eyes of some of our people who are not in sympathy with what we have done," Fred Gresham explained, certain that he and the other protestors in Cedar Rapids voiced the "sentiment of all the progressive citizens." His words collapsed the distance, both ideologically and spatially, between the campaign in Cedar Rapids and the protest in New York.[66]

Black newspapers not only rallied support for the protests, they also actively participated in the organization of the campaigns. When the black Ohioans managed to bar *The Birth of a Nation* from the state by appealing to its Department of Film Censorship, a *Chicago Defender* correspondent "immediately rushed and wired the home office" explaining how the protestors had used the newspaper "to show [the] board how the race was fighting."[67] Besides sending reporters to support local initiatives against Griffith's film, black newspapers like the *Defender* offered to send out press kits with articles and other information that bolstered the efforts of campaign organizers. Charles A. Campbell, the president of a Michigan-based alliance organized to fight *The Birth of a Nation,* employed the help of the *Defender* to build a moral and legal case against the film. He sent the paper twenty-five cents, requesting "5 copies of your paper" and "any literature that we could use in our protest."[68] The newspaper responded with clippings "showing how the Birth of a Nation was received in different parts of the United States" which, the alliance reported, were of "inestimable value to us in the fight."[69] Of course, papers such as the *Defender* also benefited financially as interest in the campaigns increased: its readership grew from 16,000 at the beginning of the campaign to 65,000 copies by the end of 1916.[70]

When thousands of blacks and several hundred white allies gathered in front of Boston's Faneuil Hall after the April 17 Tremont Theatre demonstration, tens of thousands of African Americans followed the story in the black press. They learned how the crowds sang "We'll Hang Tom Di[x]on to a Sour Apple Tree," and that black women passed around hats to collect money for the fines levied against the protestors.[71] "Nothing has ever occurred in the history of Boston equal to this crowd at the State house," the *Savannah Tribune* announced to its black southern readership.[72] The papers reported, somewhat inaccurately, not only that William Monroe Trotter and Aaron Puller had been completely vindicated but that the discriminatory ticket seller and the plainclothes officer involved in the case were reprimanded.[73] In order to sustain the momentum of the movement, the black press called on its readers to score more victories against the film "by all means" possible.[74]

The women of the Cedar Rapids Bethel AME Church had followed the campaigns in the papers at least since the mobilizations in New York, and they were probably elated to hear of the successes in Boston. At any rate, they were not easily deterred when they discovered that *The Nigger* was still being advertised at the Palace Theatre despite the city council's promise that the film would be blocked. Several black citizens confronted the chief of police, who insisted that since the lynching and burning scenes were to be cut from the film, it would be suitable for screening. The mayor offered no more help, chiding the protestors for being overly sensitive.[75] On Sunday, May 9, local black leaders called a meeting at Bethel AME. Exasperated with the local government's handling of the affair, Luther Lawrey made a motion to create a Cedar Rapids branch of the NAACP. Their campaign could have been orchestrated under the umbrella of their churches, but they decided instead to link themselves to the national organization. The church members voted unanimously to contact the national branch in New York City. "As soon as the organizer for the NAACP can arrange to come to Cedar Rapids," they explained, "we will go on record as citizens working for the uplift of the race."[76]

The campaigns were not just traveling through old networks—they were forging new bonds. As with earlier black encounters with the moving pictures, the events of 1915–1917 generated unexpected alliances. Many of the participants in the campaigns still viewed the moving pictures as an immoral pastime and envisioned the campaign against *The Birth of a Nation* as part of a greater movement against all commercial motion pictures. Others decided it was best to respond to Griffith's film with their own film productions. At the Quinn Chapel in Chicago, where Archibald J. Carey had once lobbied against the Pekin Theatre, church members gathered to hear about plans for a photoplay that would "show the Negro to himself."[77] The church's former minister, Carey, also found himself face-to-face with the medium in some rather unexpected places. After leaving Quinn, the minister served a stint on the Chicago Board of Moving Picture Censors, where he reviewed the type of "sinful" moving pictures he had so long protested.[78] Still unconvinced of the merits of commercial amusements, Carey supported the campaign against Griffith's film.[79] Suddenly, he was aligned with his longtime enemies, including Ida B. Wells, Reverdy Ransom, and correspondents from the *Broad Ax.* Neither Carey nor Wells, Ransom, and the *Broad Ax* had changed as much as the ground beneath their feet had shifted. The moving picture industry had taken on new proportions, overshadowing what once seemed an insurmountable divide between these black leaders.

As the protests spread quickly across the Midwest, down the Eastern Seaboard, and across the South, reports of victories and new strategies sustained the movement. Even when local campaigns fizzled, the momentum of the national movement was propelled forward by the successive inauguration of new local efforts. Protestors kept abreast of developments in other cities and utilized the tactics and the legal and moral precedents for their own campaigns. "The entire colored population" of Cheyenne, Wyoming, reported the *Freeman,* was "breathlessly watching the fight the citizens in Denver have put up against the playing of the 'Birth of a Nation.'"[80] After 5,000 black protestors in St. Paul, Minnesota, demonstrated outside the Auditorium Theatre, G. H. Woodson, a graduate of Howard Law School, seized upon the legal successes of the Minnesota movement in order to argue his case before the Davenport city council in Iowa.[81] Citizens of Greenville, Mississippi, also cited the successes of protests in other "leading cities" in their petitions to the Greenville Opera House, the mayor, and local city officials.[82] When local campaigns faced hardships and setbacks, leaders such as Ida B. Wells argued that Chicago's black leaders should adopt some of the strategies used elsewhere.[83]

In the summer and fall of 1915, picketing, marching, vandalism, physical altercations, and other forms of direct action became more common. The movement in Boston, for example, continued into the summer as the city's black residents manipulated the city's "sauntering law" to avoid arrest. The ordinance prohibited "sauntering and loitering" for a "period of more than seven minutes after being directed by a police officer to move on."[84] Demonstrators would stay in the vicinity of the Tremont Theatre, where *The Birth of a Nation* was being shown, for six minutes and would then cross to the Commons before circulating back to the theater.[85] Some tactics—stink bombs, eggs, and tussles with the police—were too extreme to sit well with the middle-class leadership of groups such as the NAACP. But conservative organizers, at least for now, generally refrained from publicly denouncing the behavior of their fiery counterparts.[86] Even when the IWW member threw an egg at the Liberty Theatre in April, the NAACP offered only a halfhearted repudiation of the act. The organization was careful to dissociate itself from the action, of course, explaining, "Persons unconnected with this organization threw rotten eggs at the screen in New York City," but the organization's mouthpiece, the *Crisis,* included the incident in an article listing the movement's "Chronological Record of the Fight against the 'Clansman' in the Moving Pictures," thereby connecting the action with the broader movement against *The Birth of a Nation.*[87]

In fact, a few middle-class leaders were even beginning to call for direct action. It was clear that court injunctions and meetings with city councils and censorship boards were having only minor effects on the film. In December, a janitor named Bennie Johnson was arrested in Mason City, Iowa, for stealing and destroying six reels of the Cecil Theatre's ten-reel copy of *The Birth of a Nation.* The *Chicago Defender,* a paper that championed middle-class sensibilities, hailed the theft as "THE ACT OF A PATRIOT" with "Rich, Red Blood in His Veins." The correspondent ominously warned that continued exhibitions of *The Birth of a Nation* justified even more drastic measures: "Lawlessness begets lawlessness," the article explained, "IF IT IS LAWFUL FOR YOU TO TELL A LIE AND INJURE ANOTHER, IT IS LAWFUL FOR THAT OTHER PERSON TO COMMIT *VIOLENCE* AGAINST YOU."[88]

The growing militancy of the black press's coverage of the events was also particularly apparent in the coverage of the Philadelphia campaign that unfolded in the fall. Grassroots mobilizations in Philadelphia had begun as soon as the courts refused to assist with the suppression of the pictures. On September 20, a "printed card" was distributed in the black districts of the city:

> Rally! Rally! Rally!
> All colored citizens and their white friends and sympathizers are earnestly urged to assemble at the Forrest Theater, Broad and Sansom streets, on Monday night at 8 o'clock to make a dignified protest against the photoplay known as "The Birth of a Nation," which is a horrible libel on and a most aggravating insult to every Afro-American.

That evening, a thousand black protestors gathered outside the Forrest Theatre, where they were met by a hundred armed police officers. When one of the protestors threw a brick through the upper glass of the theater, the police charged with "drawn clubs and revolvers."[89] "Hats flew in the air, negroes were knocked to the ground, and the larger part of the *offending mob* fled down the street," a white paper, the *Springfield Daily News,* reported.[90] Four days later, the Chicago *Broad Ax,* a paper edited by a black Democrat, Julius F. Taylor, published a similar account of the same event. His article explained, "Hats flew in the air, Negroes were knocked to the ground, and the great majority of them fled down the street." Once again, hats had been sent upward and black folks were pushed to the ground, but there were important differences between the *Broad Ax*'s description and the report in the white paper. The *Broad Ax* replaced the phrase "offending mob" with "them"—the pronoun "them" referring to the "Negroes," a word that the black paper capitalized.[91]

The *Broad Ax*'s interpretation continued to veer from that of the *Springfield Daily News* as it reported a black man's assault on a police officer. The white paper reported,

> A second disturbance was begun at the corner of Walnut and Broad. There a negro threw a brick, which struck Patrolman Wal[l]ace Striker on the right arm. The officer turned on his assailant with a club and the negro ran with the policeman in pursuit. Fully 50 comrades followed Striker and they were joined by a yelling mob of 1000 whites, but the negro assailant escaped.

In contrast, the *Broad Ax* actively reinterpreted the same event. The paper not only avoided identifying the protestor with coded language that equated blackness with criminality, it also added a tacit approval of the assailant's actions. According to the *Broad Ax,*

> A second disturbance at the corner of Walnut and Broad was caused when a Negro threw a brick, striking a policeman. The latter turned on his assailant, but the Negro was the better runner.[92]

A third account of the event, published in the *Chicago Defender,* was even more incendiary. This time, the paper implied that the protestors involved in this incident were men. Upon seeing "how the policemen had beaten up their women their blood boiled." According to the *Defender,* the following then occurred:

> Another riot took place at Walnut and Broad Streets. *A man threw a brick and struck a policeman on the head, and he tumbled over for dead.* Other

> policemen were seriously hurt. There was no such thing as fleeing, each man of the race standing to his guns like their fathers in the civil war. They felt it was a matter of race loyalty.[93]

In the white paper, the brick hit the right arm of Wallace Striker, whose injuries were minor enough for the officer to swing around with a club and chase his assailant down the street. By the time the *Defender* reported the story, Striker was mortally wounded, surrounded on all sides by a crowd of militant black men. The divergent details in these reports reveal a conscious effort on the part of black papers to revise the narrative of the protests in a way that glorified a more belligerent and oppositional brand of demonstration.[94] The *Broad Ax* refused, for example, to describe the black protestors as having been "pounced" upon, and the *Defender* reported on the protestors' physically aggressive behavior, their refusal to flee, and their rescue of women in distress. This type of militancy was more common to the often-contentious *Broad Ax*, but for such ideas to be promoted by papers with a decidedly middle-class readership such as that of the *Chicago Defender* or the *Freeman* was remarkable. Such uncharacteristic responses from some of the most conspicuous voices in the movement suggest not only that the campaigns were attracting more radical participants but also that these participants and their ideas were influencing the language and demands of their more conservative counterparts.

With the exception of men like William Monroe Trotter, those arrested for participating in direct action were usually from the upper ranks of the working class. Bennie Johnson, who stole the reel of film in Mason City, Iowa, was a janitor. Fred Banks, who was arrested for disturbing the peace outside the Tremont Theatre, was a porter for a cleaning company. And the Boston egg-thrower, Charles Ray, made his living as a waiter.[95] Of course, occupation alone did not determine class status, and not all working-class blacks could afford to (or wanted to) participate in the demonstrations. Nevertheless, examining the risks and profits such individuals may have encountered when participating in the campaigns and protests provides some important insights into their internal dynamics. Fred Gresham, a railroad porter who earned $360 a year in 1914—less than the national median income of around $680, but enough to afford a very modest home—expressed his frustration at the citizens of Cedar Rapids who "were afraid [joining the campaign] would hurt them in their work."[96] But Gresham's moralizing failed to account for the more limited resources, hungry families, and unpaid bills of many of his counterparts. Other blacks in Cedar Rapids refrained because they did not want to risk losing access to enjoyments such as "going to the picture show." But what did Gresham and his acquaintance—a porter who announced that "if raising his voice against such insults to the race [made] him lose his job he was not afraid to seek another"—believe they could gain?[97]

Working-class African Americans had clearly begun investing their racial identities in images of blackness on-screen by 1910, when they celebrated Jack Johnson's films as evidence of the strength and virility of black manhood. But other factors also motivated black workers to join the collective movement against Griffith's film. In Philadelphia, residents organized a protest parade with "numerous floats and bands" that combined the pleasures of music and collective socialization in the service of the campaign against *The Birth of a Nation.*[98] In other cases, participants risked their jobs or subjected themselves to violence or arrest because everyday frustrations could be hinged to the larger, more powerful movement against Griffith's film. At times, the magnitude of the campaigns swept those with only nominal complaints against the film into the protests. After black waiter John C. Hinds was arrested for loitering outside the Tremont Theater, he testified that he had gone there in order to look for his injured wife, not to protest the film. Officers directed him to move on, but since they did not similarly order the white onlookers to move, Hinds refused to leave.[99] His anger was clearly fixated on the police officers, as he made little reference to Griffith's picture. Even if Hinds had headed to the Tremont to join his wife in protest, his actions and his criticisms were directed at the unfair way he was treated by the racist police officers.

In such cases, black concerns over on-screen racial representation melded with discontents that were only peripherally related to cinematic representation. *The Birth of a Nation,* of course, was more than a projected image and a narrative. It was part of a fast-growing industry, exhibiting for the most part in segregated theaters, protected by the police and promoted by white supremacists. Within the orbit of the mobilizations, therefore, was a constellation of critiques ranging from police harassment and brutality to theater discrimination, economic privilege, state-sanctioned violence, and demands for the right to access public space and leisure venues.

In examining the black response to *The Birth of a Nation,* cinema scholar Jane Gaines has focused on analyzing the "paranoia" that drove the protestors to action. Referring to the egg-throwing incidents, she has questioned the "semiotic aptitude" of the individual who "aims at the world and hits the screen."[100] In other words, when protestors aimed their yolky weapons at the screen, was their target the representation of blackness or the representation of "real life" black people? This is an important question, but by pulling back from the individual case to the larger movement, the collective meaning of protestors' actions comes into sharper focus. Consider, for example, the long history of riotous behavior that has occurred in the space of the theater. In 1849, laboring whites in New York City pelted high-toned British actor William Macready with rotten eggs and tomatoes in a protest of the city's growing class divisions. The Astor Place Riot expressed the growing social and cultural divisions among New York's laboring and middle classes in the antebellum period.[101] And just as important as the question of where the egg ultimately landed is the question of what compelled previously disconnected people to make the same *motions* in tandem with one another. There are only a few printed reports of eggs thrown at Griffith's film, but if it had indeed become a widespread tactic—an arsenal of the quotidian foodstuff hurled at the omnipresent amusement—it would indicate a different sort of identification: that of one living subject with another. By adopting a shared aesthetic politics, these geographically dispersed egg-throwers publicly presented themselves as members of a larger, more powerful movement.

Unlike court battles and city council meetings, working-class protestors could more easily participate in the campaigns through direct action. Starlight Boyd, a saloon owner and kingpin of Cleveland's underworld, acknowledged as much when he led a group of working-class black men to demonstrate against *The Birth of a Nation* in Ohio. Having gathered a crowd in front of the theater, Boyd announced, "Boys, we have done all we can do: we have created a riot."[102] The *Cleveland Gazette* derisively described the "boys" standing quietly "in front of the Cleveland Opera House waving little American flags" but admitted that more than 125 people were in attendance.[103] Additionally, after Boyd's "mob" of the "lowest Negroes in the avenue" left the Opera House, they proceeded to attack a streetcar and break a tailor shop window on Central Avenue. It is unclear whether the owner of the tailor shop had practiced discriminatory policies toward the black citizens of Cleveland, but for several years the black population had been fighting a very public and tense battle against Jim Crow policies in the neighborhood's streetcars.[104] Only a year after the protestors vandalized the Central Avenue streetcar, mistreatment by streetcar operators just one street south, on Quincy Avenue, led to "near riots."[105] During the protests in Philadelphia, black women had hurled stones at the police-protected Forrest Theatre.[106] Indeed, demonstrations that targeted private property were far more common than those involving eggs hurled at moving picture screens, and when bricks were thrown through the windows of moving picture theaters, there was little ambiguity in terms of the protestors' target.

The participation of women in the protests further illustrates the range of motivations and tactics the mobilizations encompassed. Black women protestors, such as the women in Philadelphia, could be especially confrontational.[107] In Boston, for example, Clara Foskey, the wife of a railroad porter, was arrested for striking the police and attempting to use her hatpin as a weapon against them.[108] This type of behavior was condoned by the black press, which uncharacteristically praised black women protestors for being aggressive and even physically violent.[109] At certain times, black women may have been more outspoken activists because they posed less of a threat to the white masculine power system.[110] Women like Foskey worked at home and may have faced fewer economic repercussions, such as loss of a job, for her participation in the campaigns. Nonetheless, members of elite colored women's organizations, including the National Federation of Colored Women's Clubs and local chapters such as the Arizona Colored Women's Clubs, abstained from engaging in physical altercations. Yet these women were able to register their discontent with *The Birth of a Nation* and actively participate in the campaigns by organizing petitions, lectures, and fundraisers—activities that comfortably fit with their middle-class sensibilities.[111]

By the beginning of 1916, tens of thousands of African Americans had joined the protests against the "libelous pictures."[112] Participants marveled at the unprecedented number of black Americans in the campaigns. In Charleston, South Carolina, protestors claimed, "No such unity of action has ever been witnessed before in this or any other city."[113] "The colored people of St. Paul" were reportedly "more highly wrought up over the showing of the pictures of 'The Birth of a Nation' than anything that has happened in St. Paul Before."[114] In San Francisco, where "every Negro church in the city, political and social organization" worked "in perfect harmony," organizers celebrated the revival of the "spirit of the '60s."[115] At the same time, however, reports of unprecedented unity could not mask the growing tensions over strategy and leadership.

When the negotiations, willful misunderstandings, and benign neglect that had masked earlier tensions within the movement failed, protestors turned to silencing, denouncing, and shaming their opponents by making accusations of disloyalty to the race.[116] The black public constituted an ever-shifting conglomeration of voices and interests whose formation was always *in process.*

Not even the venerable Booker T. Washington could escape taking a position on the campaigns. Washington initially refrained from making a public statement about Griffith's moving picture, in part because of his distaste for W. E. B. Du Bois and the NAACP. But eventually public pressure compelled him to speak on the subject. The *Freeman* published Washington's telegraph to S. E. Courtney in which he feigned ignorance of the photoplay's exhibition in Boston: "Did not know 'Birth of a Nation' being played in Boston until very recently. From all I can hear it is a vicious and hurtful play."[117] With a sigh of relief, the author of the article celebrated Washington's lukewarm condemnation of the film by announcing, "The many friends of Dr. Booker T. Washington will be pleased to learn that he has announced himself so decidedly against the thing which promises so much harm."[118] As the movement spread, participation became a symbol of "race pride." The "colored citizens of Anderson [Indiana] were disgraced," Primitive Baptist minister William Martin explained, because "they permitted, without protest, the show, 'The Birth of a Nation' to throw its scenes on the largest canvas in their city."[119] In Providence, Rhode Island, the black citizens felt compelled to clear up any public misunderstandings about their disapproval of the film by announcing, "We wish to say that we have never given our consent for *The Birth of a Nation* to come to Providence, but did protest vigorously against it."[120] And when editor Alexander Manning of the *Indianapolis World* and editor George L. Knox of the *Freeman* faltered in their support of the campaign, protestors labeled them traitors.[121] Two years after the Los Angeles branch of the NAACP lodged its first complaint against Griffith's picture, thousands of protestors gathered in Cleveland for a meeting held at St. John's A.M.E. to protest the film—and the wayward editors.[122] Rumors even spread that ministers were expelled from the NAACP because they endorsed *The Birth of a Nation.*[123]

The NAACP received the greatest amount of credit for the campaigns, but the spotlight also highlighted the complaints of the organization's critics. By 1916, Harry C. Smith, editor of the *Cleveland Gazette,* was fed up with the "egotistic and dishonest" W. E. B. Du Bois, who Smith believed was unfairly taking credit for organizing the Ohio campaign against *The Birth of a Nation.*[124] In a searing article, Smith "exposed" the NAACP's claims, and told "Prof. Alphabetical" to "put that in [his] Turkish cigarette and smoke it."[125] The NAACP had learned, however, the benefits of publicity. The organization's membership grew at a tremendous rate as the NAACP became a household name by touting its role in the campaigns. In December of 1915, the *Crisis* acknowledged that the goal of the campaigns was not merely to block Griffith's film. Acknowledging the odds stacked against it and the failure of its legal battles, the organization reflected: "It will not be a bad thing after all, if *The Birth of a Nation* jolts the Negro into a campaign of counter publicity that will give America so many interesting facts of Negro History."[126] The *Crisis* recognized the modern paradox of public relations, which made the spectacle and visibility almost as important as the message. The NAACP's membership ranks grew from approximately 5,000 in the beginning of the campaign to more than 10,000 by the end of 1915. The protests were briefly put on hold during America's participation in World War I, but when exhibitions of the photoplay resumed, branch offices—recognizing that the battle against *The Birth of a Nation* could "swell membership ranks"—continued to fight the film. By 1919, the battle was waged by a national membership that had grown to more than 90,000.[127]

Despite their disagreements, Harry C. Smith and W. E. B. Du Bois employed common terms in their critiques of Griffith's film and other moving pictures. Besides claiming that *The Birth of a Nation* would "incite race hatred," the protestors most frequently charged the film with "libel" and "overcharacterization."[128] The highly respected C. Sumner Wormley and his acquaintances inaugurated a committee in Washington, D.C., that decried the picture as "mischievous and libelous"; some 2,500 miles away, another protestor, a black minister from Spokane, Washington, echoed the sentiment when he shouted down the film as a "terrible libel."[129] In the Deep South, William Watkins, chairman of a delegation representing the Negro Business Men's League of Montgomery, Alabama, condemed *The Birth of a Nation* as "a libel on the race."[130] In focusing on the "libelous" aspects of the characterizations, these claims referenced the language of state and municipal defamation laws. Usually used in reference to a specified group of people such as members of a family or an organization, group libel suits had little precedent for defending the rights of racial or ethnic groups.[131] This legal strategy, which would find more success in the World War II era, developed in dialogue with the mass protest movement.

But as keywords in the vocabulary of the campaign, such terms revealed far more than a desire for legal action. Claims of "libel" conveyed shared conceptions of the representational power of the screen and of blackness itself. Protestors criticized Griffith's depictions of supposedly true "historical" events, but they also described his fictional characters as "slanderous." They suggested or outright asserted that there was a certain type of black character that could accurately represent the entire race.[132] Moreover, this shared language of protest was not just deployed by those seeking legal recourse.[133] Even as police escorted the unnamed black man (the associate of Howard Schaeffle) from the Liberty Theatre, he "protested loudly, 'that play's a libel on a race.' "[134] Having participated in the egg-throwing incident, the man clearly did not view legal tactics as the only, or best, way to challenge the film.

Equally prevalent was the language of basic rights, which protestors used to criticize Griffith's film and to stake claims to self-representation on behalf of the race. In St. Paul, Minnesota, black residents admitted they had only been able to eliminate a few scenes from the film but believed their demonstrations "showed that we do not intend to have our rights utterly ignored or ruthlessly trod upon without protest."[135] The *Chicago Defender* was especially vocal on the issue of rights in regard to *The Birth of a Nation.* In a classic call to action, the paper argued that the film's mischaracterizations of the race threatened the freedom of black Americans. "Let us always register our protest, often unheeded, against violation of our natural rights, and the despoliation of the privileges of our citizenship," the paper announced.[136] A correspondent for the *Freeman* similarly saw Griffith's film as a strike against the civil rights of black citizens. " 'The Birth of a Nation,' " the writer lamented, "is meant as the Negroes' civil death."[137] Framed as a "natural" or "civil" right, these demands for on-screen self-representation helped fuel the simultaneous emergence of a new black film production industry.

Politicians watched nervously as black subjects used the protests to mobilize and express their demands as a political constituency. "The 'Birth of a Nation' agitation in Boston was carried to the polls," the *Freeman* reported in November of 1915.[138] Other black newspapers noted that black voters had pressured mayors John Mitchel in New York, James Rolph in San Francisco, and Walter H. Creamer of Lynn, Massachusetts, to speak in support of the ban.[139] In Ohio, black residents of the state reminded Governor Frank B. Willis of his responsibility to his black electorate during their letter-writing campaign against *The Birth of a Nation.* Willis acknowledged the demands of the black public in a letter to the *Cleveland Gazette:* "So far as I have power to prevent it," he promised, "no films which reflect upon any class of our *citizens* will be exhibited in this state."[140] With the exception of a short period during James M. Cox's term as governor, the film was banned in Ohio until 1954.[141]

For David A. Graham, the political campaign against Griffith's film culminated nearly two decades of linking his goals of black progress to the motion pictures. While Graham was minister of the Bethel AME Church in Indianapolis, Indiana, his church hosted some of the first black film exhibitions in the country. Graham had since moved to Spokane, Washington, where he helped spearhead the campaign in the city. Spokane's black citizens orchestrated a sophisticated political maneuver against *The Birth of the Nation.* After losing a battle to block the film in 1915, Graham wrote, "we marked the men [politicians] responsible for the failure." A few months later, during the November elections, the protestors selected three candidates "whom we could count upon" for support. "With wonderful unanimity," black Spokane successfully campaigned for their victory. "Our next move after our new men had been inducted into office," Graham proudly explained, "was to frame a city ordinance prohibiting plays that tend to incite race riot or race hatred."[142]

Compounding the demands for black citizenship rights was the looming shadow of war. Black Americans warned their politicians and the larger American public that racial representation had become linked to issues of political and "social equality."[143] A nation that did not respect the rights of its black citizens, protestors explained, could not count on their contributions to the nation's military efforts. In August of 1915, black soldiers of the 25th Infantry in Honolulu walked out in protest against a screening of *James Kirby,* a film they deemed racist.[144] A few months later in Douglas, Arizona, nine hundred black soldiers stationed at a military base succeeded in blocking *The Birth of a Nation* from local theaters.[145] Black protestors grew more vocal after the United States officially entered World War I in April of 1917.[146] The following year, members of the Colored Civic League of Marshall, Texas, wrote a letter to Secretary of War Newton D. Baker, listing the reasons why "the photoplay known as the 'Birth of a Nation' [should] be put under the ban through the entire United States." The government's support in suppressing the film would benefit the nation's war effort, the group explained: "In these trying hours, when the Government needs the whole-hearted support of all its citizens, we believe it is extremely unwise and unsafe to permit anything that is calculated to engender a division [of] spirit among our citizens."[147]

Sensing a threat to national security, the U.S. federal government monitored the black response to *The Birth of a Nation* as World War I drew near. The investigations of "friction between the races" caused by Griffith's film were conducted by the War Department. In July of 1918, the department delivered a collection consisting of "quite a deal of data, communications, etc., concerning 'THE BIRTH OF A NATION' photo-play" to Joel Spingarn, chairman of the NAACP. The package included a message from Emmett Scott, special assistant to the secretary of war in charge of "negro affairs." Scott explained that it was "highly desirable that no stone be left unturned to bring about the suppression of this prejudice-breeding production." On September 30, 1918, G. E. Perkins, chief of the Military Morale Section, apparently acting on behalf of the "desires of the Secretary of War," Newton D. Baker, followed up on Scott's suggestions after a "serious race riot took place in Norfolk, Va." The subject of the memo addressed to Captain J. J. Gleason was the "Suppression of Race Moving Pictures." "It would seem that in view of the fact that both of the above named pictures [*The Birth of a Nation* and *Uncle Tom's Cabin*] have caused considerable trouble in places where they have been shown, a further showing of them should be forthwith prevented as a military measure," the memo read, specifically citing the "Military Morale" of "colored soldiers." Thus the efficacy of the protest campaigns was directly affected by larger geopolitical forces. When J. J. Gleason approached the Epoch Producing Corporation, which distributed *The Birth of a Nation,* about "withdrawing the objectionable motion picture," the federal government's mild intervention was an unprecedented action on the behalf of black demands for fair representation.[148] As throughout the campaign against *The Birth of a Nation,* unplanned developments such as the United States' involvement in the war had realigned the possibilities for change, even if for just a short while.[149]

A final question remains regarding the women of the Bethel AME Church, the answer to which may provide insight into how the forces that drew the mobilizations together could, in time, also propel them apart. This is the issue of *The Nigger.* The women of Cedar Rapids joined the mobilizations against that "detrimental" production in early May of 1915. In the weeks leading up to their campaign, other protests against *The Nigger* were reported in Auburn, New York, where black citizens prevented exhibition of the film marketed there as "The New Governor"; in Ohio, where the editor of the *Cleveland*

Gazette, Harry Smith, led a battle against the film; and in Schenectady, New York, where Reverend J. C. Temple petitioned against it.[150] These scattered protests, however, attracted only a fraction of the publicity and support of the mobilizations against *The Birth of a Nation.* Why then did the black residents of Cedar Rapids focus their energies primarily on protesting this William Fox feature while the rest of black America waged a war against *The Birth of a Nation?*

The answer is simple but telling. *The Birth of a Nation* had not been released in the city, nor would it premiere for several months. Local theaters had shown photoplays with similarly "degrading" qualities before 1915, but the residents of Cedar Rapids decided to act in the spring of 1915 because of a pressing desire to join a national movement that supported their demands and represented their broader goals for racial advancement. Yet equally critical were their ability to mobilize around a local site and their familiarity with the parties with whom protestors intended to lobby or challenge. The black residents of Cedar Rapids could have written letters to the mayors of the cities where *The Birth of a Nation* was being exhibited; they could have signed a petition or collected money and sent it off to the NAACP's headquarters in New York City; but the campaign against the local theater was just as critical as drawing the connection to the national movement. The physical proximity of the Cedar Rapids Palace Theatre and the city council to the local campaign may have offered protestors more immediate channels for making demands, access to the tangible results of their campaigns, a means of connecting other local or personal discontents to the campaign, or the ability to quickly communicate with other organizers and to work closely with friends and family members. Whatever their reasons, they were not alone in their desire to have an immediate, physical proximity to the object around which they could organize their protests. When reports of new exhibitions of Griffith's film ebbed, the *Freeman* noted that *The Birth of a Nation* was "not 'locatable' this week." Comparing the photoplay to the *Kronprinz,* a German warship, the paper promised to resume its battle as soon as the film reappeared in a new theater. "When it takes midocean again (the pictures) the scouts will be hot on their trail."[151]

The women of the Bethel AME Church connected their campaign to *The Birth of a Nation* protests with the belief that *The Nigger* was similarly offensive to other members of the race.[152] Based on Edward Sheldon's 1910 play, *The Nigger* shows scenes of a black man, drunk and foaming at the mouth before he assaults a white girl in the woods and "flames indicating the lynching and burning at the stake."[153] The black rapist—whom Sheldon described in his play as a "huge, very black young African"—clearly references the trope of the predatory "black buck," which Griffith had incorporated into his Gus and Silas Lynch characters.[154] A subtitle in the film referred to the attack as "the usual crime."[155] The lynching, however, serves in *The Nigger* primarily as a backdrop to the story of Philip Morrow, a wealthy Democrat who is elected governor of a southern state. When Morrow decides to support a prohibition bill, he runs afoul of a powerful whiskey distiller who threatens to make public a long-buried family secret: Morrow's grandmother was black. The governor is shocked by the revelation of his racial identity, but decides to sacrifice his reputation and the privileges of being white in order to ensure the bill is passed.[156]

To the black protestors of Cedar Rapids, *The Nigger* contained offensive scenes that put the film on a par with *The Birth of a Nation.* They quickly learned, however, that their aesthetic sensibilities were not as representative of the "Afro American with race pride" as they had once assumed. "Opinion differs in regard to *The Nigger,*" the *Crisis* explained.[157] While R. W. Thompson of the National Negro Press Association believed *The Nigger* had "redeeming traits," Harry C. Smith agreed with the assessment of the Bethel AME women.[158] The film was "equally as bad and mob-inciting" as *The Birth of a Nation,* he asserted in a letter to Newton D. Baker, the mayor of Cleveland. The *Freeman* reported that *The Nigger* was "a very ugly sounding title, but as we understand it, an inoffensive production as it concerns our race."[159] And for Baptist minister J. Milton Waldron, *The Nigger*'s depiction of the evils of liquor alone "justifie[d] its existence."[160] The black residents of Cedar Rapids were perhaps most profoundly disappointed that their campaign was dismissed by their counterparts in Des Moines, Iowa. A committee from the Des Moines NAACP branch concluded that "there was nothing in it [*The Nigger*] as shown which would make it possible to bring action under the theater ordinance."[161]

Complex factors intersected to produce and sustain the mass movement against *The Birth of a Nation.* If the growing size of the movement and expanding sense of simultaneity produced its gravitational pull, the relationships among the individual participants operated as magnetic forces that repelled or attracted them to one another. Drawn together by a modern sensibility of space and time, the protestors bridged their local campaigns to the national movement. They viewed their respective critiques, legal procedures, and direct actions as part of a larger collective mobilization. Benedict Anderson has described a similar sense of existing together in time in his study *Imagined Communities*.[162] While there are critical differences between modern black identities and Anderson's imagined political communities, both formations rely on the assumption of a shared temporality—the belief that their members are together "moving steadily through history."[163] Anderson argued that "print capitalism" promoted this sense of temporality: profits motivated book producers to create texts in a common vernacular, which standardized certain languages and facilitated the belief in a parallel existence within linear time. The "visual capitalism" of the moving pictures brought moving picture theaters and a nationwide system of film distribution to the doorsteps of millions of black Americans. By responding to these systems and by utilizing their own overlapping spheres of print and cinema culture, black Americans came to imagine their physically dispersed local campaigns jointly progressing through time toward a common goal, even though most participants would never directly communicate with one another.[164]

The mass protest movement against *The Birth of a Nation* was rooted in the longer history of cinema and black life. Without accounting for these earlier developments, it would be impossible to understand, for example, how St. Philip AME—the black church that once exhibited a film depicting the murders of Will Cato and Paul Reid at Statesboro—became the center of the mass protest movement in Savannah a decade later.[165] These events were part of a longer process that reached back, in the very least, to the waning years of the previous century: to the court decisions, the modern inventions, and the terrible storm that demolished St. Philip's edifice in 1896; to the film exhibitions (William Craft's passion plays, Mary Stone's illustrated concerts, C. E. Hawk's life motion pictures, and the spectacles of L. L. Blair) that raised money for the New Brick Church Fund; and to the proceeds and the determination that rebuilt, brick by brick, St. Philip's church—the very building in which the protestors held their mass meetings in 1916 to protest depictions of lynchings on-screen. Black residents of Savannah had celebrated the construction of properties such as St. Philip's and the nearby Pekin Theatre for staking black claims to public space. As the moving pictures became an increasingly conspicuous aspect of black American life, ideas once linked to public space had expanded to include the realm of visual representation. These new sensibilities, especially the modern demand for visual self-determination, set off the explosive events of 1915–1917.

Between 1896 and 1915, African Americans' diverse dreams for racial progress and their claims to the promises of modern life converged time and time again in the moving pictures. Cinema contributed to and was shaped by the formation of black institutions, businesses, urban leisure practices, and the construction of new properties, artistic productions, and political demands. Indeed, it became implicated in the very notion of what it meant to be black and to be free. Armed with these beliefs, black Americans turned to new vistas. The envisioned community that emerged during the mass protest movement against *The Birth of a Nation* continued to develop in dialogue with modern black life with the emergence of the race film industry.

7

Race Films and the Transnational Frontier

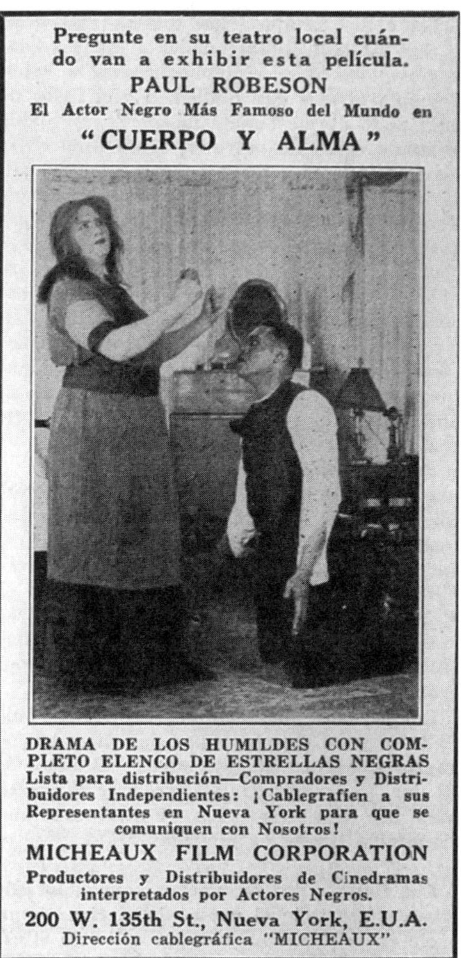
Pregunte en su teatro local cuándo van a exhibir esta película.
PAUL ROBESON
El Actor Negro Más Famoso del Mundo en
"CUERPO Y ALMA"
DRAMA DE LOS HUMILDES CON COMPLETO ELENCO DE ESTRELLAS NEGRAS
Lista para distribución—Compradores y Distribuidores Independientes: ¡Cablegrafíen a sus Representantes en Nueva York para que se comuniquen con Nosotros!
MICHEAUX FILM CORPORATION
Productores y Distribuidores de Cinedramas interpretados por Actores Negros.
200 W. 135th St., Nueva York, E.U.A.
Dirección cablegráfica "MICHEAUX"

Independent race filmmakers such as Oscar Micheaux hoped their motion pictures would appeal to audiences across the world. (*Cuerpo y alma,* 1926. From *Cine-Mundial*, May 1926, p. 330.)

In 1904, twenty-year-old Oscar Devereaux, a young black Pullman porter and enthusiastic supporter of Booker T. Washington, happened upon a poem by the frontier settler John James Ingalls. The poem resonated with Devereaux. Opportunity knocks "once at every gate," Ingalls's poem promised, but those who "doubt[ed] or hesitate[d]" were "condemned to failure." With this, Devereaux readily agreed. In fact, his persistent declarations of these beliefs had earned him a rather disagreeable reputation among his peers, who rolled their eyes at his fulminations against the colored race's "lack of ambition."

"There [are] not enough competent colored people to grasp the many opportunities that presented themselves," Devereaux lectured to anyone who would listen. "If white people could possess such nice homes, wealth and luxuries, so in time could the colored people."

"You're a fool," his listeners replied.

Ignoring the disapproval and wagging tongues of his city-dwelling black acquaintances, Devereaux decided to head west. In 1904, the U.S. government was still distributing cheap 160-acre tracts of land to American citizens through the Homestead Act. Devereaux knew little of farming, but he had some money and a sense of adventure. In "the spirit of Horace Greeley" he embarked for the "land of real beginning."[1] Devereaux purchased a homestead on a former Indian reservation in South Dakota, where he endured long bitter winters and endless summer droughts in a drafty sod house. All the while, he endeavored to make the most of the opportunities presented to him. The conquest of the West meant more to Devereaux than his individual success—it was a symbol of racial progress.

Such is the beginning of *The Conquest: The Story of a Negro Pioneer,* written by Oscar Micheaux in 1913. The sweeping tale of black life on the frontier was Micheaux's debut novel, but the story had basis in fact. *The Conquest* included thinly veiled accounts of people and events from Micheaux's own life, including his experiences as a homesteader in Gregory, South Dakota. Throughout the book, Micheaux reflected on black enterprise and racial progress on the frontier—ideas that endured in his work for decades. Both in his fascination with an uncharted territory in which the race could pursue collective advancement and in the medium he ultimately employed to disseminate his ideas, the moving pictures, Micheaux was not alone. The myth of the frontier and dreams of self-sufficient racial progress captured the imaginations of an entire generation of black filmmakers who, like Micheaux, produced motion pictures marketed to black and mixed-race audiences.

These black filmmaking pioneers formed what is known as the "race film" industry.[2] Independent race film companies such as the Foster Photoplay Company, the Lincoln Motion Picture Company, and the Micheaux Film Corporation produced hundreds of moving pictures in the interwar years. In their endeavors, race film producers sought to conquer a frontier that promised even greater freedom and prosperity than the Trans-Mississippi West of movie myths: the untapped global market for "authentic" black film. They believed that the ten million black residents of the United States and the millions more overseas, together, constituted a market with tremendous potential. Hollywood had virtually ignored, even reviled black audiences in its rise to global power. Race filmmakers announced that they would fulfill black demands for visual self-determination in the United States and past the "deserts and seas remote," to a frontier that spanned the world's vast black populations.[3]

Between the 1910s and World War II, black filmmakers envisioned and promoted transnational conceptions of racial progress. Ironically, this was often most apparent when black filmmakers mobilized the cultural motifs of American patriotism, loyalty, and rugged individualism in their productions. Race filmmakers such as Oscar Micheaux and William Foster featured heroic "colored troops" and the mythical American West on-screen.[4] But at the same time, their marketing strategies endorsed more ambitious and worldly notions of collective black progress. The tensions at the core of their endeavors were indicative of the pragmatism and ambivalence of interwar black cultural politics. Race films asserted black rights to American citizenship and equal treatment under the law.[5] Yet instead of uncritically embracing a narrative of triumphant U.S. exceptionalism, race filmmakers negotiated between their political and economic goals. On-screen, they drew on the visual iconography of American nationalism, but in the marketplace, they gestured to the type of diasporic conceptualizations of "the race" embraced by contemporary figures like Pan-Africanist Marcus Garvey, who famously implored his followers to invest in his Black Star shipping line with the motto, "Be Black, Buy Black, Think Black, and all else will take care of itself!"[6]

Race filmmakers described their ambitions in far-reaching terms: they would distribute their films to black audiences in the United States *and* export them to Europe, South America, Africa, and the Caribbean, where they believed the markets for motion pictures were unspoiled by the color line and racial attitudes of white U.S. audiences. Their films, they believed, would earn millions of dollars by answering the global demand for "authentic" images of the race and by claiming black rights to visual self-representation around the world. Like other black entrepreneurs of the era, race filmmakers viewed self-sufficient black industries as essential to the collective advancement of the race, but the scale of the international motion picture industry made them especially attuned to their place within the global economy. The race film industry's attempts to turn its globe-spanning conceptions of blackness into actual investments, box office receipts, and ultimately profits once again complicate our understanding of modern black racial formation.

Indeed, black encounters with the moving pictures were never neatly framed by the boundaries of the nation-state. Even as the U.S. government attempted to regulate the mobility of black images on-screen by patrolling its national borders, or as black protest movements against racist films galvanized the rise of national civil rights organizations, railways and ocean liners brought American motion pictures to international markets, and transported black filmgoers, exhibitors, and producers across the world. From the very beginning, itinerant film exhibitors traveled to Mexico, Canada, the Bahamas, and Cuba. In 1910, Jack Johnson's fight pictures (and the ensuing controversies) reached the Philippines, South Africa, and England. By World War I, new articulations of black diasporic consciousness had merged with the aspirations of the race film industry. This history illuminates the often unexpected routes through which black people came to understand their shared place in the world, as well as the limitations they faced when attempting to bridge their sensibilities and interests across geographic and linguistic divides. Just as Micheaux and other homesteaders discovered that the "open" and "free" American frontier was, in fact, profoundly shaped by corporate and governmental power, the race film industry's dreams of a vast international market and a shared global conception of blackness collided with far more complex realities.

At the turn of the twentieth century, America was flush with popular mythologies of transformation. The myth of the frontier not only promised opportunities for economic wealth, it also suggested a pathway for acquiring the type of rugged, manly independence idealized during the social and economic upheavals of the era. The nineteenth-century historian Frederick Jackson Turner described the American West as a site of innovation, economic mobility, political democracy, and social equality, a place where men would be tested by their abilities rather than their heritage. This romantic vision of the West appealed to leaders such as Teddy Roosevelt, who championed Turner's ideas and hailed the frontier for spawning a new American race. Even as Turner warned of the "closing" of the frontier in his famous 1893 address to the American Historical Association, the frontier myth continued to thrive in the booming new "Western" moving picture genre.[7]

Turner's frontier thesis, notwithstanding its imperial ambitions and racialized assumptions, shared some common features with the notion of "exodus" central to modern black narratives of transformation. Both ideas linked freedom to an idealized geographic location; by migrating, an oppressed people suffering from the bonds of ancient oppression could escape to a land of new opportunities. The popular American mythologies of the West and black dreams of exodus converged in the Kansas Exoduster movement of the 1870s. As the historian Nell Irvin Painter has written, in the aftermath of Radical Reconstruction freedmen imagined the West as the "land of hope"—a place not far removed from the "open frontier" described by Turner, where European-American migrants supposedly escaped the hierarchies, archaic customs, and oppressive wage-work of the eastern factory system.[8] Similar aspirations swelled the black settlements of Kansas, including the towns where John E. Lewis toured with his motion picture show at the turn of the century. Optimistic visions of a new life in the West also inspired James McFall and John McMurray to recruit moving picture projectionist Harry Wallace to join them in the all-black township of Boley, Oklahoma, in 1913.[9]

The motion picture enterprises of John E. Lewis and the Boley promoters reflected a broader spirit of racial progress that was remapping the geography of black social and cultural relations in the early twentieth century.[10] Black entrepreneurs sought out new and undiscovered markets in the hope of earning personal wealth and advancing the interests of the race. Capitalist-minded separatists and integrationists alike argued that black-owned businesses created jobs, respectability, capital, and access to goods and services that were otherwise unavailable to black clientele. Seeing the black public as a market with distinct desires and needs based on shared experiences, cultural sensibilities, or similar physiological characteristics, these businesses generated new consumer-based conceptions of racial belonging. Just as colored theater proprietors designed their programming and situated their properties for an envisioned market of black commercial filmgoers, early race film producers considered black settlement patterns and the modes and venues of black film exhibition when identifying potential consumers for their motion pictures.[11]

During the heyday of the traveling picture show, African American filmmakers produced motion pictures for markets that overlapped with the routes of turn-of-the-century black film exhibition. An exhibition-based model of production, rather than one formulated around mass-production and distribution, guided the creation of these films. Early black-produced motion pictures were relatively small in scale, intended for presentation by a specific individual (such as traveling showman William G. Hynes) or an organization (like the Knights of Pythias), in black churches and lodges or, later, in the local colored theater. Even those who traversed vast territories, such as H. C. and Mrs. Conley, intended to exhibit the films they produced themselves, rather than rent or sell copies for widespread commercial distribution.[12] Exhibition plans might include venues in Kansas, Texas, and Northern Mexico, but not the northeastern United States or Canada. The content of these early black films often reflected their plans for exhibition. Frequently commissioned by local black institutions, motion pictures depicted scenes such as the opening ceremony for a colored church, images of a community's race leaders, or even shots of ordinary black folk passing through a familiar thoroughfare. But even more elaborate endeavors could be intended for limited theatrical release. Elder James Morris Webb, author of *Jesus and Solomon Were Negroes by Birth* and *The Black Man, the Father of Civilization Proven by Biblical History,* decided in 1912 to produce a biblical moving picture of Jesus as "a man of color" for exhibition at a single theater, Motts's Pekin in Chicago.[13] Although Webb likely hoped to eventually distribute his film to other colored theaters outside Illinois, his immediate exhibition plans exemplified the scale of nearly all black film production prior to the rise of the race film industry during World War I.

But among these early black filmmakers, there were a few notable producers who adopted business practices that bridged the exhibition and mass production and distribution models of motion picture production. Tuskegee Normal and Industrial Institute, one of the most powerful black organizations of the era, saw the motion pictures as a means to profitably publicize its ideas and promote collective racial progress across the ever-broadening networks of black life.[14] Long frustrated by its inability to show people thousands of miles away "just what the school is actually doing," Booker T. Washington cooperated with at least two groups of black filmmakers to produce motion pictures of the school. In 1909, a group of black investors led by George W. Broome of Boston, Massachusetts, produced *A Trip to Tuskegee,* which featured the school's students working in the fields, milking cows, building roads, and heading off to chapel.[15] Four years later, in 1913, the Anderson-Watkins Film Exhibition Company, led by Louis B. Anderson, a local politician from Chicago, and W. F. Watkins, a dentist from Montgomery, Alabama, produced *A Day at Tuskegee.* The three-reel feature, nearly forty minutes in length, included more than a hundred "activities and scenes of the institute." Among the highlights of the film were images of Booker T. Washington and the impressive grounds of the vocational school.[16]

In many respects, these Tuskegee films followed in the footsteps of the earliest itinerant black exhibitors, who used their motion pictures to raise money and broadcast a particular institution's efforts in the cause of racial uplift. "It has been the plan of this company to send its pictures about the country and show them in colored churches," the Broome Exhibition Company announced in 1910.[17] Washington featured *A Trip to Tuskegee* (1909) in his national lecture tour, and the National Negro Business League sponsored exhibitions of the pictures in churches and lodges across the country.[18] Likewise, *A Day at Tuskegee* (1913) was described as "an education within itself" and screened in similar venues, "halls, colleges, and schools," perhaps even reaching black audiences as far away as South Africa.[19] In 1920, newspaper editor and Pan-Africanist Solomon Plaatje traveled to the United States, where he acquired a motion picture camera and films of Tuskegee from Washington's successor, Robert R. Moton.[20] After Plaatje returned home, he exhibited the films in cities and small villages across South Africa. "Mr. Plaatje was complimented on the excellence of his Show," the *Umteteli was Bantu (Mouthpiece of the People)* explained of his program, which combined the Tuskegee films with other motion pictures, much in the fashion of black itinerant film exhibitions in the United States.[21]

But Broome and Anderson-Watkins were not only interested in broadcasting the achievements of the Tuskegee institution; they intended to benefit financially from their endeavors. Both producers incorporated plans for distribution into their business models. With the same interconnected goals of earning "a paying investment" and "show[ing] Negroes what Negroes are doing," Broome and his fellow investors also produced pictures of the cotton industry and the [colored] Tenth Cavalry at Fort Ethan, Vermont.[22] The Anderson-Watkins Company modeled its distribution policies after those standardized by the white Motion Picture Patents Company. Shortly after their company was incorporated in 1913, Anderson and Watkins copyrighted *A Day at Tuskegee* and publicly announced that the film was "ready for distribution."[23] They offered exclusive "states' rights" to exhibit the three-reel moving picture, and posted advertisements that explained the films could be "rented by the day or week."[24] Despite these efforts, neither *A Trip to Tuskegee* nor *A Day at Tuskegee* generated the type of profits their investors had envisioned. Broome soon left film production for the music recording industry, but like most middle-class blacks of his generation, his finances were precarious, and he supplemented his creative endeavors by working as a waiter and railroad porter.[25] After their 1913 venture with Tuskegee, Anderson and Watkins, too, retired from the business of motion picture production, at least as primary investors. *A Day at Tuskegee* appears to be both the first and last film produced by their company.[26]

William Foster was another early race filmmaker who pursued a distribution-based model of motion picture production. An experienced entrepreneur, Foster had dabbled in an assortment of commercial endeavors, from investing in racehorses to manufacturing buttons of Jack Johnson before entering the field of motion picture production. In 1913, he boasted that his newest venture, the production of "high class" "colored pictures," would show the world the "best of the race."[27] Foster's first production featured a YMCA dedication ceremony and the black Chicago American Giants baseball team, whose owner, Rube Foster, was close friends with the still-exiled Jack Johnson. (Rube likely disguised himself as Johnson in order to help the pugilist escape the country after his conviction under the Mann Act).[28] In August 1913, Foster released *The Pullman Porter,* which became an instant hit on the Stroll. The comedy told the story of "Mr. Husband," a Pullman porter, who discovers his "wifey" dining with a fashionably dressed waiter "palm[ing] himself off as [the] proprietor" of a fancy State Street café.[29] Over the following months, Foster continued to thrill local audiences with his two-reel comedies, including *The Butler, The Grafter and the Girl,* and *The Fall Guy.* Foster appears to have possessed only a single copy of each film, meaning his photoplays could only be shown in one theater at a time. The films first screened in Chicago, circulating between the Grand, the Pekin, and Majestic theaters before they were then sent off to New York and Ohio.[30] By December of 1913, however, Foster had a new set of ambitions. Determined to expand his operations, he left Chicago on a tour to promote his films and attract investments.

In 1914, Foster reorganized the new Foster Photoplay Company. Eager to tap into the global market for "Afro American Comedies," he officially licensed the business, and arranged to build a motion picture studio in Jacksonville, Florida, a city whose early foray into itinerant exhibition and colored theaters had established it as a center of black cinema culture in the South. The black press reported "that the great demand for colored comedies in Europe brought about the deal [for Foster's company]."[31] Believing that moving pictures were "the first big opportunity ever presented to race business men to make money," Foster argued it was time for black film companies to capture the international market for motion pictures depicting the race. He told the *Chicago Defender* that white-owned companies were already capitalizing on this demand. "Strange as it may seem," he pointed out, "Afro-American moving pictures are a big hit throughout Europe. Every big manufacturer in the country has made photoplays of the race and sent them to the old country." Race pictures would show blacks in a different light, Foster believed, unlike the pictures exported by the Lubin Company and other film producers, which were based on the "white man's idea of Negro life." It would be foolish to let whites profit off of the global demand for products that black Americans were better equipped to produce.[32]

But Foster's plans to open a motion picture studio in Florida were short-lived. Although the details are unclear, Sylvester Russell, the surly theater critic for the *Chicago Defender,* blamed the failed venture on Foster's unsuccessful dealings with certain unscrupulous "white businessmen." Foster had gotten "nothing of it," Russell reported, and had returned to Chicago "penniless after [his] trip South as a defunct moving picture purveyor."[33] Still, Foster did not give up on his dreams of worldwide film distribution.[34] While he temporarily shelved his plans to construct a big motion picture studio, he continued to produce motion pictures through the 1920s. All the while, he reminded the black public of the promises film production offered for the social and economic advancement of the race. From the heroics of Frederick Douglass to the triumphs of Haitian revolutionary Toussaint L'Ouverture, he explained, certain stories could be told only "by the Negroes themselves."[35] Answering the demand for such films, especially in Europe and South America, was "the Negro business man's only international chance to make money and put his race right in the world."[36]

Black film producers would soon heed Foster's call. The race film industry was already maturing slowly by 1915, but the spectacular protests against *The*

Birth of a Nation that year accelerated its development. The campaign vividly demonstrated that black Americans were deeply invested in the ideology of visual self-determination on-screen and that they understood that neither Hollywood nor the government could be entrusted with fairly representing the race. Griffith's film, which earned millions in worldwide revenue, also made clear the potential of the motion pictures to earn untold profits in the global film market. The black public responded to reports of *The Birth of a Nation*'s financial success abroad with both awe and disgust. Echoing the transnational responses to Jack Johnson's 1910 prizefight pictures, black critics argued that white American filmmakers were exporting their racist ideologies across the world though their motion pictures. These concerns grew more acute when World War I decimated the film production capabilities of European producers, pushing U.S. film exports to unprecedented heights. As race film producers attempted to enter the international film market at this pivotal moment of global realignment, they would reconfigure their understanding of themselves and their place in the world.

Among those at the forefront of these changes were two men who grew up far from the bright lights of Hollywood and the bustling streets of black Chicago and Harlem. Noble and George Johnson, like so many of their generation, followed a long and circuitous path before happening, quite unexpectedly, upon their careers in the race film industry. The brothers were born a few years apart in the 1880s and raised in Colorado. When their mother died during George's early youth, he was sent to live with a widowed black woman who was employed by a wealthy white family on the other side of town. While Noble worked with his father training horses, George grew up in an elite white neighborhood where he went to school and attended parties with his white peers.[37] Raised apart, the brothers could be hardly more different from one another. Noble had been raised to perform manual labor and George had acquired the type of education usually reserved for middle-class white children.

As adults, the brothers headed in different directions. Noble moved farther west in search of mining and ranching work, and George became Omaha, Nebraska's first black postal clerk. But years later, their diverse skills brought them together again in the business of motion picture production. Noble ventured into the industry first. With his expertise in horsemanship and his striking good looks, he found work as an actor playing ethnic characters, especially Indians and Mexicans, in moving pictures set in the American West. In 1915, Noble was living in Los Angeles when the local black population ignited the national campaign against *The Birth of a Nation.* Heeding the growing demand for black self-representation on-screen, Noble, fellow actor Clarence Brooks, and pharmacist James Thomas Smith decided to organize a moving picture company. The men incorporated the Lincoln Motion Picture Company in 1917, making it their mission to "to produce and distribute nationally photoplays of and by Negroes."[38] In need of assistance with the business side of the operation, Noble invited his bookish younger brother, George, to join the company. The younger Johnson had no particular interest in the moving pictures, he later recalled, but at his older brother's behest, he joined the company as the Lincoln Motion Picture Company's general booking manager.[39]

The Lincoln Company and other interwar race film companies transformed the business of independent black filmmaking. They continued to produce films for local and itinerant exhibition, but increasingly turned their sights to the potential of mass distribution. Armed with the belief that "moving picture producers and distributors have the biggest political influence of any industry in the world," dozens of newly formed race film companies announced plans to produce pictures for the international market.[40] By explicitly linking racial progress to profits, race filmmakers brought the colored theater industry's philosophy of self-help into this expanding field of black film enterprise. Fittingly, Booker T. Washington proposed making a moving picture based on his autobiography.[41] The Photoplay Corporation directly challenged *The Birth of a Nation* with its mixed-race production, *The Birth of a Race,* an epic tale of interracial cooperation and humanity that began in the Garden of Eden and continued into the twentieth century. The film solicited nearly half a million dollars in investments.[42] While the world of independent race filmmaking was only a fraction of the size of Hollywood, it had acquired the critical mass of economic investment and public visibility necessary to transform itself into a distinct industry.

The potential for profits in the global market attracted speculators and experienced investors into the race film industry. Long before he began producing motion pictures, Hunter C. Haynes had established a successful business and was famously known as the "largest consigner of merchandise ever shipped from the United States by a Negro manufacturer."[43] He had earned his fortune manufacturing ready-to-use razor strops, which he sold in the United States, in Canada, and throughout Europe, a market he had carefully studied during his numerous trips abroad. Haynes could recite nearly any fact pertaining to the tonsorial trade, from the cost of a haircut at a second-class London barbershop (three pence) to the almost universal inability of European hairdressers to master the popular "curling mustache."[44]

Haynes's interests turned to motion pictures in 1913. He approached this business with the same "pull yourself up by the razor strops" attitude and meticulous research of his previous endeavors. In just one year, he explained, the U.S. film industry had exported enough film to wrap "one time around the earth," and created thirty new American millionaires. "The Negro who has money [should] invest now in the moving picture industry," he advised the readers of the *Indianapolis Freeman*.[45] In August 1914, Haynes organized the Haynes Photoplay Company, eventually producing *Uncle Remus' First Visit to New York,* a comedy about miscommunication between city-dwelling blacks and their country cousins.[46]

Both seasoned capitalists, like Haynes, and novices, such as George P. Johnson, portrayed their organizations as agents of black progress at home and abroad. Having assumed the burden of "representing" the race, the most successful black film producers understood the stakes of establishing a positive public reputation. Indeed, the public image of black production companies was almost as critical as the content of their films.[47] Companies encouraged the black public to associate social and political uplift with their filmmaking endeavors by incorporating their businesses under names such as Crispus Attucks News Review, Crusader Films, and the Progress Film Production Company. In their marketing materials, they emphasized the accomplishments of their most distinguished board members and directors. "Our official body is composed of men of reputation and responsibility," the Florentine Film Manufacturing Company eagerly assured its prospective investors.[48] Other companies included endorsements from well-known political and business leaders. Although most race film companies had at least a few white members, advertisements were careful to highlight the contributions of their black participants.[49] Reflecting the greater spirit of the race film industry, the Monumental Corporation's motto, "Organized by Negroes. To Make Money for Negroes," combined the goals of black capitalist enterprise with a politicized assertion of black rights to fair representation on-screen.[50] By referencing the Gettysburg Address and its call for representational democracy "by the people, for the people," the company suggested its films could contribute to the long-promised "new birth of freedom."[51]

When raising capital for their endeavors, race film companies underscored the importance of black visual self-determination. Black folk were "disgusted in seeing themselves being burlesqued and made the 'goat,'" Lincoln producers explained in advertisements for the company's stocks.[52] The assumption that black audiences across the world demanded "authentic" representations of themselves on-screen underwrote both the industry's profit model and its claims to racial progress. By answering the demands of an eager, ready-made market of global black consumers for "positive" representations of blackness, the race film industry would counter the degrading racial stereotypes promulgated by Hollywood cinema. By 1916, the *Chicago Defender, Indianapolis Freeman,* and *New York Age* were filled with advertisements calling on the black public to prove its commitment to racial progress and international recognition by purchasing stock in their companies.[53]

Some companies even attempted to capitalize unscrupulously on the race film "craze" by boasting of their international markets in the black press. For example, the white-owned Delight Film Corporation of Chicago, Illinois, run by Stephen Von Lorthy, claimed to have connections to the industry "both in this country and abroad." Delight "flooded the United States with circulars, mail and half page advertisements" with plans to film an all-black version of *Othello.* Investigations later revealed that the company was "swindling" funds with no actual plans to produce moving pictures.[54] Another white-owned company, the Democracy Film Corporation, targeted poor black workers in its efforts to raise capital. The company's ads boldly asserted that black people had a "duty" to purchase the company's stocks, as its planned production, *Injustice,* would "bring sympathy for the race throughout the world." For those with limited liquid assets, Democracy accepted "liberty bonds," U.S. government–issued war bonds associated with patriotic duty during World War I, in exchange for stocks. "You were loyal to your country, now be loyal to your race," the company commanded.[55]

Other would-be race film producers were more sincere in their aspirations, but equally fruitless in their endeavors. The Constellation Film Corporation advertised its "Class A stock" in the *Crisis.* Describing itself as an enterprise devoted to the "elevation and the picturization of [the race's] brightest side," the company estimated that its foreign business in the West Indies and South America would substantially increase its profits. Relying too heavily on these undeveloped markets may have contributed to Constellation's eventual collapse.[56] But even organizations with impressive backing, such as the Monumental Film Company, had difficulties. Listing W. E. B. Du Bois, the poet and journalist Alice Dunbar Nelson, and Leila Walker Wilson, the daughter of Madame C. J. Walker, America's first self-made black millionaire, on its advisory board, Monumental claimed its productions would "attract national and international attention." Nevertheless, the company produced only one or two films during its short existence.[57] For companies to succeed in the highly competitive global film industry, they would need much more than illustrious names on their advisory boards.

To draw global interest to their productions, race filmmakers also experimented with the content of their motion pictures. They cast actors whose names and faces could capture the attention of audiences both at home and abroad. Jack Johnson, whose 1910 victory had made him an international celebrity, was invited to appear in several productions. According to the *Chicago Defender,* the pugilist's "popularity through Mexico [was] the principal reason" that the Douglas Photoplay syndicate was "eager to secure him for a part at any cost."[58] Additionally, race filmmakers developed projects with storylines and themes that were explicitly diasporic. In 1920, Clarence Muse (an accomplished stage actor who performed with Evelyn Preer in the black theatrical troupe, the Lafayette Players) helped found the Delsarte Film Corporation. Muse, who once described himself as "close friends" with Marcus Garvey, threw his energy into producing a film about the Haitian revolutionary, Toussaint L'Ouverture.[59] Delsarte offered stock to "careful investors" interested in the film, which Muse had written about "The Abraham Lincoln of Haiti." The marketing campaign for the film depicted L'Ouverture as a common hero for all black people; his accomplishments and the Haitian emancipation were a victory for the entire race. According to an Associated Negro Press report, the picture was to screen simultaneously in Broadway theaters and in Paris, France, for ten weeks in 1921. Afterward, the producers announced, the film would be exhibited throughout the world.[60] Like so many race films of the era, further records of the film's distribution have been lost.

Race filmmakers also hoped motion pictures with iconic "American" images and themes would appeal abroad. The "colored Western" or "black cowboy" film quickly became a popular trope within the already specialized genre of the race film. When the Lincoln Company filmed *By Right of Birth*, a frontier tale about a young woman who discovers she is heir to a plot of oil-rich land in Oklahoma, the producers shared Muse's aspirations for global distribution.[61] This type of niche genre motion picture resembled the specialized productions of filmmakers in Europe and Asia. After World War I decimated the European film industry and fueled the growing dominance of Hollywood, French, German, and Japanese filmmakers began to develop new strategies to improve the marketability of their films at home and abroad. Instead of attempting to replicate the styles or match the production values of big-budget imported Hollywood features, filmmakers emphasized the unique characteristics of their "national" cinemas. In the Weimar Republic, for example, German Expressionist filmmakers highlighted the differences between the dramatic and highly stylized sets, subjective points of view, and uncanny imagery of their films and the linear, objective depictions of reality idealized by classical Hollywood filmmakers.[62]

Black film producers similarly responded to the popularity of Hollywood cinema by attempting to cultivate their own niche market. They employed some of the conventions of Hollywood, but highlighted the unique qualities, especially the "novelty" and "authenticity," of black-produced race pictures, which they argued Hollywood could not duplicate. In specializing in such films, race producers may have also been aware of the popularity of the Western among black filmgoers across the diaspora. From the 1920s to the post–World War II era, the demand for Westerns outpaced that of all other genres in Kenya, the Rhodesias, and South Africa.[63] The global appeal of the genre indicated that audiences around the world, like black filmmakers in the United States, interpreted the quintessentially "American" characters, themes, and landscapes of the Western genre in ways that fit their own personal experiences and sensibilities. One woman from the Copperbelt in Zambia, for example, explained that she liked "cowboy films best" because "I like to see how to throw good blows, so that I can kick anybody who interferes with my business; for example, if my husband interferes."[64] Black Westerns similarly emphasized desires that were hardly unique to the United States. In films such as *The Homesteader* (Micheaux, 1919), *By Right of Birth* (Lincoln, 1921), and *The Trail* (Sidney P. Dones, 1921), black protagonists overcame seemingly insurmountable obstacles and fought to achieve their dreams.[65] These narratives of democracy, independence, and upward economic mobility had the potential to appeal to black audiences everywhere.[66]

The tensions between racial belonging and national identity played out most explicitly in productions about heroic black soldiers. The fictionalized story lines and documentary footage of *The Trooper of Troop K, Mother,* and *Heroic Black Soldiers of the War* emphasized the pivotal, and often unacknowledged, role that black troops played in America's military.[67] As film scholars have pointed out, these motion pictures served as "a source of patriotic identity" for many African Americans by highlighting the courage, manliness, and extraordinary martial abilities of black servicemen.[68] Yet the transatlantic discourse of the interwar years and the marketing strategies of black producers bring to relief a simultaneous investment in broader notions of racial belonging. In fact, motion pictures of "colored troops" appeared at the nexus of two important black diasporic concerns during the interwar years: black martial citizenship and racial representation on-screen.

As black people and their ideas circulated across the Atlantic, they collectively formulated critiques of racial injustice by comparing their experiences and circumstances across national and regional contexts. Black Americans and black French subjects, in particular, emphasized their shared demands for martial citizenship rights, which asserted democracy and equal opportunity should be accorded to anyone who had fought on behalf of the nation to defend those ideals. Equally widespread was the collective belief in fair representation on-screen. Shortly after World War I, these ideas converged during a protest against *The Birth of a Nation* in Paris. When "two Colored princes from Dahomey, both French subjects, were ordered by the management [of the El Garòn nightclub in Montmartre] to leave the place in order to avoid trouble with his American clientele," black residents of the city, including a contingent of Senegalese officials, directly connected the incident to the influence of racist American cinema.[69] They demanded that French premier Raymond Poincaré ban *Naissance d'une nation (The Birth of a Nation),* which was scheduled for exhibition at the Salle Marivaux Theater in Paris.[70] Across the ocean, African Americans supported the black Senegalese subjects in their fight against the "vicious propaganda."[71] The *Pittsburgh Courier* explained France could not "afford militarily to affront her North African citizens."[72] And the *Chicago Defender,* citing the contributions of France's Senegalese troops to the war, concluded that permitting the exhibition of *The Birth of a Nation* in Paris "would amount to political suicide" for the nation.[73] At the same time that such critiques nodded to the black American veterans of World War I, they expressed a shared investment in a larger struggle for black equality, democracy, and the rights of fair representation.[74]

In light of the prominence of these beliefs, it is unsurprising that films of "colored troops," regardless of nationality, appealed to such a wide swath of black audiences. Black Americans clamored to watch films of black U.S. troops, especially when they might see a friend or loved one on-screen, but motion pictures of foreign black soldiers were also popular in the United States. In fact, when French and African American troops appeared together in documentary footage, the Lincoln Company and other race film producers frequently described the two groups with a single phrase: "Negro troops."[75] Whether this label was an attempt to erase the French origins of certain footage when screened for American audiences or an affirmative claim about the solidarities among French and American blacks, the notion that these soldiers could either pass as—or constituted—one group indicated the ever-present knowledge that blackness could not simply serve as a synecdoche for U.S. American national identity. While the United States' Committee on Public Information (CPI) assumed its films of white soldiers represented the entire nation, blackness was understood as a separate category.[76] Race, in essence, pushed against the borders of national belonging.

Likewise, films of black U.S. soldiers appealed to audiences outside of the United States. In 1918, William Foster produced a documentary film with scenes of the black "Fighting Eighth" Regiment for local black audiences in Chicago, and for the "big film houses in London and Paris."[77] In fact, some films of black U.S. soldiers were directly financed by *foreign* investors for audiences outside the United States. In 1914, a group of "South American businessmen" commissioned black photographer Peter P. Jones to produce motion pictures for exhibition in "Brazil and other South American countries."[78] Shortly after the deal was announced, Jones produced *For Honor of the 8th Ill., U.S.A.,* depicting black troops from the Spanish-American War "marching to Cuba" and taking "San Juan Hill."[79]

Films of "colored troops" even appealed to those directly opposed to the national mission of the United States. By situating black people as the contingent factor in the nation's very survival, black soldier motion pictures had the potential to trouble self-assured narratives of American Manifest Destiny. At times, the larger black discourse over black soldiers shaded toward a veiled threat: that continued second-class citizenship could engender desertion by black soldiers and active disloyalty that could cripple the nation in a time of crisis. The young man who attended an exhibition of the "Negro troop" film, *From Harlem to the Rhine* at Harlem's Lafayette Theatre in 1920 may have shared these sentiments. During the opening performance of "The Star-Spangled Banner," the young man refused to remove his cap. When other members of the audience questioned his behavior, he told them "the American flag meant nothing to him."[80]

Explicit pronunciations of patriotism and notions of diasporic belonging were not contradictory; rather, films with these themes reflected a pragmatic interpretation of citizenship shared by black subjects across the diaspora. Black filmmakers mobilized the cultural motifs of patriotism in their productions—triumphant images and narratives that celebrated the supposed common culture and cultural origins of the United States. But the industry's business practices and broader discourse conveyed an understanding of citizenship foremost as a "legal status" that provided citizens state protection and fair treatment in exchange for fulfilling certain obligations (including military service).[81] William Foster produced motion pictures with "patriotic flavor," including a six-reel drama, *Mother,* which presented black contributions to World War I and footage of the Eighth Regiment in 1918 "as they marched under Old Glory."[82] Yet under his pseudonym, "Juli Jones, Jr.," he explained that, rather than glorify the United States, race films could "present to the world" images "that would make the whole American nation feel ashamed of themselves."[83] Such claims situated the black population and its interests outside the nation, rather than within it.[84] And when the United States did not fulfill its commitment to its black citizens, critics pointed to the superiority of other nations' political systems. Disturbed by the absence of black soldiers in the CPI's World War I films, Lester Walton of the *New York Age* claimed the French were proudly "showing the [motion] pictures of the Senegalese and Soudanese [soldiers]."[85] This demonstrated, he argued, the superiority of French democracy.

Distribution presented another challenge for independent race film producers. Individuals such as George Johnson (who knew nothing about the business of motion pictures when he accepted his position at the Lincoln Motion Picture Company) had to establish their channels of domestic and international film distribution almost from scratch. The debut of the company's first fiction picture, *The Realization of a Negro's Ambition,* alerted Johnson to the magnitude of his responsibilities. He rented the den of the boarding house where he lived in Omaha, Nebraska, hired a part-time stenographer, and set to work. Every day, from eight in the morning to two o'clock in the afternoon, Johnson conducted business for the production company, then set out for his second full-time job as a mail carrier, which ended at midnight. Despite this grueling schedule and his inexperience in the industry, Johnson had at least one advantage. He had edited a black weekly newspaper, the *Tulsa Guide,* before joining Lincoln. He was, therefore, familiar with the distribution practices of the black press and knew exactly where to turn for industry advice. With considerable foresight, he contacted the drama editor of the *Chicago Defender,* Tony Langston.[86] Langston introduced Johnson to "the fine points of film distribution," and the two men went on to form one of the country's first black film booking organizations.[87]

The booking business opened Johnson's eyes to the prospects, and challenges, of selling Lincoln films in Mexico, the Caribbean, and farther overseas to a "vast field" that was "not confined to our Race alone or to America."[88] By 1918, the company adopted a hybrid distribution system that utilized the networks and practices established by early itinerant black film exhibitors while borrowing from the techniques of Hollywood film distributors. Johnson opened local branch booking offices throughout the country to arrange rentals of Lincoln's pictures. These offices were similar to the domestic film exchange branches of white production companies such as Paramount.[89] But Johnson also needed a system whereby smaller theaters, colored churches, and halls "who could not afford to pay our daily rates could also show the Lincoln films."[90] The solution was to hire two traveling representatives to tour across the country with the Lincoln pictures. It was a familiar arrangement: the Lincoln representatives traveled by rail to cities with considerable black populations, where they offered to split their profits, 60/40, with venues unable to shoulder the cost of a show by themselves. "In this manner we gambled with the theatre owner," Johnson recalled. "If for any reason, rain and so forth, there was no showing, we were the losers."[91] Yet like the generations of traveling black showmen and -women that preceded them, Lincoln's producers benefited from this relationship and the established local audiences and venues it provided. Among the company's greatest successes were traveling film exhibitions in the Bahamas and Cuba, where *A Man's Duty* "played to packed houses."[92]

At the same time, Lincoln courted international film exchanges, companies that specialized in the distribution and marketing of foreign motion pictures. In 1917, for example, Johnson was in negotiation with several companies that had expressed interest in representing Lincoln pictures abroad. That year, he received a Western Union telegram from New York that requested, "Wire price per foot on Trooper [*The Trooper of Troop K*] export to South American [*sic*] must have immediately private show."[93] The message may have concerned a special screening of Lincoln pictures in New York City that took place in May, for "representatives of the world's leading export companies."[94] An announcement of the private exhibition was quickly added to the Lincoln's advertisements, which bragged that Lincoln films were desired in "Spain, Europe, Africa, Cuba, Hayti, Hawaii, Australia, [and] South America."[95] Lincoln would continue to emphasize the global interest in their films, which reached as far as the Philippines. In one letter to the production company, a theater proprietor in Opon [currently Lapu-Lapu City] wrote that he wanted to exhibit Lincoln pictures "so as to show the people here the class of films we are making in the United States."[96]

Because their interests overlapped, black production companies and newspapers quickly formed a symbiotic relationship aimed at expanding one another's markets.[97] By the 1920s, motion picture advertisements constituted an important percentage of newspaper revenue.[98] In order to expand their influence and attract more advertisements, the black press pursued a wide readership in the United States and abroad. Even small Midwestern papers such as *The Bystander* of Des Moines, Iowa, promised Lincoln that its advertisements would reach "thirty-eight states and two foreign countries."[99] Other newspapers provided filmmakers with advice on how to expand their shared markets. For example, Romeo Dougherty of the *New York Amsterdam News* suggested that the Lincoln Company distribute its films in the Caribbean:

> Our papers are being circulated to a great extent in the new Virgin Islands and as they have at least one moving picture house, I was wondering if you could not get in touch with the people there and try to do some business . . . they have never seen a colored motion picture acted by colored people. I figure it would be a knock-out as the bulk of the population is colored. If you so desire you can write to Mr. E. Sebastian.[100]

By coordinating business practices, race film companies and the black press worked together for their mutual benefit. Indeed, the boundary between the two was nearly indistinguishable at times. William Foster, Clarence Muse, Oscar Micheaux, and dozens of other race film producers doubled as writers or editors of black newspapers. Attuned to the pulse of the black public, and enmeshed in its ever-broadening networks of communication, few individuals were better positioned to recognize the breadth of this rapidly expanding field of black commercial amusements.

Of the scores of interwar black filmmakers who attempted to distribute their films abroad, Oscar Micheaux was the most successful. He was "one of the most colorful characters in the history of the Negro motion pictures," recalled Micheaux's onetime business associate and occasional adversary George Johnson. Arguably, it was Micheaux's willingness for experimentation paired with an uncanny ability to adapt to new circumstances that enabled the filmmaker to outlast so many of his peers in the highly competitive business of moving pictures. Micheaux seldom hesitated when presented with new opportunities, and he consistently reevaluated his strategies as he attempted to keep apace with the ever-changing demands of the market. Throughout his thirty-year career, these characteristics guided him toward his evolving conceptualization of his market and in turn his ideas of the shared interests and geographic coordinates of "the race."

In the spring of 1912, Oscar Micheaux's life was in shambles. A drought had destroyed the crops on his South Dakota homestead, and the banks were foreclosing on his property. More distressing, however, was the state of his marriage. His new wife, Orlean McCracken, had abandoned their homestead and returned to her family's home in Chicago. To make matters worse, Orlean's protective father, the well-known minister Elder McCracken, had prohibited Micheaux from communicating with her. In these dismal times, Micheaux decided to become the author of his own destiny. He picked up a pen and paper and turned his hardships into his debut novel, *The Conquest*.[101]

Unable to find a publisher for his work, Micheaux had copies of the books printed himself and began selling them to his neighbors, mostly white farmers who were intrigued by the black homesteader's take on the local population. Encouraged by the response to his book, he launched into a new career as a writer and publisher with the same enthusiasm he had once dedicated to homesteading. Micheaux incorporated the Western Book and Supply Company in Sioux City, Iowa, completed another novel, *The Forged Note,* and began selling his work through mail order. He boosted sales with a spirited marketing campaign. In his advertisements, he pitched himself as the era's

"Foremost Negro Novelist" and boldly described *The Forged Note* as "The Literary Sensation of the Decade."[102] He was "attracting wide attention" for his novels by the time he published his third book, *The Homesteader,* a tale of interracial romance set in the plains of South Dakota.[103] The novel was less autobiographical than *The Conquest,* but it also featured a black pioneer with a French name, Jean Baptiste, and several characters who resembled people from Micheaux's own life, including his now ex-wife, Orlean McCracken. Micheaux once again organized an energetic marketing campaign for his latest book through the pages of the black press. One of his advertisements in the *Chicago Defender* caught George Johnson's eye. Intrigued, Johnson wrote to Micheaux to ask whether the Lincoln Motion Picture Company might produce a film based on *The Homesteader.*[104]

Micheaux agreed to the terms of Lincoln's offer, contracts were drawn up, and the production company began preparations to film *The Homesteader* in Los Angeles. At the last minute, however, Micheaux had a change of heart. He wrote to Johnson, explaining that he wanted to direct the film himself. "With no connections or actual experience of film directing," Johnson recalled, "Lincoln could not agree to such a proposition."[105] Realizing that the production company would refuse to budge, Micheaux decided to produce the film himself. Over the next twelve months, he taught himself the intricacies of film production, organized the Micheaux Book and Film Company, raised $15,000 in investments, rented a studio, and strolled down a Chicago thoroughfare where he happened upon a young Evelyn Preer, whom he cast in his film. By the end of it all, Oscar Micheaux had produced the first-ever feature-length film directed by an African American. *The Homesteader* was released in February 1919.[106]

While scholars have emphasized Micheaux's rugged American individualism and his distaste for internationalist politics, his understanding of his place in the world and of "the race" was far from myopic. While Micheaux may not have officially associated himself with Pan-Africanism, perhaps more than any of his contemporaries, he invested his time and resources in pursing the international motion picture market.[107] By 1919, Micheaux had already resolved to begin exporting his motion pictures abroad. While in production for his second feature film, *Within Our Gates,* Micheaux sent a letter to George Johnson detailing his plans: after finishing the film, he intended to shoot one more picture and then find "somebody to go abroad in the interest of our pictures for world distribution" so he could dedicate his time to production.[108]

Micheaux probably expected his representative to find a film exchange that could handle not only his latest features but also older films.[109] Yet his plans soon changed; perhaps unable to find a suitable candidate to travel overseas for his company, he decided against sending a representative abroad. In January 1920, he announced that he would make the trip himself: "The appreciation my people have shown my maiden efforts convinces me that they want Racial photoplays, depicting Racial life, and to that task I have consecrated my mind and efforts."[110] By "my people," Micheaux was referring simultaneously to his fellow black Americans and to the global black audiences he hoped to encounter during his journey.

It is unclear if Micheaux journeyed to Europe. His name does not appear on the entry or exit records of major American and Western European ports that year, and no further accounts provide evidence of his travels.[111] Instead, he may have left the task to Joseph Pierre Lamy, a white Jewish immigrant who had moved to New York from France in 1913. Lamy was well suited to the business of film export. He could read and write in French and English and possibly also Spanish, given that he lived with his Spanish-speaking mother-in-law.[112] During World War I, he had worked in some capacity exporting films for Fox Film Corporation, which by 1928 had the largest number of European subsidiaries of all American production companies.[113] Lamy and Micheaux may have met in New York after Oscar moved his company to Harlem from Chicago in 1920. It is unclear whether Micheaux sought out Lamy, perhaps through mutual acquaintances or by finding his name in a professional directory, or if Lamy recruited Micheaux, knowing the demand for "colored films" in Europe. In any case, Micheaux entrusted his films in Europe to Lamy, who traveled between New York, France, and England in 1920 and 1921.[114]

In the fall of 1921, Swan Micheaux, Oscar's brother and business partner, proudly announced that the company had just completed a deal to sell "all of our Foreign Rights on *Within Our Gates* and *The Brute*." On September 7, Swan told George P. Johnson that the company was "shipping a bunch of prints this week."[115] The Micheaux Film Company's letterhead was also updated to include "Foreign Distributions by Joseph P. Lamy NEW YORK LONDON PARIS."[116] Additionally, in the January–February 1921 issue of *Competitor Magazine*, Oscar Micheaux stated that his films were "being shown in all the leading countries of Europe, including England, France, Italy, Spain, and in Africa and in the leading South American Republics."[117]

Once his appetite for an international market was whetted, Micheaux worked to improve his marketability abroad. He was able to induce a major company, Pathé Exchange, to distribute his films, but Micheaux still needed to act as the primary salesperson for his work.[118] In 1924, he told the *Chicago Defender* that *Birthright* was breaking records from Atlanta, Georgia, to the Caribbean island of Nassau.[119] During these years, Micheaux produced several films that grappled with diasporic themes, including *Marcus Garland,* based upon the life of Marcus Garvey, and *A Daughter of the Congo.* The controversy that unfolded after the premiere of *A Daughter of the Congo* demonstrated the enduring conflicts that accompanied the notion of "accurate" and "positive" representations of the race on-screen. Black critics viewed Micheaux's film as a Eurocentric tale of "intraracial color feti[s]hism" and as a "realistic" depiction of Africa.[120] Set in a mythical republic in Africa, the film told the tale of "a beautiful mulatto girl," Lupeita, who was kidnapped as a child, enslaved, and rescued by a black American soldier. Rife with tropes of uncivilized Africans, "wear[ing] their birthday suits and some feathers," while also humanizing the supposedly "savage" Lupeita, the film presented an ambivalent take on the relationship between African Americans and black Africans.[121] As the merits of Micheaux's film were contested, they generated a public dialogue about black aesthetics, imperialism, and the relationship of various diasporic subjects to one another.

Micheaux's clever casting was perhaps his most effective tactic in his efforts to attract international audiences. He capitalized on Paul Robeson's fame in England in order to boost domestic and international sales of *Body and Soul* (1925). In 1924, Robeson's performance in Eugene O'Neill's stage play *All God's Chillun Got Wings* had garnered international attention.[122] The black press in the United States proudly described Robeson's accomplishments overseas, boasting that he had become "an actor of note" for his work on the London stage.[123] Micheaux was cognizant of Robeson's fame abroad when he cast the actor to play the dual role of Isaiah T. Jenkins and his twin brother, Sylvester, in *Body and Soul.* On both sides of the Atlantic, advertisements for the film prominently featured Robeson as the star "who electrified London audiences with his masterly acting."[124] Ads for *Cuerpo y alma* (Body and Soul) in *Cine-Mundial,* the Spanish-language version of *Motion Picture World,* included a still of Robeson from the film, describing the star as "The most famous black actor in the world."[125]

When *Body and Soul* was in postproduction, Micheaux once again announced plans to travel across the Atlantic.[126] The limited profits he was earning from his films were making it difficult for him to compete with Hollywood, even in the United States. As film critic D. Ireland Thomas reported, "the producer of Race pictures is forced to get his profit out of a few Race theaters, while the white productions encircle the globe. Mary Pickford is just as popular in China as she is in America, etc."[127] Micheaux believed race filmmakers were "pathfinders," but without "active encouragement and financial backing" it was unfair to hold them to the same standards as those set by Hollywood pictures. "If the race has any pride," he explained, "it is well to interest itself in and morally to encourage such efforts."[128] Micheaux planned to depart the country in April, only one month after he finished shooting *Body and Soul.* The purpose of his trip, he explained, was to "obtain world distribution of Micheaux films."[129] His itinerary included "all the larger cities on the continent" and several stops in Russia.[130] Micheaux also hoped to obtain distribution in Egypt, explaining that he would probably visit Cairo during his journey.[131] Little is known about the ultimate success of Micheaux's plan. Again, his name does not seem to appear in the records of any major ports.

Micheaux may have exaggerated the extent of his distribution overseas, but his films were more widely screened across Europe than previously assumed. Evidence of his efforts emerged when *Within Our Gates,* a film previously considered lost, was discovered in Spain with Spanish subtitles in the 1970s. Renamed *La Negra,* the Spanish version of the film is the only extant version of Micheaux's original work.[132] Another Micheaux film, *The Symbol of the Unconquered,* was uncovered in Belgium with French and Flemish subtitles. Since Lamy specialized in exports to Belgium, France, and Switzerland, it is possible that he played a part in the deal. Additionally, the international distributor First National Pictures, Ltd., submitted *Body and Soul* to the British Board of Film Censorship shortly after its release date in the United States. The film was classified and approved for exhibition in England in 1927.[133] The same company held subsidiaries across Europe, including a branch of Associated First National Pictures in Sweden where *Within Our Gates, The Brute,* and *The Symbol of the Unconquered* were imported for exhibition between 1921 and 1925.[134]

In the winter of 1925, Micheaux's sights were still set on the international distribution, but some of his goals had changed. He planned to embark on a journey to South America, where he intended to "place the Micheaux Products" in the West Indies and South America.[135] For the first time, his itinerary focused primarily on regions with large black populations. He explained that a "publicity campaign will also be launched to acquaint the citizens with colored productions."[136] In the same year, Micheaux filed for a New York State license to screen his film *Marcus Garland*.[137] Although copies of the film are no longer in existence, historian Thomas Cripps has written that the film "parodied Garvey as a mountebank who exploited the weakness of the black lower class."[138] Micheaux's plans to visit the West Indies and his desire to produce topical films may have motivated him to direct a film about the well-known Jamaican Pan-Africanist. According to the *Pittsburgh Courier*, the "exciting story of love, intrigue and the gamble for the control of a continent" began production in 1928.[139]

Although Micheaux achieved greater international visibility than his counterparts, his experiences in the international film market followed a trajectory similar to those of other race film producers. At first, the perception of international demand for "positive" depictions of black folk on-screen suggested that there might be a broad global market for films in the genre. But despite their efforts, race film producers such as Micheaux were not able to carve out a sustainable niche for their work abroad. The industry was ruled by the "great film companies who seem[ed] to have a monopoly of the business," black newspaper correspondent Maybelle Brown explained.[140] By 1937, Micheaux no longer boasted of international distribution for his films. His market, he explained, was "circumscribed to the few houses which cater to colored patronage exclusively and a few white houses on a midnight bill." He implored black audiences to understand the limitations within which race films had to compete for market share: "The theatregoer often expects a colored picture to reach the same standard set by Hollywood productions which have millions to spend and a world-wide market from which to extract a return on their investment."[141]

The widespread implementation of expensive synchronized sound technology in 1927 and the Depression had made it nearly impossible for the independent race film industry to compete with Hollywood.[142] In 1936, Ralph Mathews of the *Afro-American* mourned the dispersal and death of the leaders of the race film industry. Even Micheaux, whose career had endured far longer and had been more prolific than those of other filmmakers, he explained, had fallen "on evil days and ha[d] produced no films in the past year."[143] World War II dealt yet another blow to the race film industry, not because of the loss of what was then an almost nonexistent foreign market, but because Hollywood turned inward in its search for new audiences. White production companies produced a growing number of films for black audiences. Lillian Johnson of the *Afro-American* noted that Hollywood, "with many of its foreign markets closed because of the war, has cast down its bucket where it is, so to speak, and has looked around for the small fellows who might have something to spend for entertainment."[144] Emblematic of these changes was Hattie McDaniel's 1940 Oscar for her role as Scarlett O'Hara's loyal servant, Mammy, in *Gone with the Wind.*

The race film industry developed in dialogue with interwar reconceptualizations of "the race"—its geographic boundaries, common interests, and shared oppressions around the world. Some of these ideas were the product of actual face-to-face encounters with other diasporic subjects. Other beliefs emerged from interactions mediated by the page or the screen. Black journalists and professionals from the race film industry corresponded through letters, telegrams, and in the pages of the black press. Motion pictures and posters appeared in faraway theaters. These experiences were informed by earlier iterations of black cinema culture. At the same time they contributed to new understandings of blackness and its place in the world. The economic networks of exchange and social and cultural formations of black cinema were always broader than the nation-state; they constantly ebbed and flowed, sometimes coursing powerfully across untrodden territories and other times seeming to evaporate into thin air.

During his stints as a black newspaper editor, race film producer, and finally, chief of a "Negro news bureau," George Johnson vividly demonstrated how black social and cultural formations could be transported from one arena of black life to another. Like his fellow Lincoln agents, Johnson likely presented the company's motion pictures in Cuba and elsewhere in the Caribbean.[145] He wrote press releases, negotiated with foreign distributors, and corresponded with theater managers abroad. After Lincoln folded, he translated his connections and knowledge into a new career. In 1923, he organized the Pacific Coast News Bureau, a Los Angeles–based business dedicated to "disseminating Racial News of National and Inter-national Importance."[146] The bureau compiled reports Johnson deemed "of interest" to the race and, perhaps not surprisingly, specialized in entertainment news.[147] Johnson's dispatches reflected a broad conception of the shared interests of the race, from German censorship of "off color" depictions of Africans to reports of black actors in Italy and Haitian protests against Hollywood films.[148] Reprinted in black newspapers distributed across the world, these stories supported a sense of simultaneity, the notion that black people across the globe were moving together through time and participating in a common struggle in which they were all invested.

While the international ambitions of early black filmmakers were often thwarted, the independent race film industry was nonetheless deeply enmeshed in the vibrant transnational discourse on race and national belonging of the interwar years. The diasporic visions of black filmmakers took many forms, blended at times with imperialist desires and at other moments fused with aspirations for radical political transformation. Thus even the iconography of patriotism and national pride could be mobilized to promote modern conceptions of democracy that situated black citizenship in a global context. As black filmmakers attempted to carve out a market for their films, they attempted to put their shared notions of black identity into action through collaborations and alliances that reconfigured their understanding of themselves and their shared place in the world.

Conclusion

Picturing the Future

In the winter of 1939, as the economy struggled out of the Great Depression and the threat of another Great War loomed large on the horizon, the "spotlight of the world" turned momentarily to Atlanta, Georgia.[1] When *Gone with the Wind* debuted in the city that December, nearly 300,000 people gathered to witness the parades and festivities.[2] Loew's Grand Theatre, the site of the premiere, was decorated with Grecian columns and the white façade of an antebellum plantation.[3] Brilliant pillars of light illuminated the building and swept across the night sky. It was "the biggest event to happen in the South in my lifetime," Jimmy Carter recalled years later.[4] At the celebrity-filled gala the evening before the show, black members of the Ebenezer Church Choir, including ten-year-old Martin Luther King Jr., sang "I Want Jesus to Walk with Me" and "Get on Board Little Children" for an all-white audience.[5] Auretha Jolly English recalled the apprehensions of a few of her fellow choir members before the performance. They had heard "through the grapevine that other churches had been invited to perform but refused," and some felt the costumes were too "slave-like."[6] Members of the Atlanta Baptist Ministers' Union described the church's participation in the event as a disgrace. Soon after the premier, ministers in the union formally censured the Ebenezer's pastor, Martin Luther King Sr., for his contribution to the celebrations.[7]

Similar controversies erupted outside Atlanta and far beyond the boundaries of the Mason-Dixon line. Across the world, black and colonial subjects debated the significance of the motion picture. Business and religious leaders in Chicago, Illinois, called on "all 'lovers of freedom and democracy'" to condemn the film's romanticized vision of slavery and skewed depiction of the Civil War and Reconstruction. Oscar Micheaux announced he would direct a film more epic than *Gone with the Wind.*[8] In London, England, a group of Indians, Egyptians, and West Indians assailed the film's portrayal of "Negroes as lazy and servile and content to be in slavery."[9] Anticapitalist black radical C. L. R. James published a scathing essay that condemned the "dangerous" film but even more emphatically denounced the campaign of the Communist *Daily Worker* against the picture, which James described as a disingenuous attempt to curry black support for the Soviet Union.[10] In Mason, Michigan, a teenage boy named Malcolm Little attended *Gone with the Wind* in an all-white theater; the memory so haunted him that he spoke of it decades later when he had risen to the top of the Nation of Islam and replaced his last name with the letter *X.*[11]

Meanwhile, another chorus of black voices commended *Gone with the Wind.* The film's inclusion of black actors in featured roles, they argued, was a sign of racial progress. In particular, they celebrated Hattie McDaniel, the true star of the "CINEMA EXTRAVAGANZA," for her performance as Scarlett O'Hara's loyal servant, "Mammy."[12] Responding to criticisms that Mammy was a fantasy of the Old South, McDaniel's supporters argued the actress had imbued an otherwise flat character with humanity. Dean Gordon B. Hancock of the Associated Negro Press claimed "New Negro[es]" disapproved of Mammy only because they were embarrassed by images of unsophisticated, laboring black women.[13] Actor and former race filmmaker Clarence Muse described McDaniel's Academy Award for her role—the first ever awarded to a black actor—as part of her family's long lineage of struggle for freedom. McDaniel's father, a former slave, had dedicated his life to the progress of the race as a veteran of the Civil War, Exoduster, and itinerant minister. Muse explained that Hattie McDaniel's achievement was "a great step forward" for "the Negro [who] must be emancipated, even today."[14] McDaniel herself described the award in the classical language of racial uplift. "I consider this recognition a step further for the race, rather than personal progress," she announced shortly after accepting her Oscar.[15]

Whether concerned with integration, political allegiance, artistic production, or even proper attire, the black public negotiated the meaning of racial progress through their interactions with the motion pictures. These varied and highly public responses bore the traces of a much older history. Between 1896 and the interwar years, cinema developed in dialogue with black life. As exhibitors, filmgoers, producers, and critics, black people made sense of their shared place in the world—their collective interests, common oppressions, and united (or divergent) demands for freedom and equality. Across three decades and hundreds of thousands of miles and amid unspeakable violence, economic exploitation, and racial segregation, the history of black cinema is one of both constrained possibilities and astonishing creativity. Only by accounting for this history is it possible to fathom how "the race" came to invest its dreams of progress so deeply in the motion pictures. From the first moving picture exhibitions for black audiences in churches, lodges, and schools to the growth of colored theaters and the development of an independent film industry, black Americans navigated toward their goals of freedom on an uncharted and ever-shifting terrain.

Motion pictures became integral to two critical arenas of black public life: the physical sites in which individuals congregated and the realm of mass media. In black urban centers, motion picture shows raised money for building and operating black-controlled properties. As Mamie Garvin Smith recalled of her childhood in South Carolina, black communities viewed the construction of their own churches as "part of getting their freedom."[16] Black churches and halls, and later, colored theaters, not only served as symbols of racial progress, they were also the "public spaces" where black people congregated. These sites were critical to ensuring the permanency, stability, and autonomy of black urban populations, especially in the Jim Crow city. By providing amusements for leisure-hungry urban dwellers, they formed the backbone of black social life, a fact reflected in their very architecture. Whether housed in a shabby storefront or fancy brick edifice, black churches, halls, and schools—like colored theaters—possessed common spaces suitable for the exhibition of motion pictures. In these places, cinema was first understood as a force for racial progress.

By 1910, images on-screen became a critical site of public knowledge and racial representation. The shift occured when colored theaters began to compete with black religious institutions, pitting the two central values of racial uplift—piety and profits—against one another, thus encouraging middle-class black Americans to begin critiquing on-screen representations of the race. But it was not until other factors converged—the collision of two global leisure industries and the worldwide response to Jack Johnson's 1910 victory—that members of the black working class would invest their racial identities with images of blackness on-screen. The transformation of the screen into a critical site of racial meaning was informed by the longer history of visual culture but was inexorably tied to the specific developments that occurred through black engagements with the moving pictures. The response to Johnson's victory and the controversies over his motion pictures crystallized the screen into a critical site of racial representation. Afterward, the black public not only criticized "negative" images on-screen, it also protested against the absence of "positive" black images from this critical "place of blackness."

As black folk exhibited, created, and critiqued motion pictures, they generated new geographies of black social and institutional relations. At a pivotal moment when black migration, industrialization, and Jim Crow segregation reordered black populations across the South and West, the easily transportable and widely popular medium of motion pictures brought black people together within cities of new black settlement and across the pathways of black migration. Forged in motion across geographic space, these cultural practices trickled upward, from the working class to the middle class, and from the South to the West and North. Black cinema culture was especially important in two overlapping formations, modern black institutions and an urban commercial leisure culture, as they developed across the widely dispersed and rapidly changing landscape of twentieth-century black life. In turn, these reconfigured geographies of black social life provided the systems of communication and relationships that enabled the growth of successive generations of black organizations, networks, political strategies, and transnational articulations of racial belonging.

By remapping black people's understanding of their shared place in the world, cinema informed the emergence of new conceptions of freedom, equality, and rights. If black people with diverse interests could not settle on a definition of what constituted "positive" or "negative" images, they came to share the belief that they should control and create images of themselves on-screen. Conceptions of progress based on these new sensibilities brought individuals with diverse interests, political beliefs, and motivations into the first mass protest movement of the twentieth century. By envisioning freedom and racial progress as inexorably tied to moving picture representations of the race, black political demands increasingly included fair representation and the belief that mischaracterizations in film constituted a violation of "natural rights." By World War I, the demand for visual self-determination converged with the enterprising spirit of the philosophy of racial uplift to inform the development of the race film industry. As race filmmakers sought out larger markets for their moving pictures, they promoted an even more expansive conception of rights that reached far beyond the shores of the United States.

The particular place of cinema in the black public sphere, geographies of social and institutional relations, and conception of rights developed along long and winding routes. From the mass political campaigns of the World War I era to the transatlantic cultural productions of the 1920s and the rise of the race film industry, black cinema culture was the product of a long and complicated history, not simply an inevitable reaction to degradations and humiliations of the race in white-produced motion pictures. Black interactions with cinema created alliances among individuals with shared investments, actively reconfigured various discontents and desires into a specific type of critique, and most importantly, transformed those critiques into institutions, networks, cultural productions, and collective action. Such responses undermine the still-powerful myth of a static *national* (e.g., African American) or even *global* (e.g., diasporic) sense of black identity, suddenly mobilized by the Civil Rights, Negritude, Black Power, and Black Nationalist movements of the post–World War II era.

There is still much that remains unexplored in the history of early black cinema. I hope that future scholars will continue to look at organizations such as the black Baptists and the Knights of Pythias, institutions that, as this study has demonstrated, were pioneers of modern cinema. I am certain such research will enable us to better piece together how specific individuals acquired their film exhibition equipment and learned how to operate their moving picture outfits. While figures such as C. E. Hawk and the Conleys left relatively extensive records of their tours, in other cases, I have had to rely on conjecture based on personal relationships, geographic coordinates, and organizational affiliations to determine the patterns through which other early itinerant exhibitors, such as S. A. Bunn, learned of the moving pictures. Finally, this book has followed many of the critical pathways through which black cinema practices developed in the twentieth century, but there are many more geographies that deserve further attention. This includes not only rural black institutions, fairs, and tent shows in the United States—places where individuals such as Harry Royston showed their films—but also spaces across Canada, Cuba, Mexico, South America, and Europe.

The enduring significance of the motion pictures in black life makes clear how rich and profoundly important this history has been. In 1992, in perhaps the longest campaign against a moving picture, William F. Gibson, chair of the NAACP's national board of directors, wrote a letter to the *Los Angeles Times* protesting the Library of Congress's decision to include *Birth of a Nation* in the National Film Registry. The picture, he argued, was an "insult to more than 30 million African-Americans and every fair-minded moviegoer in America."[17] In response, Jill Brett of the Library of Congress's Public Affairs Office wrote a public letter to Gibson, in which she explained, "The noted African-American director, John Singleton, a board member, told the *Hollywood Reporter* (Dec. 8) that he had personally nominated Griffith's racist film for the registry as a 'history lesson.'"[18] Gibson and Brett's debate and the responses it generated linked the film to older disagreements about racial representation and historical memory, as well as more recent concerns over diversity and liberal inclusion. While opinions of the motion picture continue to be varied, they illuminate the persistence—and malleability—of cinema in facilitating the ongoing public interactions about race and progress.

These beliefs have endured not only through the demands of black cultural and political movements but also in the ways that a broad swath of Americans have come to understand their own rights and freedoms. Whenever there are celebrations of underrepresented groups in the movies, petitions for diverse casting and story lines on television, and campaigns against stereotypical and demeaning representations on-screen, there are echoes of the language and conceptions of rights first articulated nearly a century ago. Because token gestures and superficial acts of multiculturalism attempt to divorce these contemporary demands from the structural and legal mechanisms of race and inequality, it is important not to forget the very significant history through which forms of popular culture such as "the movies" emerged and how they were mobilized for social, economic, and political advancement. Through the moving pictures, black folk forged a culture of freedom—one that staked a claim to the public spaces and channels of communication foundational to democracy, community formation, and equality in the modern world.

Notes

Acknowledgments

Index

Notes

Abbreviations

AA	*Baltimore Afro-American*
AT	*Atlanta Constitution*
BA	*Broad Ax*
CA	*Colored American*
CC	*Colored Citizen*
CD	*Chicago Defender*
CG	*Cleveland Gazette*
CP	*Cleveland Plain Dealer*
GPJ, 1916–1977	*George P. Johnson Negro Film Collection, 1916–1977,* University of California, Los Angeles Library, Photographic Department
GPJ-CNFH	George P. Johnson: Collector of Negro Film History, University of California, Los Angeles Oral History Program (Bancroft Library, Los Angeles)
IF	*Indianapolis Freeman*
IR	*Indianapolis Recorder*
NYA	*New York Age*
NYT	*New York Times*
OE	*Omaha Enterprise*
PI	*Philadelphia Inquirer*
RP	*Richmond Planet*
ST	*Savannah Tribune*
TP	*Topeka Plaindealer*
WB	*Washington Bee*
WS	*Wichita Searchlight*

Introduction

1. *New York Herald Tribune,* Nov. 11, 1895, p. 1.

2. *Oregonian* (Portland, OR), Nov. 1, 1895, p. 2; *Kansas City Star,* Oct. 31, 1895, p. 1; *Biloxi Herald,* Nov. 16, 1895, p. 6.

3. *Oregonian* (Portland, OR), Nov. 1, 1895, p. 2; *Wheeling Register,* Nov. 1, 1895, p. 1.

4. *Charlotte Observer,* Mar. 23, 1897, p. 4; *Philadelphia Inquirer* [hereafter *PI*], May 16, 1896, p. 9; *Boston Journal,* May 18, 1896, p. 5.

5. Projected moving pictures were presented to the American public before the Koster and Bial exhibition, but the Vitascope's "official" debut as a commercial machine occurred on April 23, 1896. This exhibition was the most publicized debut of the technology. *St. Louis Republic,* Apr. 4, 1896, p. 15; *New York Times* [hereafter *NYT*], Apr. 14, 1896, p. 5; *NYT,* Apr. 19, 1896, p. 11; *NYT,* Apr. 24, 1896, p. 5.

6. Claims that the motion picture industry was the fourth largest industry in the United States were likely exaggerated, but politicians and Progressive reformers' widespread assumptions about the size of the industry suggest the enormity of its economic and cultural power. Philip C. DiMare, *Movies in American History: An Encyclopedia* (Santa Barbara, CA: ABC-CLIO, 2011), 873; Ellis Paxson Oberholtzer, *The Morals of the Movie* (Philadelphia: Penn Publishing Company, 1922), 13.

7. *Biloxi Herald,* Mar. 13, 1897, p. 8.

8. *Plessy v. Ferguson,* 163 U.S. 537 (1896).

9. Blanche Jarvis saw this reconciliation remake the terrain outside her front door. Stephen D. Lee and Ulysses S. Grant jointly petitioned in 1895 to transform the Vicksburg battlefield into a leisure park. The park would be segregated. *Ohio Plain Dealer,* May 23, 1905, p. 3; *PI,* Nov. 24, 1895, p. 7; *Daily Inter Ocean,* Dec. 1, 1895, p. 11; *Boston Journal,* Apr. 3, 1896, p. 6; David W. Blight, *Race and Reunion: The Civil War in American Memory* (Cambridge, MA: Belknap Press of Harvard University Press, 2001), 30, 134–135.

10. C. Vann Woodward, *Origins of the New South, 1877–1913* (Baton Rouge: Louisiana State University Press, 1951); Neil R. McMillen, *Dark Journey: Black Mississippians in the Age of Jim Crow* (Urbana: University of Illinois Press, 1989); Christopher Waldrep, *Vicksburg's Long Shadow: The Civil War Legacy of Race and Remembrance* (Lanham, MD: Rowman and Littlefield, 2005); Michael Newton, *The Ku Klux Klan in Mississippi: A History* (Jefferson, NC: McFarland, 2010).

11. Sister Francesca Thompson, "'From Shadows 'n Shufflin' to Spolights and Cinema': The Lafayette Players, 1915–1932," in Pearl Bowser, Jane Gaines, and Charles Musser, eds. and curators, *Oscar Micheaux and His Circle: African-American Filmmaking and Race Cinema of the Silent Era* (Bloomington: Indiana University Press, 2001), 19–33; Thomas Cripps, *Slow Fade to Black: The Negro in American Film, 1900–1942* ([1977] New York: Oxford University Press, 1993), 170–202.

12. Glenda Elizabeth Gilmore, *Gender and Jim Crow: Women and the Politics of White Supremacy in North Carolina, 1896–1920* (Chapel Hill: University of North Carolina Press, 1996); Leon F. Litwack, *Trouble in Mind: Black Southerners in the Age of Jim Crow* (New York: Knopf, 1998); Glenda Elizabeth Gilmore, *Defying Dixie: The Radical Roots of Civil Rights, 1919–1950* (New York: W. W. Norton, 2008); Michele Mitchell, *Righteous Propagation: African Americans and the Politics of Racial Destiny after Reconstruction* (Chapel Hill: University of North Carolina Press, 2004).

13. Evelyn Brooks Higginbotham, *Righteous Discontent: The Women's Movement in the Black Baptist Church, 1880–1920* (Cambridge, MA: Harvard University Press, 1993); Juliet E. K. Walker, *The History of Black Business in America: Capitalism, Race, Entrepreneurship* (New York: Macmillan Library Reference USA, 1998); Deborah G. White, *Too Heavy a Load: Black Women in Defense of Themselves, 1894–1994* (New York: W. W. Norton, 1999); Eric Foner, *Reconstruction: America's Unfinished Revolution, 1863–1877* (New York: Perennial Classics, 2002); Steven Hahn, *A Nation under Our Feet: Black Political Struggles in the Rural South, from Slavery to the Great Migration* (Cambridge, MA: Harvard University Press, 2003).

14. The first black Pentecostal revivals occurred in Mississippi in the 1890s. This may have been the moment at which Blanche Jarvis became a convert of the Pentecostal Holiness Church. Estrelda Alexander, *Black Fire: One Hundred Years of African American Pentecostalism* (Downers Grove, IL: Intervarsity Academic Press, 2011); Michael Battle, *The Black Church in America: African American Christian Spirituality* (Malden, MA: Blackwell, 2006).

15. *Topeka Plaindealer* [hereafter *TP*], Mar. 21, 1919, p. 1; *Broad Ax* [hereafter *BA*], Mar. 10, 1923, p. 2.

16. *Indianapolis Freeman* [hereafter *IF*], May 13, 1916, p. 5; *IF*, May 27, 1916, p. 5; *Frank Preer Death Certificate,* Illinois Deaths and Stillbirths Index, 1916–1947, Ancestry.com, http://www.ancestrylibrary.com; *TP*, Mar. 16, 1923, p. 1.

17. *Cleveland Gazette* [hereafter *CG*], Sept. 4, 1920, p. 1.

18. *Negro Star,* Dec. 23, 1932, p. 1; *BA,* Jan. 27, 1923, p. 1; *Kansas City Plaindealer,* Nov. 25, 1932, p. 2; *Ernestine Brooks,* Illinois Deaths and Stillbirths Index, 1916–1947, Ancestry.com, http://www.ancestrylibrary.com; *Twelfth Census of the United States—1900,* Bureau of the Census, Schedule No. 1—Population, 1900, Ancestry.com, http://www.ancestrylibrary.com; *Thirteenth Census of the United States: 1910—Population,* U.S. Department of Commerce and Labor, Bureau of the Census, 1913, Ancestry.com, http://www.ancestrylibrary.com; *Fourteenth Census of the United States: 1920—Population,* U.S. Department of Commerce and Labor, Bureau of the Census, 1922, Ancestry.com, http://www.ancestrylibrary.com; Thompson, "'From Shadows 'n Shufflin' to Spotlights and Cinema,'" 19–33; Cripps, *Slow Fade to Black,* 102, 184–187.

19. At the turn of the century, the U.S. Census Bureau defined urban population as having 2,500 people or more. In 1880, 14.3 percent of the total black population was urbanized. In 1910, the number was 27.4 percent. This is a change of 13.1 percent.

The Great Migration, which began around 1910 and continued into the 1930s, caused an additional change of 16.3 percent. *1880 Census of Population and Housing* (Washington, DC: Government Printing Office, 1880); *1900 Census of Population and Housing* (Washington, DC: Government Printing Office, 1902); *1910 Census of Population and Housing* (Washington, DC: Government Printing Office, 1913). John Kellogg, "Negro Urban Clusters in the Postbellum South," *Geographical Review* 67, no. 3 (1977): 310–321.

20. Joel Williamson argued that fears of sex between white women and black men fueled Jim Crow. Joel Williamson, *The Crucible of Race: Black/White Relations in the American South since Emancipation* (New York: Oxford University Press, 1984), 11–179. See also Steven Hahn, *The Roots of Southern Populism: Yeoman Farmers and the Transformation of the Georgia Upcountry, 1850–1890* (New York: Oxford University Press, 1983).

21. Historians have argued over when the color line began, some seeing antebellum antecedents in the South and the North, but they have largely agreed on its urban characteristics. C. Vann Woodward, *The Strange Career of Jim Crow* (New York: Oxford University Press, 1955); Howard N. Rabinowitz, *Race Relations in the Urban South, 1865–1890* (Urbana: University of Illinois Press, 1980); John Whitson Cell, *The Highest Stage of White Supremacy: The Origins of Segregation in South Africa and the American South* (Cambridge: Cambridge University Press, 1982).

22. I borrow the phrase "culture of freedom" from Herman Bennett. Herman L. Bennett, *Colonial Blackness: A History of Afro-Mexico* (Bloomington: Indiana University Press, 2009), 16.

23. Mandy Smith, interview by Sadie B. Hornsby, "The Three Sisters" GA-31, ed. Sarah H. Hall, *Work Progress Administration* (1939), March 24, 1939, Athens, Georgia, 2086.

24. Daniel O. Price, ed., U.S. Bureau of the Census, *Changing Characteristics of the Negro Population* (Washington, DC: Government Printing Office, 1969), 41–184.

25. Historians of working-class leisure have demonstrated the critical role that public amusements played in community formation, cultural practices, and the institutional life of urban wageworkers at the turn of the twentieth century. Herbert George Gutman, *Work, Culture, and Society in Industrializing America: Essays in American Working-Class and Social History* (New York: Knopf, 1976); Roy Rosenzweig, *Eight Hours for What We Will: Workers and Leisure in an Industrial City, 1870–1920* (Cambridge: Cambridge University Press, 1983); Elizabeth Ewen, *Immigrant Women in the Land of Dollars: Life and Culture on the Lower East Side, 1890–1925* (New York: Monthly Review Press, 1985); Kathy Peiss, *Cheap Amusements: Working Women and Leisure in Turn-of-the-Century New York* (Philadelphia: Temple University Press, 1986); Lizabeth Cohen, *A Consumers' Republic: The Politics of Mass Consumption in Postwar America* (New York: Knopf, 2003); David Nasaw, *Going Out: The Rise and Fall of Public Amusements* (New York: Basic Books, 1993); Robin D. G. Kelley, *Race*

Rebels: Culture, Politics, and the Black Working Class (New York: The Free Press, 1996); Tera W. Hunter, *To 'Joy My Freedom: Southern Black Women's Lives and Labors after the Civil War* (Cambridge, MA: Harvard University Press, 1997); Davarian L. Baldwin, *Chicago's New Negroes: Modernity, the Great Migration, and Black Urban Life* (Chapel Hill: University of North Carolina Press, 2007).

26. Here, the term "middle-class" refers more to a system of beliefs and a cultural status than to material wealth. As historians of nineteenth-century class identity have shown, acknowledging the complexities of class during this changing period forces us to reexamine the older equation of class identity with wealth and occupation for all Americans. This is particularly true for black Americans. The demographics of those who embraced the philosophies central to black middle-class identity show the difficulty of creating invariable economic class definitions for a population whose lives were marked by transition. References here to the "middle-class blacks" include "wealthy blacks," "black elites," "black reformers," and the "aspiring class," a group Michele Mitchell has distinguished "as a means of differentiating African American strivers from contemporaneous middle-class white Americans and to acknowledge the quickening of class stratification within African American communities." When I am specifying income, I use additional descriptives or terms such as "poor" and "wealthy" in addition to "middle-class." Mitchell, *Righteous Propagation,* xx.

27. W. E. B. Du Bois, "The Problem of Amusement" (1897), in W. E. B. Du Bois, *W. E. B. Du Bois on Sociology and the Black Community,* ed. Dan S. Green and Edwin D. Driver (Chicago: University of Chicago Press, 1980), 231. Black workers built up bustling amusement districts that drew in white pleasure-seekers, alarming the black middle class and white politicians. Kevin J. Mumford, *Interzones: Black/White Sex Districts in Chicago and New York in the Early Twentieth Century* (New York: Columbia University Press, 1997); George Chauncey, *Gay New York: Gender, Urban Culture, and the Makings of the Gay Male World, 1890–1940* (New York: Basic Books, 1994), 227–268.

28. As Leo Charney and Vanessa Schwartz explain, cinema's emphasis on visual and cognitive stimulation provided it with an exceptional ability to express and mediate the experience of modernity. Both ephemeral and spectacular, the movies fit well into the fast-paced, quickly changing tempo of urban industrial life. Leo Charney and Vanessa R. Schwartz, *Cinema and the Invention of Modern Life* (Berkeley: University of California Press, 1995); Tom Gunning, "The Cinema of Attractions: Early Film, Its Spectator, and the Avant-Garde," in Thomas Elsaesser, ed., with Adam Barker, *Early Cinema: Space, Frame, Narrative* (London: BFI, 1990), 56–62.

29. Liberal emancipation and the emergence of a black wage-earning leisure culture were directly tied to the development and growth of industrial capitalism. Eric Foner, *Free Soil, Free Labor, Free Men: The Ideology of the Republican Party before the Civil War* (New York: Oxford University Press, 1970); Thomas C. Holt, *The Problem*

of Freedom: Race, Labor, and Politics in Jamaica and Britain, 1832–1938 (Baltimore, MD: Johns Hopkins University Press, 1992).

30. These developments began in the antebellum period, as described by Daniel Walker Howe. Daniel Walker Howe, *What Hath God Wrought: The Transformation of America, 1815–1848* (New York: Oxford University Press, 2007).

31. As Donna Gabaccia has shown, the settlement of migrants via the rail system produced concentrated populations of settlers from specific locations. Donna R. Gabaccia, "Constructing North America: Railroad Building and the Rise of Continental Migrations, 1850–1914," in Marc S. Rodriguez, ed., *Repositioning North American Migration History: New Directions in Modern Continental Migration, Citizenship, and Community* (Rochester, NY: University of Rochester Press, 2004), 27–53.

32. Film historians debate whether early moving pictures appealed to the middle class, but most scholars agree that immigrants and the working class were the primary consumers of cinema in the first decade of exhibition. Robert C. Allen, "Manhattan Nickelodeons: New Data on Audiences and Exhibitors," *Cinema Journal* 34, no. 3 (1995): 5–35; Robert C. Allen, "Manhattan Myopia; or, Oh! Iowa! Robert C. Allen on Ben Singer's 'Manhattan Nickelodeons: New Data on Audiences and Exhibitors,'" *Cinema Journal* 35, no. 3 (1996): 75–103; Ben Singer, "New York, Just Like I Pictured It: Ben Singer Responds," *Cinema Journal* 35, no. 3 (1996): 104–128. The search for larger markets was a preoccupation of American industry (not just film). Government and business interests increasingly encouraged greater consumption vertically (to all classes of Americans), and horizontally (to broader geographies). Stuart Ewen, *Captains of Consciousness: Advertising and the Social Roots of the Consumer Culture* (New York: McGraw-Hill, 1976).

33. Also, according to Gerald Mast, by 1908, nickelodeons in the United States were already selling more than 80 million tickets a week, a number that is particularly remarkable in light of the fact that the population was only about 100 million and that the movies were still primarily viewed by the working class. Gerald Mast, *A Short History of the Movies* (London: Macmillan, 1986), 43.

34. Nasaw, *Going Out,* 47–61; Michael Rogin, *Blackface, White Noise: Jewish Immigrants in the Hollywood Melting Pot* (Berkeley: University of California Press, 1998).

35. Kevin K. Gaines, *Uplifting the Race: Black Leadership, Politics, and Culture in the Twentieth Century* (Chapel Hill: University of North Carolina Press, 1996).

36. As migration historians such as James Grossman and Carole Marks have explained, the periodization and geographic claims of the Great Migration have oversimplified the story of black out-migration from the rural South. Recent scholarship, including J. Trent Alexander's research that considers migrants' cities of birth (rather than the U.S. Census, which lists only the state of birth) and data from the University of Minnesota's Integrated Public Use Microdata Series (IPUMS) have further supported the importance of the "step-migration" north and west. Jack S. Blocker, "Writing African American Migrations," *Journal of the Gilded Age and Progressive*

Era 10, no. 1 (2011): 3–22; James R. Grossman, *Land of Hope: Chicago, Black Southerners, and the Great Migration* (Chicago: University of Chicago Press, 1989); J. Trent Alexander, "The Great Migration in Comparative Perspective: Interpreting the Urban Origins of Southern Black Migrants to Depression-Era Pittsburgh," *Social Science History* 22, no. 3 (1998): 349–376; Carole Marks, *Farewell—We're Good and Gone: The Great Black Migration* (Bloomington: Indiana University Press, 1989), 13; Louis M. Kyriakoudes, *The Social Origins of the Urban South: Race, Gender, and Migration in Nashville and Middle Tennessee, 1890–1930* (Chapel Hill: University of North Carolina Press, 2003); Joe William Trotter Jr., *River Jordan: African American Urban Life in the Ohio Valley* (Lexington: University Press of Kentucky, 1998).

37. I date the "Great Urbanization" from the late nineteenth century because it was during this time that large numbers of migrants moved to the city with a new conception of freedom less based on land ownership. However, it is also possible to date the urban shift from the 1860s, when large numbers of freedmen embarked for the city during and after the Civil War (Grossman, *Land of Hope*). White Americans also urbanized and migrated in mass numbers during this period. James N. Gregory, *The Southern Diaspora: How the Great Migrations of Black and White Southerners Transformed America* (Chapel Hill: University of North Carolina Press, 2005).

38. Additionally, Carole Marks has pointed out that migrants were largely urbanized and skilled before moving to the industrial North. Marks, *Farewell—We're Good and Gone;* Hunter, *To 'Joy My Freedom;* Kimberley L. Phillips, *AlabamaNorth: African-American Migrants, Community, and Working-Class Activism in Cleveland, 1915–45* (Urbana: University of Illinois Press, 1999).

39. Also, as Milton Sernett has pointed out, early migration studies, as a whole, left out considerations of culture. Milton C. Sernett, *Bound for the Promised Land: African American Religion and the Great Migration* (Durham, NC: Duke University Press, 1997).

40. See, for example, Isabel Wilkerson's award-winning *The Warmth of Other Suns* and websites such as A&E Television Network's History.com, which explains, "during the Great Migration [1916 to 1970], African Americans *began* to build a new place for themselves in public life, actively confronting economic, political and social challenges and creating a new black urban culture that would exert enormous influence in the decades to come" (my emphasis). History.com, http://www.history.com/topics/great-migration; Isabel Wilkerson, *The Warmth of Other Suns: The Epic Story of America's Great Migration* (New York: Random House, 2010).

41. Jacqueline Najuma Stewart, *Migrating to the Movies: Cinema and Black Urban Modernity* (Berkeley: University of California Press, 2005); Paula J. Massood, *Black City Cinema: African American Urban Experiences in Film* (Philadelphia: Temple University Press, 2003); Baldwin, *Chicago's New Negroes.*

42. In doing so, the history of early black cinema extends recent arguments by scholars that argue African American and African diasporic history reconfigures

previous assumptions about modernity, particularly in terms of secularization. For example, see Michael Angelo Gomez, *Exchanging Our Country Marks: The Transformation of African Identities in the Colonial and Antebellum South* (Chapel Hill: University of North Carolina Press, 1998); Saidiya V. Hartman, *Scenes of Subjection: Terror, Slavery, and Self-Making in Nineteenth-Century America* (New York: Oxford University Press, 1997); Stephan Palmie, *Wizards and Scientists: Explorations in Afro-Cuban Modernity and Tradition* (Durham, NC: Duke University Press, 2002); John M. Giggie, *After Redemption: Jim Crow and the Transformation of African American Religion in the Delta, 1875–1915* (New York: Oxford University Press, 2008). Davarian Baldwin and Jacqueline Stewart have also pointed out this oversight specifically in regard to cinema. Baldwin, *Chicago's New Negroes;* Stewart, *Migrating to the Movies.*

43. Martin Heidegger, "The Age of the World Picture [1938]," in William Lovitt, ed., *The Question Concerning Technology and Other Essays* (New York: Harper & Row, 1977), 147; Jürgen Habermas, *The Theory of Communicative Action* (Boston: Beacon Press, 1984). Talal Asad has pointed out that the very definition of what constitutes the "religious" in the Western lexicon is based on a European notion. Talal Asad, *Formations of the Secular: Christianity, Islam, Modernity* (Stanford, CA: Stanford University Press, 2003). Jared Hickman has argued that racism itself is a form of spiritual belief. Jared Hickman, "Globalization and the Gods, or the Political Theology of Race," *Early American Literature* 45, no. 1 (2010): 145–182.

44. Higginbotham, *Righteous Discontent,* 7.

45. W. E. B. Du Bois, ed., *Efforts for Social Betterment among Negro Americans,* The Atlanta University Publications, No. 14 (Atlanta: Atlanta University Press, 1909), 16; W. E. B. Du Bois, ed., *The Negro Church* (Atlanta: Atlanta University Press, 1903), 38; Carter G. Woodson, *The History of the Negro Church* (Washington, DC: Associated Publishers, 1921), 287.

46. Francesca Thompson, "Evelyn Preer: Early Dramatic Film and Stage Star," *Black Masks* 15, no. 4 (July–Aug. 2002): 7.

47. *Chicago Defender* [hereafter *CD*], Dec. 10, 1932, p. 9.

48. Cripps, *Slow Fade to Black,* 262–308.

1. Exhibitions of Faith and Fellowship

1. *Omaha Enterprise* [hereafter *OE*], Jan. 9, 1897, p. 4. Church description based on *OE,* Oct. 24, 1896, p. 4; *OE,* Nov. 14, 1896, p. 4; E. Arlington Wilson, "Introduction," in Samuel William Bacote, ed., *Who's Who among the Colored Baptists of the United States* (Kansas City, MO: Franklin Hudson, 1913), 5; *Kansas City (KS) Plaindealer,* May 3, 1946, p. 18; Josephine A. Payne, *Second Baptist Church,* 1983, Kansas City Public Library Missouri Valley Special Collections, Kansas City Public Library, 11.

2. Description of the Second Baptist film exhibition is based on a composite of early film exhibitions in black churches, with technical details from motion picture manuals and newspaper reports. See, for example, *Indianapolis Recorder* [hereafter

IR], Mar. 31, 1900, p. 4; *Colored American* [hereafter *CA*], Oct. 14, 1899, p. 8; *Kansas City Star,* July 25, 1986, p. 8; C. Francis Jenkins, *Animated Pictures* (Washington, DC: Press of M. L. McQueen, 1898).

3. *Kansas City Daily Journal,* July 26, 1896, p. 12.

4. The church's Sunday evening entertainment program followed quickly on the heels of Kansas City's first advertised exhibition at Fairmount Park in late July of 1896. *Kansas City Star,* July 25, 1896, p. 8; Charles E. Coulter, *Take Up the Black Man's Burden: Kansas City's African American Communities, 1865–1939* (Columbia: University of Missouri Press, 2006), 236–237.

5. Allan Bethel, "The Moving Picture," *Conestoga Magazine* 1 (May 1907), quoted in Kathryn Helgesen Fuller, "You Can Have the Strand in Your Own Town: The Marginalization of Small Town Film Exhibition in the Silent Film Era," *Film History* 6 (Summer 1994): 166.

6. *Wichita Searchlight* [hereafter *WS*], Nov. 11, 1900, p. 2.

7. Payne, *Second Baptist Church,* 7.

8. *PI,* Oct. 11, 1861, p. 2; Paul B. Jenkins, *The Battle of Westport* (Kansas City, MO: Franklin Hudson, 1906); Asa E. Martin, *Our Negro Population: A Sociological Study of the Negroes of Kansas City, Missouri* (Kansas City, MO: Franklin Hudson, 1913); Leigh Ann Little and John M. Olinskey, *Early Kansas City, Missouri* (Charleston, SC: Arcadia Publishing, 2013), 35–36.

9. Payne, *Second Baptist Church,* 7.

10. Joseph Heathcott, "Black Archipelago: Politics and Civic Life in the Jim Crow City," *Journal of Social History* 38 (Spring 2005): 705–736.

11. Kansas City, Missouri, had fewer than 200 black residents before the war; more than 17,000 resided in the city by the turn of the century. U.S. Department of the Interior, Census Office, *Compendium of the Eighth Census: 1860,* pt. 1: *Population* (Washington, DC: Government Printing Office, 1864), 183–195; U.S. Department of the Interior, Census Office, *Compendium of the Eleventh Census: 1890,* pt. 1: *Population* (Washington, DC: Government Printing Office, 1895), 466; U.S. Department of the Interior, Census Office, *Compendium of the Twelfth Census: 1900,* pt. 1: *Population* (Washington, DC: Government Printing Office, 1902), 625. For more on the growth of the black population, see Martin, *Our Negro Population.*

12. Details of the Second Baptist Church's history from Payne, *Second Baptist Church,* 7, and Martin, *Our Negro Population,* 179–192.

13. Donald Bogle, *Toms, Coons, Mulattoes, Mammies, and Bucks: An Interpretive History of Blacks in American Films* (New York: Viking Press, 1973); James P. Murray, *To Find an Image: Black Films from Uncle Tom to Superfly* (Indianapolis, IN: Bobbs-Merrill, 1973); Daniel Leab, *From Sambo to Superspade* (Boston: Houghton Mifflin, 1975). Also see David Nasaw, *Going Out: The Rise and Fall of Public Amusements* (New York: Basic Books, 1993); Douglas Gomery, *Shared Pleasures: A History of Movie Presentation in the United States* (Madison: University of Wisconsin Press, 1992).

14. These scholars, nonetheless, have made critical contributions to the study of early cinema in black life. This book is indebted to their pioneering research. In particular, see Thomas Cripps's groundbreaking research on race and early black cinema: Thomas Cripps, *Slow Fade to Black: The Negro in American Film, 1900–1942* ([1977] New York: Oxford University Press, 1993). Articles and book chapters on colored theaters and black filmgoing in the West and South include Gregory A. Waller, "Another Audience: Black Moviegoing, 1907–16," *Cinema Journal* 31, no. 2 (1992): 3–25; Dan Streible, "The Harlem Theater: Black Film Exhibition in Austin, Texas: 1920–1973," in Manthia Diawara, ed., *Black American Cinema* (London: Routledge, 1993); Douglas Gomery, "The Two Public Spaces of a Moviegoing Capital: Race and the History of Film Exhibition in Washington, D.C.," *Spectator* 18, no. 2 (1998): 8–17; Charlene Regester, "From the Buzzard's Roost: Black Movie-Going in Durham and Other North Carolina Cities during the Early Period of American Cinema," *Film History* 17 (2005): 113–124; Elizabeth Abel, "Double Take: Photography, Cinema, and the Segregated Theater," *Critical Inquiry* 34, no. s2 (2008): s2–s20.

Studies of black filmgoing in the North include Jacqueline Najuma Stewart, *Migrating to the Movies: Cinema and Black Urban Modernity* (Berkeley: University of California Press, 2005); Mary Carbine, "The Finest Outside the Loop," *Camera Obscura: Feminism, Culture, and Media Studies* 8, no. 23 (1990): 8–41; Alison Griffiths and James Latham, "Film and Ethnic Identity in Harlem, 1896–1915," in Melvyn Stokes and Richard Maltby, eds., *American Movie Audiences: From the Turn of the Century to the Early Sound Era* (London: British Film Institute, 1999), 46–63; Desiree J. Garcia, "Subversive Sounds: Ethnic Spectatorship and Boston's Nickelodeon Theatres, 1907–1914," *Film History* 19, no. 3 (2007): 213–227; Davarian L. Baldwin, *Chicago's New Negroes: Modernity, the Great Migration, and Black Urban Life* (Chapel Hill: University of North Carolina Press, 2007).

References to early black film exhibitions in lodges and churches have been made in Waller, "Another Audience"; Michele Wallace, "Passing, Lynching, and Jim Crow: A Genealogy of Race and Gender in U.S. Visual Culture, 1895–1929" (PhD diss., New York University, 1999); Pearl Bowser and Louise Spence, *Writing Himself into History: Oscar Micheaux, His Silent Films, and His Audiences* (New Brunswick, NJ: Rutgers University Press, 2000); and especially in Henry T. Sampson, *Blacks in Black and White: A Source Book on Black Films* (Lanham, MD: Scarecrow Press, 1995). Judith Weisenfeld has examined African American religion and film after the silent film era: Judith Weisenfeld, *Hollywood Be Thy Name: African American Religion in American Film, 1929–1949* (Berkeley: University of California Press, 2007). Allyson Field's forthcoming book on uplift cinema will also make a critical contribution to our understanding of nontheatrical black film exhibition. Allyson Nadia Field, *Uplift Cinema: The Emergence of African American Film and the Possibility of Black Modernity* (Duke University Press, forthcoming 2015).

15. Kevin Kelly Gaines, *Uplifting the Race: Black Leadership, Politics, and Culture in the Twentieth Century* (Chapel Hill: University of North Carolina Press, 1996);

Michele Mitchell, *Righteous Propagation: African Americans and the Politics of Racial Destiny after Reconstruction* (Chapel Hill: University of North Carolina Press, 2004); Touré F. Reed, *Not Alms but Opportunity: The Urban League and the Politics of Racial Uplift, 1910–1950* (Chapel Hill: University of North Carolina Press, 2008).

16. Tera W. Hunter, *To 'Joy My Freedom: Southern Black Women's Lives and Labors after the Civil War* (Cambridge, MA: Harvard University Press, 1997); Leon F. Litwack, *Been in the Storm So Long: The Aftermath of Slavery* (New York: Vintage Books, 1980); Eric Foner, *Reconstruction: America's Unfinished Revolution, 1863–1877* (New York: Perennial Classics, 2002); Steven Hahn, *A Nation under Our Feet: Black Political Struggles in the Rural South, from Slavery to the Great Migration* (Cambridge, MA: Harvard University Press, 2003).

17. Mitchell, *Righteous Propagation;* Edward Franklin Frazier and C. Eric Lincoln, *The Negro Church in America* (New York: Schocken Books, 1974); Evelyn Brooks Higginbotham, *Righteous Discontent: The Women's Movement in the Black Baptist Church, 1880–1920* (Cambridge, MA: Harvard University Press, 1993).

18. W. E. B. Du Bois, *The Philadelphia Negro* (Philadelphia: University of Pennsylvania, 1899), 76. According to Joe William Trotter Jr., "More blacks migrated to southern cities between 1900 and 1920 than to northern ones. . . . Before moving to northern cities like Philadelphia, Boston, and New York, for example, rural migrants first moved to southern cities like New Orleans, Jacksonville, Savannah, Memphis, Charleston, and Birmingham." Joe William Trotter Jr., "The Great Migration," *OAH Magazine of History* 17, no. 1 (2002): 32.

19. Joe William Trotter Jr., ed., *The Great Migration in Historical Perspective: New Dimensions of Race, Class, and Gender* (Bloomington: Indiana University Press, 1991), xi–xii.

20. Based on the U.S. Census definition of "urban" as having 2,500 or more inhabitants. Carole Marks, *Farewell—We're Good and Gone: The Great Black Migration* (Bloomington: Indiana University Press, 1989), 34; Daniel O. Price, ed., U.S. Bureau of the Census, *Changing Characteristics of the Negro Population* (Washington, DC: U.S. Government Printing Office, 1969), 39.

21. *Rising Son,* Dec. 15, 1906, p. 4.

22. Despite being the son of slaves, Samuel Bacote began with some considerable advantages over other children of freedmen in his community. A member of the mulatto class, his father was a respected citizen and a local appointed official. Samuel William Bacote, *Who's Who among the Colored Baptists of the United States* (Kansas City, MO: Franklin Hudson, 1913), 9.

23. *(Kansas City, KS) Plaindealer,* May 3, 1946, p. 1; Payne, *Second Baptist Church,* 11.

24. Wilson, "Introduction," 9.

25. W. E. B. Du Bois, ed. *The Negro Church* (Atlanta: Atlanta University Press, 1903), 84.

26. W. E. B. Du Bois, ed., *Efforts for Social Betterment among Negro Americans,* The Atlanta University Publications no. 14 (Atlanta: Atlanta University Press, 1909),

16. While only a few scattered structures existed at the end of the Civil War, by 1890, there were 23,770 black churches in the United States. The era also witnessed the construction of thousands of black schools and halls, often in conjunction with efforts undertaken by black religious institutions. By 1909 there was a net increase of 11,390 church edifices—which did not include the construction of edifices for congregations moving from one building to another. Du Bois, *Negro Church,* 38. According to Carter G. Woodson, "Comparing these statistics of 1906 with those of 1890, one sees the rapid growth of the Negro church. Although the Negro population increased only 26.1 per cent during these sixteen years, the number of church organizations increased 56.7 per cent; the number of communicants, 37.8 per cent; the number of edifices, 47.9; the seating capacity, 54.1 per cent; and the value of church property, 112.7 per cent." Carter G. Woodson, *The History of the Negro Church* (Washington, DC: Associated Publishers, 1921), 287. Gunnar Myrdal pointed out that the problem of church property debt continued into the 1940s. Gunnar Myrdal and Sissela Bok, *An American Dilemma: The Negro Problem and Modern Democracy* (New Brunswick, NJ: Transaction Publishers, 1996), 941.

27. Thorstein Veblen, *The Theory of the Leisure Class* (New York: Macmillan, 1899).

28. Robert A. McGuinn, *The Race Problem in the Churches* (Baltimore, MD: Printing office of J. F. Weishampel, 1890), 39–41.

29. W. E. B. Du Bois and Augustus Granvile Dill, eds., *Morals and Manners among Negro Americans,* The Atlanta University Publications no. 18 (Atlanta: Atlanta University Press, 1914), 110.

30. Ibid., 111.

31. The Atchison, Topeka and Santa Fe Railway was known colloquially as the "Santa Fe." Wilson, "Introduction," 9.

32. Bethel AME was in debt $6,800 in January 1897 and was paying off about "$100 per month." "Bethel AME Notes," *IF,* Jan. 9, 1897, p. 8; "Bethel A.M.E. Church," *IF,* Jan. 20, 1900, p. 4.

33. "The Cinematograph at Bethel," *IF,* Apr. 24, 1897, p. 8.

34. *Chicago Daily Inter Ocean,* Aug. 25, 1895, p. 16; *Chicago Daily Inter Ocean,* Aug. 9, 1896, p. 33.

35. Charles Musser, *The Emergence of Cinema: The American Screen to 1907* (Berkeley: University of California Press, 1990); Nasaw, *Going Out.*

36. "The Cinematograph at Bethel," *IF,* Apr. 24, 1897, p. 8.

37. Richard Abel, *The Ciné Goes to Town: French Cinema, 1896–1914* (Berkeley: University of California Press, 1998), 17.

38. *IF,* Apr. 24, 1897, p. 8.

39. The statistics on income are based on W. E. B. Du Bois's study of another midwestern city, Xenia, Ohio, in 1903. Nearly 58 percent of the five-member families in the city earned less than $9.62 a week, or $1.92 per person. The estimated annual

expenditure for the basic food, clothing, shelter, and other needs of a family of five was $266.50, or $5.13 per week. W. E. B. Du Bois, *The Negro American Family* (Atlanta: Atlanta University Press, 1908), 112.

40. *CG,* Jan. 30, 1897, p. 2.

41. Bacote believed "great men . . . combine in themselves the constructive agencies that comprise the bone and sinew of the people." Bacote, *Who's Who among the Colored Baptists of the United States,* 5–6.

42. Quote in text by Graham, in response to lynching and racial oppression, *IR,* June 10, 1899, p. 3.

43. *IF,* April 24, 1897, p. 8.

44. For example, in January, for Bethel AME, "collections for the [services last Sunday] amounted to $16.00, which was an increase of $5.00 over the previous Sunday," "Bethel AME Notes," *IF,* Jan. 16, 1897, p. 8. Bazaar proceeds listed in "Bethel A.M.E. Notes," *IF,* June 5, 1897, p. 8; *IF,* May 22, 1897, p. 8.

45. *OE,* Jan. 9, 1897, p. 4.

46. *OE,* Jan. 23, 1897, p. 4.

47. Frank Lincoln Mather, ed., *Who's Who of the Colored Race: A General Biographical Dictionary of Men and Women of African Descent* (Chicago: University of Michigan, 1915), 15; Wilson, "Introduction," 9. By 1913, the church had constructed a property valued at "$100,000 that was entirely free from debt." Martin, *Our Negro Population,* 187.

48. Isabel Eaton, "A Special Report on Domestic Service," in Du Bois, *Philadelphia Negro,* 470.

49. *Afro-American* [hereafter *AA*], Dec. 23, 1905, p. 8.

50. *Richmond Planet* [hereafter *RP*], Oct. 28, 1899, p. 1; *Gloversville Daily Leader,* Aug. 31, 1901; *CA,* Jan. 11, 1902, p. 9.

51. Charles Musser and Carol Nelson, *High-Class Moving Pictures: Lyman H. Howe and the Forgotten Era of Traveling Exhibition, 1880–1920* (Princeton, NJ: Princeton University Press, 1991), 22–46.

52. *TP,* Sept. 28, 1906, p. 3; *TP,* Oct. 5, 1906, p. 5; *TP,* Nov. 2, 1906, p. 3; *TP,* Nov. 16, 1906, p. 2.

53. The earliest example I have found of *The Devil's Cook Kitchen* moving picture show is in *IF,* Oct. 21, 1905, p. 5.

54. *Savannah Tribune* [hereafter *ST*], July 27, 1901, p. 2, "St. Philips Church Dots," *ST,* Jan. 25, 1902, p. 3; "St. Philips Church Dots," *ST,* Apr. 26, 1902, p. 2; *IF,* June 28, 1902, p. 4; *TP,* June 19, 1903, p. 2; *Sedalia Times,* June 13, 1903, p. 2; *American Citizen,* May 11, 1906, p. 1; *IF,* Oct. 9, 1909, p. 4.

55. *PI,* Apr. 3, 1897, p. 3. New models of motion picture projectors became progressively lighter and easier to transport. David Nasaw, for example, explained that in 1899, F. M. Prescott was selling an easily transportable cineograph that weighed only twenty-five pounds. Nasaw, *Going Out,* 142.

56. Gaines Chapel (Savannah, GA); the Willowtree "Negro Church" (Atlanta, GA); Burns Chapel (Sedalia, MO); and the Bethlehem Baptist Church (Savannah, GA) all cost ten cents. *ST,* Oct. 15, 1904, p. 3; *Atlanta Constitution* [hereafter *AT*], Apr. 21, 1904, p. 2; *Sedalia Weekly Conservator,* Dec. 2, 1904, p. 4; *ST,* Feb. 8, 1908, p. 4.

57. *WS,* Dec. 25, 1909, p. 1.

58. *Pittsburgh Courier,* July 1, 1911, p. 6; *ST,* Jan. 25, 1902, p. 3; *ST,* Apr. 26, 1902, p. 2; *ST,* Oct. 15, 1904, p. 3; *ST,* Aug. 5, 1905, p. 2; *ST,* Feb. 22, 1908, p. 4.

59. *Milwaukee Wisconsin Weekly Advocate,* Nov. 2, 1905, p. 1; *IF,* Nov. 11, 1905, p. 7.

60. Du Bois, *Negro Church,* 111.

61. James Melvin Washington, *Frustrated Fellowship: The Black Baptist Quest for Social Power* (Macon, GA: Mercer University Press, 1986); Higginbotham, *Righteous Discontent;* U.S. Bureau of the Census, *Religious Bodies: 1916,* pt. 2 (Washington, DC: Government Printing Office, 1919), 97–99.

62. *IF,* Nov. 11, 1905, p. 7; *Wisconsin Weekly Advocate,* Nov. 2, 1905, p. 1; *TP,* Oct. 20, 1905, p. 6. The Women's Convention was an organization that grew out of the black Baptist women's demands for greater autonomy within the church. Higginbotham, *Righteous Discontent.*

63. *Columbia South Carolina State,* Oct. 20, 1905, p. 8; *IF,* Nov. 4, 1905, p. 7.

64. *Washington Bee* [hereafter *WB*], Aug. 31, 1907, p. 5; *WB,* Sept. 7, 1907, p. 8; *WB,* Oct. 5, 1907, p. 8; *WB,* Sept. 28, 1907, p. 8; *WB,* Sept. 14, 1907, p. 8; *WB,* Sept. 21, 1907, p. 8; *WB,* Sept. 7, 1907, p. 8.

65. *WB,* Sept. 7, 1907, p. 5. The pictures were to be in the style of "Burton Holmes," who was famous for his moving picture travelogues. *PI,* Feb. 25, 1905, p. 7.

66. *WB,* Sept. 28, 1907, p. 5.

67. Siegmund Lubin also attempted to recruit black scenario writers through his advertisements in a black newspaper, the *New York Age* [hereafter *NYA*], which promised readers the opportunity to make money by proposing stories for "the Negro stock company of the Comedy section of the Lubin Company." *NYA,* Feb. 2, 1914, p. 6.

68. Tom Gunning, "The Cinema of Attractions: Early Film, Its Spectator, and the Avant-Garde," in Thomas Elsaesser with Adam Barker, eds., *Early Cinema: Space, Frame, Narrative* (Berkeley: University of California Press, 1990), 56–62.

69. *TP,* Dec. 28, 1906, p. 5.

70. This description is based on a summary of Pope's earlier "Black Hand" lecture, which was later integrated into his moving picture show. *CA,* Jan. 11, 1902, p. 9.

71. *IF,* Dec. 29, 1900, p. 3.

72. Ibid.

73. Joseph P. Eckhardt, *The King of the Movies: Film Pioneer Siegmund Lubin* (London: Fairleigh Dickinson University Press, 1997), 22–28.

74. Advertisement for "Lubin's Cineograph," in C. Francis Jenkins, *Animated Pictures* (Washington, DC: Press of M. L. McQueen, 1898), 134; *IF,* Nov. 11, 1899, p. 5.

75. Royston's show lasted two hours. He did not explicitly acknowledge that his films were reenactments in advertisements. *IF,* Nov. 11, 1899, p. 5; *IF,* Sept. 9, 1899, p. 5.

76. *IF,* Aug. 25, 1900, p. 5.

77. *IF,* Sept. 9, 1899, p. 5.

78. *IR,* Mar. 24, 1900, p. 4; *IR,* Mar. 31, 1900, p. 4; *TP,* Mar. 8, 1901, p. 1; *Colored Citizen* [hereafter *CC*], Aug. 29, 1903, p. 2.

79. Bettis's machine was likely the "projecting Kinetoscope," an Edison film projector. *TP,* Mar. 8, 1901, p. 1; *CC,* Aug. 29, 1903, p. 2; *Kansas Headlight,* Sept. 14, 1894, p. 2; *Kansas Whip,* June 24, 1938, p. 1.

80. T. S. Arthur, *Ten Nights in a Bar-Room* (Philadelphia: J. W. Bradley, 1854).

81. Lubin's *Ten Nights in a Bar-Room,* the earliest film version of the story that I am familiar with, was released in 1903, but it may have not been distributed before the fall. The film exhibition at Hyde Park Chapel was on April 28, 1903. *NY Clipper,* Oct. 24, 1903, p. 844; *Grand Forks Herald,* Jan. 10, 1904, p. 4.

82. *BA,* Apr. 18, 1903, p. 4.

83. *WS,* Dec. 25, 1909, p. 1.

84. Musser, *Emergence of Cinema,* 218.

85. Gerald Horne, *Race Woman: The Lives of Shirley Graham Du Bois* (New York: New York University Press, 2000).

86. *IR,* Apr. 22, 1899, p. 1; *IR,* May 6, 1899, p. 4.

87. *IF,* Jan. 21, 1905, p. 5; *IF,* Feb. 4, 1905, p. 5; *IF,* Mar. 4, 1905, p. 5; *IF,* Mar. 25, 1905, p. 5.

88. *CA,* Apr. 26, 1902, p. 16; *CA,* Nov. 14, 1903, p. 16.

89. *CA,* Apr. 26, 1902, p. 16; *RP,* May 28, 1904, p. 1; *Columbia South Carolina State,* Nov. 15, 1907, p. 10.

90. *AA,* June 5, 1909, p. 8; *AA,* Mar. 28, 1914, p. 5; *AA,* Nov. 12, 1910, p. 4.

91. *WS,* Dec. 15, 1909, p. 1.

92. Members of J. E. Henry and Co. were white. A few white companies exhibited movies in black churches, but most were black-owned and -operated, or sometimes interracial. *AA,* Dec. 23, 1905, p. 8.

93. *The African Methodist Episcopal Hymn and Tune Book: Adapted to the Doctrine and Usages of the Church* (Philadelphia: African Methodist Episcopal Book Concern, 902), xii.

94. For more on early white noncommercial venues and itinerant film exhibition, see Musser and Nelson, *High-Class Moving Pictures;* Terry Lindvall, *Sanctuary Cinema: Origins of the Christian Film Industry* (New York: New York University Press, 2007).

95. In particular, the white Methodist Episcopal Church promoted the exhibition of certain pictures in their churches. However, many white progressives and religious leaders eyed motion pictures with ambivalence or outright hostility. Musser, *Emergence of Cinema,* 208–221.

96. Nasaw, *Going Out,* 47–61.

97. *IF,* May 16, 1903, p. 5; *AA,* June 17, 1905, p. 1; *CG,* June 24, 1905, p. 1.

98. For example, in 1897, "all the colored Baptist ministers of the state of Indiana" were called to meet in Marion to listen to Reverend L. W. Gray speak about "The Benefit of Co-operation" and "business of vast importance, claiming the attention of the entire denomination." *IF,* June 12, 1897, p. 5.

99. The black members of the Methodist Episcopal Church (CME), the African Methodist Episcopal (AME) Church, and Baptist churches maintained publishing houses. The bishop of the AME Church, Henry McNeal Turner, published a manual on "the Machinery of Methodism," which attempted to standardize the doctrines, rules, and procedures of church administration. Henry McNeal Turner, *The Genius and Theory of Methodist Polity* (Philadelphia: A.M.E. Church, 1885); U.S. Bureau of the Census, *Religious Bodies: 1916,* pt. 2, 129–140.

100. In 1895, when traveling from Hope to promote his educational work, Henry Clay Yerger established a teacher training school "west of the Mississippi." *Hope's First Century: A Commemorative History of Hope, Arkansas, 1875–1975* (Hope, AR: Etter Print Co., 1974). Also see "Church and Social News," *IF,* Mar. 28, 1903, p. 1.

101. Richmond held patents for a machine gun and two for burial devices, from the U.S. Patent Office. By 1910, he worked as an iron molder and lived in a Nebraska poor house. With his meager salary, he would have had difficulty affording a moving picture projector. "Burial-Derrick," Apr. 2, 1895; "Automatic Machine Gun," Dec. 9, 1896, "Burial Device," Mar. 30, 1897, U.S. Patent Office, United States. "Romulus Richmond," Lancaster, Nebraska, *1910 United States Federal Census*—Population, Ancestry.com, http://www.ancestrylibrary.com; *IF,* Mar. 4, 1916, p. 8; *Sedalia Times,* Feb. 14, 1903, p. 1.

102. Distance played a significant role in determining the gender demographics of short- and long-distance migration. Black women left their rural homes for nearby cities and towns in order to supplement their families' incomes. In urban centers across the South, black migrant women found employment as domestic laborers or in other low-paid, unskilled work. In contrast, the wave of migration to the West was substantially smaller than the rural-to-urban shift within the South; in the move to most territories west of the Mississippi, black men outnumbered women. In rural areas of the South, black men outnumbered women. Kimberley L. Phillips, *AlabamaNorth: African-American Migrants, Community, and Working-Class Activism in Cleveland, 1915–45* (Urbana: University of Illinois Press, 1999); Walter F. Willcox, "The Negro Population," U.S. Department of Commerce and Labor, Bureau of the Census, Bulletin 8, *Negroes in the United States* (Washington, DC: Government Printing Office, 1904), 35.

103. Du Bois and Dill, *Morals and Manners among Negro Americans,* 105.

104. Jualynne E. Dodson, *Engendering Church: Women, Power, and the AME Church* (Lanham, MD: Rowman and Littlefield, 2002); Higginbotham, *Righteous*

Discontent; Belinda Robnett, *How Long? How Long? African-American Women in the Struggle for Civil Rights* (New York: Oxford University Press, 1997).

105. *RP,* May 10, 1902, p. 1.

106. *AA,* Sept. 18, 1909, p. 5; *AA,* Oct. 29, 1910, p. 8; *AA,* May 14, 1910, p. 8; *AA,* Nov. 2, 1912, p. 5.

107. *Philadelphia Tribune,* Sept. 28, 1912, p. 5.

108. The Walkers began with a stereopticon, then used a Kinetoscope, and then probably used projected motion pictures by 1903. Fleetwood "Fleet" Walker was the last black player in the U.S. major leagues until 1947. He was also a talented writer. David Zang, *Fleet Walker's Divided Heart: The Life of Baseball's First Black Major Leaguer* (Lincoln: University of Nebraska Press, 1995), 82.

109. As S. A. Bunn's notoriety grew, her "magnificent" shows became highly publicized. She exhibited at the Trinity AME Church on December 19, 1907. Bunn returned home to Philadelphia on December 27 for a short interlude before resuming her show in the South. *AA,* Nov. 30, 1907, p. 8; *AA,* Dec. 28, 1907, p. 8.

110. White women participated in other areas of the early motion picture industry, but there appears to be a much smaller proportion of white women *traveling* exhibitors to white men, especially compared to the number of black women traveling exhibitors in the profession. The film historian Charles Musser, in referring to white film exhibitors, argued that "almost every exhibitor from this period was male." Musser and Nelson, *High-Class Moving Pictures,* 315. For more on women and early American cinema, see Hilary Hallett, *Go West, Young Women! The Rise of Early Hollywood* (Berkeley: University of California Press, 2013); Karen Ward Mahar, *Women Filmmakers in Early Hollywood* (Baltimore, MD: Johns Hopkins University Press, 2006).

111. Women owned motion picture theaters but were arguably much more vulnerable to economic exploitation and physical danger as itinerant exhibitors on the *commercial* exhibition circuit.

112. Mrs. H. C. Conley was a musician and a delegate of the National Negro Business League. *WB,* Aug. 9, 1908, p. 4.

113. G. W. Hawkins and his wife were identified as a couple from Philadelphia, and may have been George and Lillian Hawkins of 1010 Chadwick Street, Philadelphia, Pennsylvania; *Thirteenth Census of the United States, 1910* (microfilm, 1,178 reels, NARA Microfilm Publication) Records of the Bureau of the Census, Record Group 29 (National Archives, Washington, DC) in *1910 United States Federal Census,* available at Ancestry.com, http://www.ancestrylibrary.com; *IF,* Mar. 4, 1916, p. 8.

114. McGuinn, *Race Problem in the Churches,* 41–42.

115. *AA,* Feb. 7, 1914, p. 5.

116. William Craft was stationed at the time in Nashville, Tennessee, the center of some of the nation's most important black Baptist institutions, including the Publishing Board of the National Baptist Convention.

117. *IF,* Oct. 27, 1900, p. 1; *AT,* Apr. 21, 1904, p. 2. Also see Gregory A. Waller, *Main Street Amusements: Movies and Commercial Entertainment in a Southern City, 1896–1930* (Washington, DC: Smithsonian Institution Press, 1995), 52, 166.

118. Craft exhibited at the First A. B. Church, Franklin Square, Mt. Bethel Church, St. Philip Church, and St. John Baptist Church; *ST,* July 27, 1901, p. 2.

119. *ST,* July 27, 1901, p. 2.

120. *ST,* Jan. 25, 1902, p. 3.

121. *ST,* Apr. 26, 1902, p. 2; *ST,* Oct. 15, 1904, p. 3; *ST,* Aug. 5, 1905, p. 2; *ST,* Feb. 22, 1908, p. 4.

122. Historians of black migration note the significance of institutions and kith and kin networks in determining the destination of settlement. Trotter, "Great Migration," 31–33; Phillips, *AlabamaNorth;* Jack S. Blocker Jr., "Black Migration to Muncie, 1860–1930," *Indiana Magazine of History* 92, no. 4 (1996): 297–320; Louis M. Kyriakoudes, *The Social Origins of the Urban South: Race, Gender, and Migration in Nashville and Middle Tennessee, 1890–1930* (Chapel Hill: University of North Carolina Press, 2003); Marks, *Farewell—We're Good and Gone.*

123. See Giggie's excellent study of the relationship between religion, black capitalism, and the railroads. John M. Giggie, *After Redemption: Jim Crow and the Transformation of African American Religion in the Delta, 1875–1915* (New York: Oxford University Press, 2008), 24.

124. *AA,* Dec. 28, 1907, p. 8; *WB,* Sept. 28, 1907, p. 5; *AA,* July 4, 1914, p. 8.

125. The Missouri-Kansas-Texas Railroad (the Katy), the Atchison, Topeka and Santa Fe Railway (Santa Fe), the Saint Louis–San Francisco Railway (the Frisco), Southern Railway, the Pennsylvania (Pennsy), and the Baltimore and Ohio (B&O) were especially critical for the development of itinerant moving picture exhibitions.

126. Donna R. Gabaccia, "Constructing North America: Railroad Building and the Rise of Continental Migrations, 1850–1914," in Marc S. Rodriguez, ed., *Repositioning North American Migration History* (Rochester, NY: University of Rochester Press, 2004), 27–53.

127. Joe William Trotter Jr. explained: "The Southern, Louisville, Nashville, the St. Louis and San Francisco, and the Illinois Central railroads all traveled northward from Birmingham and Bessemer, making the Jefferson County cities the major distribution points for blacks going north from Alabama. In Georgia, cities like Columbus, Americus, and Albany served as distribution points for blacks leaving from western Georgia and eastern Alabama, while Valdosta, Waycross, Brunswick, and Savannah served as distribution centers for blacks leaving the depressed agricultural counties of southern and southeastern Georgia." Trotter, "Great Migration," 32.

128. Film reels, in particular, added to the expense of a motion picture operation. Musser, *Emergence of Cinema,* 99–101.

129. For example, see *IF,* Mar. 28, 1903, p. 1; *IF,* May 16, 1903, p. 5. Lebanon, Kentucky, had a total population of 3,043 people in 1900; there were 1,051 black residents.

U.S. Department of the Interior, Census Office, *Compendium of the Twelfth Census: 1900,* pt. 1: *Population,* 618.

130. Burton W. Peretti, *Lift Every Voice: The History of African American Music* (Lanham, MD: Rowman and Littlefield, 2009). Sedalia's population in 1900 was 15,231; there were 1,725 black residents. U.S. Department of the Interior, Census Office, *Compendium of the Twelfth Census: 1900,* pt. 1: *Population,* 626. *Sedalia Times,* June 13, 1903, p. 2; *Sedalia Times,* Feb. 14, 1903, p. 1; *Sedalia Weekly Conservator,* Dec. 30, 1904, p. 1.

131. *AA,* Nov. 30, 1907, p. 8.

132. *NYA,* June 25, 1908, p. 3.

133. *IF,* Dec. 21, 1901, p. 5.

134. *CG,* Mar. 28, 1903, p. 1.

135. *CG,* Mar. 8, 1902, p. 1; *CG,* Mar. 28, 1903, p. 1; Zang, *Fleet Walker's Divided Heart.*

136. Sedalia's Katy Depot was constructed in 1896.

137. *CG,* Mar. 22, 1902, p. 2.

138. Holly Bruno and Andrew Ehritz, *Bellaire* (Charleston, SC: Arcadia, 2009).

139. U.S. Department of the Interior, Census Office, *Compendium of the Twelfth Census: 1900,* pt. 1: *Population,* 633.

140. "Atchison, Kansas," *TP,* June 19, 1903, p. 2.

141. *IF,* June 28, 1902, p. 4.

142. *IF,* Sept. 16, 1905, p. 8.

143. Another traveling moving picture exhibitor, Reverend W. C. Williams, also knew Bacote; they served on boards together in Kansas City and were mentioned in the same society pages of the local black press. Williams, whose extensive activities in the AME Church matched that of his fellow Baptist moving picture exhibitors, traveled to Topeka, Kansas, with "one of the finest machines before the public" for a moving picture show at Saint John Church, Kansas. Afterward, in Quindara, Kansas, he presented a "moving picture lecture . . . under the auspices of the Improvement club of Allen Chapel," *Kansas City (KS) Advocate,* July 20, 1917, p. 1.

144. *WS,* Oct. 20, 1900, p. 2.

145. Exodusters were black migrants who left the South after the end of Reconstruction. For more on this topic, see Nell Irvin Painter, *Exodusters: Black Migration to Kansas after Reconstruction* (Lawrence: University Press of Kansas, 1986), 146; *Wichita National Baptist World,* Aug. 31, 1894, p. 2.

146. *Wichita Negro Star,* July 30, 1920, p. 1.

147. *WS,* Oct. 20, 1900, p. 2; *WS,* Nov. 17, 1900, p. 2; *WS,* Dec. 29, 1900, p. 4.

148. *WS,* Nov. 17, 1900, p. 2.

149. Ibid.

150. While riding on the Sante Fe Railroad, a group of "white cowboys" from Texas attempted to hang John E. Lewis. *WS,* Dec. 8, 1906, p. 4.

151. *WS,* May 8, 1909, p. 4; *WS,* Dec. 25, 1909, p. 1.

152. "The People's Forum," *AA,* July 16, 1910, p. 4.

153. Higginbotham, *Righteous Discontent,* 7.

154. Du Bois, *Efforts for Social Betterment,* 16; Du Bois, *Negro Church,* 38.

155. Louis H. Davenport was also a member of the Galilean Fishermen, a black fraternal order in Baltimore, Maryland. *Baltimore Commonwealth,* Aug. 7, 1915, p. 3. For Davenport's place of birth, see "L. H. Davenport," Bureau of the Census, Thirteenth Census of the United States, 1910, Records of the Bureau of the Census, Record Group 29, National Archives, Washington, DC, accessed on Ancestry.com, http://www.ancestrylibrary.com.

2. Cinema and the God-Given Right to Play

1. *Dallas Morning News,* Jan. 7, 1894, p. 11.

2. For example, white employers tried to extract free services from live-in domestic servants. Mamie Garvin Fields and Karen E. Fields, *Lemon Swamp and Other Places: A Carolina Memoir* (New York: Free Press Collier Macmillan, 1983); Steven Hahn, *A Nation under Our Feet: Black Political Struggles in the Rural South, from Slavery to the Great Migration* (Cambridge, MA: Harvard University Press, 2003); Eric Foner, *Nothing but Freedom: Emancipation and Its Legacy* (Baton Rouge: Louisiana State University Press, 1983).

3. *IF,* Sept. 16, 1905, p. 8; *IF,* Nov. 3, 1906, p. 6; *IF,* Mar. 30, 1907, p. 7; *IF,* Apr. 4, 1908, p. 1.

4. Jacqueline Stewart, "Discovering Black Film History: Tracing the Tyler, Texas Black Film Collection," *Film History* 23, no. 2 (2011): 147–173.

5. Historians such as Herbert Gutman have long considered the meaning of leisure, but in the 1980s, when a wave of British scholarship (particularly from the Birmingham School) crossed the Atlantic, leisure began to coalesce into a field of research. Bill Brown, *The Material Unconscious: American Amusement, Stephen Crane and the Economies of Play* (Cambridge, MA: Harvard University Press, 1996); Herbert G. Gutman, *Work, Culture, and Society in Industrializing America: Essays in American Working-Class and Social History* (New York: Knopf, 1976).

6. Just as historians have moved past the Ethnocultural School's limited definitions of class and culture to account for class formation as a "dynamic social relation, not just occupation or wealth," scholars of African American history must also account for the transitional articulations of racial identity that crystallized through leisure practices and institutions in the early twentieth century. Sean Wilentz, "On Class and Politics in Jacksonian America," *Reviews in American History* 10 (1982): 45–63.

7. Roy Rosenzweig, *Eight Hours for What We Will: Workers and Leisure in an Industrial City, 1870–1920* (Cambridge: Cambridge University Press, 1983).

8. Elizabeth Ewen, "City Lights: Immigrant Women and the Rise of the Movies," *Signs* 5, no. 3 (1980): s45–s66; Kathy Peiss, *Cheap Amusements: Working Women and Leisure in Turn-of-the-Century New York* (Philadelphia: Temple University Press, 1986); Joanne J. Meyerowitz, *Women Adrift: Independent Wage Earners in Chicago, 1880–1930* (Chicago: University of Chicago Press, 1988).

9. Robin D. G. Kelley, *Race Rebels: Culture, Politics, and the Black Working Class* (New York: Free Press, 1996), 1; David R. Roediger, *The Wages of Whiteness: Race and the Making of the American Working Class* (London: Verso, 1991); Eric Lott, *Love and Theft: Blackface Minstrelsy and the American Working Class* (New York: Oxford University Press, 1993).

10. Tera W. Hunter, *To 'Joy My Freedom: Southern Black Women's Lives and Labors after the Civil War* (Cambridge, MA: Harvard University Press, 1997).

11. For example, Anna Julia Cooper critiqued the "world's parasites, the shirks, the lazy lubbers who hang around rum shops" and argued that work must come first, but she still acknowledged the importance of well-earned leisure in vindicating the capabilities of the race. Anna J. Cooper, "A Voice from the South," in Charles Lemert and Esme Bhan, eds., *The Voice of Anna Julia Cooper* (Lanham, MD: Rowman and Littlefield, 1998), 176.

12. Of course, middle-class ideas of what constituted, for example, more "sensuous" behavior were subjective, and often hypocritical. W. E. B. Du Bois admonished the black working class, especially women, for their "loose" sexual behavior but visited prostitutes while he lived in Paris, and engaged in premarital and extramarital sex. *The Autobiography of W. E. B. DuBois: A Soliloquy on Viewing My Life from the Last Decade of Its First Century* (New York: International Publishers, 1968), p. 280.

13. *Dallas Morning News*, Jan. 7, 1894, p. 11.

14. *New York Herald*, May 8, 1885, p. 3; *Cleveland Plain Dealer* [hereafter *CP*], Dec. 29, 1885, p. 4.

15. Eric Foner, *Reconstruction: America's Unfinished Revolution, 1863–1877* (New York: Perennial Classics, 2002).

16. Historian Dylan Penningroth has indicated that black people wanted to own land in order to control their own time. If this is the case, then the shift to wage labor in the twentieth century was more of a tactical shift and less of a reconceptualization of goals. Dylan C. Penningroth, *The Claims of Kinfolk: African American Property and Community in the Nineteenth-Century South* (Chapel Hill: University of North Carolina Press, 2003), 49–54.

17. African Americans briefly worked as wage laborers after emancipation, but by 1880, most of the land in the South was leased to small farmers under the sharecropping system, which came to dominate rural agricultural production in the South after the Civil War. Hahn, *Nation under Our Feet,* 412; Steven Hahn, *The Roots of Southern Populism: Yeoman Farmers and the Transformation of the Georgia Upcountry, 1850–1890* (New York: Oxford University Press, 1983).

18. The demand for black domestics contributed to the disproportionally higher rate of black female urban migration in the region. Mary Ingram of Houston City, Ward 3, Harris in *Twelfth Census of the United States—1900,* Bureau of the Census, Schedule No. 1—Population, 1900; Julia Thompson of Tyler Ward 2, District 96 in *Twelfth Census of the United States—1900,* Bureau of the Census, Schedule No. 1—Population, 1900, Ancestry.com, http://www.ancestrylibrary.com.

19. Hunter, *To 'Joy My Freedom.*

20. Earl Lewis, "Expectations, Economic Opportunities, and Life in the Industrial Age: Black Migration to Norfolk, Virginia, 1910–1945," in Joe William Trotter Jr., ed., *The Great Migration in Historical Perspective: New Dimensions of Race, Class, and Gender* (Bloomington: Indiana University Press, 1991), 36; James R. Grossman, *Land of Hope: Chicago, Black Southerners, and the Great Migration* (Chicago: University of Chicago Press, 1989), 150.

21. Black workers and their employers, of course, clashed over hours, wages, and benefits. Eric Arnesen, *Waterfront Workers of New Orleans: Race, Class, and Politics, 1863–1923* (New York: Oxford University Press, 1991); Foner, *Nothing but Freedom;* Hunter, *To 'Joy My Freedom.*

22. W. E. B. Du Bois, "The Problem of Amusement," in *W. E. B. Du Bois on Sociology and the Black Community,* ed. Dan S. Green and Edwin D. Driver (Chicago: University of Chicago Press, 1980), 231. White employers resisted claims to independence with violence and strategies that revealed a disregard for the basic human needs of their black employees. "I am completely disgusted with negro house girls," a white hotel manager complained in Charlotte, North Carolina. Justifying the exploitation of his employees, he explained, "Give them plenty to eat and they are ready to lay off until hungry again." *Charlotte Observer,* July 7, 1898, p. 2.

23. Reprinted in *WS,* Oct. 26, 1901; originally in W. E. B. Du Bois, ed., *The Negro American Family,* The Atlanta University Publications, No. 13 (Atlanta: Atlanta University Press, 1908), 226.

24. W. E. B. Du Bois, ed., *The Negro Church* (Atlanta: Atlanta University Press, 1903), 59. When conducting his 1897 study of the Philadelphia Negro, Du Bois asked the poor, largely migrant population of Philadelphia's Seventh Ward: "Where do you get your amusements?" He found that "fully three-fourths could only answer, 'From the churches.' " Although some migrants may have hesitated before telling the twenty-eight-year-old Harvard-educated sociologist, with his prim and proper New England manners, of their more illicit pastimes, the growth of black church amusements at the turn of the century supports Du Bois's findings. W. E. B. Du Bois, *The Philadelphia Negro: A Social Study* (Philadelphia: University of Pennsylvania Press, 1899), 470; Du Bois, "Problem of Amusement," 228–229; Forrester B. Washington, "Recreational Facilities for the Negro," *Annals of the American Academy of Political and Social Science* 140 (1928): 272.

25. James Roland Coates Jr., "Recreation and Sport in the African-American Community of Baltimore, 1890–1920" (PhD diss., University of Maryland, College Park, 1991), 60; Brian E. Alnutt, "The Negro Excursions: Recreational Outings among Philadelphia African Americans, 1876–1926," *Pennsylvania Magazine of History and Biography* 129, no. 1 (2005): 84.

26. Popular dances in 1901. Jean Stearns and Marshall Stearns, *Jazz Dance: The Story of American Vernacular Dance* ([1968] New York: Da Capo Press, 1994), 24.

27. Du Bois, *Philadelphia Negro,* 319.

28. Hunter, *To 'Joy My Freedom.*

29. "It Takes a Hold on Hell!," *IF,* Mar. 3, 1894, p. 3; "Great Men at Play," *Wichita National Baptist World,* Oct. 19, 1894, p. 7; *AT,* July 30, 1903, p. 6.

30. Earl Lewis, "Expectations, Economic Opportunities, and Life in the Industrial Age Migration to Norfolk, Virginia, 910–1945," 36; Grossman, *Land of Hope,* 150; Du Bois, "Problem of Amusement," 227.

31. Du Bois also noted "in one ward of Philadelphia young people between the ages of sixteen and thirty form over a third of the population"; Du Bois, "Problem of Amusement," 227.

32. "Save the Youngsters!," *TP,* Sept. 8, 1905, p. 1.

33. Ibid; *American Citizen,* Aug. 20, 1897, p. 1.

34. "The Common Welfare," in *Charities and the Commons,* April 1908–October 1908, vol. 20 (New York: Charity Organization Society, 1908), 479.

35. Respondent from Alabama to Atlanta University's survey "Morals and Manners among Negro Americans," in W. E. B. Du Bois and Augustus Granvile Dill, eds., *Morals and Manners among Negro Americans,* The Atlanta University Publications, no. 18 (Atlanta: Atlanta University Press, 1914), 91.

36. The delegates of the Ninth Atlanta Conference blamed what they perceived as moral laxity on disruptions inherent to the "transition stage between slavery and freedom. Such a period of change [i]nvolves physical strain, mental bewilderment and moral weakeness," which produce criminality; W. E. B. Du Bois, ed., *Some Notes on Negro Crime, Particularly in Georgia; Report of a Social Study Made under the Direction of Atlanta University; Together with the Proceedings of the Ninth Conference for the Study of the Negro Problems, Held at Atlanta University, May 24, 1904* (Atlanta: Atlanta University Press, 1904); *American Citizen,* Aug. 20, 1897, p. 1.

37. Frank Lincoln Mather, ed., *Who's Who of the Colored Race: A General Biographical Dictionary of Men and Women of African Descent* (Chicago: University of Michigan, 1915).

38. Du Bois and Dill, *Morals and Manners among Negro Americans,* 92.

39. Isabel Eaton, "A Special Report on Domestic Service," in W. E. B. Du Bois, *The Philadelphia Negro: A Social Study* (Philadelphia: University of Pennsylvania Press, 1899), 470.

40. The AMEZ's Christian Education Department (CED) was formed in 1887. Sandy Dwayne Martin, *Black Baptists and African Missions: The Origins of a Movement, 1880–1915* (Macon, GA: Mercer, 1989), 166.

41. *Wichita National Baptist World,* Oct. 19, 1894, p. 4; *IF,* Jan. 11, 1902, p. 8; *ST,* Feb. 8, 1908, p. 4.

42. Black church leaders were not alone in their concerns. White churches also became preoccupied in the late nineteenth century with the conundrum of attracting young people to their churches. Like black churches, they believed they were in competition with the secular distractions of city life for the attention of wage-earning youth. In response, the interracial National Baptist Young People's Union was formed to attract young adherents to the faith, but it repeatedly excluded blacks from its ranks.

43. *AA,* Nov. 16, 1907, p. 8; *AA,* Nov. 30, 1907, p. 8; *AA,* Dec. 7, 1907, p. 8.

44. Popular dances of the day.

45. *TP,* Oct. 5, 1906, p. 5. St. Chrysostom's quote about dancing was printed in the black newspaper, *Wichita National Baptist World,* Oct. 12, 1894, p. 6.

46. Thomas County responded to a survey conducted by Atlanta University. The respondent's gender is not identified in the publication. Du Bois, *Negro Church,* 64.

47. Ibid.

48. David Nasaw, *Going Out: The Rise and Fall of Public Amusements* (New York: Basic Books, 1993). For a description of the formation of white working-class identity and leisure, see Roediger, *Wages of Whiteness;* Lott, *Love and Theft;* and Matthew Frye Jacobson, *Whiteness of a Different Color: European Immigrants and the Alchemy of Race* (Cambridge, MA: Harvard University Press, 1998). Lott, for example, argues that blackface in the nineteenth century was a cipher for expressing anxieties and desires for the newly formed white working class. Eric Arnesen, Herbert Gutman, and Daniel Letwin's work challenges the degree to which whites accepted difference as a "wage." Eric Arnesen, "Whiteness and the Historians' Imagination," *International Labor and Working-Class History* 60 (2001): 3–32; Gutman, *Work, Culture, and Society in Industrializing America;* Daniel Letwin, "Interracial Unionism, Gender, and 'Social Equality' in the Alabama Coalfields, 1878–1908," *Journal of Southern History* 61, no. 3 (1995): 519–554.

49. For examples of raids, see *AT,* Mar. 16, 1908, p. 1; *Los Angeles Times,* Oct. 1, 1905, p. 16.

50. *Washington Post,* Apr. 8, 1901, p. 2; *St. Louis Republic,* May 15, 1898, p. 8.

51. *Baltimore Sun,* Mar. 10, 1904, p. 2.

52. *Chicago Tribune,* Feb. 28, 1906, p. 1.

53. David Fort Godshalk, *Veiled Visions: The 1906 Atlanta Race Riot and the Reshaping of American Race Relations* (Chapel Hill: University of North Carolina Press, 2005), 35–37.

54. Robert Sklar, *Movie-Made America: A Social History of American Movies* (New York: Random House, 1975); Steven J. Ross, *Working-Class Hollywood: Silent Film*

and the Shaping of Class in America (Princeton, NJ: Princeton University Press, 1998). Benjamin Singer and other film historians have debated whether the audiences for early films were *primarily* from the working class. For more on this debate, see Robert C. Allen, "Manhattan Nickelodeons: New Data on Audiences and Exhibitors," *Cinema Journal* 34, no. 3 (1995): 5–35; Robert C. Allen, "Manhattan Myopia; or, Oh! Iowa! Robert C. Allen on Ben Singer's 'Manhattan Nickelodeons: New Data on Audiences and Exhibitors,'" *Cinema Journal* 35, no. 3 (1996): 75–103; Ben Singer, "New York, Just like I Pictured It: Ben Singer Responds," *Cinema Journal* 35, no. 3 (1996): 104–128.

55. Gaines Chapel (Savannah, GA); the Willowtree "Negro Church" (Atlanta, GA); Burns Chapel (Sedalia, MO); and the Bethlehem Baptist Church (Savannah, GA) all cost ten cents. *ST,* Oct. 15, 1904, p. 3; *AT,* Apr. 21, 1904, p. 2; *Sedalia Weekly Conservator,* Dec. 2, 1904, p. 4; *ST,* Feb. 8, 1908, p. 4.

56. While not as cheap as moving pictures would eventually become, church film exhibitions cost less than most theater performances, which usually ranged from twenty cents to a few dollars. Also, white arcades and theaters, especially after the rise of the nickelodeon, offered cheap amusements, but black patrons were frequently turned away, limited to midnight screenings, or sent to the "buzzard's roost."

57. Although the small coastal lumber town was not certifiably urban in size, Darien had a railroad depot and a large, concentrated population of wage workers. "Letter from Darien," *ST,* Apr. 11, 1896, p. 3; advertisement in *ST,* Jan. 28, 1899, p. 1; W. Fitzhugh Brundage, "The Darien 'Insurrection' of 1899: Black Protest during the Nadir of Race Relations," *Georgia Historical Quarterly* 74, no. 2 (Summer 1990): 234–253.

58. These films appear to be *Martyrs chrétiens: Daniel dans la fosse aux lions* [Christian Martyrs: Daniel in the Lion's Den] and *Martyrs chrétiens: Le festin de Balthazar* [Belshazzar's Feast].

59. *IF,* Apr. 21, 1906, p. 5.

60. *Vindicator,* Oct. 20, 1905, p. 1.

61. *AT,* Apr. 21, 1904, p. 2.

62. "Notes from Hawk's Moving Pictures," *IF,* Feb. 10, 1906, p. 5.

63. "It Takes a Hold on Hell!," *IF,* Mar. 3, 1894, p. 3; "Great Men at Play," *Wichita National Baptist World,* Oct. 19, 1894, p. 7.

64. Robert A. McGuinn, *The Race Problem in the Churches* (Baltimore, MD: Printing office of J. F. Weishampel, 1890), 41–42.

65. *American Citizen,* Aug. 20, 1897, p. 1.

66. *IF,* July 25, 1903, p. 1.

67. *NYA,* Jan. 20, 1910, p. 6.

68. *TP,* Oct. 5, 1906, p. 5; *WS,* Mar. 19, 1910, p. 1.

69. For example, an advertisement in the *Topeka Plaindealer* sought "A reliable man . . . minister preferred; to take half interest in a motion picture exhibition." *TP,* Sept. 24, 1909, p. 3.

70. *CC,* Aug. 29, 1903, p. 2; *TP,* Oct. 4, 1912, p. 4; *Pittsburgh Courier,* Feb. 3, 1912, p. 4; *Pittsburgh Courier,* Sept. 13, 1912, p. 3; *Philadelphia Tribune,* Sept. 28, 1912, p. 5.

71. Advertisement in the *WB,* Apr. 19, 1909, p. 5.

72. *CA,* Nov. 7, 1903, p. 16.

73. *AA,* Dec. 2, 1911, p. 5; *AA,* Dec. 9, 1911, p. 5; *AA,* Dec. 16, 1911, p. 5; *CA,* Nov. 14, 1903, p. 16; *IF,* June 17, 1911, p. 10.

74. *Leavenworth Herald,* Aug. 31, 1895, p. 3; *CG,* Nov. 16, 1895, p. 2.

75. *CG,* Nov. 16, 1895, p. 2; *Winston-Salem Journal,* Oct. 31, 1898, p. 4.

76. *Vindicator,* Jan. 6, 1905, p. 4.

77. "Monzarro, the 'Fake' African Prince," originally in the New Orleans *Southwestern Christian Advocate,* reprinted in *CG,* Dec. 7, 1895, p. 3.

78. Du Bois, *Negro Church,* 260.

79. *IF,* Jan. 14, 1905, p. 5.

80. *IF,* May 27, 1911, p. 1; *AA,* May 15, 1909, p. 6.

81. See Charles Musser's description of cinema and modernity in Charles Musser, *The Emergence of Cinema: The American Screen to 1907* (Berkeley: University of California Press, 1990); Charles Musser, "Before the Rapid Firing Kinetograph: Edison Film Production, Representation and Exploitation in the 1890s," in *Edison Motion Pictures, 1890–1906: An Annotated Filmography* (Washington, DC: Smithsonian Institution Press, 1997), 19–50, 187–189.

82. Announcements by black churches described film exhibitions as so lifelike, there were "instances in which the spectators forget the object before them is only a picture and sometimes start with a rush to find a place of safety out of the way," *CA,* Oct. 14, 1899, p. 8.

83. Lynne Kirby describes the similarities and interconnected development of railroads and modern cinema. Lynne Kirby, *Parallel Tracks: The Railroad and Silent Cinema* (Durham, NC: Duke University Press, 1997).

84. *ST,* Feb. 3, 1906, p. 5.

85. *CG,* Nov. 26, 1904, p. 4.

86. *AA,* Sept. 25, 1909, p. 8; *AA,* Feb. 19, 1910, p. 5; *AA* Feb. 12, 1910, p. 5; *AA,* Oct. 15, 1910, p. 5; *AA,* Nov. 2, 1912, p. 5; *IF,* May 27, 1911, p. 1; *Baltimore Sun,* Aug. 30, 1908, p. 5; *Charlotte Observer,* Aug. 30, 1908, p. 1; *CP,* Aug. 27, 1908, p. 1.

87. *RP,* Sept. 22, 1906, p. 1.

88. *St. Louis Palladium,* Dec. 10, 1904, p. 1.

89. Andrea Dennett has argued that dime museums "merely reaffirmed" preexisting ideas of black inferiority, but her evidence, including the exclusion of black images from the depictions of the Civil War in dime museums, supports the arguments of David Nasaw and Kirk Savage, who see a democratization of white popular culture occur at the turn of the century at the expense of black Americans. Andrea Dennett, *Weird and Wonderful: The Dime Museum in America* (New York: New York University Press, 1997), p. 146; Nasaw, *Going Out;* Kirk Savage, *Standing Soldiers,*

Kneeling Slaves: Race, War, and Monument in Nineteenth-Century America (Princeton, NJ: Princeton University Press, 1997).

90. *IF,* Jan. 21, 1905, p. 5; *IF,* May 6, 1905, p. 5.

91. *IF,* Feb. 4, 1905, p. 5.

92. *RP,* May 28, 1904, p. 1.

93. *IF,* Jun. 17, 1905, p. 6.

94. *TP,* Sept. 30, 1904, p. 2. Such celebrations, of course, overlooked Japan's own imperial ambitions. *IF,* Jan. 7, 1905, p. 4; *St. Paul Appeal,* Feb. 20, 1904, p. 2.

95. *IF,* Feb. 4, 1905, p. 5.

96. *ST,* Aug. 5, 1905, p. 2.

97. Shawn Michelle Smith, *Photography on the Color Line: W. E. B. Du Bois, Race, and Visual Culture* (Durham, NC: Duke University Press, 2004), 113–145; Dora Apel, *Imagery of Lynching: Black Men, White Women, and the Mob* (New Brunswick, NJ: Rutgers University Press, 2004), 7–45; Amy Louise Wood, *Lynching and Spectacle: Witnessing Racial Violence in America, 1890–1940* (Chapel Hill: University of North Carolina, 2009), 113–145.

98. *CA,* Oct. 14, 1899, p. 8.

99. Donald Bogle, *Toms, Coons, Mulattoes, Mammies, and Bucks: An Interpretive History of Blacks in American Films* (New York: Viking Press, 1973); Daniel J. Leab, "All-Colored but Not Much Different: Films Made for Negro Ghetto Audiences, 1913–1928," *Phylon* 36, no. 3 (1975): 321–339; Ed Guerrero, *Framing Blackness: The African American Image in Film* (Philadelphia: Temple University Press, 1993).

100. Michael Rogin, *Blackface, White Noise: Jewish Immigrants in the Hollywood Melting Pot* (Berkeley: University of California Press, 1998); Rob King, *The Fun Factory: The Keystone Film Company and the Emergence of Mass Culture* (Berkeley: University of California Press, 2009), 68–72.

101. See for example, "Not a Safe Place," *ST,* Dec. 5, 1908, p. 6.

102. Kevin Gaines has argued that it was the black middle class, rather than the working class, that was invested in protesting images of racial representation at the turn of the century. Kevin Gaines, *Uplifting the Race: Black Leadership, Politics, and Culture in the Twentieth Century* (Chapel Hill: University of North Carolina Press, 1996).

103. Eileen Bowser, *The Transformation of Cinema, 1907–1915* (Berkeley: University of California Press, 1990), 22.

104. It is unclear if "pumpkins" were used because there were no watermelons available, but Lubin approved of the film nonetheless. Joseph P. Eckhardt, *The King of the Movies: Film Pioneer Siegmund Lubin* (London: Fairleigh Dickinson University Press, 1997), 51.

105. Thomas Cripps, *Slow Fade to Black: The Negro in American Film, 1900–1942* ([1977] New York: Oxford University Press, 1993), 115.

106. A 1988 issue of the British journal *Screen* played an important role in initiating this dialogue. Jane Gaines's essay "White Privilege and Looking Relations: Race

and Gender in Feminist Film Theory" showed how race was rendered invisible in the debates over female spectatorship. Jane Gaines demonstrated how Laura Mulvey's seminal theory of film spectatorship, which argued that the filmgoer identified with the patriarchal male protagonist in Hollywood films, failed to account for the racial identity of black male spectators. Jane Gaines, "White Privilege and Looking Relations: Race and Gender in Feminist Film Theory," *Cultural Critique* 4 (1986): 59–79. In 1993, Manthia Diawara edited the seminal anthology *Black American Cinema,* which attempted to bring the diverse strands of black cinema studies into conversation with each other. Diawara's own essay examined how African Americans formed "spectatorial resistance" to films such as *The Birth of a Nation.* For American audiences of Hollywood movies, Manthia Diawara pointed out, "the dominant cinema situates Black characters primarily for the pleasure of White spectators (male or female)." Manthia Diawara, "Black Spectatorship: Problems of Identification and Resistance," in Manthia Diawara, ed., *Black American Cinema* (New York: Routledge, 1993), 211–220.

107. For example, see *ST,* July 27, 1901, p. 2; *ST,* Jan. 25, 1902, p. 3; *ST,* Mar. 7, 1903, p. 2.

108. On January 27, 1902, the church advertised a "high class moving picture exhibition" in a spectacular show with "three big entertainments in one. Come out and hear for yourself. It had the latest improved machine on the road. Admission only 10 cents." *ST,* Jan. 25, 1902, p. 3.

109. *ST,* Jan. 25, 1902, p. 3; *ST,* Apr. 26, 1902, p. 2.

110. *ST,* Apr. 26, 1902, p. 2.

111. "News of the Week," *TP,* May 26, 1905, p. 5.

112. *IF,* Jan. 15, 1910, p. 6. Segregated theaters, fairs, and traveling road shows brought other opportunities to see performances, but black churches and uplift organizations were the most frequent sites in which all-black audiences consumed moving pictures until 1907.

113. *IF,* June 28, 1902, p. 4; *RP,* May 28, 1904, p. 1; *ST,* Apr. 26, 1902, p. 2.

114. *American Citizen,* May 18, 1906, p. 1.

115. *AA,* Oct. 8, 1910, p. 5.

116. "Notes from Hawk's Moving Pictures, Jacksonville, F[l]a.," *IF,* Apr. 8, 1905, p. 5.

117. Mather, *Who's Who of the Colored Race,* 182.

118. *WB,* June 22, 1907, p. 5.

119. *TP,* Oct. 5, 1906, p. 4.

120. For more on visual culture and advertising, see Stuart Ewen, *Captains of Consciousness: Advertising and the Social Roots of the Consumer Culture* ([1976] New York: McGraw-Hill, 2001); Roland Marchand, *Advertising the American Dream: Making Way for Modernity, 1920–1940* (Berkeley: University of California Press, 1985); William Leach, *Land of Desire: Merchants, Power, and the Rise of a New American Culture* (New York: Pantheon Books, 1993).

121. Ewen, *Captains of Consciousness,* 24–25.

122. *TP,* Oct. 5, 1906, p. 5.

123. Royston introduced tamales, still a local delicacy, to Knoxville, Tennessee. *IF,* Feb. 24, 1906, p. 5.

124. *IF,* Feb. 11, 1905, p. 5.

125. "Notes from Hawk's Moving Pictures, Jacksonville, F[l]a.," *IF,* Apr. 8, 1905, p. 5.

126. *TP,* Mar. 8, 1901, p. 1; *CC,* Aug. 29, 1903, p. 2; *Kansas Headlight,* Sept. 14, 1894, p. 2. H. Charles Pope also updated the black press with news of his exhibitions. *CA,* Nov. 10, 1900, p. 11.

127. *IF,* Mar. 25, 1905, p. 5.

128. *IF,* Apr. 21, 1906, p. 5.

129. *TP,* Mar. 8, 1901, p. 1; *CC,* Aug. 29, 1903, p. 5; *WB,* Aug. 31, 1907, p. 5; *IF,* Jan. 29, 1910, p. 6.

130. *IF,* Jan. 29, 1910, p. 6; *George P. Johnson Negro Film Collection, 1916–1977* (microfilm, 12 reels, University of California, Los Angeles Library, Photographic Department, 1974), reel 7.

131. Sharecropping families were also expected to perform services for their white landlords. For example, Du Bois described a black family from Farmville, Virginia, whose members were expected to drop whatever they were doing at any time of day when the white landlord rang a bell, at which time they were supposed to help him. Du Bois, "The Negroes of Farmville, Virginia," in *W. E. B. Du Bois on Sociology and the Black Community,* ed. Dan S. Green and Edwin D. Driver (Chicago: University of Chicago Press, 1980), 207.

132. In both strikes, workers demanded a ten-hour day. Roger Wallace Shugg, "The New Orleans General Strike of 1892," *Louisiana Historical Quarterly* 21, no. 2 (1938): 547–560; Daniel Rosenberg, *New Orleans Dockworkers: Race, Labor, and Unionism, 1892–1923* (Albany: State University of New York Press, 1988); Paul Ortiz, *Emancipation Betrayed: The Hidden History of Black Organizing and White Violence in Florida from Reconstruction to the Bloody Election of 1920* (Berkeley: University of California Press, 2005). See also *Governor Fleming to E. M. Montgomery, Jan 22, 1890,* Florida Governor's Letterbooks, Florida State Archives; "Riotous Negro Strikers in Florida," *New York Daily Tribune,* Jan. 22, 1890; "Riotous Blacks," Pensacola *Daily News,* Jan. 22, 1890.

133. Touré F. Reed, *Not Alms but Opportunity: The Urban League and the Politics of Racial Uplift, 1910–1950;* Kelley, *Race Rebels;* Kimberley L. Phillips, *AlabamaNorth: African-American Migrants, Community, and Working-Class Activism in Cleveland, 1915–45* (Urbana: University of Illinois Press, 1999).

134. Du Bois, "Problem of Amusement"; *Michigan Plaindealer,* Dec. 4, 1891, p. 4.

135. *Moving Picture World,* June 8, 1907, p. 216; W. D. Weatherford, *Negro Life in the South* (New York: Young Men's Christian Association Press, 1910), 139.

3. Colored Theaters in the Jim Crow City

1. *Tenth Census of the United States—1880,* Bureau of the Census, Schedule No. 1—Inhabitants, 1880, Ancestry.com, http://www.ancestrylibrary.com; *Thirteenth Census of the United States: 1910—Population,* U.S. Department of Commerce and Labor, Bureau of the Census, 1910, Ancestry.com, http://www.ancestrylibrary.com; *IF,* Sept. 19, 1908, p. 5; *IF,* Oct. 17, 1908, p. 5; *IF,* Sept. 19, 1908, p. 5.

2. Monroe N. Work, *Negro Year Book and Annual Encyclopedia of the Negro* (Tuskegee, AL: Tuskegee Normal and Industrial Institute, 1912), 24.

3. Commercial moving picture exhibition was still a risky venture; some of these theaters closed shortly after they opened. A moving picture theater on Cedar Street in Nashville, Tennessee, for example, survived for only ten days before it had to close its doors, *CG,* Mar. 4, 1911, p. 2; Truman Kella Gibson exhibited in Maryland, Virginia, and North Carolina for a short six months in 1908 before giving up on the industry. Frank Lincoln Mather, ed., *Who's Who of the Colored Race: A General Biographical Dictionary of Men and Women of African Descent* (Chicago: University of Michigan, 1915), 115.

4. The Lincoln Theater seems to have replaced the Thirteenth Street/New Pekin Theater at the Odd Fellows Hall in August 1909. The Lincoln featured one-act plays and moving pictures, and may have later moved down the street to Walnut and Main streets (*IF,* Aug. 7, 1909, p. 1). Taft's Amusement Company, which showed "polite vaudeville and moving pictures," took over a space in the Odd Fellows Hall in December 1909, naming it the Taft Theatre (*IF,* Dec. 18, 1909, p. 5), and Joseph Clarke's Walnut Street Park Theatre (1912) was a block away (*IF,* July 31, 1909, p. 11). The Lyre featured vaudeville and "high-class feature films" (*IF,* Aug. 20, 1910, p. 5), the Olio promised "everything that there is in the moving picture world" (*IF,* Feb. 14, 1914, p. 4), and the Ruby was opened by the powerful theater owner S. H. Dudley (*IF,* Dec. 20, 1913, p. 4).

5. Juliet E. K. Walker, *The History of Black Business in America: Capitalism, Race, Entrepreneurship* (New York: MacMillan Library Reference USA, 1998).

6. On the black beauty industry, see Kathy Peiss, *Hope in a Jar: The Making of America's Beauty Culture* (New York: Metropolitan Books, 1998); Susannah Walker, *Style and Status: Selling Beauty to African American Women, 1920–1975* (Lexington: University Press of Kentucky, 2007). On black insurance companies, see Robert C. Puth, "Supreme Life: The History of a Negro Life Insurance Company, 1919–1962," *Business History Review* 43, no. 1 (1969): 1–20; Alexa Benson Henderson, *Atlanta Life Insurance Company: Guardian of Black Economic Dignity* (Tuscaloosa: University of Alabama Press, 1990); R. E. Weems, "A Crumbling Legacy: The Decline of African American Insurance Companies in Contemporary America," *Review of Black Political Economy* 23, no. 2 (1994): 25–37. On shipping, see Michelle Ann Stephens, *Black Empire: The Masculine Global Imaginary of Caribbean Intellectuals in the United*

States, 1914–1962 (Durham, NC: Duke University Press, 2005); Ramla M. Bandele, *Black Star: African American Activism in the International Political Economy* (Urbana: University of Illinois Press, 2008). There are numerous studies of the black music industry and the black press. A few examples include Tim Brooks and Richard K. Spottswood, *Lost Sounds: Blacks and the Birth of the Recording Industry, 1890–1919* (Urbana: University of Illinois Press, 2004); R. A. Lawson, *Jim Crow's Counterculture: The Blues and Black Southerners, 1890–1945* (Baton Rouge: Louisiana State University Press, 2010); Henry Lewis Suggs, *The Black Press in the South, 1865–1979* (Westport, CT: Greenwood Press, 1983); Armistead Scott Pride and Clint C. Wilson, *A History of the Black Press* (Washington, DC: Howard University Press, 1997).

7. Colored theaters are defined here as black-operated theaters that catered primarily to black patrons.

8. Although white churches also hosted moving pictures, commercial venues vastly outnumbered white church exhibitions. Seating for blacks in white theaters was limited—galleries reserved for black patrons were disproportionally smaller than those reserved for whites. At other times, blacks were prohibited from participating in commercial amusements at the same time as whites.

9. Loren Schweninger, *Black Property Owners in the South, 1790–1915* (Urbana: University of Illinois Press, 1990); Walker, *History of Black Business in America;* Robert C. Kenzer, *Enterprising Southerners: Black Economic Success in North Carolina, 1865–1915* (Charlottesville: University Press of Virginia, 1997); Walter B. Weare, *Black Business in the New South: A Social History of the North Carolina Mutual Life Insurance Company* (Urbana: University of Illinois Press, 1973).

10. Ida B. Wells, *Southern Horrors: Lynch Law in All Its Phases* (New York: New York Age Print, 1892), ch. 4.

11. These binary categories limit more than just our understanding of the black experience. As Kathleen Franz has pointed out, they limit our understanding of modern consumerism in general. Kathleen Franz, "Producing Consumers," *American Quarterly* 58, no. 4 (December 2006): 1229–1230. Also see Michel de Certeau's description of tactics in Michel de Certeau, *The Practice of Everyday Life,* trans. Steven Rendall (Berkeley: University of California Press, 1984).

12. Terry Ramsaye, *A Million and One Nights: A History of the Motion Picture through 1925* (New York: Simon and Schuster, 1926), 264; Garth Jowett, *Film: The Democratic Art* (Boston: Little, Brown, 1976), 29; Charles Musser, "Another Look at the 'Chaser Theory,'" *Studies in Visual Communication* 10, no. 4 (Fall 1984): 37–41.

Robert C. Allen disagreed with the "chaser theory." See Robert C. Allen, "Contra the Chase Theory," in John L. Fell, ed., *Film before Griffith* (Berkeley: University of California Press, 1983), 105–115.

13. "Storefront picture shows continued to operate [between 1900 and 1903], particularly in the Far West, but only for short periods." Charles Musser, *The Emergence*

of Cinema: The American Screen to 1907 (Berkeley: University of California Press, 1990), 303.

14. In the later nickelodeon period, white theaters with limited resources turned to these strategies to differentiate their programs, too. Rick Altman, *Silent Film Sound* (New York: Columbia University Press, 2004), 124.

15. It was impractical and financially unsustainable for most itinerants to support the large numbers of live performers that were common at white vaudeville theaters. This was especially so in the Jim Crow South, and in the absence of a consolidated circuit of exhibition venues. Although black itinerants performed in multiple churches or lodges during each stop, their programs appeared once or twice at a single venue, rather than continuously throughout the day.

16. Charles Musser and Carol Nelson, *High-Class Moving Pictures: Lyman H. Howe and the Forgotten Era of Traveling Exhibition, 1880–1920* (Princeton, NJ: Princeton University Press, 1991).

17. *St. Louis Palladium,* Dec. 10, 1904, p. 1.

18. *National Review,* Oct. 25, 1913, p. 1; *St. Louis Palladium,* Dec. 10, 1904, p. 1.

19. White traveling exhibitions in commercial venues also reached an all-time low during this period. Musser, *Emergence of Cinema,* 299.

20. Ibid., 365–368.

21. Film historians generally periodize the "nickelodeon period" from 1905 or 1906 to 1914. Russell Merritt, "The Nickelodeon Theater, 1905–1914: Building an Audience for the Movies," in Ina Rae Hark, ed., *Exhibition, the Film Reader* (London: Routledge, 2002).

22. Before this time, theater managers segregated black patrons based on race, but at times this policy might be erratically and unevenly enforced. David Nasaw, *Going Out: The Rise and Fall of Public Amusements* (New York: Basic Books, 1993), 47–49.

23. *National Review,* Oct. 25, 1913, p. 1.

24. F. H. Richardson, *Motion Picture Handbook: A Guide for Managers and Operators of Motion Picture Theaters* (New York: The Moving Picture World, 1910), 160. Richardson's text was first published in 1908 and quickly became a widely read authority on operating movie theaters. Richardson's book was published in several editions into the 1940s.

25. Nasaw, *Going Out;* Mary Carbine, "The Finest Outside the Loop" in Philip Simpson, Andrew Utterson, and K. J. Shepherdson, eds., *Film Theory: Critical Concepts in Media and Cultural Studies* (New York: Routledge, 2003); Alison Griffiths and James Latham, "Film and Ethnic Identity in Harlem, 1896–1915," in Melvyn Stokes and Richard Maltby, eds., *American Movie Audiences: From the Turn of the Century to the Early Sound Era* (London: British Film Institute, 1999), 46–63; Charlene Regester, "From the Buzzard's Roost: Black Movie-Going in Durham and Other North Carolina Cities during the Early Period of American Cinema," *Film History* 17 (2005): 113–124; Gregory A. Waller, *Main Street Amusements: Movies and*

Commercial Entertainment in a Southern City, 1896–1930 (Washington, DC: Smithsonian Institution Press, 1995); Gregory A. Waller, "Another Audience: Black Moviegoing, 1907–16," *Cinema Journal* 31, no. 2 (1992): 3–25; Douglas Gomery, "The Two Public Spaces of a Moviegoing Capital: Race and the History of Film Exhibition in Washington, D.C.," *Spectator* 18, no. 2 (1998): 8–17.

26. Theaters in the North practiced racial segregation before the nickelodeon period, but it was during this time that these policies were standardized.

27. Frank Uriah Quillin, *The Color Line in Ohio* (Ann Arbor, MI: G. Wahr, 1913), 111.

28. Heralding these changes was the nation's first blockbuster film, *The Birth of a Nation.* The triumphant story of white brotherhood not only suppressed the memory of slavery as a "forgotten quarrel" of the Civil War, it also precluded the possibility of black participation in the creation of a new nation. White spectators watched the film in segregated spaces that reinforced the on-screen narrative; the lucrative "democratization" of white cross-class leisure had simultaneously relegated black people to the periphery of white movie theaters. By 1929, when three-fourths of the American population attended the movies weekly, most patrons were escorted to their seats by Jim Crow. For more on the reconciliation of the North and South, see David W. Blight, *Race and Reunion: The Civil War in American Memory* (Cambridge, MA: Belknap Press of Harvard University Press, 2001). For more on race, early film, and American popular culture, see Daniel Bernardi, ed., *The Birth of Whiteness: Race and the Emergence of U.S. Cinema* (New Brunswick, NJ: Rutgers University Press, 1996), 1–11. For weekly attendance races, see F. Andrew Hanssen, "Revenue Sharing and the Coming of Sound," in John Sedgwick and Michael Pokorny, eds., *An Economic History of Film* (New York: Routledge, 2005), 92.

29. *Montgomery Advertiser,* May 4, 1905, p. 10.

30. "Unofficial 'Jim Crow' Laws," *Montgomery Advertiser,* Mar. 22, 1904, p. 4.

31. Film scholars and historians have argued that segregation in theaters and racial characterizations of blackness on-screen invited ethnic white immigrants to partake in the social and cultural benefits of being white. Eric Lott, *Love and Theft: Blackface Minstrelsy and the American Working Class* (New York: Oxford University Press, 1993); Michael Rogin, *Blackface, White Noise: Jewish Immigrants in the Hollywood Melting Pot* (Berkeley: University of California Press, 1998); Bernardi, *Birth of Whiteness.*

32. *WB,* Mar. 21, 1908, p. 3.

33. "One Cent Damages for Ejecting a Negro," *Boston Journal,* Nov. 22, 1900, p. 1. Also see Quillin, *Color Line in Ohio.*

34. Letter to Sidney Bieber, Chairman of the Election Committee, Washington, D.C., "The New Ticket-Bieber and 'Jim-Crowism,'" *WB,* Mar. 21, 1908, p. 1.

35. *WB,* May 2, 1908, p. 4.

36. Ibid; *WB,* Nov. 4, 1911, p. 4; *BA,* Nov. 11, 1911, p. 2; *WB,* Feb. 10, 1912, p. 4.

37. *WB,* Feb. 10, 1912, p. 4.

38. William Howland Kenney III, "The Influence of Black Vaudeville on Early Jazz," *The Black Perspective in Music* 14, no. 3 (1986): 233.

39. Bridging both the spirit of uplift reform and commerce, colored fairs, which celebrated self-sufficiency through business enterprise, also hosted motion picture exhibitions. These events lasted anywhere from a few days to a few weeks, bringing together black people for pleasure and business opportunities. The theaters built and promoted by members of uplift reform and fraternal organizations were more explicitly commercial. Most frequently, church and uplift reform organizations sponsored motion picture shows, but the medium was also integrated into other black amusement ventures. Individuals and companies organized excursions outside the city such as the Twilight Social Club's Annual Picnic and Moving Picture Panorama to Bloemeck's Grove in Missouri, or the "Moonlight Excursion" from Savannah to Springfield; *St. Louis Palladium,* June 24, 1905, p. 1 (announcements also in *St. Louis Palladium,* July 1 and 8, 1905, issues); "Moonlight Excursion," *ST,* May 1, 1909, p. 5.

40. Theda Skocpol and Jennifer Lynn Oser, "Organization Despite Adversity: The Origins and Development of African American Fraternal Associations," *Social Science History* 28, no. 3 (2004): 387.

41. For the history of black fraternal organizations in Louisville, see the excellent study by George C. Wright, *Life behind a Veil: Blacks in Louisville, Kentucky* (Baton Rouge: Louisiana State University Press, 1985), 132–134.

42. Also John E. Lewis belonged to the Knights of Pythias; *WS,* Dec. 8, 1906, p. 4; Samuel Bacote was a high-ranking (32-degree) Mason; Mather, *Who's Who of the Colored Race,* 15; *IF,* July 27, 1912, p. 8; *IF,* Sept. 7, 1912, p. 4; "Sanborn Insurance Maps of Rocky Mount, Nash and Edgecombe Counties, North Carolina, August 1917," North Carolina Collection, Wilson Library, University of North Carolina, Chapel Hill; Julius Cahn and Gus Hill, *The Julius Cahn–Gus Hill Theatrical Guide and Moving Picture Directory Supplement* (Orange, NJ: Chronicle, 1922), 118–134; Monroe N. Work, *Negro Year Book: An Annual Encyclopedia of the Negro 1921–1922* (Tuskegee, AL: Negro Year Book Publishing Company, Tuskegee Institute, 1922), 305.

43. "Knights of Pythias at Columbia, MO," *IF,* Apr. 19, 1913, p. 8; *AA,* May 15, 1909, p. 6; *IF,* Apr. 4, 1908, p. 1; Cahn and Hill, *Julius Cahn–Gus Hill Theatrical Guide,* 135.

44. Prince Hall Freemason, Dickson Lodge no. 11: *CD,* Jan. 21, 1911, p. 3; *CD,* Sept. 9, 1911, p. 8.

45. Work, *Negro Year Book,* 309; Cahn and Hill, *Julius Cahn-Gus Hill Theatrical Guide,* 135; *AA,* May 15, 1909, p. 6. Alhambra in Charleston: *IF,* Aug. 19, 1916, p. 2; Sherman, TX: *IF,* Apr. 4, 1908, p. 1.

46. *AA,* Oct. 11, 1913.

47. This description and that of the airdome theaters are from Maggie Valentine, *The Show Starts on the Sidewalk: An Architectural History of the Movie Theatre, Starring S. Charles Lee* (New Haven, CT: Yale University Press, 1996), 22.

48. *BA,* Feb. 3, 1906, p. 1.

49. *IF,* Oct. 3, 1908, p. 5.

50. *IF,* Dec. 7, 1912, p. 6.

51. *IF,* Dec. 7, 1912, p. 6; Work, *Negro Year Book,* 309; Cahn and Hill, *Julius Cahn–Gus Hill Theatrical Guide,* 135.

52. *WB,* Aug. 22, 1908, p. 5.

53. *IF,* June 5, 1909, p. 4.

54. The advertisements ran for several weeks in the *Washington Bee.* The above quotes of advertisements are from *WB,* Sept. 18, 1909, p. 6.

55. *WB,* Nov. 13, 1909, p. 4.

56. Eric Ledell Smith, *African American Theater Buildings: An Illustrated Historical Directory, 1900–1955* (Jefferson, NC: McFarland, 2003), 41.

57. David Zang, *Fleet Walker's Divided Heart: The Life of Baseball's First Black Major Leaguer* (Lincoln: University of Nebraska Press, 1995), 108–112.

58. Macbeth likely performed in a play he wrote about Teddy Roosevelt: *Teddy's African Hunt: Play in Three Acts. Maryland Historical Magazine* (Baltimore, MD: Maryland Historical Society, 1969), 413.

59. Mather, *Who's Who of the Colored Race,* 182.

60. *IF,* Oct. 23, 1909, p. 5.

61. *IF,* Jan. 29, 1910, p. 6.

62. *IF,* May 14, 1910, p. 6.

63. *IF,* Jan. 29, 1910, p. 5.

64. Including the local Bethel AME Church; *AA,* Apr. 18, 1914, p. 3; *AA,* Apr. 25, 1914, p. 3.

65. *IF,* July 16, 1910, p. 5; *IF,* Sept. 19, 1908, p. 5.

Eddie Lee also hoped to plug into the circuit of black theaters in the South. Lee contacted Jewish entrepreneurs Lionel D. Joel and Glickerstein of Jacksonville, Florida, who had built a reputation for opening moving picture houses for black patrons. *IF,* June 26, 1909, p. 1; Bess J. Stein, interviewed by Micki Goldman, Samuel Proctor Oral History Program, Department of History, University of Florida, Apr. 24, 1980, pp. 2–3.

66. *Monthly Abstract Bulletin* (Rochester, NY: Eastman Kodak, January 1922), 39–40. "Fleet Walker Scores Big," *CG,* July 2, 1921, p. 1.

67. Mather, *Who's Who of the Colored Race,* 182; *Official Gazette of the United States Patent Office,* June 1922, vol. 299 (Washington, DC: Government Printing Office, 1922), 271.

68. *AA,* Jan. 15, 1910, p. 5.

69. Investing in the commercial amusement industry was one way in which uplift reformers could both profit and bring progress to the race. Instead of operating projectors or even managing the theaters themselves, many of these new black investors instead hired individuals with the requisite skills to operate their businesses. Veteran

exhibitors sought larger markets for their ideas and more potential profits. As Conley's business grew, for example, he retired from the road and concentrated on managing his company, hiring Prof. R. T. Greener Smith to exhibit his "illustrated lecture with animated views on the Negro in America and abroad."

70. *Secretary's Second Report, Harvard College Class of 1908, Sexennial Celebration* (Cambridge, MA: Harvard College, June 1914), 133.

71. *IF,* Apr. 20, 1907, p. 5.

72. These individuals presented on topics including poultry, photography, and shoe polish, exemplifying the diverse groups that participated in the black film industry. *IF,* Aug. 27, 1904, p. 4; *IF,* Oct. 23, 1909, p. 5.

73. *CG,* Jan. 15, 1910, p. 3.

74. *IF,* June 10, 1905, p. 5.

75. *IF,* Oct. 8, 1904, p. 5; *IF,* Feb. 11, 1905, p. 5.

76. *IF,* Oct. 24, 1908, p. 5. The black Knights of Pythias Temple was located nearby on Tenth and Chestnut streets, which according to George Wright was "rapidly becoming the heart of the black district." Wright, *Life behind a Veil,* 134.

77. *IF,* Aug. 8, 1908, p. 5.

78. *IF,* Sept. 19, 1908, p. 5; *WS,* May 14, 1910, p. 1; *WS,* May 21, 1910, p. 1; *WS,* May 21, 1910, p. 4; *WS,* May 28, 1910, p. 8; *ST,* Sept. 13, 1913, p. 8; *ST,* Oct. 25, 1913, p. 8.

79. The couple delegated tasks; when Eddie exhibited his moving picture shows around the state, Tish took charge of the theater; her "ability to 'manage,'" remarked the *Indianapolis Freeman,* was "equal to her popular husband's." Tish, in essence, was a New Woman before most Americans had even heard of the term; *IF,* Sept. 19, 1908, p. 5.

80. *WB,* Oct. 2, 1909, p. 4.

81. In the nickelodeon era, chatting and other types of noisemaking were woven into the cinema experience. White-owned theaters regulated the rowdy, noisy, conspicuous displays of black bodies and black voices by prohibiting admission to blacks or shifting to white-only seating policies. But black patrons still made their presence known when peanut shells and spilled drinks rained upon the heads of the white patrons seated below.

82. *WB,* Oct. 2, 1909, p. 4.

83. *WB,* Apr. 15, 1911, p. 3; *WB* June 17, 1911, p. 3; *WB,* July 8, 1911, p. 3; *WB,* Sept. 18, 1909, p. 5; *AA,* July 6, 1912, p. 8.

84. "This Week in Society," *WB,* Sept. 18, 1909, p. 5.

85. Walter Benjamin, *Charles Baudelaire: A Lyric Poet in the Era of High Capitalism* (New York: Verso, 1997), 40.

86. *Birmingham Reporter* quoted in *IF,* Jan. 15, 1910, p. 2.

87. W. E. B. Du Bois, *The Souls of Black Folk: Essays and Sketches* (Chicago: A. C. McClurg, 1903), 3.

88. *IF,* Mar. 13, 1909, p. 5.

89. *CG,* June 10, 1905, p. 3.

90. "Blind" Harris could not see the pictures on-screen, which may suggest the duo prepared their program in advance. *IF,* Oct. 20, 1906, p. 8; *IR,* Nov. 11, 1899, p. 1.

91. *AA,* Oct. 16, 1909, p. 5; *AA,* Oct. 16, 1909, p. 4; *AA,* Oct. 12, 1912, p. 8; *AA,* July 6, 1912, p. 3; *AA,* May 28, 1910, p. 4; *AA,* Jan. 20, 1912, p. 3; *AA,* Oct. 11, 1913, p. 8; Smith, *African American Theater Buildings,* 41.

92. Kenney, "Influence of Black Vaudeville on Early Jazz."

93. *IF,* Aug. 27, 1910, p. 5.

94. *IF,* Dec. 17, 1910, p. 5.

95. Cahn and Hill, *Julius Cahn–Gus Hill Theatrical Guide,* 133–139.

96. Work, *Negro Year Book,* 303–312.

97. *IF,* Nov. 30, 1912, p. 4; *Columbus Ledger,* Oct. 13, 1912, p. 5.

98. "Advertisement," *IF,* Dec. 5, 1914, p. 8; *IF,* Dec. 18, 1915, p. 6; J. Francis Mores, "Dreamland Theatre, Tulsa, Oklahoma," *IF,* Jan. 2, 1915, p. 5; "Race Woman Theatrical Magnate," *TP,* Nov. 28, 1919, p. 1.

99. *IF,* Dec. 23, 1911, p. 17.

100. Until World War I, white working-class and middle-class audiences less commonly viewed moving pictures in cross-class venues.

101. Though black theaters often announced that they were open to both races, most knew that white patrons would not realistically be a major source of revenue, at least in the immediate future. Early black commercial exhibitors experimented by combining amusements to please the diverse interests of their patrons. In Boston, C. W. Lewis, J. S. Price, and S. Pysant integrated moving pictures into their dances, setting up a large canvas next to the dance floor. *AA,* May 15, 1909, p. 6.

102. *IF,* Mar. 13, 1909, p. 5.

103. My italics. *IF,* Sept. 26, 1914, p. 5.

104. Gilbert Osofsky, *Harlem, the Making of a Ghetto: Negro New York, 1890–1930* (Chicago: Ivan R. Dee, 1996), 4.

105. Homosocial white working-class amusements were also regarded with suspicion.

106. *WS,* May 14, 1910, p. 1.

107. *IF,* Sept. 7, 1912, p. 5.

108. "Grand Opening, An Extraordinary Event," *IF,* Apr. 23, 1910, p. 8.

109. "From Little Acorns, Big Trees Grow," Jones explained in reference to the thriving industry. *IF,* Mar. 13, 1909, p. 5.

110. The Queen appears to have opened in 1907; it was transferred to white ownership in 1909. *AA,* Mar. 20, 1909, p. 8; *AA,* Nov. 13, 1909, p. 5; *AA,* Oct. 16, 1909, p. 5; *AA,* Apr. 17, 1909, p. 5; *AA,* Mar. 6, 1909, p. 5; *AA,* Sept. 11, 1909, p. 8; *AA,* Oct. 12, 1912, p. 8; *AA,* July 6, 1912, p. 3; *AA,* May 28, 1910, p. 4; *AA,* Jan. 20, 1912, p. 3; *AA,* Oct. 11, 1913, p. 8.

111. *IF,* Mar. 6, 1909, p. 1.

112. It was not until Woodrow Wilson took office in 1913 that the capital's system of segregation was fully implemented.

113. In 1880, slightly more than 52,000 blacks lived in the nation's capital. The pace of migration picked up in the 1890s. By 1910, there were 236,128. *1880 Census of Population and Housing* (Washington, DC: Government Printing Office, 1882); *1910 Census of Population and Housing* (Washington, DC: Government Printing Office, 1913).

114. *AA,* Nov. 6, 1909, p. 1.

115. For example: "The Negro's opportunity is good in Canada as I see it. . . . There are several prominent men in the real estate business, one moving picture show controlled exclusively by Negroes," wrote C. Francis Forster. *CD,* Sept. 28, 1912, p. 3.

116. *WB,* Sept. 18, 1909, p. 6; *IF,* Oct. 3, 1908, p. 5.

117. *CG,* May 7, 1910, p. 3.

118. *IF,* Apr. 18, 1908, p. 5.

119. *Macon Daily Telegraph,* Mar. 26, 1906, p. 1.

120. *IF,* Mar. 30, 1907, p. 7.

121. Ibid.

122. *IF,* May 20, 1911, p. 5.

123. *TP,* July 16, 1909, p. 8.

124. *WB,* Dec. 7, 1912, p. 4.

125. *AA,* June 12, 1909, p. 8.

126. C. Eric Lincoln and Lawrence H. Mamiya, *The Black Church in the African-American Experience* (Durham, NC: Duke University Press, 1990).

127. *IF,* Dec. 23, 1911, p. 17; *AA,* July 6, 1912, p. 3.

128. *IF,* Jan. 15, 1910, p. 2.

129. *WB,* Sept. 18, 1909, p. 6.

130. *IF,* Dec. 7, 1907, p. 5.

131. *IF,* Sept. 26, 1914, p. 5.

132. *IF,* Aug. 3, 1912, p. 2.

133. McFall's parents migrated to Kansas, but like many Exodusters they left the state for new territories in the 1890s. James D. and Lucy McFall migrated to Boley after their fifth child, Emma, was born in 1894. *Thirteenth Census of the United States: 1910—Population,* U.S. Department of Commerce and Labor, Bureau of the Census, 1910, Ancestry.com, http://www.ancestrylibrary.com.

134. Boley was incorporated in 1905. The *Boley Progress* newspaper, with enthusiastic endorsements from Booker T. Washington, and booklets such as "Facts about Boley, Oklahoma," published by the Commercial Club of Boley, had helped the population grow to 4,000 residents by 1911. *Facts about Boley, Oklahoma: The Largest and Wealthiest Exclusive Negro City in the World* (Boley, OK: Boley Commercial Club, 1911).

135. *National Review,* Oct. 25, 1913, p. 1.

136. *IF,* Oct. 17, 1908, p. 5.

137. Ibid.

138. "Notes of Racial Progress," *ST,* Nov. 14, 1908, p. 4; *IF,* Nov. 14, 1908, p. 5; *IF,* Oct. 17, 1908, p. 5.

139. *TP,* July 23, 1909, p. 4.

140. The black middle class applauded a "promising young businessman" such as T. Wheeler, who purchased Dayton's Enterprise Hall with plans of turning the bottom floor into a picture house. *CG,* May 1, 1909, p. 1; *IF,* Sept. 14, 1907, p. 2; *CD,* Oct. 1, 1910, p. 6.

141. *CA,* Aug. 11, 1900, p. 1.

142. "What has been needed in this city for a great number of years, and which is about to materialize, is a theatre owned and controlled by the Negroes." *WB,* Sept. 11, 1909, p. 4.

143. *IF,* Aug. 8, 1908, p. 5.

144. Exhibitions in church facilities reached a new peak in 1908.

145. *WS,* May 14, 1910, p. 1; *ST,* Aug. 2, 1913, p. 4.

146. *IF,* Aug. 8, 1908, p. 5.

147. Ibid., p. 5.

148. *IF,* Mar. 6, 1909, p. 1.

149. Examples of protest against the theater's seating policy can be found in *ST,* Nov. 16, 1901, p. 2 and Nov. 29, 1902, p. 2. Walter E. Campbell explained, "On September 15, 1906, the *Tribune* urged black young people to stay out of the 'peanut gallery' in the theater and warned them that the newspaper would take snapshots from time to time of any 'winding steps climbers.'" Walter E. Campbell, "Profit, Prejudice, and Protest," *Georgia Historical Quarterly* 70, no. 2 (Summer 1986): 197–231.

150. The "gallery gods" often became unruly, showering the audience below with peanut shells and foul language. This tradition began before the moving pictures and continued well into the twentieth century. *Macon Daily Telegraph,* Dec. 7, 1883, p. 1; *Kansas City Plaindealer,* Mar. 5, 1937, p. 2.

151. *Macon Daily Telegraph,* Nov. 18, 1890, p. 5.

152. "Observations of Our Special Correspondent in Ohio," *IF,* June 22 1907, p. 5.

153. *TP,* Aug. 16, 1912, p. 5.

154. *WS,* May 14, 1910, p. 1.

155. However, entrepreneurial blacks advocated "race pride" more often than color blindness when it came to marketing their goods and services.

156. Martin Anthony Summers, *Manliness and Its Discontents: The Black Middle Class and the Transformation of Masculinity, 1900–1930* (Chapel Hill: University of North Carolina Press, 2004), 3–4.

157. As Gail Bederman, Dan Streible, and Theresa Runstedtler have stated, the cinema became an important site for the expression of manliness at the turn of the

century. Gail Bederman, *Manliness and Civilization: A Cultural History of Gender and Race in the United States, 1880–1917* (Chicago: University of Chicago Press, 1995), 3; Dan Streible, *Fight Pictures: A History of Boxing and Early Cinema* (Berkeley: University of California Press, 2008), 165; Theresa Runstedtler, *Jack Johnson, Rebel Sojourner: Boxing in the Shadow of the Global Color Line* (Berkeley: University of California Press, 2012), 70–73.

158. *BA,* Dec. 2, 1899, p. 1.

159. *CA,* Aug. 11, 1900, p. 1.

160. *IF,* Mar. 13, 1909, p. 5.

161. Ibid.

162. At first, the industry marketed primarily to the middle class; but when nickelodeons began to meet the demand for inexpensive entertainment with their nickel shows, the movies exploded in popularity. Millions of laborers and immigrants flooded into nickelodeon theaters, bringing the industry handsome profits—and a reputation for seediness and vulgarity. The creation of a larger cross-class consumer market, as David Nasaw has pointed out, could have occurred only if these concerns were somehow alleviated. Nasaw, *Going Out.*

163. Dan Streible, "Race and the Reception of Jack Johnson Fight Films," in Daniel Bernardi, ed., *The Birth of Whiteness: Race and the Emergence of U.S. Cinema* (New Brunswick, NJ: Rutgers University Press, 1996), 196.

164. *IF,* Apr. 18, 1908, p. 5.

165. *IF,* Oct. 24, 1908, p. 5.

166. *IF,* Aug. 23, 1913, p. 6.

167. *IF,* May 18, 1912, p. 5; *IF,* Oct. 2, 1909, p. 5; *IF,* Aug. 7, 1909, p. 5.

168. Work, *Negro Year Book;* Smith, *African American Theater Buildings. Going to the Show,* Documenting the American South. University Library, University of North Carolina at Chapel Hill, 2008, http://docsouth.unc.edu/gtts/venue/1070.

169. There were two TOBAs. F. A. Barrasso (a white) of Memphis, Tennessee, organized the primarily white Theater Owners and Booking Agency (TOBA) circa 1907. The first TOBA created an official circuit for black entertainers, which consisted of approximately forty theaters located primarily in the South. Later, the Theater Owners' Booking Association (TOBA) was formed to compete with Dudley. C. H. Douglass, who managed the Ocmulgee Park Theatre in Macon, Georgia, joined the board of the mostly white and often exploitative organization. Black performers commonly joked that TOBA meant "Tough On Black Asses." Errol Hill and James Vernon Hatch, *A History of African American Theatre* (New York: Cambridge University Press, 2003), 206–207; Bernard L. Peterson, *The African American Theatre Directory, 1816–1960: A Comprehensive Guide to Early Black Theatre Organizations, Companies, Theatres, and Performing Groups* (Westport, CT: Greenwood Press, 1997), 194.

4. Monuments of Progress

1. Miles Mark Fisher, "The History of the Olivet Baptist Church" (MA thesis, University of Chicago, 1922); Miles Mark Fisher, *The Master's Slave, Elijah John Fisher: A Biography* (Philadelphia, PA: Judson Press, 1922).

2. *BA*, Feb. 22, 1902, p. 1. Also see Mark H. Haller, "Policy Gambling, Entertainment, and the Emergence of Black Politics: Chicago from 1900 to 1940," *Journal of Social History* 24, no. 4 (1991): 723; Edward A. Robinson, "The Pekin: The Genesis of American Black Theater," *Black American Literature Forum* 16 (1982): 136–138.

3. Fisher, *Master's Slave,* 55.

4. Ida B. Wells-Barnett, *Crusade for Justice: The Autobiography of Ida B. Wells* (Chicago: University of Chicago Press, 1970), 292.

5. Fisher, *Master's Slave,* 161–172.

6. *BA,* Aug. 7, 1915, p. 1; Fisher, *Master's Slave,* 171.

7. Wells-Barnett, *Crusade for Justice,* 294–295.

8. Leo Charney and Vanessa R. Schwartz explained that the "elements of modern life . . . created sufficient epistemological pressure to produce cinema." Leo Charney and Vanessa R. Schwartz, *Cinema and the Invention of Modern Life* (Berkeley: University of California Press, 1995), 10.

9. Langston Hughes, "One Way Ticket," in Arnold Rampersad and David E. Roessel, eds., *The Collected Poems of Langston Hughes* (New York: Knopf, 1994), 361.

10. Fisher, *Master's Slave,* 1–55.

11. Langston Hughes, *The Big Sea: An Autobiography* (New York: Alfred A. Knopf, 1940); Langston Hughes, *I Wonder as I Wander: An Autobiographical Journey* (New York: Hill and Wang 1993).

12. Emmett J. Scott, "Letters of Negro Migrants of 1916–1918," *Journal of Negro History* 4, no. 3 (1919): 290–340; Emmett J. Scott, "Additional Letters of Negro Migrants of 1916–1918," *Journal of Negro History* 4, no. 3 (1919): 412–465; James R. Grossman, *Land of Hope: Chicago, Black Southerners, and the Great Migration* (Chicago: University of Chicago Press, 1989).

13. Kimberley L. Phillips, *AlabamaNorth: African-American Migrants, Community, and Working-Class Activism in Cleveland, 1915–45* (Urbana: University of Illinois Press, 1999).

14. *Philadelphia Tribune,* June 27, 1914, p. 1.

15. On the movement of culture from the South across the routes of twentieth-century migration, see Nicholas Lemann, *The Promised Land: The Great Black Migration and How It Changed America* (New York: Knopf, 1991); James N. Gregory, *The Southern Diaspora: How the Great Migrations of Black and White Southerners Transformed America* (Chapel Hill: University of North Carolina Press, 2005).

16. Milton C. Sernett, *Bound for the Promised Land: African American Religion and the Great Migration* (Durham, NC: Duke University Press, 1997), 3–4.

17. For example, Hurston explained that the "average southern child, white and black, is raised on simile and invective." Zora Neale Hurston, *Dust Tracks on a Road: An Autobiography* (New York: Harper Perennial Modern Classics, 2006), 104.

18. *AA,* Mar. 12, 1910, p. 8; *IF,* July 23, 1910, p. 6; *ST,* Sept. 13, 1913, p. 8; *ST,* Oct. 25, 1913, p. 8.

19. Theaters such as the Chicago New Grand advertised "continuous vaudeville, moving pictures"; Baltimore, Maryland's Holliday promised shows from 1 P.M. to 1 A.M.; Durham, North Carolina's Rex Theatre exhibited from noon to midnight. *IF,* Oct. 21, 1911, p. 6; *CD,* Nov. 16, 1912, p. 2; *CD,* Oct. 19, 1912, p. 5; *IF,* Dec. 20, 1913, p. 4; *IF,* May 31, 1913, p. 6; *AA,* May 9, 1908, p. 8; *Durham Morning Herald,* Mar. 8, 1920 listed in "Rex Theatre—Ad—opening notice," *Going to the Show,* Documenting the American South, University Library, The University of North Carolina at Chapel Hill, 2008, http://docsouth.unc.edu/gtts/content/716.

20. *ST,* Apr. 15, 1911, p. 7.

21. Pictures were changed Mondays, Wednesdays, and Fridays at the Avenue Theatre; *AA,* Dec. 21, 1907; *AA,* Nov. 6, 1909, p. 8; *AA,* Nov. 20, 1909, p. 8; *AA,* Nov. 27, 1909, p. 8; *AA,* Dec. 11, 1909, p. 8; *AA,* Dec. 18, 1909, p. 8; *AA,* Dec. 25, 1909, p. 8.

22. *ST,* May 17, 1913, p. 4; *IF,* July 6, 1912, p. 6.

23. "'We Tho[ugh]t State Street Would Be Heaven Itself': Black Migrants Speak Out," History Matters, http://historymatters.gmu.edu/d/5337/, originally from Charles S. Johnson, "Chicago Study, Migration Interviews," [1917], Box 86, Series 6, Records of the National Urban League, Library of Congress, Washington, DC.

24. Christopher Robert Reed, *Black Chicago's First Century,* vol. 1: *1833–1900* (Columbia: University of Missouri Press, 2005), 238.

25. Sylvester Johnson, "The Black Church," in *The Blackwell Companion to Religion in America,* ed. Philip Goff (Malden, MA: Wiley-Blackwell, 2010), 457–458.

26. Fisher, "History of the Olivet Baptist Church," 52.

27. The church went from 1,485 to 843 members. Fisher, "History of the Olivet Baptist Church," 53.

28. Fisher, "History of the Olivet Baptist Church," 56–57.

29. Haller, "Policy Gambling," 723.

30. *BA,* Feb. 22, 1902, p. 1.

31. As mentioned in Chapter 3, access to public space in the South was legislated through housing regulations and restrictions on facilities, and further enforced through violent reprisals. In most northern cities, Jim Crow exclusion was technically prohibited but was in widespread practice. Moreover, in response to the influx of black migrants and European immigrants, white Progressive reformers lobbied for stricter zoning and regulation of urban space. City planners and politicians as well as black entrepreneurs vied to build the city according to their own visions. Robin Faith Bachin, *Building the South Side: Urban Space and Civic Culture in Chicago, 1890–1919* (Chicago:University of Chicago Press, 2004); Edward A. Robinson specu-

lated that Motts chose the "oriental sounding name" "Pekin" to "conjure images of the otherwordly, allowing audiences to disavow the stark realities that were part of their daily lives." This may or may not be true, but it is important to note that "Pekin" was also a town in Illinois. Robinson, "The Pekin: The Genesis of American Black Theater," 136.

32. Wells, quoted in Dempsey Travis, *An Autobiography of Black Jazz* (Chicago: Urban Research Institute, 1983), 34; *IF,* Apr. 2, 1910, p. 1.

33. Film historians have pointed out the discrepancies regarding the evolution of the Pekin Theatre, asking if the Douglass Center event occurred in 1905 or 1906. As Jacqueline Najuma Stewart has pointed out, "Dates regarding the Pekin's evolution . . . are conflicting." Part of the confusion may be because Anne Meis Knupfer's *Toward a Tenderer Humanity and a Nobler Womanhood* cited a May 5, 1905, *Broad Ax* article about the Douglass Center that took place at the New Pekin Theatre. This contradicts Ida B. Wells's description of the event, which occurred soon before the 1906 San Francisco earthquake. It appears that Wells was correct. The Chicago *Broad Ax* was not published on May 5, 1905. Thus Knupfer's description of the Pekin event was probably misdated. Jacqueline Najuma Stewart, *Migrating to the Movies: Cinema and Black Urban Modernity* (Berkeley: University of California Press, 2005), 292 n.22; Anne Meis Knupfer, *Toward a Tenderer Humanity and a Nobler Womanhood* (New York: New York University Press, 1996), 125–126.

34. The press took special pleasure in ridiculing Motts's relationship with Thomas. It was reported that Thomas sent Motts a turkey on Thanksgiving Day in 1902, with Motts returning the favor with a generous donation "so he would advertise him and his den from the pulpit." *BA,* Feb. 22, 1902, p. 1.

35. Chicago's black population continued to grow, peaking in World War I when nativist hysteria and the war closed off the supply of cheap immigrant laborers from southern and eastern Europe and factories began hiring more black employees. Grossman, *Land of Hope,* 13–14.

36. *IF,* Apr. 29, 1905, p. 1; *IF,* Oct. 28, 1905, p. 5; *BA,* July 15, 1911, p. 1.

37. Gilbert Osofsky, *Harlem, the Making of a Ghetto: Negro New York, 1890–1930* (Chicago: Ivan R. Dee, 1996), 79, 115.

38. Alison Griffiths and James Latham, "Film and Ethnic Identity in Harlem, 1896–1915," in Melvyn Stokes and Richard Maltby, eds., *American Movie Audiences: From the Turn of the Century to the Early Sound Era* (London: British Film Institute, 1999), 46–63.

39. The Crescent Theater was owned by white investors. When the Palace Theatre opened almost immediately afterward, it was deemed "destined to become as popular as the Crescent Theater in Harlem." *NYA,* May 26, 1910, p. 6; *NYA,* Jan. 7, 1909, p. 6.

40. *AA,* July 6, 1912, p. 8.

41. "Crescent Theater," *NYA,* Mar. 19, 1914, p. 6.

42. The black urban dweller, of course, differed from his Parisian bourgeois counterpart, who was "unwilling to forgo the life of a gentleman of leisure"—the black flâneur's leisure was generative of a new black self. Walter Benjamin, "Paris of the Second Empire," in Michael W. Jennings, ed., *The Writer of Modern Life: Essays on Charles Baudelaire* (Cambridge, MA: Harvard University Press, 2006), 84. *AA,* July 6, 1912, p. 3; *AA,* Aug. 26, 1911, p. 7.

43. *CD,* May 2, 1914, p. 1.

44. The ticket booth also exists today. According to Reverend James M. Moody, both were installed in the early 1890s because the church was meant to function as a venue for black social life. James M. Moody and Christopher Reed, during a tour of the Quinn AME "Black Metropolis," American Historical Association Chicago Tours, Jan. 6, 2012.

45. *IF,* Apr. 14, 1906, p. 6.

46. "The Moving Picture House Is Taking the Day," *IF,* Jan. 15, 1910, p. 6.

47. "But the spiritual function of the church was always first," Mark Miles Fisher explained. Fisher, *Master's Slave,* 87.

48. *IF,* Apr. 7, 1906, p. 5; *BA,* July 15, 1911, p. 6; Wells-Barnett, *Crusade for Justice,* 292–295.

49. "Not So Long" was published in black newspapers including the *Cleveland Gazette,* June 1, 1907, p. 4; and the *St. Louis Palladium,* June 1, 1907, p. 7.

50. William Howland Kenney, *Chicago Jazz: A Cultural History, 1904–1930* (New York: Oxford University Press, 1993); William Howland Kenney, III, "The Influence of Black Vaudeville on Early Jazz," *Black Perspective in Music* 14, no. 3 (1986): 233–248.

51. H. Sylvester Russell rigorously defended his public image in the pages of the black press; *NYA,* June 7, 1890, p. 1; *NYA,* Dec. 19, 1891, p. 2; *IF,* Dec. 14, 1907, p. 5; *IF,* Jan. 15, 1910, p. 5.

52. *CD,* Mar. 4, 1910, p. 6; *CD,* Oct. 1, 1910, p. 6.

53. Sylvester Russell, *CD,* Feb. 12, 1910, p. 4.

54. Ibid.

55. *WB,* Jan. 15, 1910, p. 4; *WS,* Oct. 20, 1900, p. 2; *WS,* May 14, 1910, p. 1; *WS,* Aug. 12, 1911, p. 1.

56. *IF,* June 26, 1909, p. 1.

57. *IF,* Feb. 24, 1912, p. 8.

58. I. Garland Penn, *The Afro-American Press and Its Editors* (Springfield, MA: Willey, 1891), 288.

59. The theater is not identified in the article. *WB,* June 12, 1909, p. 2; *WB,* Oct. 29, 1910, p. 4; Announcement of Jenifer's theater in *NYA,* July 29, 1909, p. 3.

60. *IF,* Sept. 11, 1909, p. 1; *WB,* Oct. 2, 1909, p. 4; *CD,* Feb. 12, 1910, p. 4.

61. *WB,* Oct. 2, 1909, p. 4. Additionally, the *Bee* later printed an article that argued, "All pictures should have a moral"; *WB,* Mar. 18, 1911, p. 8.

62. *IF,* Dec. 23, 1911, p. 17.

63. A. B. Caldwell, ed., *History of the American Negro and His Institutions,* vol. 6 (Atlanta: A. B. Caldwell, 1922), 170.

64. Sernett, *Bound for the Promised Land.*

65. *WB,* Nov. 6, 1909, p. 4.

66. *NYA,* Dec. 15, 1910, p. 6.

67. "Not to Blame," *WB,* Oct. 9, 1909, p. 1.

68. *WB,* Jan. 15, 1910, p. 4.

69. *WB,* Sept. 18, 1909, p. 5.

70. The dignified spectators already knew the results. The fight had taken place several months earlier. Nelson's victory placed the title back in the hands of a white man. The audience was convinced that Gans would have won if Nelson had played fair. Ibid.

71. Ibid.

72. *WB,* Oct. 2, 1909, p. 4.

73. *WB,* Sept. 18, 1909, p. 5.

74. Lee Grieveson and Peter Krämer, *The Silent Cinema Reader* (London: Routledge, 2004), 136.

75. *AA,* Dec. 13, 1913, p. 4.

76. Ibid.

77. *BA,* Dec. 28, 1912, p. 2.

78. Ibid.

79. *CG,* Jan. 25, 1913, p. 3.

80. *ST,* Nov. 23, 1912, p. 6.

81. There were between 102 and 106 black church buildings and about ten theaters catering to black filmgoers at any one time in 1910. This included Chase's, Douglass, Dunbar, Elite, Fairyland, Foraker, Ford Dabney's, Hiawatha, Howard, and Maceo theaters. *WB,* Sept. 18, 1909, p. 5; *WB,* Nov. 6, 1909, p. 1; *WB,* Oct. 15, 1910, p. 4; *WB,* Feb. 19, 1910, p. 4; *WB,* July 23, 1910, p. 5; *WB,* Mar. 12, 1910, p. 5; *IF,* May 7, 1910 p. 6. The Howard returned to white management in November 1910. *WB,* Nov. 26, 1910, p. 4. Chase's Theatre: Eric Ledell Smith, *African American Theater Buildings: An Illustrated Historical Directory, 1900–1955* (Jefferson, NC: McFarland, 2003), 37. U.S. Bureau of the Census, *Religious Bodies: 1906* (Washington, DC: Government Printing Office, 1910), 540; U.S. Bureau of the Census, *Religious Bodies: 1916* (Washington, DC: Government Printing Office, 1920), 164.

82. *IF,* June 4, 1910, pp. 1, 5, and 6; *IF,* June 11, 1910, p. 5; *IF,* June 18, 1910, pp. 5, 6, and 8; *IF,* June 25, 1910, pp. 1, 2, 5, and 6.

83. Edmund de S. Brunner, *Church Life in the Rural South* (New York: George H. Doran, 1923), 84.

84. Motts first resisted the change by eliminating moving pictures from his theaters, but this change did not last long. "The Moving Picture House Is Taking the Day," *IF,* Jan. 15, 1910, p. 6.

85. Ibid.

86. *NYA,* Dec. 15, 1910, p. 6.

87. "Knights of Pythias at Columbia, MO," *IF,* Apr. 19, 1913, p. 8; *AA,* May 15, 1909, p. 6; *IF,* Apr. 4, 1908, p. 1.

88. Rev. D. D. Buck, *The Progression of the Race in the United States and Canada: Treating of the Great Advancement of the Colored Race* (Chicago: Atwell Printing and Binding, 1907), 421.

89. *AA,* July 27, 1912, p. 3.

90. Ps. 137:5–6 (Authorized [King James] Version).

91. *BA,* Jan. 16, 1915, p. 4; *IF,* Mar. 6, 1915, p. 1; *BA,* Apr. 10, 1915, p. 1; Wells-Barnett, *Crusade for Justice,* 292–295.

92. *ST,* Jan. 6, 1912, p. 2.

5. The Fight over Fight Pictures

1. *Variety,* July 23, 1910, quoted in Dan Streible, "Race and the Reception of Jack Johnson Fight Films," in Daniel Bernardi, ed., *The Birth of Whiteness: Race and the Emergence of U.S. Cinema* (New Brunswick, NJ: Rutgers University Press, 1996), 181.

2. *IF,* July 23, 1910, p. 2.

3. As Richard DeCordova explains, in 1907, the general public rarely knew the names of screen performers. Richard DeCordova, *Picture Personalities: The Emergence of the Star System in America* (Urbana: University of Illinois Press, 2001), 7–10.

4. Gail Bederman, *Manliness and Civilization: A Cultural History of Gender and Race in the United States, 1880–1917* (Chicago: University of Chicago Press, 1995), 1–44; Thomas R. Hietala, *The Fight of the Century: Jack Johnson, Joe Louis, and the Struggle for Racial Equality* (Armonk, NY: M. E. Sharpe, 2002); Thomas C. Holt, *The Problem of Race in the Twenty-First Century* (Cambridge, MA: Harvard University Press, 2000); Theresa Runstedtler, *Jack Johnson, Rebel Sojourner: Boxing in the Shadow of the Global Color Line* (Berkeley: University of California Press, 2012).

5. *Denver Post,* July 5, 1910, p. 1; *Baltimore Sun,* July 5, 1910, p. 1; *Mt. Vernon (OH) Democratic Banner,* July 5, 1910, p. 1; *Aberdeen Daily News,* July 5, 1910, p. 1; *CG,* July 9, 1910, p. 2.

6. *NYT,* July 6, 1910, p. 3.

7. *NYT,* July 9, 1910, p. 3.

8. This chapter is indebted to Lee Grieveson's work on Progressive-era legislation and prizefight pictures, especially his analysis of the ways in which modern definitions of cinema were constituted through legislation intended to discipline and demobilize images of black bodies. See, for example, Lee Grieveson, "Fighting Films: Race, Morality, and the Governing of Cinema, 1912–1915," *Cinema Journal* 38, no. 1 (1998): 40–72.

9. *New York Daily Tribune,* July 5, 1910, p. 2.

10. "Pictorial Representations" included moving pictures, still photographs, drawings, and other materials, but the federal government appears to have actively monitored only the moving pictures through the Act.

11. Grieveson, "Fighting Films"; Dan Streible, *Fight Pictures: A History of Boxing and Early Cinema* (Berkeley: University of California Press, 2008).

12. *Daily Long Island Farmer* (Jamaica, NY), July 5, 1910, p. 3.

13. First quote in this sentence from *Pawtucket Times,* July 7, 1910, p. 2; second from *NYT,* July 14, 1910, p. 5. Entire paragraph based on these articles and *NYA,* July 2, 1914, p. 6.

14. *IF,* July 16, 1910, p. 1.

15. *AA,* July 16, 1910, p. 4.

16. Quoted in ibid.

17. Such as Lester Walton, theater critic for the *New York Age.* Anna Everett, *Returning the Gaze: A Genealogy of Black Film Criticism, 1909–1949* (Durham, NC: Duke University Press, 2001).

18. Ida B. Wells-Barnett, *Crusade for Justice: The Autobiography of Ida B. Wells* (Chicago: University of Chicago Press, 1970), 289–295; *IF,* Apr. 29, 1905, p. 1; *BA,* May 5, 1906, p. 1.

19. *CD,* Feb. 12, 1910, p. 4.

20. *IF,* Nov. 11, 1905, p. 7; *AA,* Oct. 11, 1913, p. 8.

21. *CG,* Aug. 22, 1908, p. 1.

22. Ibid.

23. Elwood Salsbury of Luna Park described the picture as depicting "the doings of some Italian society. It has no connection with the colored race." *CG,* Aug. 29, 1909, p. 1. The American Mutoscope and Biograph Company's film *The Black Viper* was probably directed by D. W. Griffith, either entirely or in part. Tom Gunning, *D. W. Griffith and the Origins of American Narrative Film: The Early Years at Biograph* (Urbana: University of Illinois Press, 1991); "Film Review," *Moving Picture World,* July 25, 1908, p. 67. The "black viper" was most likely Italian, in reference to the species of snake native to Italy and the surrounding areas.

24. For examples of theater discrimination cases supported by Harry Clay Smith, see *CG,* Mar. 26, 1898, p. 1; *CG,* July 16, 1904, p. 3; *CG,* Apr. 18, 1908, p. 3; *CG* May 13, 1911, p. 2; *CG,* May 20, 1911, p. 1.

25. See Chapter 6 for a description of Smith's campaigns against *The Birth of a Nation* in Ohio.

26. For more on liberal emancipation, see Thomas C. Holt, *The Problem of Freedom: Race, Labor, and Politics in Jamaica and Britain, 1832–1938* (Baltimore, MD: Johns Hopkins University Press, 1992). The ascendance of visual culture in the late nineteenth century marked a pivotal moment in the development of new expressions of racial thought. Text still occupied a privileged place in the sphere of intellectual

exchange. However, the era's broadening democracy, industrial capitalism, and imperialist projects in the American West and overseas became, not coincidentally, intertwined with new technologies of mass-producing images. On visual culture and race, see Shawn Michelle Smith, *Photography on the Color Line: W. E. B. Du Bois, Race, and Visual Culture* (Durham, NC: Duke University Press, 2004); Kevin Kelly Gaines, *Uplifting the Race: Black Leadership, Politics, and Culture in the Twentieth Century* (Chapel Hill: University of North Carolina Press, 1996); Michael D. Harris, *Colored Pictures: Race and Visual Representation* (Chapel Hill: University of North Carolina Press, 2003); Amy Helene Kirschke, *Art in Crisis: W. E. B. Du Bois and the Struggle for African American Identity and Memory* (Bloomington: Indiana University Press, 2007); Anne Elizabeth Carroll, *Word, Image, and the New Negro: Representation and Identity in the Harlem Renaissance* (Bloomington: Indiana University Press, 2005); Dora Apel, *Imagery of Lynching: Black Men, White Women, and the Mob* (New Brunswick, NJ: Rutgers University Press, 2004); Kirk Savage, *Standing Soldiers, Kneeling Slaves: Race, War, and Monument in Nineteenth-Century America* (Princeton, NJ: Princeton University Press, 1997); Martha Sandweiss, *Print the Legend* (New Haven, CT: Yale University Press, 2002). This was an ongoing process. For more on the earlier history of race and visual culture, see Marcus Wood, *The Horrible Gift of Freedom: Atlantic Slavery and the Representation of Emancipation* (Athens: University of Georgia Press, 2010); Kay Dian Kriz, *Slavery, Sugar, and the Culture of Refinement: Picturing the British West Indies, 1700–1840* (New Haven, CT: Yale University Press, 2008); Elizabeth Ewen and Stuart Ewen, *Typecasting: On the Arts and Sciences of Human Inequality; A History of Dominant Ideas* (New York: Seven Stories Press, 2006).

27. Ibid.; Stephen Jay Gould, *The Mismeasure of Man* (New York: Norton, 1981).

28. Miriam Hansen, "Early Silent Cinema: Whose Public Sphere?," *New German Critique*, no. 29 (Spring–Summer 1983): 147–184.

29. Italian films were exported into Japan; French production companies distributed to Latin America; and in the United States, the International Projecting and Producing Company imported films from England, Germany, and Russia, which chipped away at the powerful Motion Picture Patents Company, a trust largely controlled by Thomas Edison. Robert Sklar, *Movie-Made America: A Cultural History of American Movies* (New York: Vintage Books, 1994), 38–46; Charles Musser, *Before the Nickelodeon: Edwin S. Porter and the Edison Manufacturing Company* (Berkeley: University of California Press, 1991), 444; Aldo Bernardini, "An Industry in Recession: The Italian Film Industry 1908–1909," *Film History* 3, no. 4 (1989): 341–368; Ana M. López, "Early Cinema and Modernity in Latin America," *Cinema Journal* 40, no. 1 (Autumn 2000): 48–78; Joan M. Minguet Batllori, "Early Spanish Cinema and the Problem of Modernity," *Film History* 16, no. 1 (2004): 92–107; Michel Ghertman and Allègre L. Hadida, "Institutional Assets and Competitive Advantages of French over U.S. Cinema, 1895–1914," *International Studies of Management and Organization* 35, no. 3 (Fall 2005): 50–81; Andrew Shail, "The Motion Picture

Story Magazine and the Origins of Popular British Film Culture," *Film History* 20, no. 2 (2008): 181–197.

30. Runstedtler, *Jack Johnson, Rebel Sojourner,* 76.

31. Theresa Runstedtler, "White Anglo-Saxon Hopes and Black Americans' Atlantic Dreams: Jack Johnson and the British Boxing Colour Bar," *Journal of World History* 21, no. 4 (2010): 657.

32. These new gender anxieties were also expressed by black men who found being Jim Crowed in the theater a particularly egregious assault on their masculinity.

33. Bederman, *Manliness and Civilization,* 19–20.

34. *NYA,* June 2, 1910, p. 6.

35. *Birmingham Reporter,* quoted in "Johnson Jeffries Fight Expression of the Negro Press," *IF,* July 23, 1910, p. 2.

36. Ibid.

37. *CD,* July 5, 1913, p. 1.

38. *AA,* Aug. 6, 1910, p. 4.

39. *Morning Mission and Riverside (CA) Enterprise,* July 12, 1910, p. 1.

40. *CD,* Mar. 21, 1914, p. 2.

41. *Richmond Planet,* Aug. 6, 1910, p. 1.

42. During the summer of 1910, at least eighteen black people were lynched or killed during racially charged violence in Anderson County, Texas. Ibid.

43. Booker T. Washington referred to Jack Johnson and "Peter Jackson," the former colored heavyweight champion from Australia. *Denver Post,* June 12, 1910, p. 26. When Johnson beat Jim Corbett in 1909, Washington refused to refer to Johnson by name, but described "a certain member of our race" who had recently traveled to Australia and refused to abide by the color line. "It is a godsend that he did win. It shows to the negro race what determination will do," Washington explained. *Boston Journal,* June 7, 1909, p. 1.

44. Randy Roberts, *Papa Jack: Jack Johnson and the Era of the White Hopes* (New York: Free Press, 1983), 103.

45. *NYA,* June 9, 1910, p. 6.

46. *San Jose Evening News,* Dec. 24, 1910, p. 5.

47. *WB,* Mar. 23, 1912, p. 1. Washington turned fully against Johnson in 1912, when the pugilist was investigated for violating the Mann Act. *Washington Post,* Oct. 21, 1912, p. 4; *BA,* Jan. 4, 1913, p. 1.

48. *IF,* July 9, 1910, p. 1.

49. *AA,* Aug. 6, 1910, p. 3.

50. Ibid.

51. "In the World of Sport," *NYA,* July 6, 1911, p. 6.

52. Ibid.

53. *Baltimore Sun,* Jan. 20, 1906, p. 10.

54. Recall, for example, L. L. Blair's exhibition of a film depicting the lynching of Will Cato and Paul Reed. *ST,* Aug. 5, 1905, p. 2.

55. For example, Walter Campbell, a black barber, bet a lifetime of free shaves if Jeffries won; if Johnson prevailed, Campbell would receive a free burial from a local white undertaker. Hietala, *Fight of the Century,* 36. Robert T. Motts also won a substantial amount of money on the fight. *IF,* July 9, 1910, p. 1.

56. *ST,* June 25, 1910, p. 8.

57. *IF,* May 21, 1910, p. 7.

58. Hietala, *Fight of the Century,* 36.

59. *IF,* July 9, 1910, p. 1.

60. The *Aberdeen Daily News* made a more conservative estimate, guessing, "The negroes of Chicago won $200,000 in bets on the fight." Their commentary expressed both the sentiment that black people were naturally lazy and a fear of the implications of black victory. *Aberdeen Daily News,* July 5, 1910, p. 1.

61. Ruby Berkley Goodwin, *It's Good to be Black* (Carbondale: Southern Illinois Press, 2013), 76.

62. *Denver Post,* July 5, 1910, p. 1; *Duluth News-Tribune,* July 6, 1910, pp. 1, 3; *Lexington Herald,* July 5, 1910, p. 8; *Baltimore Sun,* July 5, 1910, p. 1.

63. Disgruntled whites also killed a black waiter named George Crawford, and nearly lynched Nelson Turner in the working class San Juan section of town. *Baltimore Sun,* July 5, 1910, p. 1; *Denver Post,* July 5, 1910, p. 1; *Beaumont Enterprise,* July 5, 1910, p. 1.

64. Barren Island housed a fertilizer plant; it was also the dumping grounds for New York's dead animals and garbage. *NYT,* July 6, 1910, p. 3. For more on Barren Island, see Benjamin Miller, *Fat of the Land: Garbage in New York; The Last Two Hundred Years* (New York: Four Walls Eight Windows, 2000).

65. *NYT,* July 5, 1910, p. 4.

66. Ibid.

67. *Los Angeles Times,* July 6, 1910, p. 114.

68. John L. Brooke, "Consent, Civil Society, and the Public Sphere in the Age of Revolution and the Early American Republic" in Jeffrey L. Pasley, Andrew W. Robertson, and David Waldstreicher, eds., *Beyond the Founders: New Approaches to the Political History of the Early American Republic* (Chapel Hill: University of North Carolina Press, 2004), 237; Herbert G. Gutman, *Work, Culture, and Society in Industrializing America: Essays in American Working-Class and Social History* (New York: Knopf, 1976).

69. Goodwin, *It's Good to be Black,* 78–79.

70. Ibid., 79; Harriett Thompson in *Thirteenth Census of the United States—1910,* Bureau of the Census, Schedule No. 1—Population, 1910, Ancestry.com, http://www.ancestrylibrary.com.

71. The first verse quoted is by Berkley. The second quote is based on her description and black minister and composer Charles A. Tindley's "The Storm Is Passing

Over," a popular church song in the early 1900s. Goodwin, *It's Good to be Black,* 78–79; Robert Darden, *People Get Ready! A New History of Black Gospel Music* (New York: Continuum, 2005), 161.

72. *NYT,* July 6, 1910, p. 3.

73. *NYA,* July 14, 1910, p. 6.

74. White newspapers justified the violent reprisals by white mobs and sold more papers by publishing sensational accounts of "negro women" who attacked "white women as they sat at their own doorsteps" or knife-wielding black men shouting "Hurrah for Johnson" on crowded city streets. *Aberdeen Daily News,* July 5, 1910, p. 1; *Duluth News-Tribune,* July 6, 1910, p. 3.

75. *IF,* July 9, 1910, p. 1.

76. Ibid.

77. *CG,* July 30, 1910, p. 2.

78. *NYA,* June 29, 1911, p. 6; *NYA,* Sept. 7, 1911, p. 6.

79. The *New York Age* ran ads for nightly exhibitions of the Johnson–Jeffries fight pictures in Meyerrose Park. *NYA,* Aug. 4, 1910, p. 6. Daily exhibitions of the film at Olympic Field are listed in *NYA,* Aug. 11, 1910, p. 6.

80. *Macon Daily Telegraph,* Sept. 25, 1910, p. 7.

81. *Tuscon Daily Citizen,* Oct. 22, 1910, p. 8.

82. Federal Bureau of Investigation, Subject: John "Jack" Arthur Johnson, *Re: John Arthur Johnson, alias, Jack Johnson White Slave Traffic Act,* Oct. 29, 1937.

83. Jack Johnson, *Jack Johnson in the Ring and Out* (Chicago: National Sports Publishing Company, 1927), 78–79.

84. Ibid.; *Newark Advocate,* May 5, 1913, p. 1; *The United States v. John Arthur Johnson,* U.S. Circuit Court, Seventh District, Case 2017, October 1912, National Archives, Chicago, Illinois.

85. *Oakland Western Outlook,* July 16, 1910, pp. 190, 551–543; *Baltimore Sun,* July 20, 1910, p. 1.

86. *AA,* July 23, 1910, p. 4.

87. 61st Congress, 3rd Session, December 5, 1910–March 4, 1911, *Senate Documents,* vol. 21 (Washington, DC: Government Printing Office, 1911), 121.

88. David J. Langum, *Crossing over the Line: Legislating Morality and the Mann Act* (Chicago: University of Chicago Press, 1994).

89. *IF,* May 23, 1913, p. 7.

90. Alexander X. Byrd, *Captives and Voyagers: Black Migrants across the Eighteenth-Century British Atlantic World* (Baton Rouge: Louisiana State University Press, 2008); Ira Berlin, *The Making of African America: The Four Great Migrations* (New York: Penguin Books, 2010).

91. Historian Edlie Wong has pointed out that slaves' conceptions of freedom often differed from legal definitions of liberty, which made physical escape an impossible

route to freedom for those whose families remained enslaved. Edlie L. Wong, *Neither Fugitive nor Free: Atlantic Slavery, Freedom Suits, and the Legal Culture of Travel* (New York: New York University Press, 2009), 8–11.

92. Alexander Byrd has argued this point in his comparative study of enslaved blacks transported to Jamaica and free black emigration to Sierra Leone. Byrd, *Captives and Voyagers*, 5–7.

93. Johnson, *Jack Johnson in the Ring and Out,* 84–105.

94. Federal Bureau of Investigation, Subject: John "Jack" Arthur Johnson, *Re: John Arthur Johnson, alias, Jack Jonson White Slave Traffic Act,* Oct. 29, 1937.

95. *IF,* May 23, 1913, p. 7.

96. Bederman, *Manliness and Civilization,* 3.

97. Quoted in Dan Streible, "A History of the Boxing Film, 1894–1915: Social Control and Social Reform in the Progressive Era," *Film History* 3, no. 3 (1989): 246.

98. Annette Gordon-Reed, *Race on Trial: Law and Justice in American History* (Oxford: Oxford University Press, 2002), 90.

99. Grieveson, "Fighting Films," 46.

100. Roddenberry also attacked a black passenger on a streetcar in Washington, D.C., in 1911. When the man sat too closely to the congressman and reportedly "poked an elbow into the representative's ribs," Roddenberry jumped to his feet and "landed three or four stiff blows to the negro's face." *Colorado Springs Gazette,* June 2, 1911, p. 3; *Oregonian* (Portland, OR), Dec. 12, 1912, p. 17.

101. *NYT,* Sept. 2, 1916, p. 16.

102. *Springfield Daily News,* Apr. 12, 1916, p. 13; *NYT,* Sept. 2, 1916, p. 16; *Digest of Decisions of the United States Federal Court* (St. Paul, MN: West Publishing Co., 1917), 356.

103. *NYT,* Sept. 2, 1916, p. 16; Grieveson, "Fighting Films."

104. *IF,* July 16, 1910, p. 1

105. *BA,* July 30, 1910, p. 1.

106. *NYA,* June 5, 1913, p. 6.

107. Quoted in Stephen Bourne, *Black in the British Frame: Black People in British Film and Television, 1896–1996* (London: Cassell, 1998), 6.

108. Sol T. Plaatje, *Native Life in South Africa, Before and Since the European War and the Boer Rebellion* (1914; Project Gutenberg, 1998), chap. xxi, http://www.gutenberg.org/cache/epub/1452/pg1452.html.

109. *NYA,* July 18, 1912, p. 4.

110. *CD,* July 5, 1913, p. 1.

111. For example, arrangements were made in 1921 to feature Jack Johnson in a five-reel feature produced by the National Film Company; *NYT,* July 30, 1912, p. 12. The following year, Andlauer Producers invited interested parties to invest in "As the World Rolls On," starring Jack Johnson; *CD,* Feb. 11, 1922, p. 7.

112. *Valparaiso El Mercurio,* Dec. 3, 1913, p. 3; *Havana El Mundo,* Sept. 26, 1913, p. 5.

113. *Mexico City El Universal,* June 15, 1918, p. 7.

114. *IF,* June 1, 1912, p. 7.

115. *CD,* Nov.1, 1919, p. 1.

116. *WB,* Sept. 28, 1912, p. 1. Johnson also later attempted to seek an injunction in Cuba against the exhibition of his fight pictures against Jess Willard, a white boxer to whom Johnson lost his championship title in 1915. *NYT,* Apr. 9, 1915, p. 12; *NYT,* Apr. 10, 1915, p. 9.

117. Motts passed away in 1911; *BA,* July 15, 1911, p. 1; *Boston Journal,* Sept. 17, 1912, p. 1; *Miami Herald,* Sept. 20, 1912, p. 6; *CD,* Sept. 21, 1912, p. 1.

118. *IF,* Jan. 4, 1913, p. 2.

119. *Augusta Chronicle,* Oct. 25, 1921, p. 2.

120. *WB,* Dec. 10, 1912, p. 3.

121. *WB,* Dec. 10, 1921, p. 3.

122. *CD,* Aug. 27, 1932, p. 5.

123. "Negro on Censor Board," *NYA,* Mar. 26, 1914, p. 6.

124. *BA,* Feb. 22, 1902, p. 1.

125. *IF,* May 1, 1915, p. 4; *IF,* May 29, 1915, p. 4; *CD,* June 5, 1915, p. 8.

126. *IF,* Dec. 20, 1913, p. 13.

6. Mobilizing an Envisioned Community

1. *Coe College Cosmos,* May 4, 1915, p. 4; *Cedar Rapids Daily Republican,* May 8, 1915, p. 2.

2. *CD,* May 15, 1915, p. 7.

3. Ibid.

4. By 1915, the terms "photoplay" and "play" were commonly used to describe moving pictures.

5. Thomas Cripps, *Slow Fade to Black: The Negro in American Film, 1900–1942* ([1977] New York: Oxford University Press, 1993), 41–69; Janet Staiger, *Interpreting Films: Studies in the Historical Reception of American Cinema* (Princeton, NJ: Princeton University Press, 1992), 139–153; Jane Gaines, *Fire and Desire: Mixed-Race Movies in the Silent Era* (Chicago: University of Chicago Press, 2001), 219–257; Melvyn Stokes, *D. W. Griffith's "The Birth of a Nation"* (New York: Oxford University Press, 2007), 129–170; Josh Glick, "Mixed Messages: D. W. Griffith and the Black Press, 1916–1931," *Film History* 23, no. 2 (2011): 174–195; Paul Polgar, "Fighting Lightning with Fire: Black Boston's Battle against 'Birth of a Nation,'" *Massachusetts Historical Review* 10 (2008): 84–113; Kimberley Mangun, "As Citizens of Portland We Must Protest: Beatrice Morrow Cannady and the African American Response to D. W. Griffith's 'Masterpiece,'" *Oregon Historical Quarterly* 107, no. 3 (2006): 382–409; John Inscoe, "*The*

Clansman on Stage and Screen: North Carolina Reacts," *North Carolina Historical Review* 64, no. 2 (1987): 139–161; Lawrence J. Oliver and Terri L. Walker, "James Weldon Johnson's 'New York Age' Essays on 'Birth of a Nation' and the 'Southern Oligarchy,'" *South Central Review* 10, no. 4 (1993): 1–17.

6. Cripps, *Slow Fade to Black,* 67.

7. The assumption implicit in this assessment is that the primary measure of success was the campaign's ability to block *The Birth of a Nation.* The protestors and national organizations, however, often acknowledged that there were other goals such as institution building and publicity that contributed to the movement. Stokes, *D. W. Griffith's "The Birth of a Nation,"* 13–14.

8. Robert Sklar, *Movie-Made America: A Social History of American Movies* (New York: Random House, 1975), 67–69; Eileen Bowser, *The Transformation of Cinema, 1907–1915* (New York: Scribner Collier Macmillan, 1990), 159–165.

9. *BA,* June 23, 1906, p. 2.

10. The national NAACP was formed in 1909. For more on the Los Angeles NAACP branch, see Delilah Leontium Beasley, *The Negro Trail Blazers of California,* ed. Adam S. Eterdvich ([1919] San Fransisco: R and E Research Associates, 1968), 193–194; Douglas Flamming, *Bound for Freedom: Black Los Angeles in Jim Crow America* (Berkeley: University of California Press, 2005), 87–90, 143–145.

11. There are eight states for which I have not found a record of such a campaign between 1915 and 1917: Florida, Maine, Nevada, New Hampshire, North Dakota, South Dakota, Vermont, and Tennessee. In 1918, however, a protest against *The Birth of a Nation* was organized by an alliance of AME ministers in Nashville, Tennessee. *CD,* May 18, 1918, p. 16.

12. "Negro Sues Canal Zone Y.M.C.A. over 'Birth of a Nation,'" *New Orleans Times-Picayune,* Oct. 18, 1916, p. 13; Paul R. Magocsi, ed., *Encyclopedia of Canada's Peoples* (Toronto: University of Toronto Press, 1999), 165–166.

13. *NYT,* Aug. 20, 1923, p. 14; *CD,* Sept. 1, 1923, p. 12; *Pittsburg Courier,* Sept. 1, 1923, p. 13; *CD,* Sept. 15, 1923, p. 7.

14. *WB,* Mar. 10, 1906, p. 4.

15. E. Burton Ceruti to May Childs Nerney, Feb. 3, 1915, in August Meier and John Bracey, eds., *Papers of the National Association for the Advancement of Colored People* (microfilm, 30 parts) (Ann Arbor: University Publications of America, 1982), pt. 11 (36 reels), series A, reel 32; *ST,* Feb. 20, 1915, p. 3; *Crisis,* May 1915, p. 40.

16. "To the Honorable City Council of the City of Los Angeles, California," Feb. 2, 1915, in Meier and Bracey, *Papers of the NAACP,* pt. 11, series A, reel 32; Ceruti to Nerney, Feb. 3, 1915, in Meier and Bracey, *Papers of the NAACP,* pt. 11, series A, reel 32; Nerney to Ceruti, Feb. 25, 1915, in Meier and Bracey, *Papers of the NAACP,* pt. 11, series A, reel 32; Nerney to Ceruti, Feb. 25, 1915, in Meier and Bracey, *Papers of the NAACP,* pt. 11, series A, reel 32; Nerney to Ceruti, Mar. 2, 1915, in Meier and Bracey, *Papers of the NAACP,* pt. 11, series A, reel 32; Nerney to Ceruti, Mar. 4,

1915, in Meier and Bracey, *Papers of the NAACP,* pt. 11, series A, reel 32; Nerney to Ceruti, Mar. 18, 1915, in Meier and Bracey, *Papers of the NAACP,* pt. 11, series A, reel 32.

17. Gaines, *Fire and Desire,* 219–257; Staiger, *Interpreting Films,* 139–153.

18. *Los Angeles Times,* editorial, July 6, 1910.

19. *ST,* Feb. 20, 1915, p. 3.

20. My italics. *NYA,* Apr. 1, 1915, p. 4.

21. *NYA,* Apr. 8, 1915.

22. *CD,* Sept. 4, 1915, p. 7.

23. *BA,* Dec. 16, 1916, p. 1.

24. *The Clansman* was the original title of Griffith's film. Ceruti to Nerney, Feb. 3, 1915, in Meier and Bracey, *Papers of the NAACP,* pt. 11, series A, reel 32.

25. James Weldon Johnson, *NYA,* Mar. 4, 1915, p. 4.

26. Johnson, *NYA,* Apr. 22, 1915, p. 4.

27. Johnson, *NYA,* Mar. 4, 1915, p. 4.

28. *WB,* June 5, 1915, p. 2; "The Dirt of a Nation," *CD,* June 5, 1915, p. 8. These critiques continued when *Birth of a Nation* was re-released in 1921. In New York City, for example, a rally was led by Captain Eugene L. C. Davidson of the Company D, 367th Infantry, in France, who wore his Croix de Guerre military ribbon (awarded for heroism during World War I) while picketing the film. With other veterans, he picketed the Capitol Theater on May 6, 1921, with signs that read, "We represented America in France, why should *The Birth of a Nation* misrepresent us here?" in an argument that foreshadowed the Double Victory campaign of World War II. "Negroes Oppose Film," *NYT,* May 7, 1921, p. 8.

29. NAACP, *Sixth Annual Report of the National Association for the Advancement of Colored People, 1915* (New York, 1916), 11.

30. Walter Benjamin, "The Work of Art in the Age of Mechanical Reproduction," in Walter Benjamin, *Illuminations,* Harry Zohn, trans. (New York: Schocken Books, 1968), 217–251.

31. Scholars have frequently criticized Walter Benjamin for his technologically determinist descriptions of the democratic possibilities of the moving picture. Yet Benjamin also made reference to *space:* "Although paintings began to be publicly exhibited in galleries and salons," he explained, "there was no way for the masses to organize and control themselves in their reception." African Americans' "simultaneous contemplation" of the movies across space was not determined, but rather generated by the history of cinema in black life and the American film industry's extensive channels of distribution. Benjamin, "Work of Art," 234–235.

32. *Crisis,* May 1915, p. 40.

33. Meanwhile, President Woodrow Wilson screened Griffith's production at the White House, which he reportedly lauded as "history written in lightning." Thomas Cripps, "The Making of the Birth of a Race," in Daniel Bernardi, ed., *The Birth of*

Whiteness: Race and the Emergence of U.S. Cinema (New Brunswick, NJ: Rutgers University Press, 1996).

34. "Fighting a Race Calumny," *Crisis,* May 1915, p. 41.

35. Ibid.

36. *IF,* Mar. 20, 1915, p. 6.

37. As early as 1909, he had implored black New Yorkers to mobilize against racist films that were screening in the Bowery. Six years later, Walton had grown cynical. *NYA,* Aug. 5, 1909, p. 6; *NYA,* Mar. 25, 1915, p. 6.

38. *IF,* Apr. 10, 1915, p. 1.

39. *NYA,* Apr. 1, 1915, p. 7.

40. Schaeffle may have been with seven other black attendees. *Springfield Union,* Apr. 15, 1915, p. 20. Elizabeth Gurley Flynn knew Howard Schaeffle as "Howard Shaeffer." He also appears to have gone by the pen name of "Eric Howard" (The John and Phyllis Collier Collection Papers 1881–1975 [Walter P. Reuther Library, Detroit, MI]). Flynn recalled Shaeffer in 1915: "The last time I had seen Howard Shaeffer he had been ordered to leave New York City or go to jail. He had hurled rotten eggs at the screen of a Broadway theater when the anti-negro, pro-Confederacy film *The Birth of a Nation* was being shown." Elizabeth Gurley Flynn, *The Rebel Girl: An Autobiography, My First Life* (New York: International Publishers, 1994), 195–196.

41. Because the NAACP organized the first public campaign and many subsequent interventions, scholars have credited the organization with mobilizations. Certainly, the NAACP grew significantly during the protests against *The Birth of a Nation,* especially after the NAACP discovered that the campaign helped bolster its modest membership rolls and publicize its other projects. However, even during the first campaign in Los Angeles, the NAACP worked with other local organizations. *Crisis,* June 1915, p. 87.

42. My italics. *NYT,* Apr. 15, 1915, p. 1.

43. Ibid.

44. This incident has also been documented by Stokes, *D. W. Griffith's "Birth of a Nation,"* 146; Gaines, *Fire and Desire,* 220–222; Staiger, *Interpreting Films,* 144.

45. *NYT,* Sept. 26, 1911, p. 8.

46. *NYT,* Mar. 5, 1914, p. 1; *NYT,* June 16, 1914, p. 6; *NYT,* Mar. 31, 1915, p. 8.

47. *NYT,* Apr. 15, 1915, p. 1.

48. Allen was organizing an event honoring Booker T. Washington; he also planned an annual event honoring the work of Harriet Beecher Stowe; Cleveland G. Allen Papers, 1915–1953 (Schomburg Center for Research in Black Culture, New York, NY).

49. He was removed from the theater but was not arrested, nor did he appear later at the police station along with the black attorney and his "delegation" that was sent to assist the two arrested Wobblies.

50. *Sun,* Apr. 18, 1915, p. 1; *Boston Sunday Globe,* Apr. 18, 1915, p. 3.

51. Ibid. Two men were ejected from the theater that evening for throwing rotten eggs at the screen. Trotter's insistence that his eggs were fresh may have been calculated to disassociate his action from that of the other egg thrower. *Sun,* Apr. 18, 1915.

52. *NYT,* Apr. 18, 1915, p. 15; *IF,* May 8, 1915, p. 6; *Boston Sunday Globe,* Apr. 18, 1915, p. 3.

53. According to his census records, Charles P. Ray lived with his mother and appears to have struggled financially. *Fourteenth Census of the United States: 1920—Population,* U.S. Department of Commerce and Labor, Bureau of the Census, 1920; *Fifteenth Census of the United States: 1930—Population,* U.S. Department of Commerce and Labor, Bureau of the Census, 1930, Ancestry.com, http://www.ancestrylibrary.com.

54. The reporters intentionally reported as a literal truth what was likely meant as a metaphor. *NYT,* June 23, 1903, p. 1; *NYT,* June 29, 1903, p. 1.

55. Stephen R. Fox, *The Guardian of Boston: William Monroe Trotter* (New York: Atheneum, 1970).

56. *Boston Sunday Globe,* Apr. 18, 1915, p. 3.

57. *CG,* Feb. 12, 1916, p. 2.

58. Meier and Bracey, *Papers of the NAACP,* pt. 11, series A, reel 32.

59. May Childs Nerney to "Our Branches and Locals," Apr. 7, 1915; Meier and Bracey, *Papers of the NAACP,* pt. 11, series A, reel 32.

60. Jennie M. Proctor to May Childs Nerney, Apr. 19, 1915, in Meier and Bracey, *Papers of the NAACP,* pt. 11, series A, reel 32.

61. *Crisis,* May 1915, p. 40.

62. *TP,* Feb. 4, 1916, p. 1.

63. In order to avoid censorship, protestors argued, the film was occasionally advertised with different titles. *CD,* Aug. 21, 1915, p. 2.

64. *CG,* July 24, 1915, p. 2.

65. *IF,* Sept. 25, 1915, p. 6.

66. *CD,* May 15, 1915, p. 7.

67. *CD,* Oct. 2, 1915, p. 1.

68. *CD,* Oct. 2, 1915, p. 8; Francis H. Warren, *Michigan Manual of Freedmen's Progress* [1915], Western Michigan University Archives and Regional History Collections, Kalamazoo, Michigan, http://www.wmich.edu/library/digi/collections/freedmen/.

69. *CD,* Oct. 2, 1915, p. 8.

70. James N. Gregory, *The Southern Diaspora: How the Great Migrations of Black and White Southerners Transformed America* (Chapel Hill: University of North Carolina Press, 2005), 50; Aurora Wallace, *Newspapers and the Making of Modern America* (Westport, CT: Greenwood Press, 2005); W. Augustus Low, ed., *Encyclopedia of Black America* (New York: Da Capo Press, 1981); James Grossman estimated that each issue was read by four people; James Grossman, "Southern Distribution of Chicago

Defender, 1919," *Encyclopedia of Chicago,* http://www.encyclopedia.chicagohistory.org/pages/3714.html.

71. *ST,* Apr. 24, 1915, p. 1.

72. *CD,* May 8, 1915, p. 1.

73. *IF,* May 8, 1915, p. 6.

74. *CD,* Apr. 24, 1915, p. 4.

75. Fred H. Gresham, "Race Men Oppose Showing the Nigger," *CD,* May 15, 1915, p. 7.

76. Ibid.

77. *BA,* Dec. 16, 1916, p. 1.

78. Joseph A. Logsdon, *The Rev. Archibald J. Carey and the Negro in Chicago Politics* (MA thesis, University of Chicago, 1961).

79. Beth Tompkins Bates, *Pullman Porters and the Rise of Protest Politics in Black America: 1925–1945* (Chapel Hill: University of North Carolina Press, 2001), 204.

80. *IF,* Jan. 1, 1916, p. 4.

81. *IR,* May 18, 1912, p. 1; Mrs. Thos. Brown, "Twin Cities News," *CD,* Oct. 30, 1915, p. 3; "Protest Sustained by Minnesota's Court," *CD,* Dec. 11, 1915, p. 5.

82. "Greenville in Righteous Protest," *CD,* Oct. 30, 1915, p. 1.

83. Ida B. Wells-Barnett, *Crusade for Justice: The Autobiography of Ida B. Wells* (Chicago: University of Chicago Press, 1970), 344.

84. Boston Ordinance, Title 14, Section 286.

85. "Police Beat and Arrest Boston Women Protesting against *The Birth of a Nation,*" *CD,* June 19, 1915, p. 1.

86. This changed after 1915.

87. *Crisis,* May 1915, pp. 40–42.

88. My italics. *CD,* Dec. 18, 1915, p. 7.

89. *Springfield Daily News,* Sept. 21, 1915, p. 5.

90. Ibid. My italics.

91. *Broad Ax* also capitalized "Negroes," unlike the earlier *Springfield Daily News* article. *Springfield Daily News,* Sept. 21, 1915, p. 5; *BA,* Sept. 25, 1915, p. 1.

92. *BA,* Sept. 25, 1915, p. 1.

93. My italics. *CD,* Sept. 25, 1915, p. 1.

94. As discussed in Chapters 3 and 5, new definitions of manhood flourished in the first decades of the twentieth century as black men moved away from hinging their identities on their productive capabilities and began seeing their gender identities based on their consumer and leisure practices. Martin Summers, *Manliness and Its Discontents: The Black Middle Class and the Transformation of Masculinity, 1900–1930* (Chapel Hill: University of North Carolina Press, 2004), 7–9.

95. *Thirteenth Census of the United States: 1910—Population,* U.S. Department of Commerce and Labor, Bureau of the Census, 1913, Ancestry.com, http://www.ancestrylibrary.com.

96. Fred H. Gresham, 1915 Iowa State Census Collection, Ancestry.com, http://www.ancestrylibrary.com; *CD,* May 15, 1915, p. 7.

97. *CD,* May 15, 1915, p. 7.

98. *CD,* Sept. 18, 1915, p. 4.

99. *Boston Evening Transcript,* Apr. 28, 1915, p. 2.

100. Gaines, *Fire and Desire,* 22.

101. Lawrence W. Levine, *Highbrow/Lowbrow: The Emergence of Cultural Hierarchy in America* (Cambridge, MA: Harvard University Press, 1988), 63–69; Sean Wilentz, *Chants Democratic: New York City and the Rise of the American Working Class, 1788–1850* (New York: Oxford University Press, 1984), 359; Eric Lott, *Love and Theft: Blackface Minstrelsy and the American Working Class* (New York: Oxford University Press, 1993), 66–67.

102. Protestors included Henry Taylor and Syd Thompson. *CG,* Apr. 21, 1917, p. 3.

103. *CG,* Apr. 21, 1917, p. 3

104. *CG,* Jan. 9, 1915, p. 3; *CG,* Aug. 17, 1918, p. 3.

105. *CG,* Aug. 17, 1918, p. 3.

106. "Colored Women Run *Birth of a Nation* out of Philadelphia," *CD,* Sept. 25, 1915, p. 1.

107. "We intend to fight as long as this play shows here," declared one of the leading black women of the city, who, according to the *Chicago Defender,* was "taking an active part in the defense of Afro-American womanhood." "Women of Race Fighting against *The Birth of a Nation,*" *CD,* June 26, 1915, p. 3.

108. "Police Beat and Arrest Boston Women Protesting against *The Birth of a Nation,*" *CD,* June 19, 1915, p. 1.

109. "Colored Women Run *Birth of a Nation* Out of Philadelphia," *CD,* Sept. 25, 1915, p. 1.

110. In 1911, the Bethel AME Church had seventy-nine members. The church was organized in 1870; its edifice was constructed in 1874 and was valued at $5,000 in 1911. *History of Linn County Iowa* (Chicago: Pioneer Publishing Company, 1911), 398.

111. "Mrs. White Presides," *CD,* Apr. 15, 1916, p. 6. Like other black organizations, the Colored Women's Clubs worked together with other local civic and religious organizations to join in fighting the film, including the CME Church, the AME Church, the Baptist Church, and the Colored Men's Protective League. In Baltimore, Maryland, more than a thousand people gathered at the Bethel Church in Druid Hill at the tenth annual session of the Federation of Women's Clubs to listen to Ruth Bennett, president of the Chester, Pennsylvania, branch speak of her organization's struggle against *The Birth of a Nation.* "Federation of Women's Clubs Elects Mrs. Mary Talbert Press," *CD,* Aug. 19, 1916, p. 3.

112. *CD,* Oct. 30, 1915, p. 1; *CD,* Dec. 11, 1915, p. 3; *ST,* Nov. 20, 1915, p. 8.

113. *NYA,* Dec. 30, 1915, p. 2.

114. *St. Paul Appeal,* Oct. 30, 1915, p. 3.

115. *IF,* Jan. 15, 1916, p. 2.

116. Black identity, Brent Edwards has argued, should be thought of as a set of practices—systems of exchange through which ideas of race were continuously reformulated and translated. Actions, debates, alliances, and other collective mobilizations forced participants to put their ideas of a shared identity into practice. Brent Hayes Edwards, *The Practice of Diaspora: Literature, Translation, and the Rise of Black Internationalism* (Cambridge, MA: Harvard University Press, 2003), 7.

117. *IF,* May 1, 1915, p. 4.

118. Ibid.

119. *IF,* Mar. 11, 1916, p. 3.

120. *NYA,* Nov. 4, 1915, p. 4.

121. *IF,* Mar. 11, 1916, p. 3; *CD,* Nov. 6, 1915, p. 1. Anna Everett also wrote that the *Philadelphia Tribune* disagreed with the protests. Anna Everett, *Returning the Gaze: A Genealogy of Black Film Criticism, 1909–1949* (Durham, NC: Duke University Press, 2001), 81.

122. "Cleveland People Fight 'The Birth of a Nation' Film," *CD,* Mar. 31, 1917, p. 1.

123. "At His Old Games," *CG,* Jan. 5, 1918, p. 1.

124. *CG,* Apr. 29, 1916, p. 2.

125. Ibid.

126. "The Slanderous Film," *Crisis,* Dec. 1915, p. 77.

127. Charles Flint Kellogg, *N.A.A.C.P.: A History of the National Association for the Advancement of Colored People* (Baltimore, MD: Johns Hopkins University Press, 1973).

128. *IF,* Aug. 5, 1916, p. 3.

129. C. Sumner Wormley hailed from the powerful and wealthy Wormley family, which was based in Virginia and Washington, D.C. *WB,* Apr. 8, 1916, p. 5; *IF,* Aug. 5, 1916, p. 3. The accusations of "libel" continued past World War I. For example, protestors in Atlantic City complained that Griffith's film "libels the race." *Advocate,* Feb. 22, 1918, p. 1.

130. *Montgomery Advertiser,* Feb. 2, 1916, p. 12.

131. Edward E. Kallgren, *California Law Review* 41, no. 2 (Summer 1953): 290–299; Evan P. Schultz, "Group Rights, American Jews, and the Failure of Group Libel Laws, 1913–1952," *Brooklyn Law Review* 66 (Spring 2000): 71–145.

132. *IF,* May 1, 1915, p. 4.

133. *CG,* May 22, 1915, p. 1.

134. *NYT,* Apr. 15, 1915 p. 1.

135. *St. Paul Appeal,* Oct. 30, 1915, p. 3.

136. *CD,* June 5, 1915, p. 8

137. *IF,* May 29, 1915, p. 4.

138. *IF,* Nov. 13, 1915, p. 4.

139. In San Francisco, the Negro Welfare League and other black organizations "left no stone unturned to stop it and its filthy work," eventually forcing Mayor Rolph and the Board of Supervisors to support their ban of the film. *CD,* Jan. 15, 1916, p. 1. Reverend W. A. Lynch of Lynn, Massachusetts, the chairman of the executive committee of the Equal Rights League, led a demonstration and convinced the mayor to bar the film from the town. "Vicious Film Play Barred by Mayor's Action," *CD,* May 18, 1918.

140. *CG,* Sept. 4, 1915, p. 2.

141. The Supreme Court's 1952 decision in *Joseph Burstyn, Inc. v. Wilson* delegitimized state censorship boards by providing the moving pictures the protections of the First Amendment. Paul McEwan, "Lawyers, Bibliographies, and the Klan: Griffith's Resources in the Censorship Battle over *The Birth of a Nation* in Ohio," *Film History* 20, no. 3 (2008): 358.

142. *IF,* Aug. 5, 1916, p. 3.

143. *WB,* Apr. 13, 1918, p. 4.

144. *NYA,* Aug. 12, 1915, p. 1.

145. *Crisis,* Oct. 1915, p. 268.

146. G. E. Perkins, Chief of the Military Morale Section, to Captain J. J. Gleason, Office of Staff, Executive Division, Military Intelligence Branch, War Department, Sept. 30, 1918, *Correspondence of the Military Intelligence Division Relating to "Negro Subversion," 1917–1941* (microfilm, 6 reels, National Archives Trust Fund Board, National Archives and Records Administration, 1987), National Archives and Records Administration, reel 3; *Crisis,* Oct. 1915, p. 268.

147. *WB,* Apr. 13, 1918, p. 4.

148. Mary Dudziak has written that in the later Civil Rights–Cold War era, U.S. federal government politicians began supporting civil rights legislation to improve America's image abroad. Although the protests of 1915–1917 occurred much earlier than the classical Civil Rights period, the government's response to the protests during World War I demonstrate the interplay between foreign and domestic policy. Mary L. Dudziak, *Cold War Civil Rights: Race and the Image of American Democracy* (Princeton, NJ: Princeton University Press, 2000).

149. Perkins, *Correspondence of the Military Intelligence Division Relating to "Negro Subversion,"* reel 3.

150. *NYA,* May 6, 1915, p. 1; *NYA,* Apr. 15, 1915, p. 1.

151. *IF,* May 8, 1915, p. 4.

152. *ST,* Sept. 4, 1915, p. 1; *CG,* May 12, 1917, p. 2.

153. *CG,* Apr. 10, 1915, p. 2.

154. Donald Bogle identified several enduring stereotypes of black characters onscreen, including the "black buck," in Donald Bogle, *Toms, Coons, Mulattoes, Mammies, and Bucks: An Interpretive History of Blacks in American Films* (New York: Viking, 1973), 13.

155. "The usual crime" was also a line from the play. *Moving Picture World* quoted in William W. Griffin, *African Americans and the Color Line in Ohio, 1915–1930* (Columbus: Ohio State University Press, 2002), 72.

156. Alan Gevinson, ed., *American Film Institute Catalog, Within Our Gates: Ethnicity in American Feature Films, 1911–1960* (Berkeley: University of California Press, 1997), 713; Edward Sheldon, *The Nigger: An American Play in Three Acts* (New York: Macmillan Company, 1910), 60.

157. *Crisis,* Oct. 1915, p. 293.

158. *CG,* Apr. 10, 1915, p. 2; *IF,* Sept. 25, 1915, p. 6.

159. *IF,* May 22, 1915, p. 4.

160. *IF,* May 15, 1915, p. 4.

161. *Crisis,* Oct. 1915, p. 293.

162. Benedict Anderson, *Imagined Communities: Reflections on the Origin and Spread of Nationalism* (London: Verso, 1983), 37–46.

163. Ibid.

164. Also see Gabriel Tarde's analysis of media and communication without a physical presence, as discussed by Stuart Ewen. Stuart Ewen, *PR! A Social History of Spin* (New York: Basic Books, 1996), 67–71.

165. *ST,* Jan. 29, 1916, p. 7; *ST,* Feb. 5, 1916, p. 7.

7. Race Films and the Transnational Frontier

1. Oscar Micheaux, *The Conquest: The Story of a Negro Pioneer* (Lincoln, NE: Woodruff Press, 1913), 47.

2. In this chapter, "race films" and the "race film industry" refers to independent race film companies. Hollywood also produced "race films," but I will delineate these throughout. Scholars who have pioneered the study of race films include Donald Bogle, *Toms, Coons, Mulattoes, Mammies, and Bucks: An Interpretive History of Blacks in American Films* (New York: Continuum, 2003), 101–158; Henry T. Sampson, *Blacks in Black and White: A Source Book on Films* (Metuchen, NJ: Scarecrow Press, 1995); Thomas Cripps, *Slow Fade to Black: The Negro in American Film, 1900–1942* (New York: Oxford University Press, 1993), 170–202. Many independent race film companies included at least a few white investors or producers. Jane Gaines, *Fire and Desire: Mixed-Race Movies in the Silent Era* (Chicago: University of Chicago Press, 2001).

3. Oscar Micheaux, *The Conquest,* 9; Patricia Nelson Limerick, *The Legacy of Conquest: The Unbroken Past of the American West* (New York: W. W. Norton, 1987), 26; Richard White, *"It's Your Misfortune and None of My Own": A History of the American West* (Norman: University of Oklahoma Press, 1991), 613–632.

4. Correspondence between French Pictorial Service and Lincoln Motion Picture Company, *George P. Johnson Negro Film Collection, 1916–1977* [hereafter *GPJ, 1916–1977*]

(microfilm, 12 reels, University of California, Los Angeles Library, Photographic Department, 1974) [1918], reel 1.

5. Jacqueline Stewart, *Migrating to the Movies: Cinema and Black Urban Modernity* (Berkeley: University of California Press, 2005), 191; J. Ronald Green, *Straight Lick: The Cinema of Oscar Micheaux* (Bloomington: Indiana University Press, 2000); Pearl Bowser and Louise Spence, *Writing Himself into History: Oscar Micheaux, His Silent Films, and His Audience* (New Brunswick, NJ: Rutgers University Press, 2000), 109–113; Dan Moos, "Reclaiming the Frontier: Oscar Micheaux as Black Turnerian," *African American Review* 36 (2002): 356–381.

6. A few films were produced for noncommercial use. Sol Plaatje exhibited self-produced films alongside those he procured from the Tuskegee Institute's Robert Russa Moton throughout South Africa. Glenn Whiley Reynolds, "Image and Empire: Cinema, Race, and Mass Black Spectatorship in Southern Africa, 1920–1940" (PhD diss., SUNY Stony Brook, 2005), 26.

7. Frederick Jackson Turner, "The Significance of the Frontier in American History," in *The Frontier in American History* (New York: Henry Holt, 1921).

8. Nell Irvin Painter, *Exodusters: Black Migration to Kansas after Reconstruction* (Lawrence: University Press of Kansas, 1986), 195–196.

9. *National Review,* Oct. 25, 1913, p. 1.

10. *CD,* Mar. 19, 1910, p. 1.

11. For more on black consumer culture, see Chapter 3.

12. H. C. Conley, Mrs. Conley, and their company traveled to Canada and Mexico with moving pictures featuring "scenes of their travels [and] the progress of the successful Afro-Americans," *WB,* Aug. 31, 1907, p. 5; *AA,* Feb. 7, 1914, p. 3; *IF,* Nov. 4, 1905, p. 7; *NYA,* Jan. 20, 1910, p. 6.

13. *CD,* Dec. 7, 1912, p. 5. An advertisement in the *Crisis* indicates that James Morris Webb completed the film prior to April 1914. *Crisis,* Apr. 1914, p. 306.

14. *CD,* Dec. 31, 1910, p. 3.

15. *NYA,* Jan. 20, 1910, p. 6.

16. *IF,* Mar. 8, 1913, p. 1.

17. *NYA,* Jan. 20, 1910, p. 6.

18. *NYA,* Aug. 4, 1910, p. 6; *Cleveland Gazette,* Jan. 15, 1910, p. 3.

19. Cary B. Lewis, "A Day at Tuskegee," *IF,* Mar. 22, 1913, p. 1.

20. Other film producers went on to make motion pictures of Tuskegee. It is unclear which films were given to Plaatje.

21. *Umteteli was Bantu,* Dec. 25, 1925, quoted in Ntongela Masilela, "New African Movement and the Beginnings of Film Culture in South Africa," in Isabel Balseiro and Ntongela Masilela, eds., *To Change Reels: Film and Culture in South Africa* (Detroit: Wayne State University Press, 2003), 19.

22. The pictures were also exhibited in white venues such as Carnegie Hall. *IR,* Jan. 29, 1910, p. 1.

23. *IF,* Mar. 8, 1913, p. 1.

24. *IF,* Nov. 1, 1913, p. 6.

25. Tim Brooks, *Lost Sounds: Blacks and the Birth of the Recording Industry* (Urbana-Champaign: University of Illinois Press, 2004), 464.

26. *CD,* Mar. 29, 1913, p. 8.

27. *CD,* Jun. 21, 1913, p. 2; *CD,* Feb. 1, 1936, p. 14. Foster's ads for the Jack Johnson buttons ran in papers such as the *New York Age. NYA,* May 26, 1910, p. 6; *GPJ, 1916–1977,* reel 4.

28. *IF,* Aug. 9, 1913, p. 5.

29. *CD,* Aug. 9, 1913, p. 6; *NYA,* Sept. 25, 1913, p. 6.

30. *CD,* July 5, 1913, p. 6; *IF,* Sept. 6, 1913, p. 5; *CD,* Sept. 27, 1913, p. 6; *IF,* Oct. 4, 1913, p. 5; *CD,* Oct. 18, 1913, p. 6.

31. *NYA,* Apr. 9, 1914, p. 6.

32. *CD,* June 20, 1914, p. 4.

33. Russell made the revelation after a "falling out" between the two men. Foster had suggested the Grand Theatre eliminate its live performances and convert entirely into a motion picture venue, which incensed Russell. *IF,* June 12, 1915, p. 5.

34. Sampson, *Blacks in Black and White,* 172–176.

35. *CD,* Oct. 9, 1915, p. 6.

36. Ibid.

37. George P. Johnson, interviewed by Elizabeth Dixon and Adelaide Tusler, George P. Johnson Collector of Negro Film History [hereafter GPJ-CNFH] (1970), July 21, 1967, transcript, 1–3, University of California, Los Angeles Oral History Program (Bancroft Library, Los Angeles).

38. GPJ-CNFH (1970), July 28, 1967, transcript, 45a.

39. Ibid.

40. "President Wilson Killed the Bill," *CD,* June 19, 1920, p. 20.

41. Quoted from Thomas Cripps, "The Making of a Birth of a Race," in Daniel Bernardi, ed., *The Birth of Whiteness: Race and the Emergence of U.S. Cinema* (New Brunswick, NJ: Rutgers University Press, 1996), 43.

42. Cripps, "Making of a Birth of a Race."

43. *IF,* June 18, 1904, p. 7

44. *IF,* Jan. 21, 1905, p. 7.

45. *IF,* June 13, 1914, p. 6.

46. His first foray into motion picture production was in 1913, as general manager of the white-owned Afro-American Film Company. *IF,* Aug. 1, 1914, p. 6.

47. *GPJ, 1916–1977,* reels 1–4.

48. *GPJ, 1916–1977,* reel 4.

49. Such as black critic Lester Walton of the Quality Amusement Corporation, *GPJ, 1916–1977,* reel 7.

50. *GPJ, 1916–1977,* reel 8. Also see Sampson, *Blacks in Black and White,* 188, 209–212, 457, 629–630.

51. Gettysburg Address.

52. *Kansas City (KS) Advocate,* May 18, 1917, p. 4.

53. *GPJ, 1916–1977,* reel 4.

54. "Delight" and "Special Investigation Report Delight Film Co., Chicago, Ill.," *GPJ, 1916–1977,* reel 4.

55. "Democracy Film Corporation," *GPJ, 1916–1977,* reel 4; *GPJ, 1916–1977,* reel 7.

56. "Constellation," *GPJ, 1916–1977,* reel 3.

57. "Monumental Picture Corporation," *GPJ, 1916–1977,* reel 8; *GPJ, 1916–1977,* reel 7.

58. "Jack Johnson a Movie Star," *CD,* Nov. 1, 1919, p. 1.

59. Personal Correspondence, Clarence Muse to Claude A. Barnett, Sept. 25, 1934, p. 2, Claude A. Barnett Papers, Box 285, folder 5. ProQuest (Black Freedom II set).

60. Clarence Muse organized Delsarte in 1920. Muse wrote the screenplay and played the title role in what was reported as a $90,000 production. *GPJ, 1916–1977,* reel 4.

61. Sampson, *Blacks in Black and White,* 290.

62. Thomas Elsaesser, for example, argued that Weimar cinema developed particular characteristics of Expressionism in order to establish a specialized niche that allowed it to compete against Hollywood imported films; Thomas Elsaesser, "Social Mobility and the Fantastic," *Wide Angle* 5, no. 2 (1982): 14–25.

63. For more on black Westerns and the global appeal of Westerns to black audiences, see Julia Leyda, "Black-Audience Westerns and the Politics of Cultural Identification in the 1930s," *Cinema Journal* 42, no. 1 (Autumn 2001): 46–70; Reynolds, "Image and Empire," 180–217; and Hortense Powdermaker, *Copper Town: Changing Africa* (New York: Harper and Row, 1962), 254–272.

64. Powdermaker, *Copper Town*, 261.

65. Sampson, *Blacks in Black and White,* 252–254, 286–289.

66. Also, genres such as Italian "Spaghetti Westerns" exemplify the versatility of genres and their expropriation into disparate cultural contexts.

67. Sampson, *Blacks in Black and White,* 255–257; *Augusta Chronicle,* May 17, 1921, p. 3.

68. Stewart, *Migrating to the Movies,* 191; Green, *Straight Lick;* Bowser and Spence, *Writing Himself into History,* 109–113; Moos, "Reclaiming the Frontier," 356–381.

69. *CD,* Sept. 15, 1923, p. 7.

70. Melvyn Stokes, "Kojo Touvalou Houénou: An Assessment," *Transatlantica* 1 (2009), http://transatlantica.revues.org.

71. *AA,* July 27, 1923, p. 1.

72. *Pittsburgh Courier,* Sept. 15, 1923.

73. *CD,* Sept. 1, 1923, p. 12; *CD,* Nov. 17, 1923, p. 2.

74. *NYA,* Aug. 20, 1923, p. 14; *CD,* Sept. 1, 1923, p. 12; *Pittsburgh Courier,* Sept. 1, 1923, p. 13; *CD,* Sept. 15, 1923, p. 7.

75. *GPJ, 1916–1977,* reel 1.

76. *NYA,* Nov. 30, 1918, quoted in Sampson, *Blacks in Black and White,* 234.

77. *CD,* July 20, 1918, p. 5; *CD,* Apr. 27, 1918, p. 4; *CD,* Oct. 26, 1918, p. 10.

78. *CD,* May 23, 1914, p. 1; *CD,* June 13, 1914, p. 6.

79. *CD,* Sept. 12, 1914, p. 6.

80. The young man was reportedly Cuban. *NYA,* May 22, 1920, p. 6.

81. As Mae Ngai has written of citizenship in the context of interned Japanese Americans, who "understood that citizenship is, in the first instance, a formal status with explicit legal rights and obligations, and that loyalty is a matter of political, not cultural, practice." Mae Ngai, *Impossible Subjects: Illegal Aliens and the Making of Modern America* (Princeton, NJ: Princeton University Press, 2004), 201.

82. "Foster Photo Play Corporation," *GPJ, 1916–1977,* reel 4; *CD,* Apr. 27, 1918, p. 4.

83. *CD,* May 22, 1915, p. 2.

84. Foster's ambivalence is further demonstrated by his imperialist description of "the heathen" "in the jungle of Africa" who nonetheless "has more soul than the degenerate white Southern cracker." *CD,* May 22, 1915, p. 2.

85. *NYA,* Nov. 30, 1918, quoted in Sampson, *Blacks in Black and White,* 234.

86. GPJ-CNFH (1970), July 28, 1967, transcript, 46.

87. GPJ-CNFH (1970), July 28, 1967, transcript, 45a.

88. *Kansas City (KS) Advocate,* June 8, 1917, p. 4.

89. Max Alvarez, "The Origins of the Film Exchange," *Film History* 17, no. 4 (2005): 431–465.

90. GPJ-CNFH (1970), July 28, 1967, transcript, 47.

91. Ibid., transcript, 48.

92. Sampson, *Blacks in Black and White,* 141.

93. Western Union Telegram to George P. Johnson, *GPJ, 1916–1977,* reel 7.

94. Ibid.

95. *Kansas City (KS) Advocate,* May 18, 1917, p. 4.

96. It is unclear if "we" referred to a common national or racial identity with Lincoln's management and whether the "people here" were Filipino or black American soldiers stationed overseas, but in either case, the news of Lincoln's pictures had reached far across the global networks of black social life. "Scenes from Lincoln Productions," *GPJ, 1916–1977,* reel 7.

97. The black press had diverse interests and could also disparage and be unsupportive of race film projects, especially after the period in which the industry first emerged (1915–1917).

98. See, for example, marketing materials and letters addressed to George P. Johnson, *GPJ, 1916–1977,* reel 7.

99. "Letter from *The Bystander* to George P. Johnson," *GPJ, 1916–1977,* reel 7.

100. "Letter from Romeo Dougherty to George P. Johnson," Aug. 7, 1917, *GPJ, 1916–1977,* reel 7.

101. Bowser and Spence, *Writing Himself into History;* Green, *Straight Lick;* Betti Carol Van Epps–Taylor, *Oscar Micheaux: Dakota Homesteader, Author, Pioneer Film Maker* (Sioux Falls, SD: Dakota West Books, 1999).

102. *IF,* Sept. 9, 1916, p. 4.

103. *CD,* Jan. 8, 1916, p. 1.

104. Van Epps–Taylor, *Oscar Micheaux*, 96.

105. GPJ-CNFH (1970), July 28, 1967, transcript.

106. Cripps, *Slow Fade to Black;* Bowser and Spence, *Writing Himself into History;* Green, *Straight Lick;* Van Epps–Taylor, *Oscar Micheaux.*

107. Brent Edwards, "Pan-Africanism and 'pan-Africanism': Some Historical Notes," *Phylon* 23 (Winter 1962): 346–358.

108. "Extracts from letter from Oscar Micheaux," *GPJ, 1916–1977,* reel 8.

109. The journey may have been exhausting, for Micheaux offered a job to Johnson when he returned in March. *GPJ, 1916–1977,* reel 8. Also see GPJ-CNFH (1970), July 28, 1967.

110. *CD,* Jan. 31, 1920, p. 8.

111. Neither my own research nor that of other film scholars has seemed to produce evidence of Micheaux's travels to Europe during this period. However, because of the unreliability of many import and export records and the number of alternative routes he might have taken, this cannot serve as conclusive evidence for or against his international travel.

112. Fourteenth Census of the United States Federal Census Record—1920, Census Place: Manhattan Assembly District 7, New York, New York, Ancestry.com, http://www.ancestrylibrary.com.

113. Frank Allen Southard, *American Industry in Europe: Origins and Development of the Multinational Corporation* ([1931] New York: Arno Press, 1976), 94–95.

114. 15 Dec. 1920. Port of Arrival: Key West, Florida (Departure: Havana, Cuba), *Florida Passenger Lists, 1898–1951;* 2 Feb 1921 Port of Arrival: Plymouth England, *UK Incoming Passenger Lists, 1878–1960,* original data: Board of Trade: Commercial and Statistical Department and successors: Inwards Passenger Lists. Kew, Surrey, England: National Archives of the UK (TNA). Series BT26, 1,472 pieces. 21 July, 1921. Port of Arrival: New York, New York (Departure: Boulogne-Sur-Mer), *New York Passenger Lists, 1820–1957.*

115. "Swan Micheaux to George P. Johnson," September 7, 1921, *GPJ, 1916–1977,* reel 8.

116. *GPJ, 1916–1977,* reel 8.

117. Quoted in Bowser and Spence, *Writing Himself into History,* 30.

118. Patrick McGilligan, *Oscar Micheaux: The Great and Only: The Life of America's First Black Filmmaker* (New York: HarperCollins e-books, 2009), 195.

119. D. Ireland Thomas, *CD,* Aug. 16, 1924, 7a.

120. *New York Amsterdam News,* Apr. 16, 1930, p. 10; *Pittsburgh Courier,* Aug. 30, 1930, p. A7.

121. *New York Amsterdam News,* Apr. 16, 1930, p. 10.

122. Stephen Bourne, *Black in the British Frame: The Black Experience in Film and Television* (London: Continuum, 2001), 10–31.

123. *BA,* Dec. 2, 1922, p. 2.

124. *Pittsburgh Courier,* Dec. 12, 1925, p. 11.

125. The advertisement described Robeson as "El Actor Negro Más Famoso de Mundo," *Cine-Mundial,* June 1926, p. 400.

126. *Pittsburgh Courier,* Feb. 14, 1925, p. 3. This trip may have been planned in place of his delayed 1924 journey.

127. *CD,* Jan. 10, 1925, p. 6.

128. *AA,* Dec. 27, 1924, p. 7.

129. *Pittsburgh Courier,* Feb. 14, 1925, p. 3.

130. Ibid.

131. Ibid.

132. Pearl Bowser, Jane Gaines, and Charles Musser, eds. and curators, *Oscar Micheaux and His Circle: African-American Filmmaking and Race Cinema of the Silent Era* (Bloomington: Indiana University Press, 2001), 233–236.

133. According to the British Board of Film Classification (BBFC), two minutes and forty seconds of footage were cut from the film. The "A" rating suggested that some councils had ruled that minors must be accompanied by adults in order to see the film. British Board of Film Classification, "Body and Soul Classified 26 July, 1927," http://www.bbfc.co.uk. I accessed this information on July 29, 2012; a representative from the British Board of Film Classification confirmed that the British Board of Film Censors processed *Body and Soul* in 1927.

134. Tommy Gustafsson, "The Visual Re-creation of Black People in a 'White' Country: Oscar Micheaux and Swedish Film Culture in the 1920s," *Cinema Journal* 47, no. 4 (Summer 2008): 30–49; Southard, *American Industry in Europe,* 94–95.

135. *AA,* Dec. 12, 1925, p. 4.

136. Ibid.

137. Bernard L. Peterson Jr., "The Films of Oscar Micheaux: America's First Fabulous Black Filmmaker," *Crisis* 86 (April 1979): 138. Also see Bowser, Gaines, and Musser, *Oscar Micheaux and His Circle,* 276.

138. Thomas Cripps, " 'Race Movies' as Voices of the Black Bourgeois: The Scar of Shame," in Valerie Smith, ed., *Representing Blackness: Issues in Film and Video* (New Brunswick, NJ: Rutgers University Press, 1997), 50. Also see: Kenneth White Munden, *American Film Institute Catalogue* (Berkeley: University of California Press, 1976), 492.

139. *Pittsburgh Courier,* Aug. 25, 1928, p. 2.

140. *AA,* Jan. 8, 1927, p. 11.

141. *AA,* Feb. 27, 1937, p. 11.

142. Cripps, *Slow Fade to Black*; Ralph Mathews, "The Villain of 'The Wages of Sin,'" *AA,* Jan. 18, 1936.

143. Mathews, "The Villain of 'The Wages of Sin.'"

144. Lillian Johnson, "Light and Shadow," *AA,* Jan. 13, 1940, p. 13.

145. For example, in a telegram to the writer and theater manager D. Ireland Thomas, Johnson wrote that he had confirmed bookings in the South and was considering a stop in Cuba. "Telegram of George P. Johnson to D. Ireland Thomas," December 2, 1921, *GPJ, 1916–1977,* reel 7.

146. The agency's reports were published by black newspapers across the country. Its international coverage was varied, reporting on Haitian airline services, the French treatment of black American soldiers, and curious items such as the story of a black South African who had been hired as a valet for a pig in Johannesburg. *GPJ, 1916–1977,* reel 10 (Pacific Coast News Bureau folder).

147. Johnson's coverage included topics such as "Porto Rican" cotton laborers, Liberian Trading Companies, and the scientific history of Ethiopia. Ibid.

148. *Pittsburgh Courier,* Sept. 3, 1927, sm2.

Conclusion

1. *Atlanta Daily World,* Dec. 14, 1939, p. 1; M. Carmen Gómez-Galisteo, *The Wind Is Never Gone: Sequels, Parodies and Rewritings of* Gone with the Wind (Jefferson, NC: McFarland, 2011), 70.

2. Ibid.

3. *Life,* Dec. 25, 1939, pp. 11–13.

4. Hamilton Cravens, *Great Depression: People and Perspectives* (Santa Barbara, CA: ABC-CLIO, 2009), 221.

5. Martin Luther King Jr. would one day sing those very same "freedom hymns" while marching on Albany and Selma. Wyatt T. Walker, "The Soulful Journey of the Negro Spiritual: Freedom's Song," *Negro Digest,* July 1963, pp. 84–95; M. Jonathan Rieder, *The Word of the Lord Is upon Me: The Righteous Performance of Martin Luther King, Jr.* (Cambridge, MA: Harvard University Press, 2009), 181; Gómez-Galisteo, *Wind Is Never Gone,* 70.

6. Memoirs of Auretha Jolly English in Jeanie Sutton Lambright, *They Also Served: Women's Stories from the World War II Era* (Bloomington, IN: Xlibris, 2003), 34.

7. Stephen G. N. Tuck, *Beyond Atlanta: The Struggle for Racial Equality in Georgia, 1940–1980* (Athens: University of Georgia Press, 2001), 10; Taylor Branch, *Parting the Waters: America in the King Years 1954–63* (New York: Simon and Schuster, 1988), 55.

8. *AA,* Jan. 20, 1940, p. 14.

9. "Demand London Ban 'Gone with the Wind,'" *Negro Star,* June 7, 1940, p. 4.

10. C. L. R. James published the essay under the name "J. R. Johnson." "To conclude, the film is dangerous and must be exposed and boycotted. But infinitely more dangerous, and therefore to be exposed and boycotted to an infinitely greater degree, is this mischievous manipulation of Negro militancy in the interest of the Moscow bureaucrats," he explained; originally published in J. R. Johnson, "On *Gone with the Wind,*" *Socialist Appeal,* Jan. 13, 1940, reprinted in C. L. R. James, *C. L. R. James and the "Negro Question,"* ed. Scott McLemee (Jackson: University Press of Mississippi, 1996), 51–55.

11. Malcolm X and Alex Haley, *The Autobiography of Malcolm X* (New York: Random House, 1964), 38.

12. "Footlights Flickers," *Kansas City (KS) Plaindealer,* Dec. 29, 1930, p. 3.

13. *Kansas City (KS) Plaindealer,* May 17, 1940, p. 7.

14. Clarence Muse, *CD,* Mar. 16, 1940, p. 21.

15. *Pittsburgh Courier,* Mar. 9, 1940, p. 20.

16. "All black people were made to sit upstairs in the gallery. Just in the same way, Negroes had to sit upstairs in the movie houses when we got those in Charleston. We called the upstairs there the 'buzzard's roost.' The churches had their 'buzzard's roosts' too," Mamie Garvin Fields explained when describing her youth in Charleston at the turn of the twentieth century. Mamie Garvin Fields and Karen E. Fields, *Lemon Swamp and Other Places: A Carolina Memoir* (New York: Free Press Collier Macmillan, 1983), 33.

17. William F. Gibson, "Library of Congress Recognition Undeserved for 'Birth of a Nation,'" *Los Angeles Times,* Dec. 28, 1992, http://articles.latimes.com/1992-12-28/entertainment/ca-2023_1_aryan-nation.

18. Jill Brett, "'The Birth of a Nation' Documents History," *Los Angeles Times,* Jan. 4, 1993, http://articles.latimes.com/1993-01-04/entertainment/ca-864_1_film-registry-national-film-preservation-board-classic-american-films.

Acknowledgments

I would not have been able to write this book without the help of an incredibly patient, talented, and generous group of individuals.

At the Graduate Center, CUNY, I had the fortune to study with faculty who helped me think broadly about the connections between politics, culture, and economics. Seminars with Kathleen McCarthy and Barbara Welter helped me articulate my research interests. Classes with Jonathan Sassi encouraged me to think differently about religion—a subject that I had once, foolishly, overlooked in relation to my interests in cinema and representation. Clarence Taylor helped me contextualize the social and political movements in the longer trajectory of civil rights campaigns. Joshua Freeman helped me frame my ideas about leisure and working class history. In the Film Studies program, Cindy Wong introduced me to exciting scholarship on film and race. My fellow graduate students read drafts and offered insights and camaraderie that sustained me.

I am indebted to Herman Bennett's generosity and wisdom. He read multiple drafts of this project and was one of its first and most vocal advocates. His invaluable feedback made me rethink the significance of my archives and the implications of the early history of black cinema. Without his guidance I would not have taken on the more intimidating—and much more rewarding—set of questions about migration, black institutional life, social formation, and visual culture that are central to this project. Joshua Brown has been a wonderful critic, supporter, and advisor. Our conversations convinced me that I wanted to begin my research in the late nineteenth century, a decision that led me to some of my most exciting discoveries. I am incredibly grateful to him for sparking my interest in this period and for providing me with acute insights and practical suggestions on my work. I met Stuart Ewen almost a decade ago as an MFA student at Hunter College. Over the years, he has been an incredible mentor and friend. His courses fueled my desire to learn more about popular culture and film. When he advised me on my thesis film project, he helped me navigate through hours of footage to find a clear narrative. With this book, he was once again instrumental in helping me find the plot and the purpose of my work. I am also thankful to the late Elizabeth Ewen for her suggestions on this project. Having long admired her pioneering work on women and early American film, I was especially honored to receive her insights on turn-of-the-century filmgoing. Five years ago, David Nasaw read the humble seminar paper that eventually led to this book. Since then, he has introduced me to countless books and ideas that fueled the development of my research. His suggestions on the craft of writing have also proven invaluable. These chapters would be much more cluttered and clumsy without his sage advice. Michele Wallace offered both encouragement and an encyclopedic knowledge of early American and African American cinema. After our conversations, I was always excited to delve deeper into the archives and get back to writing.

During three amazing years at SUNY, Old Westbury, my colleagues offered support and friendship while I was researching and writing this book. Laura Anker, Jermaine Archer, Aubrey Bonnett, John Friedman, Amanda Frisken, Karl Grossman, Joseph Manfredi, Andrew Mattson, Carol Quirke, Samara Smith, Lois Stergiopoulos, and Denton L. Watson made going to work a pleasure. We are all fortunate to live in a world were there are people like Laura Anker. Amanda Frisken was a terrific advocate whose support gave me the time and energy to complete this book. I miss afternoon chats with Carol Quirke, who helped me figure out the publishing process. Her sense of humor and keen insights always kept things in perspective. Llana Barber offered wonderful camaraderie and on-the-spot feedback. She helped me navigate my way through some of my most unwieldy arguments. Jermaine Archer, a cherished friend and a terrific co-conspirator, helped keep my spirits up. Nobody could ask for a better friend and colleague. Our conversations about race and visual culture have inspired me to keep thinking about—and looking at—the past.

Even before I began working at Indiana University, the school generously supported the completion of this book. Since joining the faculty, I have been fortunate to work with an incredible group of scholars. In particular, I would like to thank my colleagues in the Department of American Studies. Deborah Cohn has offered tremendous support from day one. I am indebted to Vivian Halloran for her invaluable guidance and for her friendship. Paula Cotner and Carol Glaze helped me stay on track even when I hit a few bumps in the road. Jason McGraw, Amrita Myers, Christina Snyder, and Ellen Wu, thank you for your advice and for making life out here fun.

Conversations with, and suggestions from, Allyson Nadia Field, Terri Francis, Hilary Hallett, Kathy Peiss, Kathryn Fuller Seeley, Jacqueline Stewart, Gregory Waller, and the organizers and participants in the Regeneration in Digital Contexts: Early Black Film Conference, organized by the Black Film Center/Archive, have made this a better book. Charles Musser offered useful advice, especially regarding itinerant and nontheatrical film exhibition. I am also grateful for the encouragement of Thavolia Glymph, and for the support and advice of the anonymous readers from the *Journal of American History,* the anonymous readers from Harvard University Press, and the anonymous panelists at the National Endowment for the Humanities. Any views, findings, conclusions, or recommendations expressed in this book do not necessarily represent those of the National Endowment for the Humanities. Frank Donnelly, the Geospatial Data Librarian at Baruch College, CUNY, helped me create the maps in this book. The multitalented Rachel Lerner-Ley helped put together the Black Film Venue Database. I am grateful for Justin Wolfe's eye for detail as I was working through the revisions. He also helped me acquire the images for this book. Brian Distelberg has been an incredible editor, whose eye for clarity and suggestions for revision have been priceless. It has been a privilege to work with him.

Several institutions enabled me to complete this book. The folks at the Black Film Center/Archive, especially Michael Martin and Brian Graney, have made IU Bloomington an exciting meeting point and resource for the study of black cinema. I am also indebted to the assistance of the librarians and staff at the Schomburg Center for Research in Black Culture, the New York Public Library for the Performing Arts, the Film Studies Center at the Museum of Modern Art, New York City (especially Charles Silver), the George Eastman House, the Historical Society of Washington, D.C., the Library of Congress, the Kansas City Public Library's Missouri Valley Special Collections, and the Howard Theater in Washington, D.C. (especially Ashley Mason-Greene). Quinn Chapel AME Church in Chicago is a living monument to the tremendous accomplishments and vision of freedom forged by turn-of-the-century black Americans. I am thankful to Reverend James M. Moody for allowing me to include an image of the church in this book, which I hope will highlight the importance of Quinn's ongoing endeavors to restore its historic edifice.

Gabrielle Aronas, Barney Collier, Kimberly Goodman, Michael Hernandez, Maki Ichikawa, Ellen Kim, Allison Kramer, Sheila Kurtz, Layla Love, Ashlee Park, Huiyuhl Yi, and Lang Yip, thank you for your friendship. I am lucky to have you in my life. Hwal Pak and Mija Pak have been amazing in all ways small and big. My siblings reminded me to celebrate along the way. Caelyn Marie Caddoo and Miranda Boen make me hopeful for the future.

My parents, Jayne Caddoo and Gary Caddoo, have given me more love and support than these sentences can convey. My dad has always believed in me, and I am grateful for all he has done to help me accomplish my dreams. I inherited my love of reading and my curiosity about the world from my mother, who as a little girl spent countless afternoons in her attic bedroom reading the encyclopedia. My parents dutifully read every chapter, even trudging through the first clumsy and barely coherent drafts. This project is dedicated to them.

Ougie Pak has lived with me through all iterations of this project. He has weathered the flood of newspaper clippings and books that regularly fill our living room, and he has listened to me babble for hours about lost films and nineteenth-century train routes. I thank him with all my heart for his unmatched patience and support, and for too many things to be enumerated here.

Index